A Study of World Trade Organisation

A Study of
World Trade Organisation

Second Revised Edition

K.R. Gupta

ATLANTIC
PUBLISHERS & DISTRIBUTORS (P) LTD

Published by

ATLANTIC

PUBLISHERS & DISTRIBUTORS (P) LTD

B-2, Vishal Enclave, Opp. Rajouri Garden,
New Delhi-110027
Phones : +91-11-25413460, 25429987, 25466842

Sales Office
7/22, Ansari Road, Darya Ganj,
New Delhi-110002
Phones : +91-11-23273880, 23275880, 23280451
Fax : +91-11-23285873
Web : www.atlanticbooks.com
E-mail : info@atlanticbooks.com

Branch Office
5, Nallathambi Street, Wallajah Road,
Chennai-600002
Phones : +91-44-64611085, 32413319
E-mail : chennai@atlanticbooks.com

ISBN 978-81-269-0976-6

Printed in India
at Nice Printing Press, Delhi

PREFACE TO THE SECOND EDITION

The book had gone out of print long back and urgent demands were received for a new edition. But being extremely busy with some other books, I could not devote time to revise the book. Now I am glad to place before readers the revised and enlarged edition of the book. A completely new chapter has been included on Doha Round of negotiations launched in late 2001 to boost world economy and fight poverty.

The Doha Round aims at working toward a global trade agreement that would liberalise markets, primarily agriculture, manufacturing and services, to reduce poverty and promote development. The trade talks are designed to help increase trade and develop the economies of poorer countries.

Despite the fact that agriculture accounts for only about eight per cent of world trade, it is the key to any deal because of its importance for developing countries. The deal has to give developing countries the same flexibility in opening up their fledgling industries, which its counterpart, that is, rich nations expect in politically sensitive farm sectors.

The book seeks to bring to light disagreements that persist on issues such as the size of tariff cuts and the special treatment that developing nations including India should receive. The most pressing issue is agriculture, in which developing nations want the rules — for both subsidies and protection — to be rebalanced in their favour. Another pressing issue is industrial tariffs, where greater market access is needed in both developing and developed countries. Also on the menu are issues such as services, dumping, trade facilitation and regional trade agreements.

Unfortunately, the Round has lurched from crisis to crisis for years over differences among rich and poor countries over cutting farm and industrial tariffs and subsidies.

The year 2008 is crucial for the outcome of the Doha Round of global trade talks. A successful completion of the Doha Round in 2008 is being considered essential because failure to reach a deal this year could push the negotiations back to 2010, given the change in the U.S. administration in early 2009.

K.R. GUPTA

PREFACE TO THE FIRST EDITION

The book attempts to analyse the various provisions of the World Trade Organisation (WTO) and examines their working in actual practice. It also examines the implications of and the need for several new provisions (e.g. those relating to labour standards, environment problems, investments agreement, competition policies, government procurement, information technology, electronic commerce etc.) proposed to be included in the WTO. It particularly studies as to how far the provisions of the WTO are consistent with the requirements of the developing countries and what modifications are required to make them suitable for the developing countries. The provisions and working of the WTO have been examined with a detached and scientific outlook. The analysis is penetrating and illuminative.

Appendix-V contains viewpoints of important countries, international organisations and regional organisations on the provisions and working of the WTO. It is hoped that the book would be found useful by the researchers and students of International Economics and International Law, business executives, Government officers concerned with formulation and execution of economic policies, parliamentarians and the common man interested in world economic affairs.

K.R. GUPTA

CONTENTS

1

ORIGIN AND EVOLUTION OF WTO

Introduction

The World Trade Organization (WTO) is the legal and institutional foundation of the multilateral trading system. It provides the principal contractual obligations determining how Governments frame and implement domestic trade legislation and regulations. And it is the platform on which trade relations among countries evolve through collective debate, negotiation and adjudication.

The WTO is based in Geneva, Switzerland. Its essential functions are :

administering and implementing the multilateral and plurilateral trade agreements which together make up the WTO;

acting as a forum for multilateral trade negotiations;

seeking to resolve trade disputes;

overseeing national trade policies; and

cooperating with other international institutions involved in global economic policy-making.

The WTO Agreement contains some 29 individual legal texts — covering everything from agriculture to textiles and clothing, and from services to government procurement, rules of origin and intellectual property. Added to these are more than 25 additional Ministerial declarations, decisions and understandings which spell out further obligations and commitments for WTO members. However, a number of simple and fundamental principles run through all of these instruments which, together, make up the multilateral trading system.

Origin and Evolution of WTO

The origin of the WTO may by traced to the Atlantic Charter issued on 14 August 1941, by the President of the United States and the Prime Minister of the United Kingdom.[1] Points 4 and 5 of the Atlantic Charter read as follows :

> They (the United States and the United Kingdom Government)[2] will endeavour, with due respect for their existing obligations, to further the enjoyment by all states, great or small, victor or vanquished, of access, on equal terms, to the trade and to the raw materials of the world which are needed for their economic prosperity.
>
> They desire to bring about the fullest collaboration between all nations in the economic field with the object of securing, for all, improved labour standards, economic advancement and social security.

The idea was further developed in Article 7 of the Mutual Aid Agreement concluded in February 1942 between the United States and the United Kingdom. The prospects of a successful termination of war brought the attention of the world towards the problems of peace.[3] It was widely recognised that political security could not be achieved without financial and commercial stability. Following the establishment, in 1946, of the International Monetary Fund and the International Bank for Reconstruction and Development to deal with the financial aspects of international economic relations, a third organisation was required to look after the trade problems of the world. The United States gave the lead and, in December 1945, published a document, prepared in consultation with the United Kingdom, entitled 'Proposals for Expansion of World Trade and Employment.' It sent copies of this document to other governments for their consideration. The proposals put forward the idea of establishing an International

---

1. Government of India, *Report of the Fiscal Commission*, 1949-50 (New Delhi, 1950), p. 272.
2. Words within parenthesis added.
3. V.A. Sayid Muhammad, *The Legal Framework of World Trade* (London, 1951), 17.

Trade Organisation. The member countries were to conduct their commercial relations in accordance with the rules and regulations provided in the charter of the organisation. The proposals contained provisions relating to trade barriers, restrictive business practices, intergovernmental commodity arrangements, international aspects of domestic employment policies and the structure of the suggested International Trade Organisation.

In February 1946, the Economic and Social Council of the United Nations, at its first meeting at the initiation of the United States, passed a resolution calling for an international conference on trade and employment to consider the question of establishing an International Trade Organisation. It established a Preparatory Committee consisting of nineteen countries to arrange for the Conference and to prepare a draft Charter for such an organisation. The Secretary-General of the United Nations sent invitations to nineteen members for participating in the Preparatory Committee. All members except the USSR agreed to participate in the work of the Committee. The USSR did not attend because at that time it was not possible for the country to devote sufficient preliminary study to the serious and far-reaching questions which were to be discussed in the Committee. The First Session of the Preparatory Committee was held in London from 15 October to 26 November 1946. Some members of the United Nations (*viz.*, Columbia, Poland, Peru, Mexico and Syria) who were not invited to the Preparatory Committee, sent official representatives to observe the proceedings of the First Session. Representatives of some intergovernmental organisations (*viz.* FAO, IBRD and IMF) attended and participated in the First Session. Representatives of some non-governmental organisations were also present, *viz.*, the International Chamber of Commerce, the International Co-operative Alliance, the World Federation of Trade Unions, and the American Federation of Labour.

Before the Preparatory Committee met, the United States prepared a Suggested Charter for the International Trade Organisation. It was an elaborated version of the Proposals cast in charter language. Copies of the Suggested Charter were sent to the Secretary-General of the United Nations and to the governments invited by the Economic and Social Council to serve on the Preparatory Committee. The Suggested Charter was prepared by the most competent and experienced technical staff of the United States Government. This was to serve as a basis for discussion and not as the fixed and final views of the United States Government.[4] Some other governments also submitted documents. A Draft Charter was submitted by Brazil. India submitted a detailed Commentary on the United States Proposals. The United Kingdom submitted a Memorandum on the employment policy. Long and detailed discussions were held on the basis of these documents particularly on the United States Suggested Charter. A draft charter was prepared in this Session. This draft was incomplete in certain respects. There was a division of opinion and no agreement could be reached to voting and other organizational questions. Provisions on state trading and treatment of non-members were not worked out. Several technical articles also remained incomplete. The First Session appointed a Drafting Committee to prepare a Draft Charter on the Report and other documents of the First Session, to edit for clarity and consistency the portions of the text on the basis of which the Preparatory Committee came to a substantial identification of views, for preparing alternative drafts of those portions on which there remained a division of opinion and to prepare suggested drafts covering such incomplete portions as were referred to it by the Preparatory Committee, together with such explanatory notes and commentaries as the Drafting Committee might consider desirable and useful.[5] The Drafting Committee was also entrusted with the work of preparing a more detailed draft of the General Agreement on Tariffs and Trade, based upon the outline drafted at the First Session.

It was felt by some of the most influential countries that the long time required for the negotiation of the International Trade Organisation should not hold up the action on the reduction of

---

4. United Nations, *The Report of the First Session of the Preparatory Committee of the United Nations Conference on Trade and Employment* (London, 1946), p. 52.

5. United Nations, *Report of the Drafting Committee of the Preparatory Committee of the United Nations Conference on Trade and Employment* (New York, 1947), p. 1.

barriers, particularly because they considered the immediate post-war period to be the most favourable time for such action. This led to the idea of holding multilateral negotiations for the reduction of tariffs. Just before the end of the session, on 8 November 1946, the United States invited the governments represented on the Preparatory Committee to negotiate tariff concessions with her. The countries invited by the United States accepted the invitation to participate in tariff negotiations. At the conclusion of the London session, the Preparatory Committee of the International Conference on Trade and Employment passed a resolution expressing the desirability of reciprocal and mutually advantageous negotiations aimed at a substantial reduction of tariffs and the elimination of preferences, and recommending the concerned governments to hold the tariff negotiations under the sponsorship of the Preparatory Committee in connection with, and as a part of, the Second Session of the Committee, in accordance with the procedures recommended in the Memorandum on Procedures approved by the Preparatory Committee at its First Session.

The Second Session of the Preparatory Committee was held in Geneva on 19 April 1947. At this session, the Preparatory Committee completed the Draft Charter which provided the basis for discussion at the World Conference. In addition, at this Session, the General Agreement on Tariffs and Trade was negotiated. In the first instance, it was a tariff agreement pursuant to Article 17 of International Trade Organisation Charter providing for negotiations aimed at a reduction of tariffs and other barriers to trade. Rules regarding the conduct of commercial policy were provided just to prevent the tariff concessions from being nullified by other measures of trade policy.[6] The general provisions of the Agreement were very similar to the corresponding provisions of the Geneva Draft of the Charter.

The World Conference was held at Havana on 21 November 1947. Fifty-six nations sent delegations to the Conference. Some governments sent representatives to observe the proceedings of

6. "International Trade Co-operation in an Expanding World", GATT Document No. Spec/121/57, October 1947, Address delivered by E.W. White before the Academy of Science, Prague (September 1957), p. 2.

the Conference. The USSR, again, did not attend the Conference. The heated and protracted discussions ended in the signing of the Final Act of the Havana Conference by fifty-three countries on 24 March 1948. There were six hundred and two amendments to the Geneva draft. Argentina and Poland refused to sign and the transmission of Turkey's authorization was delayed. The Final Act authenticated the text of the Havana Charter but did not bind any government to ratify it.

In 1947, the General Agreement was considered to be a temporary arrangement pending the establishment of International Trade Organisation with wider and more positive objectives than those of the GATT. It was thought that the concrete results of the GATT would facilitate the negotiation of International Trade Organisation. The Preparatory Committee set up by the Economic and Social Council of the United Nations expected that "the task of the World Conference would be facilitated if concrete action were taken by the principal trading nations to enter into reciprocal negotiations directed to the substantial reduction of tariffs and to the elimination of preferences on a mutually advantageous basis...."[7] It was envisaged that the GATT would be finally merged into International Trade Organisation. Article XXIX lays down :

1. The contracting parties undertake to observe to the fullest extent of their executive authority the general principles of Chapters I to VI inclusive and of Chapter IX of the Havana Charter pending their acceptance of it in accordance with their constitutional procedures.
2. Part II of this Agreement shall be suspended on the day on which the Havana Charter enters into force.

Unluckily, the Havana Charter could not come into existence. The controversies which the Charter aroused in the United States caused its ratification to be postponed until 1951 when the Government announced its intention not to resubmit the Charter for the approval of Congress. Almost simultaneously the Government of the United Kingdom declared that "there was no likelihood of

7. United Nations, *Report of the Second Session of the Preparatory Committee of the United Nations Conference on Trade and Employment* (Geneva, 1947), p. 70.

the International Trade Organisation mentioned in the Havana Charter being established and developed as an official instrument for the encouragement of international trade," adding that "it would in no case recommend to Parliament that the United Kingdom should ratify the Charter."[8] Most of the other countries did not ratify the Charter because they did not want to create the Organisation without the co-operation of the United States.

Why did the United States not ratify the Charter? The main reason was the strong opposition from the business community. It opposed the Charter on several grounds. The most important criticism was that the Charter contained numerous exceptions and escape clauses which nullified the basic principles and ideals for which it stood.[9] It did not go far enough in removing trade restrictions. Any country could comply with the provisions of the Charter without removing trade barriers under one or the other escape clause. It permitted the countries to create balance of payments difficulties by adopting domestic programmes for achieving full employment or for economic development and then to use restrictions for safeguarding the monetary reserves. It permitted the countries suffering from balance of payments deficits to discriminate between different products on the basis of essentiality and between different countries during the transitional period. It permitted the old preferential arrangements to continue. It justified the new preferential arrangements leading to the formation of customs unions or free trade areas which might be unduly prolonged. It justified protective measures for economic development and reconstruction. It did not outlaw state trading and combines and cartels. It permitted quantitative restrictions on the importation of agricultural products for the enforcement of domestic price support schemes. It permitted, and also encouraged, inter-governmental commodity agreements for restricting production and raising prices. All these were contrary to the liberal trading principles and a purely competitive market economy. The business community held that the Charter was nothing but a codification

8. United Nations Conference on Trade and Development, *The Developing Countries in GATT*, UN Conference on Trade and Development Document No. E/CONF. 46/36 (Geneva, March 1946), p. 9.

9. William Diebold, Jr., *The End of I.T.O.* (New Jersey, 1952), p. 14.

of malpractices, that practices which were not considered to be respectable had been made sacred and lawful by being embodied in the Charter.

This criticism was, however, unjustified. Firstly, it focused attention on the weaknesses of the Charter and neglected all its good points, *viz.*, the most favoured nation treatment, reduction of trade barriers and preferential arrangements, general elimination of quantitative restrictions, freedom of transit, regulation of the administration of tariffs, and other charges on imports and exports, national treatment of internal taxation and regulations, settlement of differences, provisions concerning full employment, etc. Secondly, it neglected the safeguards and limitations to which these exceptions and escape clauses were subject.[10] These minimised the chances of the misuse of the exceptions and escape clauses. Further, if a perfect Charter was not possible from the very beginning, it was not wise to forego even an imperfect Charter.[11] Something was better than nothing. Thirdly, it was not correct to assume that all members would continue taking advantage of the exceptions and escape clauses for which they had fought.[12] Many countries fought for these simply because they did not want to tie their hands. This has been well demonstrated by the working of the General Agreement. In fact, the framers of the Charter acted in a very realistic and practical manner. They knew that a rigid body of rules without any exception would not be acceptable to most of the trading countries. Under-developed countries were not ready to consider any proposal prohibiting trade restrictions unless the infant industries were exempted. The United States, the most ardent opponent of trade restrictions, was not ready to accept any proposal which did not permit it to protect its agriculture. Countries suffering from a disequilibrium in the balance of payments wanted permission to apply restrictions on imports to safeguard their monetary reserves. No country would accept any provision which hinders the preservation of its national security.

10. William Adams Brown, Jr., *The United States and the Restoration of World Trade* (Washington, D.C., 1950), p. 364.

11. *Ibid.*

12. *Ibid.*, p. 365.

A second American criticism was that the Charter imposed one-sided obligations on the United States. This criticism was based, mainly speaking, on two points. Firstly, it was held that the tariff reductions made by the United States would be effective whereas the tariff reductions made by most of the other countries, which were in balance of payments difficulties, or underdeveloped, or in need of special measures for economic reconstruction, would be nullified by the quantitative restrictions which they were entitled to apply under the exceptions and escape clauses.[13] This argument contained an element of truth. But mostly these escape clauses were of a transitory nature and would have been terminated eventually. Further, the United States would gain to the extent the Charter regulated these practices; because if the Charter did not come into force, these would have been indulged in without any regulation or safeguard. Secondly, it was argued that whenever there arose certain differences among the members, the United States was likely to be outvoted because it possessed only one vote and not a weighted vote as in the International Monetary Fund. This was particularly important because of the wider responsibilities and powers vested in the Organisation. There was, however, no basis to assume that the United States would always be outvoted. The chances of a defeat in voting were as many for the United States as for any other country; rather the chances of defeat were less for the United States because of her substantial influence over other countries in economic as well as in political spheres. At the Havana Conference, the United States succeeded in getting certain provisions accepted which were sought by her alone, *viz.*, the finality of determination on financial matters by the International Monetary Fund, quantitative restrictions on the import of agricultural products to enforce price-support schemes, greater freedom to subsidies exports of primary commodities, etc.[14] Further, most of the matters in the International Trade Organisation would be decided by consultation, investigation and co-operation. Voting was not likely to decide many issues. Voting has not played a

13. Diebold, *op. cit.*, p. 20.

14. Clair Wilcox, *A Charter for World Trade* (New York, 1949), p. 197.

very important role in deciding issues in International Monetary Fund and GATT.[15] There was no reason to expect the contrary in International Trade Organisation. International Trade Organisation was bound to accept the determination of the Fund in all financial matters and the United States casts a highly weighted vote in it. Further, even if the United States found itself repeatedly outvoted by a combine of other members, it could withdraw from the Organisation giving six months notice.

Thirdly, opposition came from the protectionists. Groups having vested interests in the protected industries warned against the danger to American economy of a free import of low-cost foreign goods.[16]

Fourthly, the provisions relating to restrictive business practices were opposed by those who did not favour the antitrust activities of even their national government.[17]

On the whole, most of the criticisms of the Havana Charter were from those sections, whose vested interests were affected by it and did not have much justification, considered objectively. In fact, the government and disinterested sections of the society were in favour of the ratification of the Charter by the United States. But business community having vested interests being very powerful in the US, the Charter could not be ratified.

Why did International Trade Organisation fail to come into existence and GATT succeeded? There are a number of reasons for this. GATT covered a narrow sphere as compared with International Trade Organisation. GATT dealt mainly with tariffs and other matters related to them. In addition to tariffs, International Trade Organisation dealt with employment, commodity agreements, restrictive business practices, etc. This, of course, is a matter of expediency rather than of merit. The Agreement, without any doubt, would have been more useful and complete if it could include certain suitable provisions concerning international commodity agreements, restrictive business practices, etc., which are very

15. Brown, *op. cit.*, p. 375.

16. Diebold, *op. cit.*, p. 23.

17. Raymond Vernon, "Organising For World Trade", *International Conciliation* (New York, November 1955), p. 186.

closely related to the provisions of the Agreement. In fact, GATT had been taking considerable interest in these problems. Secondly, participation in GATT did not require any special legislation in most of the contracting parties. They could participate in GATT as in any other commercial agreement just by the executive authority. Participation in International Trade Organisation required legislative approval. Thirdly, commitments in the Agreement were less binding than those in the International Trade Organisation. A contracting party could withdraw itself from the Agreement by giving sixty days notice while the Charter required six months' notice for withdrawal from the International Trade Organisation. This, however, had the disadvantage which created an element of uncertainty. There was always the possibility that a country might withdraw from the Agreement if it finds that its immediate interests are being injured even if the continuation of its membership is in its long-term interests.

In the beginning, only a limited number of underdeveloped countries acceded to GATT as compared to the number of countries in this category who subscribed to the Havana Charter. This has been attributed to the omission of provisions contained in the Havana Charter relating to the study and solutions of problems of instability in the world market for raw materials and foodstuffs and the provisions pertaining to economic development.[18]

The Latin American countries form a great majority of those countries which did not accede to the General Agreement. Out of the seventeen Latin American countries which signed the Havana Charter, only three were among the twenty-three original contracting parties. In 1954, the Economic Commission for Latin America conducted a survey to find out why some countries joined the GATT and others did not.[19] The seven Latin American countries

---

18. United Nations Conference on Trade and Development, *The Developing Countries in GATT*, UN Conference on Trade and Development Document No. E/CONF. 46/36 (Geneva, March 1964), p. 15.

19. Economic Commission for Latin America, *Study of Inter-Latin American Trade*, E/CN. 12/369/Rev. 1 (Geneva, April 1956), pp. 6-7. cf. United Nations Conference on Trade and Development, *The Developing Countries in GATT*, UN Conference on Trade and Development Document No. E/CONF. 46/36 (Geneva, March 1964), p. 26.

which were full members of the GATT at the time of the survey joined GATT mainly because of the following considerations :

1. Within the combined advantages and limitations of the General Agreement, countries exporting basic products can better defend their interests by becoming members of a world organisation for international trade which also includes the principal purchasers of those products.
2. Anxiety was felt to improve the tariff treatment accorded by the large buyers to certain exporters of primary products.
3. Countries with low tariffs were authorised by the GATT to make an overall increase in their custom duties before joining subsequent negotiations being based on these new tariffs.
4. Countries whose tariffs were bound by bilateral treaties were able to negotiate within the GATT with the parties to such treaties for a reduction in the import schedules covered by consolidation of tariff concessions.
5. The objectives of the GATT coincide with traditional national trade policy.

Those who stayed outside GATT probably did so because of one or more of the following reasons :

1. Membership of the GATT entailed tariff negotiations leading to mutual concessions, whose results, for various reasons, appeared of dubious value from the standpoint of an effective expansion of national exports; furthermore, it was doubtful if the economic value of the benefits obtained for exports would compensate for the possible restrictive effects of such membership upon economic development, since the text implied dependence on international approval for the application of certain protective measures covering industrial production.
2. The commitments of membership — reduction of tariffs through bilateral negotiations, and extension of the resulting concessions to the other contracting parties through the most favoured nation clause — were believed to be incompatible, despite the exceptions permitted

under Article V, with the inclination of some countries to reduce the dependence of tariffs on external commitments, in order to use them as an instrument in the diversification of the national economy and in the stabilisation of the balance of payments.

3. The contractual limitations of trade policy might be intensified if to the commitments involved in bilateral agreements were added a new obligation entailed by the membership of GATT, and rarely included in the treaties concerned, namely, that of refraining from adopting measures to restrict imports of scheduled goods.

4. The persistent disequilibrium in foreign accounts generally compels the maintenance or the increase of selective measures of various kinds, whose operation within the regulations of the GATT might be neither so far-reaching nor, above all, so well-timed and rapid as Governments deem necessary. In the same connexion, it would not be wise for countries whose external payments situation depends to an appreciable extent upon the income from certain efforts and on the proportion of convertible exchange received, to incur commitments which might hamper the adaptation of their trade policy to changing conditions in world markets.

5. In the opinion of some countries whose exports are definitely at marginal levels with the volume of world supply, the most favoured nation clause to which they had already agreed with the consumer markets would suffice to enable them to participate automatically, without new tariff commitments, in any exemption, consolidation or concessions which these markets accord to their major suppliers, whether the contracting parties of the GATT or not. Some countries thought that, if they joined GATT, circumstances might compel them to conclude the customs agreements which are of no real value to their export trade, although causing a reduction both of fiscal revenues and of the margin within which tariffs could be modified by unilateral action.

Working of GATT

GATT Trade Rounds

Year	Subjects covered	Participating countries
1947 Geneva	Tariffs	23
1949 Annecy	Tariffs	13
1951 Torquay	Tariffs	38
1956 Geneva	Tariffs	26
1960 Geneva 1961 (Dillon Round)	Tariffs	26
1964 Geneva 1967 (Kennedy Round)	Tariffs and Anti-dumping Measures	62
1973 Geneva 1979 (Tokyo Round)	Tariffs, non-tariff measures and "framework" agreements	102
1986 Geneva 1993 (Uruguay Round)	Tariffs, non-tariff measures, rules, services, intellectual property rights, dispute settlement, textiles and clothing, agriculture, establishment of the WTO etc.	123

The first round of negotiations, which gave birth to GATT, resulted in 45,000 tariff concessions affecting $10 billion — or about one-fifth — of world trade. It was also agreed that the value of these concessions should be protected by early and largely "provisional" — acceptance of some of the trade rules in the draft ITO Charter. The tariff concessions and rules together became known as the General Agreement on Tariffs and Trade and entered into force in January 1948. Despite of its provisional nature, the GATT remained the only multilateral instrument governing international trade from 1948 till the establishment of the WTO.

Although, in its 47 years, the basic legal text of the GATT remained much as it was in 1948, there were additions in the form of 'plurilateral' — voluntary membership — agreements and continual efforts to reduce tariffs. Much of this was achieved through a series of 'trade rounds'. Eight trade rounds have been conducted, the last being the Uruguay Round which gave birth to WTO.

In the beginning, several countries did not show much enthusiasm for the Agreement. Though welcoming the benefits of tariff concessions, they did not like external interference in the conduct of their commercial policy. "At best their attitude was one of reluctant acceptance of an apparent necessity."[20] After the acute postwar difficulties were over, the contracting parties started realising the value of the Agreement. Thanks to the realistic and objective approach of the Contracting Parties, GATT succeeded in firmly establishing itself.

GATT was considered by its creators to be a stop-gap arrangement, pending the coming into existence of the much more ambitious International Trade Organisation. Consequently, it had no organisation, no executive committee and no staff of its own. Its operations were conducted by the contracting parties in occasional plenary sessions. This system continued for eight years. In course of this period, makeshift arrangements shaped by necessity and experience resulted in the creation of a system which was very similar to an international organisation. An *ad hoc* committee with limited powers handled the important business in between the annual sessions. Previously, a Secretariat was borrowed from the Interim Commission for International Trade Organisation. After that, it was borrowed from the United Nations.

In October 1953, the Contracting Parties decided to conduct, at their ninth session, a comprehensive review of the General Agreement, "upon the basis of the experience gained since it had been in provisional operation, and...in the light of this review to examine to what extent it would be desirable to amend or supplement the existing provisions of the Agreement, and what modifications should be made in the arrangements for its administration, in order that the Agreement may contribute more effectively to an early progress towards the attainment of its objective."[21] It being clear that there was no immediate prospect of establishing an International Trade Organisation, the Contracting

20. E.W. White, *The First Ten Years of the GATT* (Geneva, 1958), p. 5.

21. GATT, *Basic Instruments and Selected Documents, Second Supplement* (Geneva, 1954), p. 29.

Parties decided to revise the text of the General Agreement to enable it to operate effectively on a permanent basis. There was also a growing awareness of the disappointment of the developing countries with the working of the GATT. In addition, it was felt that the institutional framework of GATT was inadequate and there was a need for some sort of organisation to administer GATT. It was hoped that this review would end the provisional character of the Agreement and establish it as a regular international organisation.

The developing countries pointed out that the operation of GATT, during the seven years it had been in force, had hindered their commercial and development prospects. In regard to the treatment received by the developing countries from the provisions of GATT and their procedural application, on some points the developing countries had common views, but on other points only certain groups placed special emphasis. The difference of views originated from the particular experience of individual countries and from differences in the degree of economic development among the less developed countries.

The developing countries pointed, *inter alia*, to the following problems:[22]

1. The procedures for the implementation of the developmental rules of Article XVIII were unduly dilatory and cumbersome. Every time a country decided to institute import restrictions for facilitating economic growth, it had to appear before the Contracting Parties during the annual session in order to explain proposed measures and seek prior approval. The International Committee never made use of its authority to convene a special session of the Contracting Parties for the purpose of considering a request under Article XVIII. In addition, the approval, if granted, might be subject to a number of limitations and qualifications.
2. The measures available under the provisions of Article XVIII were inadequate and included a concept of "infant industry" which in the opinion of the developing

22. UN Conference on Trade and Development, *op. cit.*, pp. 33-34.

countries was extremely restricted since...the original text did hot mark the distinction between economic structures as an aggregate but looked at separate industries as such.[23]

3. The failure to introduce in the General Agreement the provisions of the Havana Charter in respect of commodity arrangements had seriously affected the export interests of the developing countries.
4. While the General Agreement permitted the existing preferential arrangements to continue, it did not allow developing countries to enter into new preferential arrangements aimed at promoting their economic development.

There were some problems on which certain groups of countries placed special emphasis. Some countries emphasized the difficulties in adjusting bound tariffs, on which they depended much more than on quantitative restrictions. At the time of participation in the early round of tariff negotiations the customs duties of these countries were generally specific and also low. Subsequent development needs, or reduction in effective protection resulting from rising prices, led the Governments concerned to apply to the Contracting Parties for authorization to increase certain bound rates. In such cases, the attitude of the developed countries was not sympathetic; they were reluctant to accept modification in bound rates of duty either during or at the end of the period in which negotiated items remained bound. The Cuban delegate to the ninth session pointed out in this respect that "this negative attitude was shown not only in connection with exceptional situation, where it was necessary to ask the Contracting Parties for a special authorization to hold the corresponding negotiations, but also when the intention was simply to utilise the procedures established in Article XXVIII of the Agreement, to adjust concessions, once the assured life of the schedules had terminated".[24]

---

23. Statement made by Mr. A. Helmi at the ninth session of the Contracting Parties, 10 November 1954.

24. Statement made by Mr. G. Gutierrez at the Ninth Session of the Contracting Parties, Press Release GATT/201, 16 November 1954.

On the other hand, countries that had already achieved a certain degree of economic development and which had engaged in further elaborate development plans, like Brazil and India, laid more emphasis on their dissatisfaction with the provisions regarding quantitative restrictions. Some countries expressed concern about the manner in which developed countries were making use of Article XI of the Agreement relating to import restrictions on agricultural or fishery products imposed for the enforcement of domestic marketing or production restriction programmes.

The developing countries also pleaded for an enlargement of the scope of the Agreement to include some provisions of the Havana Charter which had previously been excluded. They stated that the General Agreement, like the Havana Charter should reflect the organic relationship between international trade and economic development.

In contrast, the developed countries stated that a major modification of the Agreement would impede the attainment of the objectives that had been sought at its inception and some of these countries suggested that the further success in the operation of the GATT depended on maintaining the discipline of its provisions.

The review ended in reaffirming the fundamental rules of the Agreement. The most important amendments adopted at the ninth session can be summarised as follows :

1. Certain drafting changes in the preamble and a reference to economic development.
2. Article XVIII relating to governmental assistance to economic development was completely revised. The revised Article recognised that contracting parties in the early stages of development should enjoy additional facilities to enable them (i) to maintain sufficient flexibility in their tariff structure to be able to grant the tariff protection required for the establishment of particular industries, and (ii) to apply quantitative restrictions to stimulate specific branches of production and to protect the balance of payments in a manner which takes full account of the continued high level of demand for

imports likely to be generated by their programmes of economic development.

3. Provisions relating to negotiated tariff rates were amended and a new article on tariff negotiations was introduced. It was decided that the periods of "firm validity" should run for three years at the end of which contracting parties have an opportunity to renegotiate individual concessions if required, provided they consult, not only with the contracting party with which the pertinent concession was initially negotiated, but also with a contracting party that is a principal-supplier or has a substantial interest in the concession. If no agreement was reached, the concession could always be withdrawn, but the interested contracting parties were entitled to modify or withdraw concessions accordingly. The revised provisions also permitted a modification or withdrawal of a concession during the period of "firm validity" if the Contracting Parties consented to it.
4. The provisions relating to anti-dumping and countervailing duties were amended in two respects : (i) it was made mandatory to grant an importing country the permission to impose countervailing duties when it found that serious injury to third countries existed or was threatened and (ii) the importing country was permitted to levy such duties without prior approval when delay would cause serious damage, subject to the condition that it must modify any action taken and withdraw the duty if it was subsequently disapproved.
5. The consultation provisions of Article XII were strengthened with a view to achieving a more effective removal of restrictions as the balance of payments situation improved and to ensure that the trade interests of other countries received due consideration.
6. Article XIV, containing exceptions to the rule of non-discrimination, was amended and simplified. Formerly, the article contained three different criteria which, if met, permitted the use of discriminatory quantitative

restrictions. The revised Article provided a simple criterion permitting the contracting party to discriminate in a manner having effects equivalent to exchange restrictions which at the time it was permitted to apply under the International Monetary Fund's Articles of Agreement or a special exchange agreement. The contracting parties practising discrimination under Article XIV were required to consult periodically.

7. The provisions of Article XVI were extended and tightened to limit the harmful effects of export subsidies. The Article prohibited the use of subsidies on non-primary products or manufactures after 1 January 1958, or at the earliest practicable date thereafter. In the meantime no new or increased subsidies were to be granted on these products. In respect of primary products, the contracting parties were under an obligation not to use subsidies which increase exports so as to obtain for themselves more than a fair share of world trade.
8. The revised Article XVIII on state trading contained a paragraph recognizing that state trading enterprises might be operated so as to create obstacles to trade and that negotiations to eliminate or reduce such obstacles were important for the expansion of international trade. It established a reporting procedure on the operations of state trading enterprises maintained by contracting parties in order to enable interested countries to see that these operations were being carried out in a manner consistent with the provisions of the Agreement.

The foregoing shows that the amendments made in the General Agreement in 1954-55 were of secondary importance and did not take into account the criticisms that had been made of the fundamental assumptions on which the original Agreement had been based. To quote the GATT report :

> Probably the most important result was the least tangible since it did not involve any change in the Agreement itself. The original Agreement had been drawn up at a time when governments had been through a major war

> and were determined to substitute co-operation for economic warfare. After seven years of actual experience with these rules, it was of paramount importance that they be either reaffirmed by governments or reshaped in a form that governments could accept and would undertake to carry out. Essentially, the review resulted in a reaffirmation of the cardinal rules of the Agreement. The amendments that were adopted were designed to make them in some cases more flexible and in other cases more firm, depending upon the lessons of practical experience. But in no case were the fundamental principles discarded.[25]

An important outcome of the review session was the conclusion of an Agreement for the establishment of the Organisation for Trade Cooperation which was to administer the General Agreement and sponsor international consultations and negotiations on trade matters. The agreement for the Organisation was not, however, ratified and, therefore, could not come into existence.

In 1965, a new chapter on trade and development was added to the General Agreement. The new Part IV of the General Agreement specifically committed developed countries to help the developing countries 'as a matter of conscious and purposeful effort.' It laid down the important new principle — applied in the Kennedy Round Negotiations — that full reciprocity in trade negotiations would not be expected from developing countries. The developed countries undertook that, except when compelling reasons made it impossible, they would refrain from increasing barriers to exports of primary and other products of special interest to developing countries, and would give high priority to reducing existing barriers, including fiscal taxes. A Committee on Trade and Development was set up. The Committee had the duty to follow all activities of GATT, ensuring that problems of concern to developing countries were given priority attention.

Trade Rounds — the Package Route to Reduction in Trade Barriers

The biggest leaps forward in international trade liberalization

25. GATT, *International Trade* 1954 (Geneva, 1955), p. 129.

have come through multilateral trade negotiations, or 'trade rounds', under the auspices of GATT — the Uruguay Round was the latest and most extensive.

Although often lengthy, trade rounds offer a package approach to trade negotiations; an approach with a number of advantages over issue-by-issue negotiations. For a start, a trade round allows participants to seek and secure advantages across a wide range of issues. Second, concessions which are necessary but would otherwise be difficult to defend in domestic political terms, can be made more easily in the context of a package which also contains politically and economically attractive benefits. Third, developing countries and other less powerful participants have a greater chance of influencing the multilateral system in the context of a round than if bilateral relationships between major trading nations are allowed to dominate. Finally, overall reform in politically-sensitive sectors of world trade can be more feasible in the context of a global package; reform of agricultural trade was a good example in the Uruguay Round.

Most of GATT's early trade rounds were devoted to continuing the process of reducing tariffs. The results of the Kennedy Round in the mid-sixties, however, included a new GATT Anti-Dumping Agreement. The Tokyo Round during the seventies was a more sweeping attempt to extend and improve the system.

The Tokyo Round — a First Attempt at Reforming the Trading System

Conducted between 1973 and 1979 and with 102 participating countries, the Tokyo Round continued GATT's efforts to progressively reduce tariffs. The results included an average one-third cut in custom duties in the world's nine major industrial markets, bringing the average tariff on manufactured products down to 4.7 per cent compared with about 40 per cent at the time of GATT's creation. The tariff reductions, phased in over a period of eight years, involved an element of harmonization, bringing the highest tariffs down proportionately more than the lowest.

Elsewhere, the Tokyo Round had mixed results. It failed to come to grips with the fundamental problems affecting farm trade and also stopped short of providing a new agreement on 'safeguards' (emergency import measures). Nevertheless, a series of agreements on non-tariff barriers did emerge from the negotiations, in some cases interpreting existing GATT rules, in others breaking entirely new ground. In most cases, only a relatively small number of, mainly industrialized, GATT members ascribed to these agreements and arrangements which, as a consequence, were often referred to as 'codes'. They included the following agreements :

Subsidies and countervailing measures — interpreting Articles VI, XVI and XXIII of the General Agreement on Tariffs and Trade

Technical barriers to trade — sometimes called the Standards Code

Import licensing procedures

Government procurement

Customs valuation — interpreting Article VII

Anti-dumping — interpreting Article VI and replacing the Kennedy Round Anti-Dumping Code

Bovine Meat Arrangement

International Dairy Arrangement

Trade in Civil Aircraft

Several of the above Codes were amended and extended in the Uruguay Round. Those on subsidies and countervailing measures, technical barriers to trade, import licensing, customs valuation and anti-dumping, are now multilateral commitments within the WTO Agreement — in other words, all WTO members are committed to them — while those on government procurement, bovine meat, dairy products and civil aircraft remain 'plurilateral' agreements.

Did GATT Succeed?

Given its provisional nature and limited field of action, the success of GATT in promoting and securing the liberalization of much of world trade over 47 years is incontestable. Continual reductions in tariffs alone helped spur very high rates of world trade growth — around 8 per cent a year on average — during the 1950s and 1960s. And the momentum of trade liberalization helped ensure that trade growth consistently outpaced production growth throughout the GATT era. The rush of new members during the Uruguay Round demonstrated that the multilateral trading system, as then represented by GATT, was recognized as an anchor for development and an instrument of economic and trade reform.

The limited achievement of the Tokyo Round, outside the tariff reduction results, was a sign of difficult times to come. GATT's success in reducing tariffs to such a low level, combined with a series of economic recessions in the 1970s and early 1980s, drove governments to devise other forms of protection for sectors facing increased overseas competition. High rates of unemployment and constant factory closures led governments in Europe and North America to seek bilateral market-sharing arrangements with competitors and to embark on a subsidies race to maintain their holds on agricultural trade. Both these changes undermined the credibility and effectiveness of GATT.

Growth of GDP and Trade by Region 1986-94

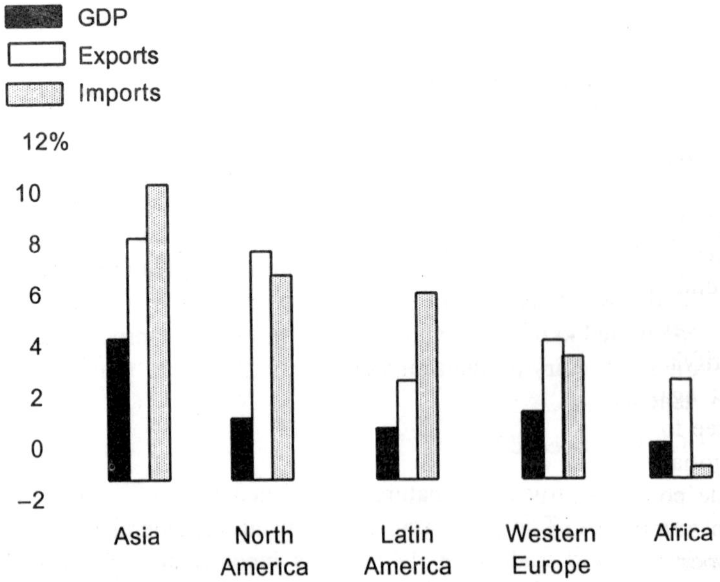

Note : Asia excl. China.
Trade refers to goods and services.

Apart from the deterioration in the trade policy environment, it also became apparent by the early 1980s that the General Agreement was no longer as relevant to the realities of world trade as it had been in the 1940s. For a start, world trade had become far more complex and important than 40 years before : the globalization of the world economy was underway, international investment was exploding and trade in services — not covered by the rules of GATT — was of major interest to more and more countries and, at the same time, closely tied to further increases in world merchandise trade. In other respects, the GATT had been found wanting : for instance, with respect to agriculture where loopholes in the multilateral system were heavily exploited — and efforts at liberalization met with little success — and in the textiles and clothing sector where an exception to the normal disciplines of GATT was negotiated in the form of the Multifibre Arrangement. Even the institutional structure of GATT and its dispute settlement system were giving cause for concern.

Together, these and other factors convinced GATT members that a new effort to reinforce and extend the multilateral system should be attempted. That effort resulted in the Uruguay Round.

The Uruguay Round — Creating a New System

The seeds of the Uruguay Round were sown in November 1982 at a Ministerial meeting of GATT members in Geneva. Although Ministers intended to launch a major new negotiation, the meeting stalled on the issue of agriculture and was widely regarded as a failure. In fact, the work programme that Ministers agreed formed the basis for what was to become the Uruguay Round negotiating agenda.

Nevertheless, it took four more years of exploring and clarifying issues and painstaking consensus-building, before Ministers met again in September 1986, in Punta del Este, Uruguay, to agree to launch the Uruguay Round. They were able to accept a negotiating agenda which covered virtually every outstanding trade policy issue including the extension of the trading system into several new areas, notably trade in services and intellectual property. It was the biggest negotiating mandate on trade ever agreed and Ministers gave themselves four years to complete it.

By 1988, the negotiations had reached the stage of a "Mid-term Review". This took the form of a Ministerial Meeting in Montreal, Canada, and led to the elaboration of the negotiating mandate for the second stage of the Round. Ministers agreed a package of early results which included concessions on market access for tropical products — aimed to assist developing countries — as well as a streamlined dispute settlement system and the Trade Policy Review Mechanism which provided for the first comprehensive, systematic and regular reviews of national trade policies and practices of GATT members.

At the Ministerial meeting in Brussels in December 1990, disagreement on the nature of commitments to future agricultural trade reform led to a decision to extend the round.

By December 1991, a comprehensive draft text of the 'Final Act', containing legal texts fulfilling every part of the Punta del Este mandate, with the exception of market access results was on the table in Geneva. For the following two years the negotiations lurched continuously from impending failure to predictions of imminent success. Several deadlines came and went; farm trade was joined by services, market access, anti-dumping rules and the proposed creation of a new institution, as the major points of conflict; and differences between the United States and European Communities became central to hopes for a final, successful conclusion. It took until 15 December 1993 for every issue to be finally resolved and for negotiations on market access for goods and services to be concluded. On 15 April 1994, the deal was signed by Ministers from most of the 125 participating governments at a meeting in Marrakesh, Morocco.

How is the WTO different from the GATT?

The World Trade Organization is not a simple extension of GATT. On the contrary, it completely replaces its predecessor and has a very different character. Among the principal differences are the following :

> The GATT was a set of rules, a multilateral agreement, with no institutional foundation, only a small associated secretariat which had its origins in the attempt to establish an International Trade Organization in the

1940s. The WTO is a permanent institution with its own secretariat.

The GATT was applied on a 'provisional basis' even if, after more than forty years, governments chose to treat it as a permanent commitment. The WTO commitments are full and permanent.

The GATT rules applied to trade in merchandise goods. In addition to goods, the WTO covers trade in services and trade-related aspects of intellectual property.

While GATT was a multilateral instrument, by the 1980s many new agreements had been added of plurilateral, and therefore selective nature. The agreements which constitute the WTO are almost all multilateral and, thus, involve commitments for the entire membership.

The WTO dispute settlement system is faster, more automatic, and thus much less susceptible to blockages, than the old GATT system. The implementation of WTO dispute findings will also be more easily assured.

The 'GATT 1947' will continue to exist until the end of 1995, thereby allowing time for all GATT member countries to accede to the WTO and permitting an overlap of activity in areas like dispute settlement. Moreover GATT lives on as 'GATT 1994', the amended and updated version of 'GATT 1947', which is an integral part of the WTO Agreement and which continues to provide the key disciplines affecting international trade in goods.

2

STRUCTURE AND MEMBERSHIP OF WTO

The Structure of the WTO

The structure of the WTO is dominated by its highest authority, the Ministerial Conference, composed of representatives of all WTO members, which is required to meet at least in every two years and which can take decisions on all matters under any of the multilateral trade agreements.

The day-to-day work of the WTO, however, falls to a number of subsidiary bodies; principally the General Council, also composed of all WTO members, which is required to report to the Ministerial Conference. As well as conducting its regular work on behalf of the Ministerial Conference, the General Council convenes in two particular forms — as the Dispute Settlement Body, to oversee the dispute settlement procedures and as the Trade Policy Review Body to conduct regular reviews of the trade policies of individual WTO members.

The General Council delegates responsibility to three other major bodies — namely the Councils for Trade in Goods, Trade in Services and Trade-Related Aspects of Intellectual Property Rights. The Council for Goods oversees the implementation and functioning of all the agreements covering trade in goods (Annex 1A of the WTO Agreement), though many such agreements have their own specific overseeing bodies. The latter two Councils have responsibility for their respective WTO agreements (Annexes 1B and 1C) and may establish their own subsidiary bodies as necessary.

Three other bodies are established by the Ministerial Conference and report to the General Council. The Committee on Trade and Development is concerned with issues relating to the developing countries and, especially, to the 'least-developed' among them. The Committee on Balance of Payments is responsible for consultations between WTO members and countries which take trade-restrictive measures, under Articles XII and XVIII of GATT, in order to cope with balance-of-payments difficulties. Finally, issues relating to WTO's financing and budget are dealt with by a Committee on Budget, Finance and Administration.

Each of the four plurilateral agreements of the WTO — those on civil aircraft, government procurement, dairy products and bovine meat — establish their own management bodies which are required to report to the General Council.

Representation in the WTO and Economic Groupings

The work of the WTO is undertaken by representatives of member governments but its roots lie in the everyday activity of industry and commerce. Trade policies and negotiating positions are formulated in capitals, usually with a substantial advisory input from private firms, business organizations, farmers as well as consumer and other interest groups. Most countries have a diplomatic mission in Geneva, sometimes headed by a special Ambassador to the WTO, whose officials attend meetings of the many negotiating and administrative bodies at WTO headquarters. Sometimes expert representatives are sent directly from capitals to put forward their governments' views on specific questions.

As a result of regional economic integration — in the form of customs unions and free trade areas — and looser political and geographic arrangements, some groups of countries act together in the WTO with a single spokesperson in meetings and negotiations.

The largest and most comprehensive grouping is the European Union and its 15 member states. The EU is a customs union with a single external trade policy and tariff. While the member states coordinate their position in Brussels and Geneva, the European Commission alone speaks for the EU at almost all WTO meetings. The EU is a WTO member in its own right as are each of its member states.

A lesser degree of economic integration has so far been achieved by the countries which are GATT members of the Association of South East Asian Nations (ASEAN) — Malaysia, Indonesia, Singapore, Philippines, Thailand and Brunei Darussalam. Nevertheless, they have many common trade interests and are frequently able to coordinate positions and to speak with a single voice.

Among other groupings which occasionally present unified. statements is the Latin American Economic System (SELA) and the African, Caribbean and Pacific Group (ACP). More recent efforts at regional economic integration — for instance, NAFTA (Canada, US and Mexico) and MERCOSUR (Brazil, Argentina, Paraguay and Uruguay) — have not yet reached the point where their constituents frequently have a single spokesperson on WTO issues.

A well-known alliance in the Uruguay Round — bringing together a similarity of trade interests rather than a regional identity — was the Cairns Group which comprised, and still comprises, agricultural exporting nations from developed, developing and Central European countries.

How the WTO Takes Decisions?

The WTO continues a long tradition in GATT of seeking to make decisions not by voting but by consensus. This procedure allows members to ensure their interests are properly considered even though, on occasion, they may decide to join a consensus in the overall interests of the multilateral trading system. Where consensus is not possible, the WTO Agreement allows for voting. In such circumstances, decisions are taken by a majority of the votes cast and on the basis of "one country, one vote".

There are four specific voting situations envisaged in the WTO Agreement. First, a majority of three-quarters of WTO members can vote to adopt an *interpretation* of any of the multilateral trade agreements. Second, and by the same majority, the Ministerial Conference may decide to *waive an obligation* imposed on a particular member by a multilateral agreement. Third, decisions to *amend* provisions of the multilateral agreements can be adopted through approval either by all members or by a

two-thirds majority depending on the nature of the provision concerned. However, such amendments only take effect for those WTO members who accept them. Finally, a decision to *admit a new member* is taken by a two-thirds majority in the Ministerial Conference.

The WTO Secretariat and Budget

The WTO Secretariat is located in Geneva. It has around 450 staff and is headed by its Director-General and four Deputy Directors-General. Its responsibilities include the servicing of WTO delegate bodies with respect to negotiations and the implementation of agreements. It has a particular responsibility to provide technical support to developing countries, and especially the least-developed countries. WTO economists and statisticians provide trade performance and trade policy analyses while its legal staff assist in the resolution of trade disputes involving the interpretation of WTO rules and precedents. Other Secretariat work is concerned with accession negotiations for new members and providing advice to governments considering membership.

The WTO budget is around US $ 83 million (105 million Swiss Francs) with individual contributions calculated on the basis of shares in the total trade conducted by WTO members. Part of the WTO budget also goes to the International Trade Centre.

How Countries Join the WTO?

Most WTO members were previously GATT members who signed the Final Act of the Uruguay Round and concluded their market access negotiations on goods and services by the Marrakesh meeting in 1994. A few countries which joined the GATT later in 1994, signed the Final Act and concluded negotiations on their goods and services schedules, and became WTO members. Other countries that had participated in the Uruguay Round negotiations, concluded their domestic ratification procedures only during the course of 1995, and became members thereafter.

Aside from these arrangements which relate to 'original' WTO membership, any other state or customs territory having full autonomy in the conduct of its trade policies may accede to the WTO on terms agreed with WTO members.

The accession process commences with the submission of a formal written request for accession pursuant to Article XII of the WTO Agreement. This request is considered by the General Council which establishes a Working Party to examine the accession request and to submit recommendations to the General Council which may include a Protocol of Accession. The Working Party is open to all Members of the WTO.

Established procedures require the applicant government to present to Working Party members a memorandum covering all aspects of its trade and legal regime. This memorandum forms the basis for detailed fact finding by the Working Party. After examining all aspects of the existing trade and legal regimes of the acceding government, the Working Party goes into the substantive part of the multilateral negotiations involved in accessions, *i.e.* determining the terms and conditions of entry. These terms and conditions, involving commitments to observe WTO rules and disciplines upon accession, and transitional periods if any, are finally incorporated in the Draft Report of the Working Party and the Protocol of Accession.

At the same time, the applicant government engages in bilateral negotiations with interested Working Party members on concessions and commitments on market access for goods and services. This bilateral process determines the specific benefits for WTO Members in permitting the applicant to accede to the WTO.

Once both the Working Party's Draft Report and Protocol of Accession and the market-access commitments in goods and services are completed to the satisfaction of members of the Working Party, the "accession package" is presented to the General Council or the Ministerial Conference for adoption. Once approved, the applicant is then free to sign the Protocol. Thirty days after the applicant government notifies the WTO Secretariat that it has completed its ratification procedures, the applicant government becomes a Member of the WTO.

Questions are often raised as to when a WTO applicant can accede to the WTO and whether it joins the WTO as a developing or a developed country. These questions are an inherent part of each WTO accession negotiation. Basically, this involves the granting of certain flexibilities in the implementation of WTO rules and disciplines — a matter determined in the negotiation process. While accession processes vary in length and can take several years to complete, much depends on the speed with which the applicant government is able to adjust its trade and legal regime to the requirements of WTO rules and disciplines.

Because each accession Working Party takes decisions by consensus, WTO Members must be in agreement that their individual concerns have been met and that all outstanding issues have been resolved in the course of their deliberations.

Since the WTO was established on 1 January 1995, seven countries have become WTO Members. These are: Ecuador, Estonia, Latvia, Kyrgyz Republic, Mongolia and Panama. The WTO is awaiting notification of ratification from Georgia.

With 31 governments still in the queue for membership to the WTO, accessions will remain a major challenge for WTO Members in the years ahead.

Applicants

The following 31 governments have requested to join the WTO. Their applications are currently being considered by WTO accession working parties. Each of the governments listed below has WTO observer status.

Albania

Algeria

Andorra

Armenia

Azerbaijan

Belarus

Bosnia Herzegovina

Bhutan

Cambodia

People's Republic of China

Croatia

Jordan

Kazakhstan

Lao People's Democratic Republic

Lebanon

Lithuania

Former Yugoslav Republic of Macedonia

Moldova

Nepal

Oman, Sultanate of

Russian Federation

Samoa

Saudi Arabia

Seychelles

Sudan

Chinese Taipei

Tonga

Ukraine

Uzbekistan

Vanuatu

Vietnam

Note : The WTO is waiting for confirmation of ratification from Georgia. It will become the 136th Member of the WTO 30 days after the WTO receives confirmation of ratification.

Membership of the World Trade Organization

135 Governments as of 13 November 1999

Member	Date of Membership
Angola	1 December 1996
Antigua and Barbuda	1 January 1995
Argentina	1 January 1995
Australia	1 January 1995
Austria	1 January 1995
Bahrain	1 January 1995
Bangladesh	1 January 1995
Barbados	1 January 1995
Belgium	1 January 1995
Belize	1 January 1995
Benin	22 February 1996
Bolivia	13 September 1995
Botswana	31 May 1995
Brazil	1 January 1995
Brunei Darussalam	1 January 1995
Bulgaria	1 December 1996
Burkina Faso	3 June 1995
Burundi	23 July 1995
Cameroon	13 December 1995
Canada	1 January 1995
Central African Republic	31 May 1995
Chad	19 October 1996
Chile	1 January 1995
Colombia	30 April 1995
Congo	27 March 1997
Costa Rica	1 January 1995
Côte d'Ivoire	1 January 1995
Cuba	20 April 1995

Member	Date of membership
Cyprus	30 July 1995
Czech Republic	1 January 1995
Democratic Republic of the Congo	1 January 1997
Denmark	1 January 1995
Djibouti	31 May 1995
Dominica	1 January 1995
Dominican Republic	9 March 1995
Ecuador	21 January 1996
Egypt	30 June 1995
El Salvador	7 May 1995
Estonia	13 November 1999
European Communities	1 January 1995
Fiji	14 January 1996
Finland	1 January 1995
France	1 January 1995
Gabon	1 January 1995
Gambia	23 October 1996
Germany	1 January 1995
Ghana	1 January 1995
Greece	1 January 1995
Grenada	22 February 1996
Guatemala	21 July 1995
Guinea Bissau	31 May 1995
Guinea	25 October 1995
Guyana	1 January 1995
Haiti	30 January 1996
Honduras	1 January 1995
Hong Kong, China	1 January 1995
Hungary	1 January 1995

Member	Date of membership
Iceland	1 January 1995
India	1 January 1995
Indonesia	1 January 1995
Ireland	1 January 1995
Israel	21 April 1995
Italy	1 January 1995
Jamaica	9 March 1995
Japan	1 January 1995
Kenya	1 January 1995
Korea	1 January 1995
Kuwait	1 January 1995
Kyrgyz Republic	20 December 1998
Latvia	10 February 1999
Lesotho	31 May 1995
Liechtenstein	1 September 1995
Luxembourg	1 January 1995
Macau	1 January 1995
Madagascar	17 November 1995
Malawi	31 May 1995
Malaysia	1 January 1995
Maldives	31 May 1995
Mali	31 May 1995
Malta	1 January 1995
Mauritania	31 May 1995
Mauritius	1 January 1995
Mexico	1 January 1995
Mongolia	29 January 1997
Morocco	1 January 1995
Mozambique	26 August 1995
Myanmar	1 January 1995

Member	Date of membership
Namibia	1 January 1995
Netherlands — including Netherlands Antilles	1 January 1995
New Zealand	1 January 1995
Nicaragua	3 September 1995
Niger	13 December 1996
Nigeria	1 January 1995
Norway	1 January 1995
Pakistan	1 January 1995
Panama	6 September 1997
Papua New Guinea	9 June 1996
Paraguay	1 January 1995
Peru	1 January 1995
Philippines	1 January 1995
Poland	1 July 1995
Portugal	1 January 1995
Qatar	13 January 1996
Romania	1 January 1995
Rwanda	22 May 1996
Saint Kitts and Nevis	21 February 1996
Saint Lucia	1 January 1995
Saint Vincent & the Grenadines	1 January 1995
Senegal	1 January 1995
Sierra Leone	23 July 1995
Singapore	1 January 1995
Slovak Republic	1 January 1995
Slovenia	30 July 1995
Solomon Islands	26 July 1996
South Africa	1 January 1995
Spain	1 January 1995

Member	Date of membership
Sri Lanka	1 January 1995
Suriname	1 January 1995
Swaziland	1 January 1995
Sweden	1 January 1995
Switzerland	1 July 1995
Tanzania	1 January 1995
Thailand	1 January 1995
Togo	31 May 1995
Trinidad and Tobago	1 March 1995
Tunisia	29 March 1995
Turkey	26 March 1995
Uganda	1 January 1995
United Arab Emirates	10 April 1996
United Kingdom	1 January 1995
United States	1 January 1995
Uruguay	1 January 1995
Venezuela	1 January 1995
Zambia	1 January 1995
Zimbabwe	3 March 1995

3

SETTLEMENT OF DISPUTES

Without a means of settling disputes, the rules-based system would be worthless because the rules could not be enforced. The WTO's procedure underscores the rule of law, and it makes the trading system more secure and predictable. The system is based on clearly-defined rules, with timetables for completing a case. First rulings are made by a panel and endorsed (or rejected) by the WTO's full membership. Appeals based on points of law are possible.

However, the point is not to make rulings. The priority is to settle disputes, through consultations if possible. By early 1997, 19 out of 71 cases had been settled "out of court", without going through the full panel process.

Principles : Equitable, Fast, Effective, Mutually Acceptable

WTO members have agreed that if they believe fellow-members are violating trade rules, they will use the multilateral system of settling disputes instead of taking action unilaterally. That means abiding by the agreed procedures, and respecting judgements.

Typically, a dispute arises when one country adopts a trade policy measure or takes some action that one or more fellow-WTO members considers to be breaking the WTO agreements, or to be a failure to live up to obligations. A third group of countries can declare that they have an interest in the case and enjoy some rights.

Understanding on Rules and Procedures Governing the Settlement of Disputes.

A procedure for settling disputes existed under the old GATT, but it had no fixed timetables, rulings were easier to block, and many cases dragged on for a long time inconclusively. The Uruguay Round agreement introduced a more structured process with more clearly defined stages in the procedure. It introduced greater discipline for the length of time a case should take to be settled, with flexible deadlines set in various stages of the procedure. The agreement emphasizes that prompt settlement is essential if the WTO is to function effectively. It sets out in considerable detail the procedures and the timetable to be followed in resolving disputes. If a case runs its full course to a first ruling, it should not normally take more than about one year — 15 months if the case is appealed. The agreed time limits are flexible, and if the case is considered urgent (*e.g.* if perishable goods are involved), then the case should take three months less.

The Uruguay Round agreement also made it impossible for the country losing a case to block the adoption of the ruling. Under the previous GATT procedure, rulings could only be adopted by consensus, meaning that a single objection could block the ruling. Now, rulings are automatically adopted unless there is a consensus to reject a ruling — any country wanting to block a ruling has to persuade all other WTO members (including its adversary in the case) to share its view.

Although much of the procedure does resemble a court or tribunal, the preferred solution is for the countries concerned to discuss their problems and settle the dispute by themselves. The first stage is therefore consultations between the governments concerned, and even when the case has progressed to other stages, consultation and mediation are still always possible.

Settling disputes is the responsibility of the Dispute Settlement Body (the General Council in another guise). The Dispute Settlement Body has the sole authority to establish "panels" of experts to consider the case, and to accept or reject the panels' findings or the results of an appeal. It monitors the implementation of the rulings and recommendations, and has the power to authorize retaliation when a country does not comply with a ruling.

First stage : consultation (up to 60 days). Before taking any other actions the countries in dispute have to talk to each other to

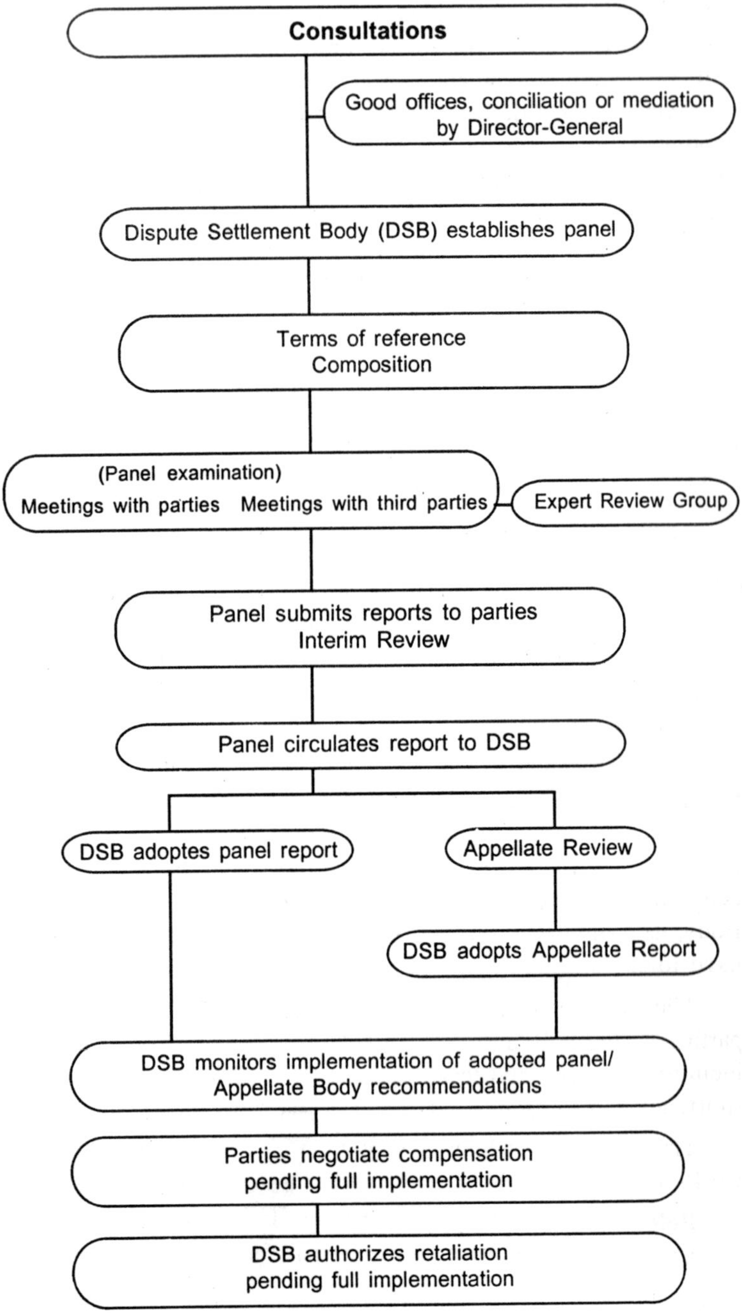
Consultations
Good offices, conciliation or mediation by Director-General
Dispute Settlement Body (DSB) establishes panel
Terms of reference
Composition
(Panel examination)
Meetings with parties
Meetings with third parties
Expert Review Group
Panel submits reports to parties
Interim Review
Panel circulates report to DSB
DSB adoptes panel report
Appellate Review
DSB adopts Appellate Report
DSB monitors implementation of adopted panel/ Appellate Body recommendations
Parties negotiate compensation pending full implementation
DSB authorizes retaliation pending full implementation

see if they can settle their differences by themselves. If that fails, they can also ask the WTO director-general to mediate or try to help in any other way.

Second stage : the panel (up to 45 days for a panel to be appointed, plus 6 months for the panel to conclude). If consultations fail, the complaining country can ask for a panel to be appointed. The country "in the dock" can block the creation of a panel once, but when the Dispute Settlement Body meets for a second time, the appointment can no longer be blocked (unless there is a consensus against appointing the panel).

Panels

Panels are like tribunals. But unlike in a normal tribunal, the panelists are usually chosen in consultation with the countries in dispute. Only if the two sides cannot agree does the WTO director-general appoint them. This only happens rarely.

Panels consist of three (occasionally five) experts from different countries who examine the evidence and decide who is right and who is wrong. The panel's report is passed to the Dispute Settlement Body, which can only reject the report by consensus.

Panellists for each case can be chosen from a permanent list of well-qualified candidates, or from elsewhere. They serve in their individual capacities. They cannot receive instructions from any government.

Officially, the panel is helping the Dispute Settlement Body make rulings or recommendations. But because the panel's report can only be rejected by consensus in the Dispute Settlement Body, its conclusions are difficult to overturn. The panel's findings have to be based on the agreements cited.

The panel's final report should normally be given to the parties to the dispute within six months. In cases of urgency, including those concerning perishable goods, the deadline is shortened to three months.

The agreement describes in some detail how the panels are to work. The main stages are :

Before the first hearing : each side in the dispute presents its case in writing to the panel.

First hearing : the case for the complaining country and defence : the complaining country (or countries), the responding country, and those that have announced they have an interest in the dispute, make their case at the panel's first hearing.

Rebuttals : the countries involved submit written rebuttals and present oral arguments at the panel's second meeting.

Experts : if one side raises scientific or other technical matters, the panel may consult experts or appoint an expert review group to prepare an advisory report.

First draft : the panel submits the descriptive (factual and argument) sections of its report to the two sides, giving them two weeks to comment. This report does not include findings and conclusions.

Interim report : The panel then submits an interim report, including its findings and conclusions, to the two sides, giving them one week to ask for a review.

Review : The period of review must not exceed two weeks. During that time, the panel may hold additional meetings with the two sides.

Final report : A final report is submitted to the two sides and three weeks later, it is circulated to all WTO members. If the panel decides that the disputed trade measure does break a WTO agreement or an obligation, it recommends that the measure be made to conform with WTO rules. The panel may suggest how this could be done.

The report becomes a ruling : The report becomes the Dispute Settlement Body's ruling or recommendation within 60 days unless a consensus rejects it. Both sides can appeal the report (and in some cases both sides do).

Appeals

Either side can appeal a panel's ruling. Sometimes both sides do so. Appeals have to be based on points of law such as legal interpretation — they cannot reexamine existing evidence or examine new evidence.

Each appeal is heard by three members of a permanent seven-member Appellate Body set up by the Dispute Settlement Body and broadly representing the range of WTO membership. Members of the Appellate Body have four-year terms. They have to be individuals with recognized standing in the field of law and international trade, not affiliated with any government.

The appeal can uphold, modify or reverse the panel's legal findings and conclusions. Normally appeals should not last more than 60 days, with an absolute maximum of 90 days.

The Dispute Settlement Body has to accept or reject the appeals report within 30 days — and rejection is only possible by consensus.

The Case has been Decided : What Next?

Go directly to jail. Do not pass Go, do not collect .... Well, not exactly. But the sentiments apply. If a country has done something wrong, it should swiftly correct its fault. And if it continues to break an agreement, it should offer compensation or suffer a suitable penalty that has some bite.

Even once the case has been decided, there is more to do before trade sanctions (the conventional form of penalty) are imposed. The priority at this stage is for the losing "defendant" to bring its policy into line with the ruling or recommendations. The dispute settlement agreement stresses that "prompt compliance with recommendations or rulings of the DSB [Dispute Settlement Body] is essential in order to ensure effective resolution of disputes to the benefit of all Members".

If the country that is the target of the complaint loses, it must follow the recommendations of the panel report or the appeals report. It must state its intention to do so at a Dispute Settlement Body meeting held within 30 days of the report's adoption. If complying with the recommendation immediately proves impractical, the member will be given a "reasonable period of time" to do so. If it fails to act within this period, it has to enter into negotiations with the complaining country (or countries) in order to determine mutually-acceptable compensation — for instancc, tariff reductions in areas of particular interest to the complaining side.

If after 20 days, no satisfactory compensation is agreed, the complaining side may ask the Dispute Settlement Body for permission to impose limited trade sanctions ("suspend concessions or obligations") against the other side. The Dispute Settlement Body should grant this authorization within 30 days of the expiry of the "reasonable period of time" unless there is a consensus against the request.

In principle, the sanctions should be imposed in the same sector as the dispute. If this is not practical or if it would not be effective, the sanctions can be imposed in a different sector of the same agreement. In turn, if this is not effective or practicable and if the circumstances are serious enough, the action can be taken under another agreement. The objective is to minimize the chances of actions spilling over into unrelated sectors while at the same time allowing the actions to be effective.

In any case, the Dispute Settlement Body monitors how adopted rulings are implemented. Any outstanding case remains on its agenda until the issue is resolved.

More Cases can be Good News

If the courts find themselves handling an increasing number of criminal cases, does that mean law and order is breaking down? Not necessarily. Sometimes it means that people have more faith in the courts and the rule of law. They are turning to the courts instead of taking the law into their own hands.

For the most part, that is what is happening in the WTO. No one likes to see countries quarrel. But if there are going to be trade disputes anyway, it is healthier that the cases are handled according to internationally agreed rules. There are strong grounds for arguing that the increasing number of disputes is simply the result of expanding world trade and the stricter rules negotiated in the Uruguay Round; and that the fact that more are coming to the WTO reflects a growing faith in the system.

The Review

The review has covered many aspects of the Dispute Settlement Understanding. Among the issues governments have highlighted are the following :

Implementation

The Dispute Settlement Understanding does not spell out clear procedures for handling a possible disagreement on whether the accused government has implemented correctly the DSB's ruling. If the accused government concedes that it has not implemented correctly by the end of the reasonable period of time for implementation, members generally agree that the complaining government can then seek compensation or authorization to retaliate (as in the "Beef-Hormone" case). Authorization is given by the DSB.

Sometimes the two sides disagree about whether the accused government has implemented correctly. Again, members agree in principle that it is first necessary to determine whether there has been proper implementation before moving to the questions of compensation and retaliation. They also agree that the judgement has to be made within the WTO system and not unilaterally.

The main difference of opinion appears to be over the amount of time needed to determine whether the accused government has implemented correctly, which in turn depends on the procedures to be followed to reach a decision.

For example, do the two sides have to try to settle this new disagreement by consulting each other, and if so, for how long? Must the DSB meet — and if so, how many times — to refer the matter to the panel or Appellate Body for a judgement?

Should the panel make the judgement with the possibility of an appeal? Or should it only be made by the Appellate Body if the original matter had been appealed, or by the panel if it had not?

Must the DSB adopt the judgement automatically or must there be a consensus to adopt? How quickly can authority to retaliate be requested? And if the amount of retaliation is challenged, how long should the arbitration take?

Transparency and access to the dispute settlement system

Panel and Appellate Body reports (and all other WTO documents relating to specific disputes) are published on the WTO website immediately after distribution to the member governments. However, panel and appeals deliberations are confidential, and there have been complaints, particularly by non-governmental organizations (NGOs), that the proceedings of the dispute settlement system lack transparency.

Some governments say the WTO system is exclusively intergovernmental in nature. In their view, if an NGO wants to make an argument to a panel it should convince one of the governments involved in the dispute to present that argument to the panel. Other governments hold the view that the credibility of the system would be enhanced if it were more open and that openness would have no significant disadvantages.

It should be noted that the Appellate Body ruled (in the "Shrimp/Turtle" case) that panels have the right to accept submissions that they have not requested from sources other than governments involved in the dispute (such as NGOs). It should also be noted that Article 18.2 of the DSU states :

> "...Nothing in this Understanding shall preclude a party to a dispute from disclosing statements of its own positions to the public. Members shall treat as confidential information submitted by another Member to the panel or the Appellate Body which that Member has designated as confidential. A party to a dispute shall also, upon request of a Member, provide a non-confidential summary of the information contained in its written submissions that could be disclosed to the public."

Developing countries and dispute settlement

Developing countries have made greater use of the WTO dispute settlement system than they made of the system under GATT (*i.e.* before 1995). To date, they have brought more than 40 disputes to the WTO system.

The DSU provides special treatment for developing countries in a number of respects. For example, it provides the possibility of a speedier process (Art.3.12), that special consideration should be given to developing countries in consultations (Arts.4.10, 12.10) and in the panel process (Arts.8.10, 12.10, 12.11) and that account should be taken of developing country interests in the surveillance stage (Arts.21.2, 21.7, 21.8). There are also special provisions for least-developed countries (Art.24).

One of the developing countries' major concerns expressed in the DSU review has been their shortage of resources for participating in the dispute settlement system. For the moment, the DSU addresses this concern by requiring the WTO Secretariat to provide legal assistance to such countries. The Secretariat also conducts a number of special training courses on dispute settlement for officials from such countries.

Disputes Facts and Stats

Situation as at 18 October 1999

To date, 183 disputes, regarding 142 distinct matters, have been brought to the WTO, of which :

- 29 were withdrawn following consultations;
- 86 are under consultations;
- 24 are being examined by panels;
- 7 subject of panel reports which have been appealed;
- 20 are in implementation stage following adoption by DSB of panel & appellate reports;
- 8 implemented;
- 7 closed without the need for implementation;
- 2 authority for panel elapsed.

Countries Involved in Disputes

Disputes involving	as complainant	as respondent	with developing countries: US/EC/Japan as complainant	with developing countries: US/EC/Japan as Respondent
United States	60	38	22	14
EC	47	28	21	11
Japan	7	12	3	0
Developing Countries	44	61	—	—

WTO Agreements Cited in the Disputes

SPS/TBT	Agriculture	Textiles	TRIMS	TRIPS	GATS
26	25	11	15	20	9

WTO Members Involved in Disputes

	As Complainant (case nos.)	Total	As Respondent (case nos.)	Total
Argentina	35, 111	2	56, 77, 121, 123, 145, 155, 157, 164, 171	9
Australia	35, 91, 169, 178	4	18, 21, 57, 106, 119, 126	6
Belgium			80, 127	2
Brazil	4, 69, 70, 71, 112, 154	6	22, 30, 46, 51, 52, 65, 81, 116, 183	9
Canada	7, 9, 10, 18, 20, 35, 46, 48, 92, 135, 137, 144, 153, 167, 180	15	31, 103, 113, 114, 117, 139, 142, 170	8
Chile	14, 97	2	87, 109, 110	3
Colombia	78	1	181	1
Costa Rica	24	1		
Czech Rep	159	1	148	1
Denmark			83	1
Ecuador	27	1	182	1
European Communities	8, 15, 38, 39, 40, 42, 53, 54, 63, 66, 73, 75, 77, 79, 81, 85, 87, 88, 96, 98, 100, 107, 108, 110, 114, 116, 117, 118, 120, 121, 136, 138, 142, 145, 146, 147, 149, 150, 151, 152, 155, 157, 160, 165, 166, 176, 183	47	7, 9, 12, 13, 14, 16, 17, 25, 26, 27, 48, 62, 69, 72, 104, 105, 115, 124, 134, 135, 137, 140, 141, 153, 154, 158, 172, 174	28

	As Complainant (case nos.)	Total	As Respondent (case nos.)	Total
France			131, 173	2
Greece			125, 128	2
Guatemala	16, 27, 158	3	60, 156	2
Honduras	16, 27, 158	3		
Hong Kong, China	29	1		
Hungary	143, 148	2	35, 159	2
India	19, 32, 33, 34, 58, 134, 140, 141, 168	9	50, 79, 90, 91, 92, 93, 9[illegible], 96, 120, 146, 149, 150, 175	13
Indonesia	123	1	54, 55, 59, 64	4
Ireland			68, 82, 129	3
Japan	6, 51, 55, 64, 95, 139, 162	7	8, 10, 11, 15, 28, 42, 44, 45, 66, 73, 76, 147	12
Korea	89, 99, 179	3	3, 5, 20, 40, 41, 75, 84, [illegible]8, 161, 163, 169	11
Malaysia	58	1	1	1
Mexico	16, 27, 49, 60, 156, 158, 182	7	53, 101, 132	3
Netherlands			130	1
New Zealand	35, 72, 93, 113, 177	5		
Pakistan	58	1	36, 107	2
Panama	105, 158	2		
Peru	12	1	112	1
Philippines	22, 61	2	74, 102	2

	As Complainant (case nos.)	Total	As Respondent (case nos.)	Total
Poland	122	1	19	1
Portugal			37	1
Singapore	1	1		
Slovak Rep			133, 143	2
South Africa			168	1
Sri Lanka	30	1		
Sweden			86	1
Switzerland	94, 119, 133	3		
Thailand	17, 35, 47, 58, 181	5	122	1
Turkey			29, 34, 43, 47	4
United Kingdom			67	1
United States	3, 5, 11, 13, 16, 21, 26, 27, 28, 31, 35, 36, 37, 41, 43, 44, 45, 50, 52, 56, 57, 59, 62, 65, 67, 68, 74, 76, 80, 82, 83, 84, 86, 90, 101, 102, 103, 104, 106, 109, 115, 124, 125, 126, 127, 128, 129, 130, 131, 132, 158, 161, 163, 164, 170, 171, 172, 173, 174, 175	60	2, 4, 6, 24, 32, 33, 38, 39, 49, 58, 61, 63, 78, 85, 88, 89, 95, 97, 99, 100, 108, 111, 118, 136, 138, 144, 151, 152, 160, 162, 165, 166, 167, 176, 177, 178, 179, 180	38
Uruguay	25	1		
Venezuela	2	1	23	1

Annual Tally of Disputes

1995	**25 Cases Filed**	
		Dispute Nos : 1—25
Settled officially in consultations stage :	9	Nos : 1, 5, 6, 7, 12, 14, 19, 20, 23
Still inactive in consultations stage :	6	Nos : 3, 13, 15, 16, 17, 25
Went to panel or beyond :	10	Nos : 2, 4, 8, 9, 10, 11, 18, 21, 22, 24

1996	**39 Cases Filed**	
		Dispute Nos : 26—64
Settled officially in consultations stage :	7	Nos : 28, 32, 36, 37, 40, 42, 43
Still inactive in consultations stage :	13	Nos : 29, 30, 39, 41, 45, 47, 49, 51, 52, 53, 57, 61, 63
Went to panel or beyond :	19	Nos : 26, 27, 31, 33, 34, 35, 38, 44, 46, 48, 50, 54, 55, 56, 58, 59, 60, 62, 64

1997	**47 Cases Filed**	
		Dispute Nos : 65—111
Settled officially in consultations stage :	12	Nos : 73, 74, 85, 86, 89, 91, 92, 93, 94, 96, 102, 106
Still inactive in consultations stage :	16	Nos : 65, 66, 71, 78, 80, 81, 82, 83, 97, 100, 101, 104, 105, 107, 109, 111
Went to panel or beyond :	19	Nos : 67, 68, 69, 70, 72, 75, 76, 77, 79, 84, 87, 88, 90, 95, 98, 99, 103, 108, 110

1998	44 Cases Filed	
		Dispute Nos : 112—155
Settled officially in consultations stage :	1	No : 119
Inactive more than 12 months in consultations stage :	18	Nos : 112, 115, 116, 117, 118, 120, 122, 123, 124, 125, 127, 128, 129, 130, 131, 133, 134, 137
Inactive 6-12 months in consultations stage :	14	Nos : 140, 141, 143, 144, 145, 146, 147, 148, 149, 150, 151, 152, 153, 154
Went to panel or beyond :	11	Nos : 113, 114, 121, 126, 132, 135, 136, 138, 139, 142, 155

1999 (1 Jan.—18 Oct.)	28 Cases Filed	
		Dispute Nos : 156—183
Settled officially in consultations stage :	0	
In consultations stage more than 6 months :	6	Nos : 157, 158, 159, 167, 168, 169
In consultations stage 3-6 months :	7	Nos : 171, 172, 173, 174, 175, 176, 177
In consultations stage less than 3 months :	6	Nos : 178, 179, 180, 181, 182, 183
Went to panel or beyond :	9	Nos : 156, 160, 161, 162, 163, 164, 165, 166, 170

OVERVIEW OF THE STATE-OF-PLAY OF WTO DISPUTES

This Overview updates the Overview dated 9 November 1999. New developments are reflected in paragraphs :

I (7) European Communities Bananas (DS27) — request under DSU 22.2

I (7) European Communities Bananas (DS27) — arbitration of level of nullification

I (24) Brazil Aircraft (DS46) — update on implementation

I (25) Canada Aircraft (DS70) — update on implementation

I (26) (a) & (b) Canada Dairy Products (DS103 & 113) — statement of intention to comply

II (9) Turkey Textiles (DS34) — adoption of Appellate Body and panel report

VI (12) Australia Salmonids (DS21) — suspension of panel proceedings

VI (21) (a) United States Safeguards (lamb) (DS177) — establishment of a panel

VI (21) (b) United States Safeguards (lamb) (DS178) — establishment of a panel

VI (22) Thailand Anti-Dumping (steel) (DS122) — establishment of a panel

VI (23) United States Anti-Dumping (steel) (DS179) — establishment of a panel

VII (63) United States Anti-Dumping (steel) (DS184) — request for consultations

VII (64) Trinidad and Tobago Imports of Pasta (DS185) — request for consultations

VIII B (31) European Communities Butter Products (DS72) — notification of settlement

	Consultation Requests	Distinct Matters	Active Cases	Completed Cases	Settled or Inactive Cases
Number	185	144	32	26	39

Table of Contents

I. Implementation Status of Adopted Reports

For descriptions of the reports adopted since 1 January 1999 see Part II of this Overview, and for those adopted earlier than 1 January 1999, see Part VIII of this Overview.

(1) *United States — Standards for Reformulated and Conventional Gasoline*, complaints by Venezuela (WT/DS2) and Brazil (WT/DS4). The US announced implementation of the recommendations of the DSB as of 19 August 1997, at the end of the 15 month reasonable period of time.

(2) *Japan — Taxes on Alcoholic Beverages*, complaints by the European Communities (WT/DS8), Canada (WT/DS10) and the United States (WT/DS11). The period for implementation was set by the Arbitrator at 15 months from the date of adoption of the reports *i.e.* it expired on 1 February 1998. Japan presented modalities for implementation which were accepted by the complainants.

(3) *United States — Restrictions on Imports of Cotton and Man-Made Fibre Underwear*, complaint by Costa Rica (WT/DS24). The US announced that the measure at issue expired as of 27 March 1997.

(4) *Brazil — Measures Affecting Desiccated Coconut*, complaint

by the Philippines (WT/DS22) — no implementation issue in view of the result.

(5) *United States — Measure Affecting Imports of Woven Wool Shirts and Blouses*, complaint by India (WT/DS33). The US announced that the measure was withdrawn as at 22 November 1996, before the Panel had concluded its work. Therefore, no implementation issue arose.

(6) *Canada — Certain Measures Concerning Periodicals*, complaint by the United States (WT/DS31). The implementation period was agreed by the parties to be 15 months from the date of adoption of the reports i.e. it expired on 30 October 1998. Canada has withdrawn the contested measure.

(7) *European Communities — Regime for the Importation, Sale and Distribution of Bananas*, complaints by Ecuador, Guatemala, Honduras, Mexico and the United States (WT/DS27). The period for implementation was set by arbitration at 15 months and 1 week from the date of the adoption of the reports *i.e.* it expired on 1 January 1999. The EC has revised the contested measures. On 18 August 1998, the complainants requested consultations with the EC (without prejudice to their rights under Article 21.5), for the resolution of the disagreement between them over the WTO-consistency of measures introduced by the EC in purported compliance with the recommendations and rulings of the Panel and Appellate Body. At the DSB meeting on 25 November 1998, the EC announced that it had adopted the second Regulation to implement the recommendations of the DSB, and that the new system will be fully operational from 1 January 1999. On 15 December 1998, the EC requested the establishment of a panel under Article 21.5 to determine that the implementing measures of the EC must be presumed to conform to WTO rules unless challenged in accordance with DSU procedures. On 18 December 1998, Ecuador requested the re-establishment of the original panel to examine whether the EC measures to implement the recommendations of the DSB are WTO-consistent. At its meeting on 12 January 1999, the DSB agreed to reconvene the original panel, pursuant to Article 21.5 of the DSU, to examine both Ecuador's and the EC's requests. Jamaica, Nicaragua, Colombia, Costa Rica, Coté d' Ivoire, Dominican Republic, Dominica, St.

Lucia, Mauritius, St. Vincent, indicated their interest to join as third parties in both requests, while Ecuador and India indicated their third-party interest only in the EC request. On 14 January 1999, the United States, pursuant to Article 22.2 of the DSU, requested authorization from the DSB for suspension of concessions to the EC in an amount of US$520 million. At the DSB meeting on 29 January 1999, the EC, pursuant to Article 22.6 of the DSU, requested arbitration on the level of suspension of concessions requested by the United States. The DSB referred the issue of the level of suspension to the original panel for arbitration. Pursuant to Article 22.6 of the DSU, the request for the suspension of concessions by the United States was deferred by the DSB until the determination, through the arbitration, of the appropriate level for the suspension of concessions. In the panel requested by the EC, pursuant to Article 21.5 of the DSU, the panel found that, because a challenge had actually been made by Ecuador regarding the WTO-consistency of the EC measures taken in implementation of the DSB recommendations, it was unable to agree with the EC that the EC must be presumed to be in compliance with the recommendations of the DSB. In the panel requested by Ecuador, pursuant to Article 21.5 of the DSU, the panel found that the implementation measures taken by the EC in compliance with the recommendations of the DSB were not fully compatible with the EC's WTO obligations. In the arbitration, under Article 22.6 of the DSU, necessitated by the EC's challenge to the level of suspension sought by the United States (US$520 million), the arbitrators found that the level of suspension sought by the United States was not equivalent to the level of nullification and impairment suffered as a result of the EC's new banana regime not being fully compatible with the WTO. The arbitrators accordingly determined the level of nullification suffered by the United States to be equal to US$191.4 million. The arbitrator's report and the reports of the panels were issued to the parties on 6 April 1999, and circulated to Members on 9 and 12 April 1999 respectively. On 9 April 1999, the United States, pursuant to Article 22.7 of the DSU, requested that the DSB authorize suspension of concessions to the EC equivalent to the level of nullification and impairment, *i.e.* US$191.4 million. On 19 April 1999, the DSB authorized the

United States to suspend concessions to the EC as requested. The report of the panel requested by Ecuador, under Article 21.5 of the DSU, was adopted by the DSB on 6 May 1999. On 8 November 1999, Ecuador requested authorization from the DSB to suspend the application to the EC of concessions or other related obligations, pursuant to Article 22.2 of the DSU, in an amount of US$450 million. At the DSB meeting on 19 November 1999, the EC, pursuant to Article 22.6 of the DSU, requested arbitration on the level of suspension of concessions requested by Ecuador and on the EC's claim that Ecuador had not followed the principles and procedures of Article 22.3 of the DSU (concerning suspension of concessions or commitments under a different agreement). The DSB referred these issues to the original panel for arbitration. Pursuant to Article 22.6 of the DSU, the request for the suspension of concessions by Ecuador was deferred by the DSB until the determination, through arbitration, of the appropriate level for the suspension of concessions and of the claim that Ecuador had not followed the principles and procedures set out in Article 22.3 of the DSU.

(8) *India — Patent Protection for Pharmaceutical and Agricultural Chemical Products*, complaint by the United States (WT/DS50). The period of implementation was agreed by the parties to be 15 months from the date of the adoption of the reports *i.e.* it expires on 16 April 1999. India has undertaken to comply with the recommendations of the DSB within the implementation period. At the DSB meeting on 28 April 1999, India presented its final status report on implementation of this matter which disclosed the enactment of the relevant legislation to implement the recommendations and rulings of the DSB.

(9) *European Communities — Measures Affecting Meat and Meat Products (Hormones)*, complaint by the United States (WT/DS26), and Canada (WT/DS48). The period for implementation was set by arbitration at 15 months from the date of the adoption of the reports *i.e.* it expires on 13 May 1999. The EC has undertaken to comply with the recommendations of the DSB within the implementation period. At the DSB meeting on 28 April 1999, the EC informed the DSB that it would consider offering compensation in view of the likelihood that it may not be

able to comply with the recommendations and rulings of the DSB by the deadline of 13 May 1999. On 3 June 1999, the United States and Canada, pursuant to Article 22.2 of the DSU, requested authorisation from the DSB for the suspension of concessions to the EC in the amount of US$202 million and Can.$75 million, respectively. The EC, pursuant to Article 22.6 of the DSU, requested arbitration on the level of suspension of concessions requested by the United States and Canada. The DSB referred the issue of the level of suspension to the original panel for arbitration. The arbitrators determined the level of nullification suffered by the United States to be equal to US$116.8 million, and the level of nullification suffered by Canada to be equal to CDN$11.3 million. The reports of the arbitrators were circulated to Members on 12 July 1999. At its meeting on 26 July 1999, the DSB authorised the suspension of concessions to the EC by the United States and Canada in the respective amounts determined by the arbitrators as being equivalent to the level of nullification suffered by them.

(10) *Argentina — Certain Measures Affecting Imports of Footwear, Textiles, Apparel and Other Items*, complaint by the United States (WT/DS56). Argentina has indicated its intention to comply with the recommendations of the DSB within the time period permissible under Article 21 of the DSU. At the DSB meeting on 22 June 1998, Argentina announced that it had reached an agreement on implementation with the US, whereby Argentina would reduce the statistical tax to 0.5% by 1 January 1999, and cap specific duties on textiles and apparel at 35% by 19 October 1998. At the DSB meeting on 26 May 1999, Argentina announced that Decree 108/99, pursuant to which no import transactions covered by the statistical tax shall be taxed in excess of the amounts agreed between it and the United States, will enter into force on 30 May 1999.

(11) *Japan — Measures Affecting Consumer Photographic Film and Paper*, complaint by the United States (WT/DS44) — no implementation issue in view of the result.

(12) *European Communities, United Kingdom, and Ireland — Customs Classification of Certain Computer Equipment*, complaint

by the United States (WT/DS62, 67, 68). No implementation issue in view of the result.

(13) *European Communities — Measures Affecting Importation of Certain Poultry Products*, complaint by Brazil (WT/DS69). The EC and Brazil announced at the DSB meeting on 21 October 1998, that they had reached a mutual agreement on a reasonable period of time for implementation, which is to be the period up to 31 March 1999.

(14) *Indonesia — Certain Measures Affecting the Automobile Industry*, complaints by the United States, the European Communities and Japan (WT/DS54, 55, 59 & 64). Indonesia indicated its intention to comply with the recommendations of the DSB within the time permissible under Article 21 of the DSU. On 8 October 1998, the EC, pursuant to Article 21.3 of the DSU, requested that the reasonable period of implementation be determined by binding arbitration. The Arbitrator determined, pursuant to Article 21.3 of the DSU, that the reasonable period of time for Indonesia to implement the recommendations and rulings of the DSB is 12 months from the date of adoption of the Panel Report *i.e.* it expires on 23 July 1999. The report of the Arbitrator was circulated to Members on 7 December 1998. By a communication dated 15 July 1999, Indonesia informed the DSB that it had issued a new automotive policy on 24 June 1999 (the 1999 Automotive Policy), which effectively implements the recommendations and rulings of the DSB in this matter.

(15) *India — Patent Protection for Pharmaceutical and Agricultural Chemical Products*, complaint by the European Communities (WT/DS79/1). India indicated at the DSB meeting of 21 October 1998, that it needed a reasonable period of time to comply with the DSB recommendations and that it intended to have bilateral consultations with the EC to agree on a mutually acceptable period of time. At the DSB meeting on 25 November 1998, India read out a joint statement done with the EC, in which it was agreed that the implementation period in this dispute would correspond to the implementation period in a similar dispute brought by the US (DS50). At the DSB meeting on 28 April 1999, India presented its final status report on implementation of DS50, which report also applies to implementation in this dispute.

The report disclosed the enactment of the relevant legislation to implement the recommendations and rulings of the DSB.

(16) *United States — Import Prohibition of Certain Shrimp and Shrimp Products*, complaint by India, Malaysia, Pakistan and Thailand (WT/DS58). Pursuant to Article 21.3 of the DSU, the US has 30 days from the date of adoption of the Panel and Appellate Body Reports (*i.e.* from 6 November 1998) to inform the DSB of its intentions regarding implementation of the recommendations and rulings of the DSB. At the DSB meeting on 25 November 1998, the US informed the DSB that it was committed to implementing the recommendations of the DSB and was looking forward to discussing with the complainants the question of implementation. The parties to the dispute have announced that they have agreed on an implementation period of 13 months from the date of adoption of the Appellate Body and Panel Reports *i.e.* it expires on 6 December 1999.

(17) *Australia — Measures Affecting the Importation of Salmon*, complaint by Canada (WT/DS18). Pursuant to Article 21.3 of the DSU, Australia has 30 days from the date of adoption of the Panel and Appellate Body Reports (*i.e.* from 6 November 1998) to inform the DSB of its intentions regarding implementation of the recommendations and rulings of the DSB. At the DSB meeting on 25 November 1998, Australia informed the DSB that it was committed to implementing the recommendations of the DSB and was looking forward to discussing with the complainants the question of implementation. On 24 December 1998, Canada requested arbitration, pursuant to Article 21.3(c) of the DSU, to determine the reasonable period of time for implementation of the recommendations of the DSB. The Arbitrator decided that the reasonable period of time for implementation is 8 months *i.e.* it expires on 6 July 1999. The report of the Arbitrator was circulated to Members on 23 February 1999. On 28 July 1999, Canada made a request to the DSB, pursuant to DSU Article 22.2, for authorisation to suspend concessions to Australia for its non-compliance with the recommendations of the DSB in this matter. Canada simultaneously made a request, pursuant to DSU Article 21.5, for determination by the original panel of whether the measures taken by Australia in implementing the recommendations of the

DSB were WTO-consistent. Australia informed the DSB that in the event that the DSB approved Canada's request under 22.2, it wished to request, pursuant to DSU 22.6, for arbitration on the level of nullification suffered by Canada.. The DSB agreed to Canada's request and referred the matter for determination of the WTO-consistency of the implementing measures to the original panel. The EC, Norway and the US reserved their third-party rights. The DSB also referred the Canadian request for suspension of concessions to arbitration in view of Australia's challenge of the level of nullification suffered by Canada.

(18) *Guatemala — Anti-Dumping Investigation Regarding Imports of Portland Cement from Mexico* (WT/DS60). In view of the result, no implementation issue arises.

(19) *Korea — Taxes on Alcoholic Beverages*, complaints by the European Communities and the United States (DS 75 & 84). At the DSB meeting on 19 March 1999, Korea informed the DSB, as required by Article 21.3 of the DSU, that it was considering options for implementation of the DSB's recommendations. On 9 April 1999, the two complainants separately requested, pursuant to Article 21.3(c) of the DSU, that the reasonable period of time for Korea to implement the recommendations of the DSB be determined by arbitration. On 23 April 1999, the three parties to the dispute, jointly informed the DSB that they had agreed on the appointment of an arbitrator for the determination of the reasonable period of time for implementation, and also that they had agreed that the arbitrator issue his arbitration award no later than 7 June 1999. On 4 June 1999, the arbitrator determined the reasonable period of time to be 11 months and two weeks. *i.e.* until 31 January 2000.

(20) *Japan — Measures Affecting Agricultural Products*, complaint by the United States (WT/DS76/1). Pursuant to Article 21.3 of the DSU, Japan informed the DSB on 13 April 1999 that it was studying ways in which to implement the recommendations of the DSB. In a joint communication, the two parties informed the DSB on 15 June 1999, that they had agreed on an implementation period of 9 months and 12 days from the date of adoption of the reports, *i.e.* from 19 March to 31 December 1999.

(21) *United States — Anti-Dumping Duty on Dynamic Random Access Memory Semiconductors (DRAMS) of One Megabit or Above from Korea*, complaint by Korea (WT/DS99/1). Pursuant to Article 21.3 of the DSU, the United States informed the DSB on 13 April 1999 that it was studying ways in which to implement the recommendations of the DSB. At the DSB meeting on 26 July 1999, the two parties notified the DSB that they had agreed on an implementation period of 8 months effective from the date of adoption of the report, *i.e.* from 19 March 1999. The reasonable period of time would therefore expire on 19 November 1999.

(22) *Australia — Subsidies Provided to Producers and Exporters of Automotive Leather*, complaint by the United States (WT/DS126/1). On 17 September 1999, Australia informed the DSB that it had implemented the recommendations and rulings of the DSB. On 4 October 1999, the United States informed the DSB that it believed that the measures taken by Australia to comply with the rulings and recommendations of the DSB were not consistent with the Subsidies Agreement and the DSU, and therefore requested that the original panel be reconvened pursuant to Article 21.5 of the DSU. The United States and Australia reached an agreement concerning certain procedures to be applicable in this case. That agreement provides, *inter alia*, that Australia will not raise any procedural objection to the establishment of a panel in accordance with Article 21.5 of the DSU, while the United States will not request authorization to suspend concessions pursuant to Article 22.2 of the DSU until after the review panel has circulated its report. Also, it has been agreed that neither party will appeal the review panel's report. At its meeting on 14 October 1999, the DSB agreed to reconvene the original panel pursuant to Article 21.5 of the DSU. The EC and Mexico reserved their third-party rights.

(23) *India — Quantitative Restrictions on Imports of Agricultural, Textile and Industrial Products* complaint by the United States (WT/DS90/1). At the DSB meeting of 14 October 1999, India stated its intention to comply with the recommendations and rulings of the DSB, at the same time drawing attention to the Panel's suggestion that the reasonable period of time for implementation in this case could be longer than 15 months in

view of the practice of the IMF, the BOP Committee and GATT and WTO panels of granting longer phase-out periods for the elimination of BOP restrictions, and in view of India's status as a developing country Member. India further indicated that it would consult with the US with a view to agreeing upon a reasonable period of time for implementation. The US stated its willingness to enter into such consultations and its expectation that India would implement the recommendations promptly.

(24) *Brazil — Export Financing Programme for Aircraft*, complaint by Canada (WT/DS46). At the DSB meeting of 19 November 1999, Brazil announced that it had withdrawn the measures at issue within 90 days and had thus implemented the recommendations and rulings of the DSB.

(25) *Canada — Measures Affecting the Export of Civilian Aircraft*, complaint by Brazil (WT/DS70). At the DSB meeting of 19 November 1999, Canada announced that it had withdrawn the measures at issue within 90 days and thus had implemented the recommendations and rulings of the DSB.

(26) (a) *Canada — Measures Affecting the Importation of Milk and the Exportation of Dairy Products*, complaint by the United States (WT/DS103/1). At the DSB meeting of 19 November 1999, Canada stated its intention to comply with the recommendations and rulings of the DSB.

(26) (b) *Canada — Measures Affecting Dairy Products*, complaint by New Zealand (WT/DS113/1). See DS103 above.

II. Appellate and Panel Reports Adopted Since 1 January 1999

(1) (a) *Korea — Taxes on Alcoholic Beverages*, complaint by the European Communities (WT/DS/75/1). This request, dated 4 April 1997, is in respect of internal taxes imposed by Korea on certain alcoholic beverages pursuant to its Liquor Tax Law and Education Law. The EC contends that the Korean Liquor Tax Law and Education Tax Law appear to be inconsistent with Korea's obligations under Article III : 2 of GATT 1994. On 10 September 1997, the EC requested the establishment of panel. At its meeting on 16 October 1997, the DSB established a panel, which would also examine the complaint by the US below.

Canada and Mexico reserved their third-party rights. The Panel found that soju (both diluted and distilled), is directly competitive and substitutable with the imported distilled alcoholic beverages that were in issue, namely, whisky, brandy, rum, gin, vodka, tequila, liqueurs and ad-mixtures. The Panel also found that Korea has taxed the imported products in a dissimilar manner and that the tax differential was more than *de minimis*, and is applied so as to afford protection to domestic production. The Panel therefore concluded that Korea had violated Article III :2 of GATT 1994. The report of the Panel (which also covers DS84 below) was circulated to Members on 17 September 1998. On 20 October 1998, Korea notified its intention to appeal certain issues of law and legal interpretations developed by the Panel. The Appellate Body upheld the panel's findings on all points. The report of the Appellate Body was circulated to Members on 18 January 1999. The DSB adopted the Panel and Appellate Body Reports on 17 February 1999.

(1) (b) *Korea — Taxes on Alcoholic Beverages*, complaint by the United States (WT/DS84/1). This request, dated 23 May 1997, is in respect of the same measures complained of by the EC in DS75 above. The US also alleges violations of Article III :2. On 10 September 1997, the US requested the establishment of a panel. At its meeting on 16 October 1997, the DSB established a panel, which would also examine the complaint by the EC above. Canada and Mexico reserved their third-party rights. See DS75 above.

(2) *Japan — Measures Affecting Agricultural Products*, complaint by the United States (WT/DS76/1). This request, dated 7 April 1997, is in respect of the prohibition by Japan, under quarantine measures, of imports of agricultural products. The US alleges that Japan prohibits the importation of each variety of a product requiring quarantine treatment until the quarantine treatment has been tested for that variety, even if the treatment has proved to be effective for other varieties of the same product. The US alleges violations of Articles 2, 5 and 8 of the SPS Agreement, Article XI of GATT 1994, and Article 4 of the Agreement on Agriculture. In addition, the US makes a claim for nullification and impairment of benefits. On 3 October 1997, the US requested

the establishment of a panel. The DSB established a panel on 18 November 1997. The EC, Hungary and Brazil reserved their third-party rights. The Panel found that Japan acted inconsistently with Articles 2.2 and 5.6 of the SPS Agreement, and Annex B and, consequently, Article 7 of the SPS Agreement. The report of the Panel was circulated to Members on 27 October 1998. On 24 November 1998, Japan notified its intention to appeal certain issues of law and legal interpretations developed by the Panel. The Appellate Body upheld the basic finding that Japan's varietal testing of apples, cherries, nectarines and walnuts is without scientific basis. The report of the Appellate Body was circulated to Members on 22 February 1999. The DSB adopted the Appellate Body Report and the Panel Report, as modified by the Appellate Body Report, on 19 March 1999.

(3) *United States — Anti-Dumping Duty on Dynamic Random Access Memory Semiconductors (DRAMS) of One Megabit or Above from Korea*, complaint by Korea (WT/DS99/1). This request, dated 14 August 1997, is in respect of a decision of the US Department of Commerce (DoC) not to revoke the anti-dumping duty on dynamic random access memory semi-conductors (DRAMS) of one megabyte or above originating from Korea. Korea contends that the DoC's decision was made despite the finding that the Korean DRAM producers have not bumped their products for a period of more than three and a half consecutive years, and despite the existence of evidence demonstrating conclusively that Korean DRAM producers will not engage in dumping DRAMS in the future. Korea considers that these measures are in violation of Articles 6 and 11 of the Anti-Dumping Agreement. On 6 November 1997, Korea requested the establishment of a panel. At its meeting on 16 January 1998, the DSB established a panel. The Panel found the measures complained of to be in violation of Article 11.2 of the Anti-Dumping Agreement. The report of the Panel was circulated on 29 January 1999. At its meeting on 19 March 1999, the DSB adopted the Panel Report.

(4) *Australia — Subsidies Provided to Producers and Exporters of Automotive Leather*, complaint by the United States (WT/DS126/1). The request, dated 4 May 1998, is in respect of prohibited subsidies allegedly provided to Australian producers

and exporters of automotive leather, including subsidies provided to Howe and Company Proprietary Ltd. (or any of its affiliated and/or parent companies), which allegedly involve preferential government loans of about A$25 million and non-commercial terms and grants of about A$30 million. The US contends that these measures violate the obligations of Australia under Article 3 of the Subsidies Agreement. On 11 June 1998, the US requested the establishment of a panel. See also WT/DS106. At its meeting on 22 June 1998, the DSB established a Panel. The Panel found that the loan from the Australian Government to Howe/ALH is not a subsidy contingent upon export performance within the meaning of Article 3.1(a) of the SCM Agreement, but that the payments under the grant contract are subsidies within the meaning of Article 1 of the SCM Agreement, which are contingent upon export performance within the meaning of Article 3.1(a) of that Agreement. The report of the Panel was circulated to Members on 25 May 1999. At its meeting on 16 June 1999, the DSB adopted the Panel report.

(5) *Brazil — Export Financing Programme for Aircraft*, complaint by Canada (WT/DS46). On 19 June 1996, Canada requested consultations with Brazil, based on Article 4 of the Subsidies Agreement, which provides for special procedures for export subsidies. Canada claims that export subsidies granted under the *Brazilian Programa de Financiamento* ás Exportações (*PROEX*), to foreign purchasers of Brazil's Embraer aircraft are inconsistent with the Subsidies Agreement Articles 3, 27.4 and 27.5. Canada requested the establishment of a panel on 16 September 1996, alleging violations of both the Subsidies Agreement and GATT 1994. The DSB considered this request at its meeting on 27 September 1996. Due to Brazil's objection to the establishment of a panel, Canada agreed to modify its request, limiting the scope of the request to the Subsidies Agreement. The modified request was submitted by Canada on 3 October 1996 but was subsequently withdrawn prior to a DSB meeting at which it was to be considered. On 10 July 1998, Canada again requested the establishment of a panel. At its meeting on 23 July 1998, the DSB established a panel. The US reserved its rights as a third-party in the dispute. The Panel found that Brazil's measures were inconsistent

with Articles 3.1(a) and 27.4 of the Subsidies Agreement. The report of the Panel was circulated to Members on 14 April 1999. On 3 May 1999, Brazil notified its intention to appeal certain issues of law and legal interpretations developed by the Panel. The Appellate Body upheld all the findings of the panel, but reversed and modified the panel's interpretation of the "material advantage" clause in item (k) of the Illustrative List of Export Subsidies in Annex I of the SCM Agreement. The report of the Appellate Body was circulated to Members on 2 August 1999. The DSB adopted the Appellate Body Report and the Panel Report, as modified by the Appellate Body Report, on 20 August 1999.

(6) *Canada — Measures Affecting the Export of Civilian Aircraft*, complaint by Brazil (WT/DS70). This request dated 10 March 1997, is in respect of certain subsidies granted by the Government of Canada or its provinces intended to support the export of civilian aircraft. The request is made pursuant to Article 4 of the Subsidies Agreement. Brazil contends that these measures are inconsistent with Article 3 of the Subsidies Agreement. On 10 July 1998, Brazil requested the establishment of a panel. At its meeting on 23 July 1998, the DSB established a panel. The US reserved its rights as a third-party in the dispute. The Panel found that certain of Canada's measures were inconsistent with Articles 3.1(a) and 3.2 of the Subsidies Agreement, but rejected Brazil's claim that EDC assistance to the Canadian regional aircraft industry constitutes export subsidies. The report of the panel was circulated to Members on 14 April 1999. On 3 May 1999, Canada notified its intention to appeal certain issues of law and legal interpretations developed by the Panel. The Appellate Body upheld the findings of the panel. The report of the Appellate Body was circulated to Members on 2 August 1999. The DSB adopted the Appellate Body and Panel Reports on 20 August 1999.

(7) *India — Quantitative Restrictions on Imports of Agricultural, Textile and Industrial Products,* complaint by the United States (WT/DS90/1). This request, dated 15 July 1997, is in respect of quantitative restrictions maintained by India on importation of a large number of agricultural, textile and industrial products. The

US contends that these quantitative restrictions, including the more than 2,700 agricultural and industrial product tariff lines notified to the WTO, are inconsistent with India's obligations under Articles XI :1 and XVIII :11 of GATT 1994, Article 4.2 of the Agreement on Agriculture, and Article 3 of the Agreement on Import Licensing Procedures. On 3 October 1997, the US requested the establishment of a panel. The DSB established a panel on 18 November 1997. The panel found that the measures at issue were inconsistent with India's obligations under Articles XI and XVIII11 of GATT 1994, and to the extent that the measures apply to products subject to the Agreement on Agriculture, are inconsistent with Article 4.2 of the Agreement on Agriculture. The panel also found the measures to be nullifying or impairing benefits accruing to the United States under GATT 1994, and the Agreement on Agriculture. The report of the Panel was circulated to Members on 6 April 1999. On 26 May 1999, India notified its intention to appeal certain issues of law and legal interpretations developed by the Panel. The Appellate Body upheld the findings of the panel. The report of the Appellate Body was circulated to Members on 23 August 1999. The DSB adopted the Panel and Appellate Body reports at its meeting on 22 September 1999.

(8) (a) *Canada — Measures Affecting the Importation of Milk and the Exportation of Dairy Products* (WT/DS103/1), complaint by the United States. This request, dated 8 October 1997, is in respect of export subsidies allegedly granted by Canada on dairy products and the administration by Canada of the tariff-rate quota on milk. The US contends that these export subsidies by Canada distort markets for dairy products and adversely affect US sales of dairy products. The US alleges violations of Article II, X and X1 of GATT 1994, Articles 3, 4, 8, 9 and 10 of the Agreement on Agriculture, Article 3 of the Subsidies Agreement, and Articles 1, 2 and 3 of the Import Licensing Agreement. On 2 February 1998, the US requested the establishment of a panel. On 25 March 1998, the DSB established a panel. Australia and Japan reserved their third-party rights. The Panel found that the measures complained against were inconsistent with Canada's obligations under Article II :1(b) of GATT 1994, and Articles 3.3 and 8 of the Agreement on Agriculture by providing export subsidies as

listed in Article 9.1(a) and 9.1(c) of the Agreement on Agriculture. The report of the Panel, which also covers DS113 below, was circulated to Members on 17 May 1999. On 15 July 1999, Canada notified its intention to appeal certain issues of law and legal interpretations developed by the Panel (which appeal also includes DS113 below). The Appellate Body reversed the Panel's interpretation of Article 9.1(a) and, in consequence, reversed the Panel's finding that Canada acted inconsistently with its obligations under Article 3.3 and 8 of the Agreement on Agriculture. However, the Appellate Body upheld the Panel's finding that Canada was in violation of Article 3.3 and 8 of the Agreement on Agriculture in respect of export subsidies listed in Article 9.1(c) of the Agreement on Agriculture. In addition, the Appellate Body partly reversed the Panel's finding that Canada acted inconsistently with its obligations under Article II :1(b) of GATT 1994. The report of the Appellate Body was circulated on 13 October 1999. At its meeting on 27 October 1999, the DSB adopted the Appellate Body report and the Panel report, as modified by the Appellate Body report.

(8) (b) *Canada — Measures Affecting Dairy Products*, complaint by New Zealand (WT/DS113/1). This request, dated 29 December 1997, is in respect of an alleged dairy export subsidy scheme commonly referred to as the "special milk classes" scheme. New Zealand contends that the Canadian "special milk classes" scheme is inconsistent with Article XI of GATT, and Articles 3, 8, 9 and 10 of the Agreement on Agriculture. On 12 March 1998, New Zealand requested the establishment of a panel. On 25 March 1998, the DSB established a panel. Australia and Japan reserved their third-party rights. Pursuant to Article 9.1 of the DSU, the DSB decided that the same panel established in respect of DS103 above, should also examine this dispute (see DS103 above).

(9) *Turkey — Restrictions on Imports of Textile and Clothing Products*, complaint by India (WT/DS34). This request, dated 21 March 1996, claims that Turkey's imposition of quantitative restrictions on imports of a broad range of textile and clothing products is inconsistent with Articles XI and XIII of GATT 1994, as well as ATC Article 2. Earlier, India had requested to be joined in the consultations between Hong Kong and Turkey on

the same subject matter (WT/DS29). On 2 February 1998, India requested the establishment of a panel. At its meeting on 13 March 1998, the DSB established a panel. Thailand, Hong Kong, China, Philippines and the United States reserved their third-party rights. The Panel found that Turkey's measures are inconsistent with Articles XI and XIII of GATT 1994, and consequently inconsistent also with Article 2.4 of the ATC. The Panel also rejected Turkey's assertion that its measures are justified by Article XXIV of GATT 1994. The report of the Panel was circulated to Members on 31 May 1999. On 26 July 1999, Turkey notified its intention to appeal certain issues of law and legal interpretations developed by the Panel. The Appellate Body upheld the Panel's conclusion that Article XXIV of GATT 1994 does not allow Turkey to adopt, upon the formation of a customs union with the EC, quantitative restrictions which were found to be inconsistent with Articles XI and XIII of GATT 1994 and Article 2.4 of the ATC. However, the Appellate Body concluded that the Panel erred in its legal reasoning in interpreting Article XXIV of GATT 1994. The report of the Appellate Body was circulated on 21 October 1999. At its meeting on 19 November 1999, the DSB adopted the Appellate Body report and the Panel report, as modified by the Appellate Body report.

III. Appellate Body Reports Issued

IV. Panel Reports Appealed

(1) (a) *Chile — Taxes on Alcoholic Beverages*, complaint by the European Communities (WT/DS87/1). This request, dated 4 June 1997, is in respect of Chile's Special Sales Tax on spirits, which allegedly imposes a higher tax on imported spirits than on *Pisco*, a locally brewed spirit. The EC contends that this differential treatment of imported spirits violates Article III :2 of GATT 1994. On 3 October 1997, the EC requested the establishment of a panel. The DSB established a panel on 18 November 1997. Canada, Mexico, Peru and the US reserved their third-party rights.

(1) (b) *Chile — Taxes on Alcoholic Beverages*, complaint by the European Communities (WT/DS110/1). This request, dated 15 December 1997, is in respect of Chile's internal tax regime for

alcoholic beverages complained of by the EC (DS87) and by the US (DS109). In essence, this new request by the EC takes issue with the modification to the law on taxation on alcoholic beverages passed by Chile to address the concerns of the EC in DS87. The EC contends that the modified law still violates Article III :2 of GATT 1994. On 9 March 1998, the EC requested the establishment of a panel. On 25 March 1998, the DSB established a panel. Pursuant to Article 9.1 of the DSU, the DSB decided that the same Panel established to examine the dispute in DS87 above should examine this dispute. Peru, Canada and the US reserved their third-party rights. The panel found that Chile's Transitional System and its New system for taxation of distilled alcoholic beverages was inconsistent with Article III :2 of GATT 1994. The report of the panel (which covers (3)(a) above) was circulated to Members on 15 June 1999. On 13 September 1999, Chile notified its intention to appeal certain issues of law and legal interpretations developed by the Panel.

(2) *Korea — Definitive Safeguard Measure on Imports of Certain Dairy Products*, complaint by the European Communities (WT/DS98/1). This request, dated 12 August 1997, is in respect of a definitive safeguard measure imposed by Korea on imports of certain dairy products. The EC contends that under the provisions of different governmental measures, Korea has imposed a safeguard measure in the form of an import quota on imports of certain dairy products. The EC considers that this measure is in violation of Articles 2, 4, 5 and 12 of the Agreement on Safeguard Measures, as well as a violation of Article XIX of GATT 1994. On 9 January 1998, the EC requested the establishment of a panel. At the DSB meeting on 22 January 1998, the EC informed the DSB that it was for the time being not pursuing the panel request. On 10 June 1998, the EC made a fresh request for a panel. At its meeting on 23 July 1998, the DSB established a panel. The panel found that Korea's measure is inconsistent with Articles 4.2(a), and 5 of the Agreement on Safeguards, but rejected the EC claims under Article XIX of GATT 1994, Articles 2.1, 12.1 (although it found that Korea's notifications to the Committee on Safeguards were not timely, and to that extent were inconsistent with Article 12.1), 12.2 and 12.3 of the Agreement

on Safeguards. The report of the panel was circulated to Members on 21 June 1999. On 15 September 1999, Korea notified its intention to appeal certain issues of law and legal interpretations developed by the Panel.

(3) *Argentina — Safeguard Measures on Imports of Footwear*, complaint by the European Communities (WT/DS121/1). This request, dated 3 April 1998, is in respect of provisional and definitive safeguard measures imposed by Argentina on imports of footwear. The EC alleges that by Resolution 226/97 of 24 February 1997, Argentina imposed a provisional safeguard measure in the form of specific duties on imports of footwear effective from 25 February 1997, which was followed by Resolution 987/97, which imposed a definitive safeguard measure on these imports effective from 13 September 1997. The EC contends that the above measures violate Articles 2, 4, 5, 6 and 12 of the Agreement on Safeguards, and Article XIX of GATT 1994. On 10 June 1998, the EC requested the establishment of a panel. At its meeting on 23 July 1998, the DSB established a panel. Brazil, Indonesia, Paraguay, the US and Uruguay reserved their rights as third-parties to the dispute. The panel found that Argentina's measure is inconsistent with Articles 2 and 4 of the Agreement on Safeguards. The report of the panel was circulated on 25 June 1999. On 15 September 1999, Argentina notified its intention to appeal certain issues of law and legal interpretations developed by the Panel.

(4) *United States — Tax Treatment for "Foreign Sales Corporations*" (WT/DS108/1), complaint by the European Communities. This request, dated 18 November 1997, is in respect of Sections 921-927 of the US Internal Revenue Code and related measures, establishing special tax treatment for "Foreign Sales Corporations" (FSC). The EC contends that these provisions are inconsistent with US obligations under Articles III :4 and XVI of the GATT 1994, Articles 3.1(a) and (b) of the Subsidies Agreement, and Articles 3 and 8 of the Agreement on Agriculture. On 1 July 1998, the EC requested the establishment of a Panel. In the request for a panel, the EC invoked Article 3.1(a) and (b) of the Subsidies Agreement, and Articles 8, 9 and 10 of the Anti-Dumping Agreement, and did not pursue the claims under the

GATT 1994. At its meeting on 22 September 1998, the DSB established a panel. Barbados, Canada and Japan reserved their rights as third-parties to the dispute. The panel found that, through the FSC scheme, the United States has acted inconsistently with its obligations under Article 3.1(a) of the Subsidies Agreement as well as with its obligations under Article 3.3 of the Agreement on Agriculture (and consequently with its obligations under Article 8 of that Agreement). The report of the panel was circulated to Members on 8 October 1999. On 28 October 1999, the US notified its intention to appeal certain issues of law and legal interpretations developed by the Panel. On 2 November 1999, the US withdrew its notice of appeal pursuant to Rule 30 of the Working Procedures for Appellate Review, stating that the withdrawal was conditional on its right to file a new notice of appeal pursuant to Rule 20 of the Working Procedures.

V. Panel Reports Issued

VI. Active Panels

(1) (a) *United States — Measure Affecting Government Procurement*, complaint by the European Communities (WT/DS88/1). This request, dated 20 June 1997, is in respect of an Act enacted by the Commonwealth of Massachusetts on 25 June 1996, entitled Act regulating State Contracts with companies doing Business with Burma (Myanmar). The Act provides, in essence, that public authorities of the Commonwealth of Massachusetts are not allowed to procure goods or services from any persons who do business with Burma. The EC contends that, as Massachusetts is covered under the US schedule to the GPA, this violates Articles VIII(B), X and XIII of the GPA Agreement. The EC also contends that the measure also nullifies benefits accruing to it under the GPA, as well as impeding the attainment of the objectives of the GPA, including that of maintaining balance of rights and obligations. On 8 September 1998, the EC requested the establishment of a panel. At its meeting on 21 October 1998, the DSB established a panel. Japan reserved its third-party right. The DSB agreed that pursuant to Article 9.1 of the DSU, a single panel would examine this dispute together with DS95 below. At the request of the complainants, dated 10

February 1999, the Panel agreed, pursuant to Article 12.12 of the DSU, to suspend the panel proceedings (which also applies to DS95 below).

(1) (b) *United States — Measure Affecting Government Procurement*, complaint by Japan (WT/DS95/1). This request, dated 18 July 1997, is in respect of the same issued raised by the EC in DS88 above. On 8 September 1998, Japan requested the establishment of a panel. At its meeting on 21 October 1998, the DSB established a panel. The DSB agreed that pursuant to Article 9.1 of the DSU, a single panel would examine this dispute together with DS88 above.

(2) *Mexico — Anti-Dumping Investigation of High-Fructose Corn Syrup (HFCS) from the United States*, complaint by the United States (DS132). This request, dated 8 May 1998, is in respect of an anti-dumping investigation of high-fructose corn syrup (HFCS) grades 42 and 55 from the US, conducted by Mexico. The US alleges that on 27 February 1997, the Government of Mexico published a notice initiating this anti-dumping investigation on the basis of an application dated 14 January 1997 from the Mexican National Chamber of Sugar and Alcohol Producers. The US further alleges that on 23 January 1998, Mexico issued a notice of final determination of dumping and injury in that investigation, and consequently imposed definitive anti-dumping measures on these imports from the United States. The US contends that the manner in which the application for an anti-dumping investigation was made, as well as the manner in which a determination of threat of injury was made, is inconsistent with Articles 2, 3, 4, 5, 6, 7, 9, 10 and 12 of the Anti-Dumping Agreement. On 8 October 1998, the US requested the establishment of a panel. The DSB established a panel at its meeting on 25 November 1998. Jamaica reserved its third-party rights.

(3) *European Communities — Measures Affecting the Prohibition of Asbestos and Asbestos Products*, complaint by Canada (WT/DS135). This request, dated 28 May 1998, is in respect of measures allegedly imposed by France, in particular Decree of 24 December 1996, with respect to the prohibition of asbestos and products containing asbestos, including a ban on imports of such goods. Canada alleges that these measures violate

Articles 2, 3 and 5 of the SPS Agreement, Article 2 of the TBT Agreement, and Articles II, XI and XIII of GATT 1994. Canada also alleges nullification and impairment of benefits accruing to it under the various agreements cited. On 8 October 1998, Canada requested the establishment of a panel. The DSB established a panel at its meeting on 25 November 1998. The US reserved its third-party rights.

(4) *Canada — Patent Protection of Pharmaceutical Products*, complaint by the European Communities (WT/DS114/1). This request, dated 19 December 1997, is in respect of the alleged lack of protection of inventions by Canada in the area of pharmaceuticals under the relevant provisions of the Canadian implementing legislation (in particular the Patent Act). The EC contends that Canada's legislation is not compatible with its obligations under the TRIPS Agreement, because it does not provide for the full protection of patented pharmaceutical inventions for the entire duration of the term of protection envisaged by Articles 27.1, 28 and 33 of the TRIPS Agreement. On 11 November 1998 the EC requested the establishment of a panel. At its meeting on 1 February 1999, the DSB established a panel. Australia, Brazil, Cuba, India, Israel, Japan, Poland, Switzerland, and the United States reserved their third-party rights.

(5) *United States — Anti-Dumping Act of 1916*, complaint by the European Communities (WT/DS136). This request, dated 9 June 1998, is in respect of the alleged failure of the United States to repeal its Anti-Dumping Act of 1916. The EC contends that the US Anti-Dumping Act of 1916 is still in force and is applicable to the import and internal sale of any foreign product irrespective of its origin, including products originating in countries which are WTO Members. The EC also alleges that the 1916 Act exists in the US statute books in parallel with the Tariff Act of 1930, as amended, which includes the US implementing legislation of multilateral Anti-Dumping provisions. The EC alleges violations of Articles III : 4, VI : 1, and VI : 2 of GATT 1994, Article XVI : 4 of the WTO Agreement, and Articles 1, 2, 3, 4 and 5 of the Anti-Dumping Agreement. On 11 November 1998, the EC requested the establishment of a panel. At its meeting on 1 February 1999,

the DSB established a panel. India, Japan, and Mexico reserved their third-party rights.

(6) (a) *Canada — Certain Measures Affecting the Automotive Industry*, complaint by Japan (WT/DS139/1). This request, dated 3 July 1998, is in respect of measures being taken by Canada in the automotive industry. Japan contends that under Canadian legislation implementing an automotive products agreement (Auto Pact) between the US and Canada, only a limited number of motor vehicle manufacturers are eligible to import vehicles into Canada duty free and to distribute the motor vehicles in Canada at the wholesale and retail distribution levels. Japan further contends that this duty-free treatment is contingent on two requirements : (i) a Canadian value-added content requirement that applies to both goods and services; and (ii) a manufacturing and sales requirement. Japan alleges that these measures are inconsistent with Articles I : 1, III : 4 and XXIV of GATT 1994, Article 2 of the TRIMs Agreement, Article 3 of the SCM Agreement, and Articles II, VI and XVII of GATS. On 12 November 1998, Japan requested the establishment of a panel. At its meeting on 1 February 1999, the DSB established a panel. Pursuant to Article 9.1 of the DSU, the DSB agreed that the panel also examine the complaint by the EC in DS141 (see below). India, Korea, and the United States reserved their third-party rights.

(6) (b) *Canada — Certain Measures Affecting the Automotive Industry*, complaint by the European Communities (WT/DS142/1). This request, dated 17 August 1998, is in respect of the same measures raised by Japan in DS139 and cites the same provisions alleged to be in violation, except for Article XXIV of GATT 1994, which was cited by Japan but is not cited by the EC. On 14 January 1998, the EC requested the establishment of a panel. At its meeting on 1 February 1999, the DSB established a panel. Pursuant to Article 9.1 of the DSU, the DSB agreed that the panel established in respect of the complaint by Japan (DS139) also examine this complaint. India, Korea, and the United States reserved their third-party rights.

(7) *United States — Imposition of Countervailing Duties on Certain Hot-rolled Lead and Bismuth Carbon Steel Products*

Originating in the United Kingdom, complaint by the European Communities (WT/DS138/1). This request, dated 30 June 1998, is in respect of the alleged imposition of countervailing duties on certain hot-rolled lead and bismuth carbon steel (leaded bars) from the UK. The EC contends that the US imposed countervailing duties of 1.69 per cent on United Engineering Steels Ltd (UES) for the review period 1 January 1994 to 31 December 1994, and of 2.4 per cent for the review period 1 January 1995 to 20 March 1995, on the basis of subsidies which had been granted to British Steel Corporation (BSC). The EC also contends that the US imposed countervailing duties on British Steel plc/British Steel Engineering Steels LTD (BSES) for the review period 1 January 1996 to 31 December 1996 on the basis of subsidies granted to BSC before its privatization in 1988. The EC alleges that these impositions of countervailing duties constitute a violation of Articles 1.1(b), 10, 14 and 19.4 of the SCM Agreement. On 14 January 1999, the EC requested the establishment of a panel. At its meeting on 17 February 1999, the DSB established a panel. Brazil and Mexico reserved their third-party rights.

(8) *United States — Sections 301-310 of the Trade Act of 1974*, complaint by the European Communities (WT/DS152/1). This dispute, dated 25 November 1998, is in respect of Title III, chapter 1 (sections 301-310) of the US Trade Act of 1974 (the Trade Act), as amended, and in particular sections 306 and 305 of this Act. The EC contends that by imposing strict time limits within which unilateral determinations must be made and trade sanctions taken, sections 306 and 305 of the Trade Act do not allow the US to comply with the rules of the DSU in situations where a prior multilateral ruling under the DSU on conformity of measures taken pursuant to implementation of DSB recommendations has not been adopted by the DSB. The EC further contends, that the DSU procedure resulting in a multilateral finding, even if initiated immediately after the end of the reasonable period of time for implementation, cannot be finalised, nor can subsequent DSU procedure for seeking compensation or suspension of concessions be complied with, within the time limits of sections 306 and 305. The EC alleges that Title III, chapter 1(sections 301-310) of the Trade Act, as amended, and in particular sections

306 and 305 of the Act, are inconsistent with Articles 3, 21, 22 and 23 of the DSU; Article XVI :4 of the WTO Agreement; and Articles I, II, III, VIII and XI of GATT 1994. The EC also alleges that the Trade Act nullifies and impairs benefits accruing, directly or indirectly, to it under GATT 1994, and also impedes the objectives of GATT 1994 and of the WTO. The EC is also seeking consultations in respect of announcements by the US, which are unilateral determinations under section 306 of the Trade Act, on retaliatory actions being prepared by the US for what it considers non-implementation by the EC of the recommendations of the DSB in the dispute *European Communities — Regime for the Importation, Sale and Distribution of Bananas* (DS27). On 26 January 1999, the EC requested the establishment of a panel. At its meeting on 2 March 1999, the DSB established a panel. Brazil, Canada, Cameroon, Colombia, Costa Rica, Cuba, Dominica, Dominican Republic, Ecuador, Hong Kong, India, Israel, Jamaica, Japan, Korea, St. Lucia and Thailand reserved their third-party rights.

(9) (a) *Korea — Measures Affecting Imports of Fresh, Chilled, and Frozen Beef*, complaint by the United States (WT/DS161/1). This dispute, dated 1 February 1999, is in respect of an alleged Korean regulatory scheme that discriminates against imported beef by *inter alia*, confining sales of imported beef to specialised stores, limiting the manner of its display, and otherwise constraining the opportunities for the sale of imported beef. The United States also alleges that Korea imposes a markup on sales of imported beef, limits import authority to certain so-called "super-groups" and the Livestock Producers Marketing Organization ("LPMO"), and provides domestic support to the cattle industry in Korea in amounts which cause Korea to exceed its aggregate measure of support as reflected in Korea's schedule. The United States contends that these restrictions apply only to imported beef, thereby denying national treatment to beef imports, and that the support to the domestic industry amounts to domestic subsidies that contravene the Agreement on Agriculture. The United States alleges violations of Articles II, III, XI, and XVII of GATT 1994; Articles 3, 4, 6, and 7 of the Agreement on Agriculture; and Articles 1 and 3 of the Import Licensing Agreement. On 15 April

1999, the United States requested the establishment of a panel. At its meeting on 26 May 1999, the DSB established a panel. Australia, Canada and New Zealand reserved their third-party rights.

(9) (b) *Korea — Measures Affecting Imports of Fresh, Chilled, and Frozen Beef*, complaint by Australia (WT/DS169/1). This request, dated 13 April 1999, is on the same basis as the US request in DS161. On 12 July 1999, Australia requested the establishment of a panel. At its meeting on 26 July 1999, the DSB established a panel. Canada, New Zealand and the United States reserved their third-party rights. At the request of Korea, the DSB agreed that, pursuant to DSU Article 9.1, this complaint would be examined by the same panel established in respect of DS161 above.

(10) *United States — Section 110(5) of the US Copyright Act*, complaint by the European Communities (WT/DS160/1). This request, dated 26 January 1999, is in respect of Section 110(5) of the US Copyright Act, as amended by the Fairness in Music Licensing Act, which was enacted on 27 October 1998. The EC contends that Section 110(5) of the US Copyright Act permits, under certain conditions, the playing of radio and television music in public places (bars, shops, restaurants, etc.) without the payment of a royalty fee. The EC considers that this statute is inconsistent with US obligations under Article 9(1) of the TRIPS Agreement, which requires Members to comply with Articles 1-21 of the Berne Convention. On 15 April 1999, the European Communities requested the establishment of a panel. At its meeting on 26 May 1999, the DSB established a panel. Australia, Japan and Switzerland reserved their third-party rights.

(11) *United States — Import Measures on Certain Products from the European Communities*, complaint by the European Communities (WT/DS165/1). This request, dated 4 March 1999, is in respect of the US decision, effective as of 3 March 1999, to withhold liquidation on imports from the EC of a series of products together valued at over $500 million on an annual basis, and to impose a contingent liability for 100% duties on each individual importation of affected products. The EC believes that this measure includes administrative provisions which foresee the

posting of a bond to cover the full potential liability. The EC contends that this measure deprives EC imports into the United States, of the products in question, of the right to a duty not in excess of the rate bound in the US Schedule. The EC further contends that, by requiring the deposit of a bond, US Customs will effectively impose 100% duties on each individual importation. The EC alleges violations of Articles 3, 21, 22 and 23 of the DSU, and Articles I, II, VIII and XI of GATT 1994. The EC also alleges nullification and impairment of benefits under GATT 1994, as well as the impediment of the objectives of the DSU and GATT 1994. The EC had requested urgent consultations pursuant to Article 4.8 of the DSU. On 11 May 1999, the EC requested the establishment of a panel. At its meeting on 16 June 1999, the DSB established a panel. Dominica, Ecuador, India, Jamaica, Japan and St.Lucia reserved their third-party rights.

(12) *Australia — Measures Affecting the Importation of Salmonids*, complaint by the United States (WT/DS21). This request for consultations, dated 17 November 1995, concerns the same regulation alleged to be in violation of the WTO Agreements in WT/DS18, in respect of which the reports of the panel and Appellate Body have already been adopted and are awaiting implementation. On 11 May 1999, the United States requested the establishment of a panel. At its meeting on 16 June 1999, the DSB established a panel. Canada, the EC, Hong Kong/China, India and Norway reserved their third party rights. At the request of the complainants, the Panel agreed on 8 November 1999 to suspend its work, pursuant to Article 12.12 of the DSU, until such time as the panelists have completed their work in the ongoing proceeding requested by Canada pursuant to Article 21.5 of the DSU (WT/DS18) or for eleven months, whichever is the earlier.

(13) *Korea — Measures Affecting Government Procurement*, complaint by the United States (WT/DS163/1). This dispute, dated 16 February 1999, is in respect of certain procurement practices of the Korean Airport Construction Authority ("KOACA"), and other entities concerned with the procurement of airport construction in Korea, which are allegedly inconsistent with Korea's obligations under the Agreement on Government

Procurement ("GPA"). These allegedly include practices relating to qualification for bidding as a prime contractor, domestic partnering, and the absence of access to challenge procedures that are in breach of the GPA. The United States contends that KOACA and the other entities are within the scope of Korea's list of central government entities as specified in Annex 1 of Korea's obligations in Appendix I of the GPA, and pursuant to Article I(1) of the GPA, apply to the procurement of airport construction. On 11 May 1999, the United States requested the establishment of a panel. At its meeting on 16 June 1999, the DSB established a panel. The EC and Japan reserved their third-party rights.

(14) *Argentina — Measures on the Export of Bovine Hides and the Import of Finished Leather*, complaint by the European Communities (WT/DS155). This request, dated 24 December 1998, concerns certain measures taken by Argentina on the export of bovine hides and the import of finished leather. The EC alleges that the de facto export prohibition on raw and semi-tanned bovine hides (which is implemented in part through the authorization granted by the Argentinian authorities to the Argentinian tanning industry to participate in customs control procedures of hides before export)is in violation of GATT Articles; XI : 1 (which outlaws de jure export prohibitions and measures of equivalent effect); and X : 3(a) (which requires uniform and impartial administration of laws and regulations) to the extent that personnel of the Argentinian Chamber for the tanning industry are authorized to assist Argentinian customs authorities. The EC also claims that the "additional value added tax" of 9 per cent on imports of products into Argentina; and the "advance turnover tax" of 3 per cent based on the price of imported goods imposed on operators when importing goods into Argentina; are in violation of GATT Article III : 2 (which prohibits tax discrimination of foreign products which are like, directly competitive or substitutable to domestic products). On 3 June 1999, the EC requested the establishment of a panel. At its meeting on 26 July 1999, the DSB established a panel.

(15) *United States — Anti-Dumping Act of 1916 (II)*, complaint by Japan (WT/DS162/1). This dispute, dated 10 February 1999, is in respect of the US Anti-Dumping Act of 1916, 15 U.S.C. 72

(1994), ("US 1916 Act"). Japan alleges that the US 1916 Act stipulates that the importation or sale of imported goods within the US market in certain circumstances is unlawful, constituting a criminal offence and inviting civil liability. Japan further alleges that judicial decisions under the US 1916 Act are made without the procedural safeguards provided for in the Anti-Dumping Agreement. Japan states that a court action has been brought under the US 1916 Act against affiliates of Japanese companies. Japan contends that the US 1916 Act is inconsistent with Articles III, VI and XI of GATT 1994, and the Anti-Dumping Agreement. The European Communities has also instituted dispute settlement proceedings against the US 1916 Act, which dispute is now pending before a panel (DS136). On 3 June 1999, Japan requested the establishment of a panel. At its meeting on 26 July 1999, the DSB established a panel. The EC and India reserved their third-party rights.

(16) *United States — Definitive Safeguard Measure on Imports of Wheat Gluten from the European Communities*, complaint by the European Communities (WT/DS166/1). This request, dated 17 March 1999, is in respect of definitive safeguard measures imposed by the United States on imports of wheat gluten from the European Communities. The EC contends that by a Proclamation of 30 May 1998, and a Memorandum of the same date, by the US President, under which the United States imposed definitive safeguard measures in the form of a quantitative limitation on imports of wheat gluten from the EC, effective as of 1 June 1998. The EC considers these measures to be in violation of Articles 2, 4, 5 and 12 of the Agreement on Safeguards; Article 4.2 of the Agreement on Agriculture; and Articles I and XIX of GATT 1994. On 3 June 1999, the EC requested the establishment of a panel. At its meeting on 26 July 1999, the DSB established a panel. Australia and New Zealand reserved their third-party rights.

(17) *Argentina — Measures Affecting Imports of Footwear*, complaint by the United States (WT/DS164/1). This dispute, dated 1 March 1999, is in respect of certain measures implemented by Argentina affecting imports of footwear. The United States contends that in November 1998, Argentina adopted Resolution

1506 modifying Resolution 987 of 10 September 1997, which had established safeguard duties on imports of footwear from non-MERCOSUR countries. Resolution 1506 allegedly imposes a tariff-rate quota (TRQ) on such footwear imports in addition to the safeguard duties previously imposed, postpones any liberalization of the original safeguard duty until 30 November 1999, and liberalizes the TRQ only once during the life of the measure. The United States further contends that Argentina has not notified this measure to the Committee on Safeguards. The United States alleges violations of Articles 5.1, 7.4 and 12 of the Agreement on Safeguards. On 3 June 1999, the US requested the establishment of a panel. See also complaint by Indonesia (DS123) and complaint by the EC (DS121). On 15 July 1999, the United States requested the establishment of a panel. At its meeting on 26 July 1999, the DSB established a panel.

(18) *Guatemala — Definitive Anti-dumping Measure regarding Grey Portland Cement from Mexico*, complaint by Mexico (WT/DS156). This request, dated 5 January 1999, concerns definitive anti-dumping duties imposed by the authorities of Guatemala on imports of grey Portland cement from Mexico and the proceedings leading thereto. Mexico alleges that the definitive anti-dumping measure is inconsistent with Articles 1, 2, 3, 5, 6, 7, 12 and 18 of the Antidumping Agreement and its Annexes I and II, as well as with Article VI of GATT 1994. See also 2(4). At its meeting on 22 September 1999, the DSB established a panel. The EC, Ecuador, Honduras and the United States reserved their third-party rights.

(19) *Canada — Patent Protection Term*, complaint by the United States (WT/DS170/1). This request, dated 6 May 1999, is in respect of the grant of patent term in Canada. The United States contends that the TRIPS Agreement obligates Members to grant a term of protection for patents that runs at least until twenty years after the filing date of the underlying protection, and requires each Member to grant this minimum term to all patents existing as of the date of the application of the Agreement to that Member. The United States alleges that under the Canadian Patent Act, the term granted to patents issued on the basis of applications filed before 1 October 1989 is 17 years from the date

on which the patent is issued. The United States contends that this situation is inconsistent with Articles 33, 65 and 70 of the TRIPS Agreement. On 15 July 1999, the United States requested the establishment of a panel. At its meeting on 22 September 1999, the DSB established a panel.

(20) *European Communities — Anti-Dumping Duties on Imports of Cotton-Type Bed-Linen from India*, complaint by India (WT/DS141/1). This request, dated 3 August 1998, is in respect of Commission Regulation (EC) No 2398/97 of 28 November 1997 on imports of cotton-type bed-linen from India. India asserts that the EC initiated anti-dumping proceedings against the import of cotton-type bed-linen from India by publishing a notice of initiation in September 1996. Provisional anti-dumping duties were imposed by EC Commission Regulation No 1069/97 of 12 June 1997. This was followed by the imposition of final duties in accordance with the above-mentioned EC Council Regulation of 28 November 1997. India contends that the determination of standing, the initiation, the determination of dumping and injury as well as the explanations of the EC authorities' findings are inconsistent with WTO law. India is also of the view that EC authorities' establishment of the facts was not proper and that the EC's evaluation of facts was not unbiased and objective. India also contends that the EC has not taken into account the special situation of India as a developing country. India alleges violations of Articles 2.2.2, 3.1, 3.2, 3.4, 3.5, 5.2, 5.3, 5.4, 5.8, 6., 12.2.2, and 15 of the Anti-Dumping Agreement, and Articles I and VI of the GATT 1994. On 7 September 1999, India requested the establishment of a panel. At its meeting on 27 October 1999, the DSB established a panel. Egypt, Japan and the US reserved their third-party rights.

(21) (a) *United States — Safeguard Measure on Imports of Fresh, Chilled or Frozen Lamb from New Zealand*, complaint by New Zealand (WT/DS177/1). This request, dated 16 July 1999, is in respect of a safeguard measure imposed by the United States on imports of lamb meat from New Zealand. New Zealand alleges that by Presidential Proclamation under Section 203 of the US Trade Act 1974, the United States imposed a definitive safeguard measure in the form of a tariff-rate quota on imports fresh, chilled, or frozen lamb meat effective from 22 July 1999.

New Zealand contends that this measure is inconsistent with Articles 2, 4, 5, 11 and 12 of the Agreement on Safeguards, and Articles I and XIX of GATT 1994. On 14 October 1999, New Zealand requested the establishment of a panel. At its meeting on 19 November 1999, the DSB established a panel. The DSB agreed that, pursuant to Article 9.1 of the DSU, this complaint would be examined by the same panel established in respect of DS178. Canada, the EC, Iceland and Japan reserved their third-party rights.

(21) (b) *United States — Safeguard Measure on Imports of Lamb Meat from Australia*, complaint by Australia (WT/DS178/1). This request, dated 23 July 1999, in respect of a definitive safeguard measure imposed by the United States on imports of lamb. Australia alleges that by Presidential Proclamation under Section 203 of the US Trade Act 1974, the United States imposed a definitive safeguard measure in the form of a tariff-rate quota on imports of fresh, chilled, or frozen lamb meat from Australia effective from 22 July 1999. Australia contends that this measure is inconsistent with Articles 2, 4, 5, 8, 11 and 12 of the Agreement on Safeguards, and Articles I, II and XIX of GATT 1994. On 14 October 1999, Australia requested the establishment of a panel. At its meeting on 19 November 1999, the DSB established a panel. The DSB agreed that, pursuant to Article 9.1 of the DSU, this complaint would be examined by the same panel established in respect of DS177. Canada, the EC, Iceland and Japan reserved their third-party rights.

(22) *Thailand — Anti-Dumping Duties on Angles, Shapes and Sections of Iron or Non-Alloy Steel; H-Beams from Poland*, complaint by Poland (WT/DS122/1). This request, dated 6 April 1998, concerns the imposition of final anti-dumping duties on imports of these products. Poland alleges that provisional anti-dumping duties were imposed by Thailand on 27 December 1996, and a final anti-dumping duty of 27.78% of CIF value for these products, produced or exported by any Polish producer or exporter, was imposed on 26 May 1997. Poland further alleges that Thailand refused two requests by Poland for disclosure of findings. Poland contends that these actions by Thailand violate Articles 2, 3, 5 and 6 of the Anti-Dumping Agreement. On 13 October 1999,

Poland requested the establishment of a panel. At its meeting on 19 November 1999, the DSB established a panel. The EC, Japan and the US reserved their third-party rights.

(23) *United States — Anti-Dumping Measures on Stainless Steel Plate in Coils and Stainless Steel Sheet and Strip from Korea*, complaint by Korea (WT/DS179). This request, dated 30 July 1999, is in respect of Preliminary and Final Determinations of the United States Department of Commerce (DOC) on Stainless Steel Plate in Coils from Korea dated 4 November 1998 and 31 March 1999 respectively, and Stainless Steel Sheet and Strip from Korea dated 20 January 1999 and 8 June 1999 respectively. Korea considers that several errors were made by the United States in those determinations which resulted in erroneous findings and deficient conclusions as well as the imposition, calculation and collection of anti-dumping margins which are incompatible with the obligation of the United States under the provisions of the Anti-Dumping Agreement and Article VI of GATT 1994 and in particular, but not necessarily exclusively, Article 2, Article 6 and Article 12 of the Anti-Dumping Agreement. Korea believes that the United States did not act in conformity with the cited provisions, among others, in its treatment of the following : certain US sales made to a bankrupt company; the calculation of two distinct exchange rate periods for export sales; and currency conversion for certain normal value sales made in US dollars. On 14 October, Korea requested the establishment of a panel. At its meeting on 19 November 1999, the DSB established a panel. The EC and Japan reserved their third-party rights.

VII. Pending Consultations (most recent listed first)

(64) *Trinidad and Tobago — Certain Measures Affecting Imports of Pasta from Costa Rica*, complaint by Costa Rica (DS185/1). This request, dated 18 November 1999, is in respect of (i) the anti-dumping investigation being carried out by Trinidad and Tobago at the request of the company "Cereal Products Limited" against imports of pasta from the Costa Rican company "Roma Prince Sociedad Anénima", (ii) proceedings undertaken as part of a preliminary hearing prior to the initiation of the anti-dumping investigation, and (iii) Articles 3 and 5 of the 1996

Antidumping and Countervailing Duties Regulation of Tobago and Trinidad. Costa Rica claims that these measures are inconsistent with Articles 2, 3, 5, 6 and 12 of the Anti-Dumping Agreement.

(63) *United States — Anti-Dumping Measures on Certain Hot-Rolled Steel Products from Japan*, complaint by Japan (DS184/1). This request, dated 18 November 1999, is in respect of the preliminary and final determinations of the US Department of Commerce and the US International Trade Commission on the anti-dumping investigation of Certain Hot-Rolled Steel Products from Japan issued on 25 and 30 November 1998, 12 February 1999, 28 April 1999 and 23 June 1999. Japan considers that these determinations are erroneous and based on deficient procedures under the US Tariff Act of 1930 and related regulations. The Japanese complaint also concerns certain provisions of the Tariff Act of 1930 and related regulations. Japan claims violations of Articles VI and X of the GATT 1994 and Articles 2, 3, 6 (including Annex II), 9 and 10 of the Anti-Dumping Agreement.

(62) *Brazil — Measures on Import Licensing and Minimum Import Prices*, complaint by the European Communities (DS183/1). This request, dated 14 October 1999, is in respect of a number of Brazilian measures, particularly Brazil's non-automatic licensing system and the minimum pricing practice, which allegedly restrict EC exports — notably of textile products, Sorbitol and Carboxymethylcellulose (CMC). The EC considers that those Brazilian measures violate, in particular, Articles II, VIII, X and XI of the GATT 1994; Article 4.2 of the Agreement on Agriculture; Articles 1, 3, 5 and 8 of the Agreement on Import Licensing Procedures; and Articles 1 through 7 of the Agreement on Implementation of Article VII of the GATT 1994.

(61) *Ecuador — Provisional Anti-Dumping Measure on Cement from Mexico*, complaint by Mexico (DS182/1). This request, dated 5 October 1999, concerns a provisional anti-dumping measure taken by Ecuador against imports of cement from Mexico as well as Ecuador's actions preceding that measure. Mexico considers that the provisional anti-dumping measure and the actions preceding it violate, inter alia, Articles 1, 2, 3, 4, 5, 6, 7, 9, 12, 18 and Annex II of the Anti-Dumping Agreement as well as Article VI of the GATT 1994.

(60) *United States — Reclassification of Certain Sugar Syrups*, complaint by Canada (DS 180/1). This request, dated 6 September 1999, is in respect of the proposed reclassification of certain sugar syrups by the US Customs Service. Canada claims that these US measures are in violation of Article II of the GATT 1994 and Article 4 of the Agreement on Agriculture. In addition, Canada alleges that these measures nullify or impair benefits accruing to it under the same provisions of the GATT and the Agreement on Agriculture.

(59) *United States — Section 211 Omnibus Appropriations Act*, complaint by the European Communities (WT/DS176/1). This request, dated 8 July 1999, is in respect of Section 211 of the US Omnibus Appropriations Act. The EC alleges that Section 211, which was signed into law on 21 October 1998, has the consequence of making impermissible the registration or renewal in the United States of a trademark, if it was previously abandoned by a trademark owner whose business and assets have been confiscated under Cuban law. The EC further alleges that this law provides that no US court shall recognize or enforce any assertion of such rights. The EC and its Member states contend that Section 211 US Omnibus Appropriations Act is not in conformity with US obligations under the TRIPS Agreement, especially Article 2 in conjunction with the Articles 3, 4, 15 to 21, 41, 42 and 62 of the Paris Convention.

(58) *India — Measures Relating to Trade and Investment in the Motor Vehicle Sector*, complaint by the United States (WT/DS175/1). This request, dated 1 May 1999, is in respect of certain Indian measures affecting trade and investment in the motor vehicle sector. The United States contends that the measures in question require manufacturing firms in the motor vehicle sector to : (i) achieve specified levels of local content; (ii) achieve a neutralization of foreign exchange by balancing the value of certain imports with the value of exports of cars and components over a stated period; and (iii) limit imports to a value based on the previous year's exports. According to the United States, these measures are enforceable under Indian law and rulings, and manufacturing firms in the motor vehicle sector must comply with these requirements in order to obtain Indian import licenses

for certain motor vehicle parts and components. The United States considers that these measures violate the obligations of India under Articles III and XI of GATT 1994, and Article 2 of the TRIMS Agreement.

(57) *European Communities — Protection of Trademarks and Geographical Indications for Agricultural Products and Foodstuffs*, complaint by the United States (WT/DS174/1). This request, dated 1 June 1999, is in respect of the alleged lack of protection of trademarks and geographical indications for agricultural products and foodstuffs in the European Communities. The United States contends that EC Regulation 2081/92, as amended, does not provide national treatment with respect to geographical indications and does not provide sufficient protection to pre-existing trademarks that are similar or identical to a geographical indication. The United States considers this situation to be inconsistent with the EC's obligations under the TRIPS Agreement, including but not necessarily limited to Articles 3, 16, 24, 63 and 65 of the TRIPS Agreement.

(56) (a) *European Communities — Measures Relating to the Development of a Flight Management System*, complaint from the United States (WT/DS172/1). This request, dated 21 May 1999, is in respect of alleged actionable subsidies granted or maintained to a French company, Sextant Avionique ("Sextant"), to develop a new flight management system ("FMS") adapted to Airbus aircraft. The United States contends that the French government has agreed to grant, and the European Commission has approved, a loan, on preferential and non-commercial terms, in the amount of 140 million French francs, to be disbursed over three years, for a project in which Sextant will develop a FMS adapted to Airbus aircraft. The United States considers this aid to be a specific subsidy within the meaning of Articles 1 and 3 of the SCM Agreement, which subsidy has caused and continues to cause adverse effects within the meaning of Article 5 of the SCM Agreement. The United States also contends that this aid has caused and continues to cause serious prejudice within the meaning of Articles 5(c) and 6 of the SCM Agreement because the subsidy may involve the direct forgiveness of debt; may displace or impede imports of FMS from the United States into France; may

displace or impede exports of FMS from the United States to third country markets; and may cause significant price undercutting by the subsidised product as compared with the price of a like product of another Member in the same market or may cause significant price suppression, price depression or lost sales in the same market. The United also believes that this aid has caused and continues to cause a nullification or impairment of benefits accruing directly or indirectly to it under GATT 1994 within the meaning of Article XXIII : 1(b) of GATT 1994, and Article 5(b) of the SCM Agreement.

(56) (b) *France — Measures Relating to the Development of a Flight Management System*, complaint by the United States (WT/DS173/1). This request is identical to the one addressed to the EC above.

(55) *Argentina — Patent Protection for Pharmaceuticals and Test Data Protection for Agricultural Chemicals*, complaint by the United States (WT/DS171/1). This request, dated 6 May 1999, is in respect of (i) the alleged absence in Argentina of either patent protection for pharmaceutical products or an effective system for providing exclusive marketing rights in such products, and (ii) Argentina's alleged failure to ensure that changes in its laws, regulations and practice during the transition period provided under Article 65.2 of the TRIPS Agreement do not result in a lesser degree of consistency with the provisions of the TRIPS Agreement. Under the first limb, the United States contends that the TRIPS Agreement does not permit WTO Members to allow third parties to market products subject to exclusive marketing rights without the consent of the right holder. According to the United States, Argentina's law does not provide product patent protection for pharmaceutical inventions, or a system that conforms to Article 70.9 of the TRIPS Agreement with regard to the grant of exclusive marketing rights. The United States therefore contends that Argentina's legal regime appears to be inconsistent with Articles 27, 65 and 70 of the TRIPS Agreement. Under the second limb, the United States contends that prior to August 1998, Argentina provided a ten year term of protection against unfair commercial use for undisclosed test data or other data submitted to Argentine regulatory authorities in support of

applications for marketing approval for agricultural chemical products. The United States further contends that since the issuance in 1998 of Regulation 440/98, which *inter alia* revoked earlier regulations, Argentina has provided no effective protection for such data against unfair commercial use. The United States therefore alleges that Argentina's legal regime is inconsistent with Article 65.5 of the TRIPS Agreement.

(54) *South Africa — Anti-dumping Duties on the Import of Certain Pharmaceutical Products from India*, complaint by India (WT/DS168/1). This request, dated 1 April 1999, is in respect of a recommendation for the imposition of definitive anti-dumping duties by the South African Board on Tariffs and Trade (BTT), contained in its Report No. 3799, dated 3 October 1997, on the import of certain pharmaceutical products from India. India alleges that South Africa initiated anti-dumping proceedings against the importation of ampicillin and amoxycillin of 250mg capsules from India. The BTT allegedly made a preliminary determination on 26 March 1997 that ampicillin and amoxycillin of 250mg and 500mg capsules, exported by M/S Randaxy Laboratories Ltd of India, were being dumped into the South African Customs Union (SACU). This was allegedly followed by a recommendation to impose final duties on these products by the BTT, which was reported on 10 September 1997. India contends that the definition and calculation by the BTT of normal value is inconsistent with South Africa's WTO obligations, because erroneous methodology was used for determining the normal value and the resulting margin of dumping. India further contends that the determination of injury was not based on positive evidence and did not include an evaluation of all relevant economic factors and indices having a bearing on the state of the industry, which led to an erroneous determination of material injury suffered by the petitioner. India is also of the view that the South African authorities' establishment of the facts was not proper and that their evaluation was not unbiased or objective. India also claims that the South African authorities have not taken into account India's special situation as a developing country. India alleges violations of Articles 2, 3, 6(a) to(c) individually and in conjunction with 12, 12 and 15 of the Anti-Dumping Agreement; and Articles I and VI of GATT 1994

(53) *United States — Countervailing Duty Investigation with respect to Live Cattle from Canada*, complaint by Canada (WT/DS167/1). This request, dated 19 March 1999, concerns the initiation of a countervailing duty investigation by the United States, on 22 December 1998, with respect to live cattle from Canada. Canada contends that the initiation of this investigation is inconsistent with US obligations under the Subsidies Agreement, including the fact that the written application filed with the US Department of Commerce was not made by or on behalf of the domestic industry, and that there was not, sufficient information provided with respect to the measures or actions alleged to be subsidies, for purpose of initiating an investigation under the SCM Agreement. Canada further contends that the measures or actions alleged to be subsidies either are not, in law or fact, subsidies within the meaning of the Subsidies Agreement, or do not confer more than a *de minimis* level of countervailing subsidy. Canada also believes that this initiation of investigation is inconsistent with US obligations under the Agreement on Agriculture relating to "due restraint". Canada alleges violations of Articles 1, 2, 10, 11.1 — 11.5, and 13.1 of the Subsidies Agreement; and Article 13 of the Agreement on Agriculture.

(52) *Hungary — Safeguard Measure on Imports of Steel Products from the Czech Republic*, complaint by the Czech Republic (WT/DS159/1). This request, dated 21 January 1999, is in respect of the imposition of quantitative restrictions by Hungary on imports of a broad range of steel products from the Czech Republic. The Czech Republic alleges that Hungary imposed a safeguard measure in the form of an import quota on imports of a broad range of steel products from the Czech Republic, and that this measure only applies to the Czech Republic. The Czech Republic contends that these quantitative restrictions are in breach of Hungary's obligations under GATT Articles I and XIX, as well as provisions of the Agreement on Safeguards.

(51) *European Communities — Regime for the Importation, Sale and Distribution of Bananas II*, complaint by Guatemala, Honduras, Mexico, Panama, and the United States (WT/DS158/1). This request, dated 20 January 1999, is in respect of the implementation of the recommendations of the DSB in *European*

Communities — Regime for the Importation, Sale and Distribution of Bananas. The complaining parties state that the 15-month reasonable period of time for the EC to implement the DSB's recommendations and rulings ended on 1 January 1999. The complaining parties contend that the EC modified its regime in a manner that will not permit this dispute to conclude at this time on the basis of a solution that is acceptable to their governments, and as a result, jointly and severally, request consultations with the EC concerning the EC banana regime established by EC Regulation 404/93, as amended and implemented by Council Regulation 1637/98 of 20 July 1998 and EC Commission Regulation 2362/98 of 28 October 1998. The complaining parties contend that their objective is to clarify and discuss in detail with the EC the various aspects of the EC's modified banana regime, including their effect on the market, their concerns about their WTO-inconsistency, and ways that the EC might modify its regime in order to produce a satisfactory settlement of this dispute.

(50) *Argentina — Anti-Dumping Measures on Imports of Drill Bits from Italy*, complaint from the European Communities. (WT/DS157/1). This request, dated 14 January 1998, is in respect of definitive anti-dumping measures allegedly imposed by Argentina on imports of drill bits from Italy. The EC states that on 12 September 1998, Argentina imposed definitive anti-dumping measures on imports of drill bits from Italy. The investigation which led to the imposition of these measures had allegedly been initiated on 21 February 1997. The EC contends that because Argentina's investigation exceeded 18 months, it was in violation of Article 1 of the Anti-Dumping Agreement.

(49) *European Communities — Measures Affecting Differential and Favourable Treatment of Coffee*, complaint by Brazil (WT/DS154/1). This dispute, dated 7 December 1998, is in respect of the special preferential treatment under the EC's Generalised System of Preferences (GSP). Brazil asserts that the EC GSP scheme is applicable to products originating in the Andean Group of countries and the Central American Common Market countries, that are conducting programs to combat drug production and trafficking. In the case of soluble coffee, this special preferential treatment, contained in Council Regulation (EC) No. 1256/96,

amounts to duty free access into the EC market. Brazil states that it is aware that there is a proposed Council Regulation which would unify all EC laws and regulations concerning the operation of the GSP scheme for both agricultural and industrial products. Brazil contends that this special treatment adversely affects the importation into the EC of soluble coffee originating in Brazil. Brazil alleges that this special treatment is inconsistent with the Enabling Clause, as well as with Article I of GATT 1994. Brazil further alleges that this special treatment nullifies or impairs benefits accruing to Brazil directly or indirectly under the cited provisions.

(48) *European Communities — Patent Protection for Pharmaceutical and Agricultural Products*, complaint by Canada (WT/DS153/1). This dispute, dated 2 December 1998, is in respect of the protection of inventions in the area of pharmaceutical and agricultural chemical products under the relevant provisions of EC legislation, particularly Council Regulation (EEC) No. 1768/92 and European Parliament and Council Regulation (EC) No. 1610/96, in relation to EC obligations under the TRIPS Agreement. Canada contends that under the above Regulations, a patent term extension scheme, which is limited to pharmaceutical and agricultural chemical products, has been implemented. Canada alleges that Regulations (EEC) No. 1768/92 and (EC) No. 1610/96 are inconsistent with the EC's obligations not to discriminate on the basis of field of technology, as provided by Article 27.1 of the TRIPS Agreement, because these Regulations only apply to pharmaceutical and agricultural products.

(47) *United States — Measures Affecting Textiles and Apparel Products*, complaint by the European Communities (WT/DS151/1). This dispute, dated 19 November 1998, is in respect of alleged changes to US rules of origin for textiles and apparel products. The EC discloses that this issue was the subject of an earlier request for consultations (DS85), in respect of which a mutually agreed solution was notified to the DSB, pursuant to Article 3.1 of the DSU. However, the EC contends that the US has not implemented its commitments as contained in that agreement with the result that, in the EC view, the US is still acting in a manner inconsistent with its obligations under the WTO. The

dispute concerns changes allegedly introduced by the US to its rules of origin for textiles and apparel products, which entered into force on 1 July 1996, which changes adversely affect exports of EC textile products to the US, in that as a result of these changes EC products are allegedly no longer recognised in the US as being of EC origin. The EC alleges violations of Articles 2.4, 4.2 and 4.4 of the ATC, Article 2 of the Agreement on Rules of Origin, Article III of GATT 1994, and Article 2 of the TBT Agreement.

(46) *India — Measures Affecting Custom Duties*, complaint by the European Communities (WT/DS150/1). This dispute, dated 30 October 1998, concerns a series of increases in customs duties allegedly implemented by India. The EC states that the measures in question relate to Schedule 1 of the 1975 Customs Tariff Act, the Special Customs Duty, and the Special Additional Duty. The EC contends that under these measures, the aggregate value of tariffs resulting from the addition of the different duties applied by India exceed India's WTO bound rates under a series of tariff headings. The EC alleges violations of Articles II:1(b) and III:2 of GATT 1994.

(45) *India — Import Restrictions*, complaint by the European Communities (WT/DS149). This dispute, dated 29 October 1998, concerns import restrictions allegedly maintained by India under its Export and Import Policy, 1997-2002, for reasons other than Article XVIII:B of GATT 1994. The EC states that India notified these restrictions to the WTO in Part A of Annex I to its notification of 20 May 1997 under paragraph 9 of the Understanding on the Balance-of-Payments Provisions of GATT 1994 (WT/BOP/N/24). India claims that these restrictions are justified under Article XX and/or Article XXI of GATT 1994. The EC contends that these import restrictions constitute an infringement of Articles III, X, XI, XIII and XVII of GATT 1994, Article 4.2 of the Agreement on Agriculture, and Articles 1, 2 and 3 of the Agreement on Import Licensing Procedures, and cannot be justified under Articles XX or XXI of GATT 1994.

(44) *Czech Republic — Measure Affecting Import Duty on Wheat from Hungary, complaint from Hungary* (WT/DS148/1). This dispute, dated 12 October 1998, is in respect of a regulation

adopted by the Czech Republic which entered into force on 9 October 1998, and which allegedly increased the import duty of wheat originating in Hungary. Hungary asserts that the increased import duty on wheat (HS1001.1000, 1001.9099) exceeds several times the respective bound rates in the Czech Schedule for 1998. Hungary also alleges that it is the only country subject to this measure. Hungary contends that this measure is inconsistent with Articles I and II of GATT 1994, and Article 4 of the Agreement on Agriculture. Hungary invokes the urgency provision of the DSU (4.8), due to the severe economic and trade losses that are being caused by this measure, which is expected to remain in force until 26 April 1999.

(43) *Japan — Tariff Quotas and Subsidies Affecting Leather*, complaint by the European Communities (WT/DS147/1). This dispute, dated 8 October 1998, concerns the management of the tariff quotas for leather and the subsidies allegedly benefiting the leather industry and "Dowa" regions in Japan. The EC states that the management of the three tariff quotas is specified in a notice published every year by the Ministry of International Trade & Industry (MITI), which is based on Article 6 of the Ministerial Order on the tariff quota system for heavy oil, crude oil, etc. The EC contends that the complexity of the management of the tariff quota system, as well as the fact that applications for licenses may only be submitted on a single day, appears open to criticism. In addition, the EC further contends that many licenses are granted for quantities without real economic interest, and some have a very short validity period. According to the EC, the system leads to a situation that deters foreign companies from establishing in Japan for purposes of importing leather directly. The EC also contends that subsidies were granted on the basis of the "Law concerning Special Fiscal Measures", which extended the duration of 15 subsidy programmes. The EC considers that these subsidies are specific and that the total value of these different subsidy programmes is liable to cause serious prejudice to its interests. The EC alleges violations of Articles 1(6), 3(5)(g), (h), (i) and (j) of the Import Licensing Agreement, and Article 6 of the Subsidies Agreement.

(42) *India — Measures Affecting the Automotive Sector*,

complaint by the European Communities (WT/DS146/1). This dispute, dated 6 October 1998, concerns certain measures affecting the automotive sector being applied by India. The EC states that the measures include the documents entitled "Export and Import Policy, 1997-2002", "ITC (HS Classification) Export and Import Policy 1997-2002" ("Classification"), and "Public Notice No. 60 (PN/97-02) of 12 December 1997, Export and Import Policy April 1997-March 2002", and any other legislative or administrative provision implemented or consolidated by these policies, as well as MoUs signed by the Indian Government with certain manufacturers of automobiles. The EC contends that under these measures, imports of complete automobiles and of certain parts and components are subject to a system of non-automatic import licenses. The EC further contends that in accordance with Public Notice No. 60, import licenses may be granted only to local joint venture manufacturers that have signed an MoU with the Indian Government, whereby they undertake, inter alia, to comply with certain local content and export balancing requirements. The EC alleges violations of Articles III and XI of GATT 1994, and Article 2 of the TRIMs Agreement.

(41) *Argentina — Countervailing Duties on Imports of Wheat Gluten from the European Communities*, complaint by the European Communities (WT/DS145/1). This dispute, dated 23 September 1998, is in respect of definitive countervailing duties allegedly imposed by Argentina on imports of wheat gluten from the EC. The EC states that Argentina imposed a countervailing duty on wheat gluten imports from the EC with effect from 23 July 1998. The investigation which led to the imposition of these duties had been initiated on 23 October 1996 and, consequently, the EC contends that the investigation exceeded 18 months, contrary to Article 11.11 of the Subsidies Agreement. The EC also claims a violation of Article 10 of the same Agreement.

(40) *United States — Certain Measures Affecting the Import of Cattle, Swine and Grain from Canada*, complaint by Canada (WT/DS144/1). This dispute, dated 25 September 1998, is in respect of certain measures, imposed by the US state of South Dakota and other states, prohibiting entry or transit to Canadian trucks carrying cattle, swine, and grain. Canada contends that

these measures adversely affect the importation into the United States of cattle, swine, and grain originating in Canada. Canada alleges violations of Articles 2, 3, 4, 5, 6, 13 and Annexes B and C of the SPS Agreement; Articles 2, 3, 5 and 7 of the TBT Agreement; Article 4 of the Agreement on Agriculture; and Articles I, III, V, XI and XXIV:12 of GATT 1994. Canada also makes a claim of nullification or impairment of benefits accruing to it under the cited Agreements. Canada invoked Article 4.8 of the DSU for expedited consultations in view of the perishable nature of the goods in question.

(39) *Slovak Republic — Measure Affecting Import Duty on Wheat from Hungary, complaint from Hungary* (WT/DS143/1). This dispute, dated 18 September 1998, is in respect of a regulation adopted by the Slovak Republic which entered into force on 10 September 1998, which allegedly increased the import duty of wheat originating in Hungary. Hungary asserts that the increased import duty on wheat (HS1001.1000, 1001.90) amounts to 2540 SKK/t which equals to approximately 70% *ad Valorem*. Hungary alleges that the bound rates for these tariff lines in the Slovak Schedule for 1998 are set at 4.4% (HS1001.1000), 27% (HS1001.9010) and 22.5% (HS1001.9091, 1001.9099). Hungary also alleges that it is the only country subject to this measure. Hungary contends that this measure is inconsistent with Articles I and II of GATT 1994, and Article 4 of the Agreement on Agriculture. Hungary invokes the urgency provision of the DSU due to the severe economic and trade losses that are being caused by this measure, which is expected to remain in force until 10 March 1999.

(38) *European Communities — Anti-Dumping Investigations Regarding Unbleached Cotton Fabrics from India*, complaint by India (WT/DS140/1). This request, dated 3 August 1998, is in respect of alleged repeated recourse by the EC to anti-dumping actions on unbleached cotton fabrics (UCF), from India. India considers, in the light of the information which has become available before and after the adoption of Regulation 773/98, that the determination of standing, the initiation, the selection of the sample, the determination of dumping and the injury are inconsistent with the EC's WTO obligations. India is also of the view that

EC's establishment of the facts was not proper and that EC's evaluation of facts was not unbiased and objective. India also contends that EC has not taken into account the special situation of India as a developing country. India alleges violations of Articles 2.2.1, 2.4.1, 2.4.2, 2.6, 3.3, 3.2, 3.4, 3.5, 4.1(I), 5.2, 5.3, 5.4, 5.5, 5.8, 6.10, 7.1(I), 7.4, 9.1, 9.2, 12.1, 12.2 and 15 of the Anti-Dumping Agreement, and Articles I and VI of GATT 1994. India also alleges nullification and impairment of benefits accruing to it under the cited agreements.

(37) *European Communities — Measures Affecting Imports of Wood of Conifers from Canada*, complaint by Canada (WT/DS137/1). This request, dated 17 June 1998, is in respect of certain measures concerning the importation into the EC market of wood of conifers from Canada. The measures include, but are not limited to, Council Directive 77/93, of 21 December 1976, as amended by Commission Directive 92/103/EEC, of 1 December 1992, and any relevant measures adopted by EC Member states affecting imports of wood of conifers from Canada into the EC. Canada alleges that these adversely affect the importation into the EC market of wood of conifers from Canada. Canada alleges violations of Articles I, III and XI of GATT 1994, Articles 2, 3, 4, 5 and 6 of the SPS Agreement, and Article 2 of the TBT Agreement. Canada is also making a claim for nullification and impairment of benefits accruing to it indirectly under the cited agreements.

Canada Contends

(36) *European Communities — Measures Affecting Import Duties on Rice*, complaint by India (DS134). This request, dated 28 May 1998, is in respect of the restrictions allegedly introduced by an EC Regulation establishing a so-called cumulative recovery system (CRS), for determining certain import duties on rice, with effect from 1 July 1997. India contends that the measures introduced through this new regulation will restrict the number of importers of rice from India, and will have a limiting effect on the export of rice from India to the EC. India alleges violations of Articles I, II, III, VII and XI of GATT 1994, Articles 1-7, 11 and Annex I of the Customs Valuation Agreement, Articles 1 and 3 of the

Import Licensing Agreement, Article 2 of the TBT Agreement, Article 2 of the SPS Agreement, and Article 4 of the Agreement on Agriculture. India also makes a claim of nullification and impairment of benefits accruing to it under the various agreements cited.

(35) *Slovak Republic — Measures Concerning the Importation of Dairy Products and the Transit of Cattle*, complaint by Switzerland (WT/DS133/1). The request, dated 11 May 1998, concerns measures imposed by the Slovak Republic (in particular, a decree of 6 July 1996) with respect to the importation of dairy products and the transit of cattle. Switzerland contends that these measures have a negative impact on Swiss exports of cheese and cattle. Switzerland alleges that some of these measures are inconsistent with Articles I, III, V, X and XI of GATT 1994, Article 5 of the SPS Agreement, and Article 5 of the Import Licensing Agreement.

(34) *France — Certain Income Tax Measures Constituting Subsidies*, complaint by the United States (WT/DS131/1). This request, dated 5 May 1998, is in respect of prohibited subsidies provided by France. The United States alleges that, based on unofficial English translations of the relevant legislation and descriptions in secondary sources, it is its understanding that under French income tax law, a French company may deduct temporarily, certain start-up expenses of its foreign operations through a tax-deductible reserve account. The United States also believes that a French company may establish a special reserve equal to ten percent of its receivable position at year end for medium-term credit risks in connection with export sales. The United States contends that each of these measures constitute an export subsidy, and that the deduction for start-up expenses constitute an import substitution subsidy, and as such both measures violate Article 3 of the SCM Agreement.

(33) *Ireland — Certain Income Tax Measures Constituting Subsidies*, complaint by the United States (WT/DS130/1). This request, dated 5 May 1998, is in respect of prohibited subsidies provided by Ireland. The United States alleges that, based on unofficial copies of the relevant legislation and descriptions in secondary sources, it is its understanding that under Irish income tax law, "special trading houses" qualify for a special tax rate in

respect of trading income from the export sale of goods manufactured in Ireland. The United States contends that this measure constitutes an export subsidy and as such violates Article 3 of the SCM Agreement.

(32) *Greece — Certain Income Tax Measures Constituting Subsidies*, complaint by the United States (WT/DS129/1). This request, dated 5 May 1998, is in respect of prohibited subsidies provided by Greece. The United States alleges that, based on unofficial English translations of relevant legislation and descriptions in secondary sources, it is its understanding that under Greek income tax law, Greek exporters are entitled to a special annual tax deduction calculated as a percentage of export income. The United States contends that this measure constitutes an export subsidy and as such violates Article 3 of the SCM Agreement.

(31) *Netherlands — Certain Income Tax Measures Constituting Subsidies*, complaint by the United States (WT/DS128/1). This request, dated 5 May 1998, is in respect of prohibited subsidies provided by the Netherlands. The United States alleges that, based on unofficial English translations of the relevant legislation and descriptions in secondary sources, it is its understanding that under Dutch income tax law, exporters may establish a special "export reserve" for income derived from export sales. The United States contends that this measure constitutes an export subsidy and as such violates Article 3 of the SCM Agreement.

(30) *Belgium — Certain Income Tax Measures Constituting Subsidies*, complaint by the United States (WT/DS127/1). This request, dated 5 May 1998, is in respect of prohibited subsidies provided by Belgium. The United States alleges that, based on unofficial English translations of relevant legislation and descriptions in secondary sources, it is its understanding that under Belgium income tax law, Belgian corporate taxpayers receive a special BEF 4,00,000 (index linked) tax exemption for recruiting a departmental head for exports (known as an "export manager"). The United States contends that this measure constitutes an export subsidy and as such violates Article 3 of the SCM Agreement.

(29) (a) *European Communities — Enforcement of Intellectual*

Property Rights for Motion Pictures and Television Programs, complaint by the United States (WT/DS124/1). This request, dated 30 April 1998, is in respect of the lack of enforcement of intellectual property rights in Greece. The US claims that a significant number of TV stations in Greece regularly broadcast copyrighted motion pictures and television programs without the authorization of copyright owners. The US contends that effective remedies against copyright infringement do not appear to be provided or enforced in Greece in respect of these broadcasts. The US alleges a violation of Articles 41 and 61 of the TRIPS Agreement.

(29) (b) *Greece — Enforcement of Intellectual Property Rights for Motion Pictures and Television Programs*, complaint by the United States (WT/DS125/1). This request, dated 30 April 1998, is in respect of the same measures raised against the EC above (DS124).

(28) *Argentina — Safeguard Measures on Imports of Footwear*, complaint by Indonesia (WT/DS123/1). This request, dated 23 April 1998, is in respect of the same provisional and definitive safeguard measures imposed by Argentina in the above dispute (DS121). On 15 April 1999, Indonesia requested the establishment of a panel. In a communication dated 10 May 1999, Indonesia informed the DSB that it was not pursuing its request for a panel at the next DSB meeting, but that this was without prejudice to its rights under the DSU to resurrect the panel request.

(27) *India — Measures Affecting Export of Certain Commodities*, complaint by the European Communities (WT/DS120/1). This request, dated 16 March 1998, is in respect of India's EXIM Policy (1997-2002), which allegedly sets up a negative list for the export of several commodities. The EC alleges that under this policy, raw hides and skins are listed as products the export of which requires an export licence, and that these licences are systematically refused. The EC contends that this is in effect an export embargo and violates Article XI of GATT 1994.

(26) *United States — Harbour Maintenance Tax*, complaint by the European Communities (WT/DS118/1). This request, dated 6 February 1998, concerns the US Harbour Maintenance Tax

(HMT), allegedly introduced by legislation in the US. The EC contends that the HMT violates Articles I, II, III, VIII and X of GATT 1994, as well as the Understanding on the Interpretation of Article II:1(B) of GATT 1994.

(25) *Canada — Measures Affecting Film Distribution Services*, complaint by the European Communities (WT/DS117/1). This request, dated 20 January 1998, is in respect of Canada's alleged measures affecting film distribution services, including the 1987 Policy Decision on film distribution and its application to European companies. The EC contends that these measures violate Articles II and III of GATS.

(24) *Brazil — Measures Affecting Payment Terms for Imports*, complaint by the European Communities (WT/DS116/1). This request, dated 9 January 1998, is in respect of measures affecting payment terms for imports allegedly introduced by the Central Bank of Brazil. The EC contends that these measures violate Articles 3 and 5 of the Agreement on Import Licensing Procedures.

(23) *Peru — Countervailing Duty Investigation against Imports of Buses from Brazil*, complaint by Brazil (WT/DS112/1). This request, dated 23 December 1997, is in respect of a countervailing duty investigation being carried out by Peru at the request of Carroceria Morillas S.A., against imports of buses from Brazil. Brazil contends that the procedures followed by the Peruvian authorities to initiate this investigation are inconsistent with Articles 11 and 13.1 of the Subsidies Agreement.

(22) *United States — Tariff Rate Quota for Imports of Groundnuts*, complaint by Argentina (WT/DS111/1). This request, dated 19 December 1997, is in respect of the alleged commercial detriment to Argentina resulting from a restrictive interpretation by the US of the tariff rate quota negotiated by the two countries during the Uruguay Round, regarding the importation of groundnuts. Argentina alleges violations of Articles II, X and XII of GATT 1994, Articles 1, 4 and 15 of the Agreement on Agriculture, Article 2 of the Agreement on Rules of Origin, and Article 1 of the Import Licensing Agreement. Nullification and impairment of benefits is also alleged.

(21) *Chile — Taxes on Alcoholic Beverages*, complaint by the

United States (WT/DS109/1). This request, dated 11 December 1997, is in respect of Chile's internal taxes on alcoholic beverages, which allegedly impose a higher tax on imported spirits than on pisco, a locally brewed spirit. The US contends that this differential treatment of imported spirits violates Article III:2 of GATT 1994. Taxes on these beverages are the subject of a complaint by the EC (DS87), in respect of which a panel has already been established.

(20) *Pakistan — Export Measures Affecting Hides and Skins* (WT/DS107/1), complaint by the European Communities. This request, dated 7 November 1997, is in respect of a Notification enacted by the Ministry of Commerce of Pakistan prohibiting the export of, *inter alia*, hides and skins and wet blue leather made from cow hides and cow calf hides. The EC contends that this measure limits access of EC industries to competitive sourcing of raw and semi-finished materials.

(19) *European Communities — Regime for the Importation, Sale and Distribution of Bananas* (WT/DS105/1), complaint by Panama. This request, dated 24 October 197, is in respect of the EC's regime for the importation, sale and distribution of bananas as established through Regulation 404/93, as well as any subsequent legislation, regulations or administrative measures adopted by the EC, including those reflecting the Framework Agreement on Bananas. Panama does not specify provisions which the EC regime violates. This is the same regime that was the subject of a successful challenge by the US, Ecuador, Guatemala, Honduras, and Mexico (DS27).

(18) *European Communities — Measures Affecting the Exportation of Processed Cheese* (WT/DS104/1), complaint by the United States. This request, dated 8 October 1997, is in respect of export subsidies allegedly granted by the EC on processed cheese without regard to the export subsidy reduction commitments of the EC. The US contends that these measures by the EC distort markets for dairy products and adversely affect US sales of dairy products. The US alleges violations of Articles 8, 9, 10 and 11 of the Agreement on Agriculture, and Article 3 of the Subsidies Agreement.

(17) *Mexico — Anti-Dumping Investigation of High-Fructose*

Corn Syrup (HFCS) from the United States, complaint by the United States (WT/DS101/1). This request, dated 4 September 1997, is in respect of an anti-dumping investigation of high-fructose corn syrup (HFCS) from the United States conducted by Mexico, resulting in a preliminary determination of dumping and injury in an investigation of 25 June 1997, and the consequent imposition of provisional measures on imports of HCFS from the United States. The US alleges violations of Articles 5.5, 6.1.3, 6.2, 6.4 and 6.5 of the Anti-Dumping Agreement. See also DS 132 under "Active panels".

(16) *United States — Measures Affecting Imports of Poultry Products*, complaint by the European Communities (WT/DS100/1). This request, dated 18 August 1997, is in respect of a ban on imports of poultry and poultry products from the EC by the US Department of Agriculture's Food Safety Inspection Service, and any related measures. The EC contends that although the ban is allegedly on grounds of product safety, the ban does not indicate the grounds upon which EC poultry products have suddenly become ineligible for entry into the US market. The EC considers that the ban is inconsistent with Articles I, III, X and XI of GATT 1994, Articles 2, 3, 4, 5, 8 and Annex C of the SPS Agreement, or Article 2 and 5 of the TBT Agreement.

(15) *United States — Countervailing Duty Investigation of Imports of Salmon from Chile*, complaint by Chile (WT/DS97/1). This request, dated 5 August 1997, is in respect of a countervailing duty investigation initiated by the US Department of Commerce against imports of salmon from Chile. Chile contends that the decision to initiate an investigation was taken in the absence of sufficient evidence of injury, in violation of Article 11.2 and 11.3. Chile also contends a violation of Article 11.4, in relation to the representative status of producers of salmon fillets.

(14) *Denmark — Measures Affecting the Enforcement of Intellectual Property Rights*, complaint by the United States (WT/DS83/1). This request, dated 14 May 1997, is in respect of Denmark's alleged failure to make provisional measures available in the context of civil proceedings involving intellectual property rights. The US contends that this failure violates Denmark's obligations under Articles 50, 63 and 65 of the TRIPS Agreement.

(13) (a) *Ireland — Measures Affecting the Grant of Copyright and Neighbouring Rights*, complaint by the United States (WT/DS82/1). This request, dated 14 May 1997, is in respect Ireland's alleged failure to grant copyright and neighbouring rights under its law. The US contends that this failure violates Ireland's obligations under Articles 9-14, 63, 65 and 70 of the TRIPS Agreement. On 9 January 1998, the United States requested the establishment of a panel.

(13) (b) *European Communities — Measures Affecting the Grant of Copyright and Neighbouring Rights*, complaint by the United States (WT/DS115/1). This request, dated 6 January 1998, raises exactly the same measures as in 16(a) above in respect of Ireland but makes the complaint to the EC. On 9 January 1998, the United States requested the establishment of a panel.

(12) *Belgium — Measures Affecting Commercial Telephone Directory Services*, complaint by the United States (WT/DS80/1). This request, dated 2 May 1997, is in respect of certain measures of the Kingdom of Belgium governing the provision of commercial telephone directory services. These measures include the imposition of conditions for obtaining a license to publish commercial directories, and the regulation of the acts, policies, and practices of BELGACOM N.V. with respect to telephone directory services. The US alleges violations of Articles II, VI, VIII and XVII of GATS, as well as nullification and impairment of benefits accruing to it under the specific GATS commitments made by the EC on behalf of Belgium.

(11) *United States — Safeguard Measure Against Imports of Broom Corn Brooms*, complaint by Colombia (WT/DS78/1). This request, dated 28 April 1997, is in respect of US Presidential Proclamation 6961 of 28 November 1996, adopting a safeguard measure against imports of broom and corn brooms. Colombia contends that the adoption of this safeguard measure is inconsistent with the obligations of the US under Articles 2, 4, 5, 9 and 12 of the Agreement on Safeguards, Articles II, XIII and XIX of GATT 1994. Colombia also makes a claim for nullification and impairment of benefits under GATT 1994.

(10) *Canada — Measures Affecting the Export of Civilian*

Aircraft, complaint by Brazil (WT/DS71). This request dated 10 March 1997, is in respect of the same measures complained of in WT/DS70. However, the request is made pursuant to Article 7 of the Subsidies Agreement. In this request, Brazil contends that the measures are actionable subsidies within the meaning of Part III of the Subsidies Agreement, and cause adverse effects within the meaning of Article 5 of the Agreement.

(9) *Japan — Measures Affecting Imports of Pork*, complaint by the European Communities, (WT/DS66). This request, dated 15 January 1997, is in respect of certain measures affecting imports of pork and its processed products imposed by Japan. The EC contends that these measures are in violation of Japan's obligations under Articles I, X : 3 and XIII of the GATT 1994. The EC also contends that these measures nullify or impair benefits accruing to it under the GATT 1994.

(8) *United States — Anti-Dumping Measures on Imports of Solid Urea from the Former German Democratic Republic*, complaint by the European Communities (WT/DS63). This request, dated 28 November 1996, is in respect of Anti-Dumping duties imposed on exports of solid urea from the former German Democratic Republic by the United States. The EC contends that theses measures violate Articles 9 and 11 of the Anti-Dumping Agreement.

(7) *United States — Import Prohibition of Certain Shrimp and Shrimp Products*, complaint by the Philippines (WT/DS61). This request, dated 25 October 1996, is in respect of a complaint by the Philippines regarding a ban on the importation of certain shrimp and shrimp products from the Philippines imposed by the United States under Section 609 of U.S. Public Law 101-62. Violations of Articles I, II, III, VIII, XI and XIII of GATT 1994 and Article 2 of the TBT Agreement are alleged. A nullification and impairment of benefits under GATT 1994 is also alleged. (See WT/DS58).

(6) *Mexico — Customs Valuation of Imports*, complaint by the European Communities (WT/DS53). This request, dated 27 August 1996, concerns the Mexican Customs Law. The EC claims that Mexico applies CIF value as the basis of customs

valuation of imports originating in non-NAFTA countries, while it applies FOB value for imports originating in NAFTA countries. Violation of GATT Article XXIV : 5(b) is alleged.

(5) (a) *Brazil — Certain Automotive Investment Measures*, complaint by Japan (WT/DS51). This request, dated 30 July 1996, concerns certain automotive investment measures taken by the Brazilian government. Violations of the TRIMs Agreement Article 2, GATT Articles I : 1, III : 4 and XI : 1 as well as the Subsidies Agreement Articles 3, 27.2 and 27.4 are alleged. In addition, Japan makes a non-violation claim under GATT Article XXIII : 1(b).

(5) (b) *Brazil — Certain Measures Affecting Trade and Investment in the Automotive Sector*, complaint by the United States (WT/DS52). This request, dated 9 August 1996, concerns the same measures as identified in Japan's request above. Violations of the TRIMs Agreement Article 2, GATT Articles I : 1 and III : 4 as well as the Subsidies Agreement Articles 3 and 27.4 are alleged. In addition, the United States also makes a non-violation claim under GATT Article XXIII : 1(b).

(5) (c) *Brazil — Certain Measures Affecting Trade and Investment in the Automotive Sector*, complaint by the United States (WT/DS65). This request, dated 10 January 1997, concerns more or less the same measures as in WT/DS52 above. However, this request also includes measures adopted by Brazil subsequent to consultations held with the United States pursuant to the request under WT/DS52, which measures confer benefits to certain companies located in Japan, the Republic of Korea, and the European Communities. The United States alleges violations under Articles I : 1 and III : 4 of GATT 1994, Article 2 of the TRIMs Agreement, and Articles 3 and 27.4 of the SCM Agreement. The United States has also made a nullification and impairment of benefits claim under Article XXIII : 1(b) of GATT 1994.

(5) (d) *Brazil — Measures Affecting Trade and Investment in the Automotive Sector*, complaint by the European Communities (WT/DS81/1). This request, dated 7 May 1997, is in respect of certain measures in the trade and investment sector implemented by Brazil, including in particular, Law No. 9440 of 14 March

1997, Law No. 9449 of 14 March 1997, and Decree No. 1987 of 20 August 1996. The EC contends that these measures violate Articles I : 1 and III : 4 of GATT 1994, Articles 3, 5 and 27.4 of the Subsidies Agreement, and Article 2 of the TRIMs Agreement. The EC also makes a claim for nullification and impairment of benefits under both GATT 1994 and the Subsidies Agreement. See also DS51, 52 and 65.

(4) *Japan — Measures Affecting Distribution Services*, complaint by the United States (WT/DS45). This request, dated 13 June 1996, concerns Japan's measures affecting distribution services (not limited to the photographic film and paper sector) through the operation of the Large-Scale Retail Store Law, which regulates the floor space, business hours and holidays of supermarkets and department stores. Violations of the GATS Article III (Transparency) and Article XVI (Market Access) are alleged. The US also alleges that these measures nullify or impair benefits accruing to the US (a non-violation claim). See 5(4) above. The United States requested further consultations with Japan on 20 September 1996, expanding the factual and legal basis of its claim.

(3) *Brazil — Countervailing Duties on Imports of Desiccated Coconut and Coconut Milk Powder from Sri Lanka*, complaint by Sri Lanka (WT/DS30). This request, dated 23 February 1996, claims that Brazil's imposition of countervailing duties on Sri Lanka's export of desiccated coconut and coconut milk powder is inconsistent with GATT Articles I, II and VI and Article 13(a) of the Agriculture Agreement (the so-called peace clause). See WT/DS22.

(2) (a) *Turkey — Restrictions on Imports of Textile and Clothing Products*, complaint by Hong Kong (WT/DS29). This request, dated 12 February 1996, claims that Turkey's quantitative restrictions on imports of textile and clothing products are in violation of GATT Articles XI and XIII. The background to this dispute is a recently concluded customs union agreement between Turkey and the European Communities. Hong Kong claims that GATT Article XXIV does not entitle Turkey to impose new quantitative restrictions in the present case.

(2) (b) *Turkey — Restrictions on Imports of Textile and*

Clothing Products, complaint by Thailand (WT/DS47). This request for consultations, dated 20 June 1996, concerns Turkey's imposition of quantitative restrictions on imports of textile and clothing products from Thailand. Violations of GATT Articles I, II, XI and XIII as well as Article 2 of the Textiles Agreement are alleged. Earlier, Hong Kong (WT/DS29) and India (WT/DS34) separately requested consultations with Turkey on the same measure.

(1) (a) *Korea — Measures Concerning the Testing and Inspection of Agricultural Products*, complaint by the United States (WT/DS3). Request circulated on 6 April 1995. The dispute involves testing and inspection requirements with respect to imports of agricultural products into Korea. The measures are alleged to be in violation of GATT Articles III or XI, Articles 2 and 5 of the Agreement on Sanitary and Phytosanitary Measures (SPS), TBT Articles 5 and 6 and Agriculture Article 4. See below.

(1) (b) *Korea — Measures Concerning Inspection of Agricultural Products*, complaint by the United States (WT/DS41). This request for consultations, dated 24 May 1996, concerns testing, inspection and other measures required for the importation of agricultural products into Korea. The United States claims these measures restrict imports and appear to be inconsistent with the WTO Agreement. Violations of GATT Articles III and XI, SPS Articles 2, 5 and 8, TBT Articles 2, 5 and 6, and Article 4 of the Agreement on Agriculture are alleged. The United States requested consultations with Korea on similar issues on 4 April 1995 (WT/DS3/1). See above.

VIII. Completed Cases (most recent listed first)

A. *Appellate and Panel Reports Adopted before 1 January 1999*

(18) *India — Patent Protection for Pharmaceutical and Agricultural Chemical Products*, complaint by the European Communities (WT/DS79/1). This request, dated 28 April 1997, is in respect of the alleged absence in India of patent protection for pharmaceutical and agricultural chemical products, and the absence of formal systems that permit the filing of patent applications of and provide exclusive marketing rights for such products. The EC contends that this is inconsistent with India's obligations under

Article 70, paragraphs 8 and 9, of the TRIPS Agreement (see similar US complaint in DS50, where the Panel and Appellate Body reports were adopted on 16 January 1998). On 9 September 1997, the EC requested the establishment of a panel. At its meeting on 16 October 1997, the DSB established a panel. The US reserved its third-party rights. The Panel found that India has not complied with its obligations under Article 70.8(a) of the TRIPS Agreement by failing to establish a legal basis that adequately preserves novelty and priority in respect of applications for product patents for pharmaceutical and agricultural chemical inventions, and was also not in compliance with Article 70.9 of the TRIPS Agreement by failing to establish a system for the grant of exclusive marketing rights. The report of the Panel was circulated to Members on 24 August 1998. At its meeting on 2 September 1998, the DSB adopted the Panel Report.

(17) *United States — Import Prohibition of Certain Shrimp and Shrimp Products*, complaint by India, Malaysia, Pakistan and Thailand (WT/DS58). This request, dated 8 October 1996, concerns a joint complaint by India, Malaysia, Pakistan and Thailand against a ban on importation of shrimp and shrimp products from these countries imposed by the United States under Section 609 of US Public Law 101-162. Violations of Articles I, XI and XIII of GATT 1994, as well nullification and impairment of benefits, are alleged. On 9 January 1997, Malaysia and Thailand requested the establishment of a panel. On 30 January 1997, Pakistan also requested the establishment of a panel. At its meeting on 25 February 1997, the DSB established a panel. Australia, Colombia, the EC, Philippines, Singapore, Hong Kong, India, Guatemala, Mexico, Japan, Nigeria and Sri Lanka reserved their third-party rights. On 25 February 1997, India also requested the establishment of a panel in the same matter. At its meeting on 10 April 1997, the DSB agreed to establish a panel in respect of India's request but agreed to incorporate this with the panel already established in respect of the other complainants. The Panel found that the import ban in shrimp and shrimp products as applied by the United States is inconsistent with Article XI:1 of GATT 1994, and cannot be justified under Article XX of GATT 1994. The report of the Panel was circulated to Members on 15 May 1998.

On 13 July 1998, the US notified its intention to appeal certain issues of law and legal interpretations developed by the Panel. The Appellate Body reversed the Panel's finding that the US measure at issue is not within the scope of measures permitted under the chapeau of Article XX of GATT 1994, but concluded that the US measure, while qualifying for provisional justification under Article XX(g), fails to meet the requirements of the chapeau of Article XX. The report of the Appellate Body was circulated to Members on 12 October 1998. The DSB adopted the Appellate Body Report and the Panel Report, as modified by the Appellate Body Report, on 6 November 1998.

(16) *Australia — Measures Affecting the Importation of Salmon*, complaint by Canada (WT/DS18). This request for consultations, dated 5 October 1995, is in respect of Australia's prohibition of imports of salmon from Canada based on a quarantine regulation. Canada alleges that the prohibition is inconsistent with GATT Articles XI and XIII, and also inconsistent with the SPS Agreement. On 7 March 1997, Canada requested the establishment of a panel. At its meeting on 10 April 1997, the DSB established a panel. The US and the European Communities reserved their third-party rights. The Panel found that Australia's measures complained against were inconsistent with Articles 2.2, 2.3, 5.1, 5.5, and 5.6 of the SPS Agreement, and also nullified or impaired benefits accruing to Canada under the SPS Agreement. The report of the Panel was circulated to Members on 12 June 1998. On 22 July 1998, Australia notified its intention to appeal certain issues of law and legal interpretations developed by the Panel. The Appellate Body reversed the Panel's reasoning with respect to Articles 5.1 and 2.2 of the SPS Agreement but nevertheless found that Australia had acted inconsistently with Articles 5.1 and 2.2 of the SPS Agreement; broadened the Panel's finding that Australia had acted inconsistently with Articles 5.5 and 2.3 of the SPS Agreement; reversed the Panel's finding that Australia had acted inconsistently with Article 5.6 of the SPS Agreement but was unable to come to a conclusion whether or not Australia's measure was consistent with Article 5.6 due to insufficient factual findings by the Panel. The report of the Appellate Body was circulated to Members on 20 October 1998. The DSB adopted the

Appellate Body Report and the Panel Report, as modified by the Appellate Body Report, on 6 November 1998.

(15) *Guatemala — Anti-Dumping Investigation Regarding Imports of Portland Cement from Mexico*, complaint by Mexico (WT/DS60). This request, dated 15 October 1996 is in respect of an anti-dumping investigation commenced by Guatemala with regard to imports of portland cement from Mexico. Mexico alleges that this investigation is in violation of Guatemala's obligations under Articles 2, 3, 5 and 7.1 of the Anti-Dumping Agreement. On 4 February 1997, Mexico requested the establishment of a panel. At its meeting on 20 March 1997, the DSB established a panel. The US, Canada, Honduras and El Salvador have reserved their third-party rights. The Panel found that Guatemala had failed to comply with the requirements of Article 5.3 of the Anti-Dumping Agreement by initiating the investigation on the basis of evidence of dumping, injury and casual link that was not "sufficient" as a justification for initiation. The report of the Panel was circulated to Members on 19 June 1998. On 4 August 1998, Guatemala notified its intention to appeal certain issues of law and legal interpretations developed by the Panel. The Appellate Body reversed the Panel's finding that the dispute was properly before the Panel, on the ground that Mexico did not comply with Article 6.2 of the DSU in its request for a panel since it did not identify the measure it was complaining against. Having found that the dispute was not properly before the Panel, the Appellate Body could not make any conclusions on the findings by the Panel on the substantive issues that were also the subject of the appeal. The Appellate Body stressed that its decision was without prejudice to Mexico's right to pursue fresh dispute settlement proceedings on this matter. The report of the Appellate Body was circulated to Members on 2 November 1998. At the DSB meeting on 25 November 1998, the DSB adopted the Appellate Body Report and the Panel Report, as reversed by the Appellate Body Report.

(14) *Argentina — Certain Measures Affecting Imports of Footwear, Textiles, Apparel and Other Items*, complaint by the United States (WT/DS56). This request, dated 4 October 1996, concerns the imposition of specific duties on these items in

excess of the bound rate and other measures by Argentina. The United States contends that these measures violate Articles II, VII, VIII and X of GATT 1994, Article 2 of the TBT Agreement, Article 1 to 8 of the Agreement on the Implementation of Article VII of GATT 1994, and Article 7 of the Agreement on Textiles and Clothing. On 9 January 1997, the United States requested the establishment of a panel. At its meeting on 25 February 1997, the DSB established a panel. The EC and India reserved their third-party rights to the dispute. The Panel found that the minimum specific duties imposed by Argentina on textiles and apparel are inconsistent with the requirements of Article II of GATT, and that the statistical tax of three per cent ad valorem imposed by Argentina on imports is inconsistent with the requirements of Article VIII of GATT. The report of the Panel was circulated on 25 November 1997. On 21 January 1998, Argentina notified its intention to appeal certain issues of law and legal interpretations developed by the Panel. The Appellate Body upheld, with some modification, the Panel's findings and conclusions. The report of the Appellate Body was circulated to Members on 27 March 1998. The Appellate Body report and the Panel report, as modified by the Appellate Body, were adopted by the DSB on 22 April 1998.

(13) *Japan — Measures Affecting Consumer Photographic Film and Paper*, complaint by the United States (WT/DS44). On 13 June 1996, the United States requested consultations with Japan concerning Japan's laws, regulations and requirements affecting the distribution, offering for sale and internal sale of imported consumer photographic film and paper. The US alleges that the Japanese Government treated imported film and paper less favourably through these measures, in violation of GATT Articles III and X. The US also alleges that these measures nullify or impair benefits accruing to the US (a non-violation claim). The United States requested the establishment of a panel on 20 September 1996 and it was established on 16 October 1996. The Panel found; that the US did not demonstrate that the Japanese 'measures' cited by the US nullified or impaired, either individually or collectively, benefits accruing to the US within the meaning of GATT Article XXIII : 1(b); that the US did not

demonstrate that the Japanese distribution 'measures' cited by the US accord less favourable treatment to imported photographic film and paper within the meaning of GATT Article III : 4; and that the US did not demonstrate that Japan failed to publish administrative rulings of general application in violation of GATT Article X : 1. The report of the Panel was circulated to Members on 31 March 1998. The Panel report was adopted by the DSB on 22 April 1998.

(12) *European Communities, United Kingdom, and Ireland — Customs Classification of Certain Computer Equipment*, complaint by the United States (WT/DS62, 67, 68). These are in respect of the reclassification by the European Communities, for tariff purposes, of certain Local Area Network (LAN) adapter equipment and personal computers with multimedia capability. The United States alleges that these measures violate Article II of GATT 1994. On 11 February 1997, the US requested the establishment of a panel. At its meeting on 25 February 1997, the DSB established a panel. Japan, the Republic of Korea, India and Singapore reserved their third-party rights. The Panel found that the EC failed to accord imports of LAN equipment from the US treatment no less favourable than that provided for in the EC Schedule of commitments, thereby acting inconsistently with Article II : 1 of GATT 1994. The report of the Panel was circulated to Members on 5 February 1998. On 24 March 1998, the EC notified its intention to appeal certain issues of law and legal interpretations developed by the Panel. The Appellate Body reversed the Panel's conclusion that the EC tariff treatment of LAN equipment is inconsistent with Article II : 1 of GATT 1994. The report of the Appellate Body was circulated to Members on 5 June 1998. At its meeting on 22 June 1998, the DSB adopted the Appellate Body report and the Panel report, as modified by the Appellate Body report. The Panel and Appellate Body reports also cover 3(b) and (c) below.

(11) *European Communities — Measures Affecting Importation of Certain Poultry Products*, complaint by Brazil (WT/DS69). This request dated 24 February 1997, is in respect of the EC regime for the importation of certain poultry products and the implementation by the EC of the Tariff Rate Quota for these products. Brazil contends that the EC measures are inconsistent

with Articles X and XXVII of GATT 1994 and Articles 1 and 3 of the Agreement on Import Licensing Procedures. Brazil also contends that the measures nullify or impair benefits accruing to it directly or indirectly under GATT 1994. On 12 June 1997, Brazil requested the establishment of a panel. At its meeting on 30 July 1997, the DSB established a panel. The US and Thailand reserved their third-party rights. The panel found that Brazil had not demonstrated that the EC had failed to implement and administer the tariff rate quota for poultry in line with its obligations under the cited agreements. The report of the Panel was circulated to Members on 12 March 1998. On 29 April 1998, Brazil notified its intention to appeal certain issues of law and legal interpretations developed by the Panel. The Appellate Body upheld most of the Panel's findings and conclusions, but reversed the Panel's finding that the EC had acted inconsistently with Article 5.1(b) of the Agreement on Agriculture. The Appellate Body, however, concluded that the EC had acted inconsistently with Article 5.5 of the Agreement on Agriculture. The report of the Appellate Body was circulated to Members on 13 July 1998. At its meeting on 23 July 1998, the DSB adopted the Appellate Body report and the Panel report, as modified by the Appellate Body report.

(10) (a) *Indonesia — Certain Measures Affecting the Automobile Industry*, complaint by Japan (WT/DS55). This request, dated 4 October 1996, concerns Indonesia's National Car Programme — basically the same measures as in WT/DS54. Japan contends that these measures are in violation of Indonesia's obligations under Articles I : 1, III : 2, III : 4 and X : 3(a) of GATT 1994, as well as Articles 2 and 5.4 of the TRIMs Agreement. On 17 April 1997, Japan requested the establishment of a panel. At its meeting on 12 June 1997, the DSB established a panel. In accordance with Article 9.1 of the DSU, the DSB decided that a single panel will examine this dispute together with DS54 and DS64. The Panel found that Indonesia was in violation of Articles I and II : 2 of GATT 1994, Article 2 of the TRIMs Agreement, Article 5(c) of the SCM Agreement, but was not in violation of Article 28.2 of the SCM Agreement. The Panel however, found that the complainants had not demonstrated that Indonesia was in violation of Articles 3 and 65.5 of the TRIPS Agreement. The report of the

Panel was circulated to Members on 2 July 1998. In view of the fact that a single Panel examined the disputes in DS55, DS64, DS54, and DS59, pursuant to Article 9.1 of the DSU, a single Panel report was issued which covers this dispute, as well as those listed below. At its meeting on 23 July 1998, the DSB adopted the Panel report.

(10) (b) *Indonesia — Certain Measures Affecting the Automobile Industry*, complaint by Japan (WT/DS64). See 5(a) above.

(10) (c) *Indonesia — Certain Measures Affecting the Automobile Industry*, complaint by the European Communities (WT/DS54). See 5(a) above.

(10) (d) *Indonesia — Certain Measures Affecting the Automobile Industry*, complaint by the United States (WT/DS59). See 5(a) above.

(9) (a) *European Communities — Measures Affecting Meat and Meat Products (Hormones)*, complaint by the United States (WT/DS26). On 25 April 1996, the United States requested the establishment of a panel in this dispute, claiming that measures taken by the EC under the Council Directive Prohibiting the Use in Livestock Farming of Certain Substances Having a Hormonal Action restrict or prohibit imports of meat and meat products from the United States, and are apparently inconsistent with GATT Articles III or XI, SPS Agreement Articles 2, 3 and 5, TBT Agreement Article 2 and the Agreement on Agriculture Article 4. A panel was established at the DSB meeting on 20 May 1996. The Panel found that the EC ban on imports of meat and meat products from cattle treated with any of six specific hormones for growth promotion purposes was inconsistent with Articles 3.1, 5.1 and 5.5 of the SPS Agreement. The report of the Panel was circulated to Members on 18 August 1997. On 24 September 1997, the EC notified its intention to appeal certain issues of law and legal interpretations developed by the Panel. The Appellate Body upheld the Panel's finding that the EC import prohibition was inconsistent with Articles 3.3 and 5.1 of the SPS Agreement, but reversed the Panel's finding that the EC import prohibition was inconsistent with Articles 3.1 and 5.5 of the SPS Agreement. On the general and procedural issues, the Appellate Body upheld

most of the findings and conclusions of the Panel, except with respect to the burden of proof in proceedings under the SPS Agreement. The report of the Appellate Body was circulated to Members on 16 January 1998. The Appellate Body report and the Panel report, as modified by the Appellate Body, were adopted by the DSB on 13 February 1998. On 16 April 1997, the respondent requested that the "reasonable period of time" for implementation of the recommendations and rulings of the DSB be determined by binding arbitration, pursuant to Article 21.3(c) of the DSU. The Arbitrator found the reasonable period of time for implementation to be 15 months from the date of adoption (*i.e.* 15 months from 13 February 1998). The report of the Arbitrator was circulated to Members on 29 May 1998.

(9) (b) *European Communities — Measures Affecting Livestock and Meat (Hormones)*, complaint by Canada (WT/DS48). On 28 June 1996, Canada requested consultations with the European Communities regarding the importation of livestock and meat from livestock that have been treated with certain substances having a hormonal action under GATT Article XXII and the corresponding provisions in the SPS, TBT and Agriculture Agreements. Violations SPS Articles 2, 3 and 5; GATT Article III or XI; TBT Article 2; and Agriculture Article 4 are alleged. The Canadian claim is essentially the same as the US claim (WT/DS26), for which a panel was established earlier. See above. The DSB established a panel on 16 October 1996. The Panel found that the EC ban on imports of meat and meat products from cattle treated with any of six specific hormones for growth promotion purposes was inconsistent with Articles 3.1, 5.1 and 5.5 of the SPS Agreement. The report of the Panel was circulated to Members on 18 August 1997. On 24 September 1997, the EC notified its intention to appeal certain issues of law and legal interpretations developed by the Panel. The Appellate Body upheld the Panel's finding that the EC import prohibition was inconsistent with Articles 3.3 and 5.1 of the SPS Agreement, but reversed the Panel's finding that the EC import prohibition was inconsistent with Articles 3.1 and 5.5 of the SPS Agreement. On the general and procedural issues, the Appellate Body upheld most of the findings and conclusions of the Panel, except with respect to the

burden of proof in proceedings under the SPS Agreement. The report of the Appellate Body was circulated to Members on 16 January 1998. The Appellate Body report and the Panel report, as modified by the Appellate Body, were adopted by the DSB on 13 February 1998. On 16 April 1997, the respondent requested that the "reasonable period of time" for implementation of the recommendations and rulings of the DSB be determined by binding arbitration, pursuant to Article 21.3(c) of the DSU. The Arbitrator found the reasonable period of time for implementation to be 15 months from the date of adoption (*i.e.* 15 months from 13 February 1998). The report of the Arbitrator was circulated to Members on 29 May 1998.

(8) *India — Patent Protection for Pharmaceutical and Agricultural Chemical Products*, complaint by the United States (WT/DS50). This request, dated 2 July 1996, concerns the alleged absence of patent protection for pharmaceutical and agricultural chemical products in India. Violations of the TRIPS Agreement Articles 27, 65 and 70 are claimed. The United States requested the establishment of a panel on 7 November 1996. The DSB established a panel at its meeting on 20 November 1996. The Panel found that India has not complied with its obligations under Article 70.8(a) or Article 63(1) and (2) of the TRIPS Agreement by failing to establish a mechanism that adequately preserves novelty and priority in respect of applications for product patents for pharmaceutical and agricultural chemical inventions, and was also not in compliance with Article 70.9 of the TRIPS Agreement by failing to establish a system for the grant of exclusive marketing rights. The report of the Panel was circulated on 5 September 1997. On 15 October 1997, India notified its intention to appeal certain issues of law and legal interpretations developed by the Panel. The Appellate Body upheld, with modifications, the Panel's findings on Articles 70.8 and 70.9, but ruled that Article 63(1) was not within the Panel's terms of reference. The report of the Appellate Body was circulated to Members on 19 December 1997. The Appellate Body report and the Panel report, as modified by the Appellate Body, were adopted by the DSB on 16 January 1998. At the DSB meeting of 22 April 1998, the parties announced that they had agreed on an implementation period of 15 months.

(7) *European Communities — Regime for the Importation, Sale and Distribution of Bananas*, complaints by Ecuador, Guatemala, Honduras, Mexico and the United States (WT/DS27). The complainants in this case other than Ecuador had requested consultations with the EC on the same issue on 28 September 1995 (WT/DS16). After Ecuador's accession to the WTO, the current complainants again requested consultations with the EC on 5 February 1996. The complainants allege that the EC's regime for importation, sale and distribution of bananas is inconsistent with GATT Articles I, II, III, X, XI and XIII as well as provisions of the Import Licensing Agreement, the Agreement on Agriculture, the TRIMs Agreement and the GATS. A panel was established at the DSB meeting on 8 May 1996. The Panel found that the EC's banana import regime, and the licensing procedures for the importation of bananas in this regime, are inconsistent with the GATT. The Panel further found that the Lomé waiver waives the inconsistency with GATT Article XIII, but not inconsistencies arising from the licensing system. The report of the Panel was circulated to Members on 22 May 1997. On 11 June 1997, the European Communities notified its intention to appeal certain issues of law and legal interpretations developed by the Panel. The Appellate Body mostly upheld the Panel's findings, but reversed the Panel's findings that the inconsistency with GATT Article XIII is waived by the Lomé waiver, and that certain aspects of the licensing regime violated Article X of GATT and the Import Licensing Agreement. The report of the Appellate Body was circulated to Members on 9 September 1997. At its meeting on 25 September 1997, the Appellate Body report and the Panel report, as modified by the Appellate Body, were adopted by the DSB. On 17 November 1997, the complainants requested that the "reasonable period of time" for implementation of the recommendations and rulings of the DSB be determined by binding arbitration, pursuant to Article 21.3(c) of the DSU. The Arbitrator found the reasonable period of time for implementation to be the period from 25 September 1997 to 1 January 1999. The report of the Arbitrator was circulated to Members on 7 January 1998.

(6) *Canada — Certain Measures Concerning Periodicals*,

complaint by the United States (WT/DS31). In its request for consultations dated 11 March 1996, the United States claims that measures prohibiting or restricting the importation into Canada of certain periodicals are in contravention of GATT Article XI. The US further alleges that the tax treatment of so-called "split-run" periodicals and the application of favourable postage rates to certain Canadian periodicals are inconsistent with GATT Article III. The DSB established a panel on 19 June 1996. The Panel found the measures applied by Canada to be in violation of GATT rules. The report of the Panel was circulated to Members on 14 March 1997. On 29 April 1997, Canada notified its intention to appeal certain issues of law and legal interpretations developed by the Panel. The Appellate Body upheld the Panel's findings and conclusions on the applicability of GATT 1994 to Part V.1 of Canada's Excise Tax Act, but reversed the Panel's finding that Part V.1 of the Excise Act is inconsistent with the first sentence of Article III : 2 of GATT 1994. The Appellate Body further concluded that Part V.1 of the Excise Act is inconsistent with the second sentence of Article III : 2 of GATT 1994. The Appellate Body also reversed the Panel's conclusion that Canada's "funded" postal rate scheme is justified by Article III : 8(b) of GATT 1994. The report of the Appellate Body was circulated to Members on 30 June 1997. At its meeting on 30 July 1997, the DSB adopted the Appellate Body report and the Panel report, as modified by the Appellate Body.

(5) *United States — Measure Affecting Imports of Woven Wool Shirts and Blouses*, complaint by India (WT/DS33). This case concerns the transitional safeguard measure imposed by the United States. India claimed that the safeguard measure is inconsistent with Articles 2, 6 and 8 of the ATC. A panel was established at the DSB meeting on 17 April 1996. The Panel found that the safeguard measure imposed by the United States violated the provisions of the ATC. The report of the Panel was circulated to Members on 6 January 1997. On 24 February 1997, India notified its intention to appeal certain issues of law and legal interpretations developed by the Panel. The Appellate Body upheld the Panel's decisions on those issues of law and legal interpretations that were appealed against. The report of the

Appellate Body was circulated to Members on 25 April 1997. The Appellate Body report and the Panel report, as upheld by the Appellate Body, were adopted by the DSB on 23 May 1997.

(4) *Brazil — Measures Affecting Desiccated Coconut*, complaint by the Philippines (WT/DS22). The Philippines claims that the countervailing duty imposed by Brazil on the Philippine's exports of desiccated coconut is inconsistent with WTO and GATT rules. The report of the Panel concluded that the provisions of the agreements relied on by the claimant were inapplicable to the dispute (WT/DS22/R). The report was circulated to members on 17 October 1996. On 16 December 1996, the Philippines notified its decision to appeal against certain issues of law and legal interpretations developed by the panel. The Appellate Body upheld the findings and legal interpretations of the Panel. The report of the Appellate Body was circulated to Members on 21 February 1997. The Appellate Body's report and the Panel report, as modified by the Appellate Body's report, were adopted by the DSB on 20 March 1997.

(3) *United States — Restrictions on Imports of Cotton and Man-Made Fibre Underwear*, complaint by Costa Rica (WT/DS24). This dispute involves US restrictions on textile imports from Costa Rica, allegedly in violation of the ATC agreement. The Panel found that the US restraints were not valid. The report of the panel was circulated to members on 8 November 1996. On 11 November 1996, Costa Rica notified its decision to appeal against one aspect of the Panel report. The Appellate Body upheld the appeal by Costa Rica on that particular point. The report of the Appellate Body was circulated to Members on 10 February 1997. The Appellate Body's report and the Panel report as modified by the Appellate report, were adopted by the DSB on 25 February 1997. At the meeting of the DSB on 10 April 1997, the US informed the meeting that the measure which had been the subject of this dispute had expired on 27 March 1997 and had not been renewed, effectively meaning that the US had immediately complied with the recommendations of the DSB.

(2) *Japan — Taxes on Alcoholic Beverages*, complaints by the European Communities (WT/DS8), Canada (WT/DS10) and the United States (WT/DS11). Complainants claimed that spirits

exported to Japan were discriminated against under the Japanese liquor tax system which, in their view, levies a substantially lower tax on "shochu" than on whisky, cognac and white spirits. A joint panel was established at the DSB meeting on 27 September 1995. The report of the panel, which found the Japanese tax system to be inconsistent with GATT Article III : 2, was circulated to Members on 11 July 1996. On 8 August 1996 Japan filed an appeal. The report of the Appellate Body was circulated to Members on 4 October 1996. The Appellate Body's Report affirmed the Panel's conclusion that the Japanese Liquor Tax Law is inconsistent with GATT Article III : 2, but pointed out several areas where the Panel had erred in its legal reasoning. The Appellate Report, together with the panel report as modified by the Appellate Report, was adopted on 1 November 1996. On 24 December 1996, the US, pursuant to Article 21(3)(c) of the DSU applied for binding arbitration to determine the reasonable period of time for implementation by Japan of the recommendations of the Appellate Body. The Arbitrator found the reasonable period for implementation of the recommendations to be 15 months. The Arbitrator's report was circulated to members on 14 February 1997.

(1) *United States — Standards for Reformulated and Conventional Gasoline*, complaints by Venezuela (WT/DS2) and Brazil (WT/DS4). A single panel considered the complaints of both Venezuela and Brazil. Complainants alleged that a U.S. gasoline regulation discriminated against complainants' gasoline in violation of GATT Articles I and III and Article 2 of the Agreement on Technical Barriers to Trade (TBT). The report of the panel found the regulation to be inconsistent with GATT Article III : 4 and not to benefit from an Article XX exception, (WT/DS2/R, 29 January 1996). The United States appealed on 21 February 1996. On 22 April, the Appellate Body issued its report (WT/DS2/AB/R), modifying the panel report on the interpretation of GATT Article XX(g), but concluding that the Article XX(g) was not applicable in this case. The Appellate Report, together with the panel report as modified by the Appellate Report, was adopted by the DSB on 20 May 1996.

B. *Settled or Inactive Cases*

(31) *European Communities — Measures Affecting Butter Products*, complaint by New Zealand (WT/DS72). This request, dated 24 March 1997, is in respect of decisions by the EC and the United Kingdom's Customs and Excise Department, to the effect that New Zealand butter manufactured by the ANMIX butter-making process and the spreadable butter-making process be classified so as to be excluded from eligibility for New Zealand's country-specific tariff quota established by the European Communities' WTO Schedule. New Zealand alleges violations of Articles II, X and XI of GATT, Article 2 of the TBT Agreement, and Article 3 of the Agreement on Import Licensing Procedures. On 6 November 1997, New Zealand requested the establishment of a panel. The DSB established a panel on 18 November 1997. The US reserved its third-party rights. At the request of the complainants, dated 24 February 1999, the Panel agreed, pursuant to Article 12.12 of the DSU, to suspend the panel proceedings. In a communication dated 11 November 1999, the parties notified a mutually agreed solution to this dispute.

(30) *Colombia — Safeguard Measure on Imports of Plain Polyester Filaments from Thailand*, complaint by Thailand (DS 181/1). This request for a panel, dated 7 September 1999 concerns a unilateral restraint allegedly imposed by Colombia against imports of plain polyester filaments from Thailand. Colombia's safeguard measure is alleged to be inconsistent with Article 2 of the Agreement on Textiles and Clothing (ATC) regarding the application of a transitional safeguard mechanism and with Article 2 of the ATC regarding the introduction and application of restrictions by Members. The safeguard measures imposed by Colombia on 26 October 1998 have been subject to the two-stage examination and review procedures by the Textiles Monitoring Body (TMB). The TMB recommended at its fiftieth meeting held on 16-19 November 1998 that Colombia rescind the measure. On 22 December 1998, Colombia notified the TMB of its inability to conform with this TMB recommendation and provided the TMB with reasons therefor. At its fifty-second meeting on 18-20 January 1999, the TMB reviewed the matter and repeated its recommendation to Colombia to rescind the safeguard measure

forthwith. At the DSB meeting on 27 October 1999, Thailand announced that it was withdrawing its request for a panel because the Colombian safeguard measure had been terminated.

(29) *Argentina — Measures Affecting Textiles and Clothing*, complaint by the European Communities (WT/DS77/1). This request dated 17 April 1997, is in respect of a range of specific duties on textiles and clothing which have allegedly resulted in increased duties and have led to applied tariffs that exceed the 35% binding made by Argentina. The EC contends that these measures are a violation of Argentina's commitments under Article II of GATT 1994, and also of Article 7 of the ATC. See similar US complaint in DS56 pending before a panel. On 10 September 1997, the EC requested the establishment of a panel. At its meeting on 16 October 1997, the DSB established a panel. The US reserved its third-party rights. The Panel suspended its work at the request of the EC on 29 July 1998. Pursuant to DSU Article 12.12, the panel's authority lapsed on 29 July 1999, 12 months having passed since the suspension of the panel's work.

(28) *Sweden — Measures Affecting the Enforcement of Intellectual Property Rights*, complaint by the United States (WT/DS86/1). This request, dated 28 May 1997, is in respect of Sweden's alleged failure to make provisional measures available in the context of civil proceedings involving intellectual property rights. The US contends that this failure violates Sweden's obligations under Articles 50, 63 and 65 of the TRIPS Agreement. In a communication dated 2 December 1998, the two parties notified a mutually agreed solution to this dispute.

(27) *United States — Anti-Dumping Duties on Imports of Colour Television Receivers from Korea*, complaint by Korea (WT/DS89/1). This request, dated 10 July 1997, is in respect of the imposition of anti-dumping duties by the US on imports of colour television receivers (CTVs) from Korea. Korea contends that the US has for the past twelve years maintained an anti-dumping order for Samsung's CTVs despite the absence of dumping and the cessation of exports from Korea, without examining the necessity of continuing to impose such duties. Korea contends that the US actions violate Articles VI.1 and VI.6(a) of GATT 1994, and Articles 1, 2, 3.1, 3.2, 3.6, 4.1, 5.4, 5.8, 5.10, 11.1 and

11.2 of the Anti-Dumping Agreement. On 6 November 1997, Korea requested the establishment of a panel. On 5 January 1998, Korea informed the DSB that it was withdrawing its request for a panel but reserving its right to reintroduce the request. At the DSB meeting on 22 September 1998, Korea announced that it was definitively withdrawing the request for a panel because the imposition of anti-dumping duties had now been revoked.

(26) *Australia — Subsidies Provided to Producers and Exporters of Automotive Leather* (WT/DS106/1), complaint by the United States. This request, dated 10 November 1997, is in respect of Australia's alleged prohibited subsidies provided to its producers and exporters of automotive leather. The US contends that these measures by Australia violate Article 3 of the Subsidies Agreement. On 9 January 1998, the United States requested the establishment of a panel. At its meeting on 22 January 1998, the DSB established a panel in accordance with the accelerated procedure under the Subsidies Agreement. On 11 June 1998, the US withdrew its request for a panel. See also WT/DS126.

(25) *Australia — Anti-dumping Measures on Imports of Coated Woodfree Paper Sheets*, complaint by Switzerland (WT/DS119/1). This request, dated 20 February 1998, is in respect of the provisional anti-dumping measures applied on the imports of coated woodfree paper sheets from Switzerland. Switzerland contends that the investigation is not in conformity with Australia's commitments under Articles 3 and 5 of the Anti-Dumping Agreement. On 13 May 1998, the two parties notified a mutually agreed solution.

(24) *United States — The Cuban Liberty and Democratic Solidarity Act*, complaint by the European Communities (WT/DS38). On 3 May 1996 the European Communities requested consultations with the United States concerning the Cuban Liberty and Democratic Solidarity (LIBERTAD) Act of 1996 and other legislation enacted by the US Congress regarding trade sanctions against Cuba. The EC claims that US trade restrictions on goods of Cuban origin, as well as the possible refusal of visas and the exclusion of non-US nationals from US territory, are inconsistent with the US obligations under the WTO Agreement. Violations of GATT Articles I, III, V, XI and XIII, and GATS Articles I, III,

VI, XVI and XVII are alleged. The EC also alleges that even if these measures by the US may not be in violation of specific provisions of GATT or GATS, they nevertheless nullify or impair its expected benefits under GATT 1994 and GATS and impede the attainment of the objectives of GATT 1994. The European Communities requested the establishment of a panel on 3 October 1996. The DSB established a panel at its meeting on 20 November 1996. At the request of the EC, dated 21 April 1997, the Panel suspended its work. The Panel's authority lapsed on 22 April 1998, pursuant to Article 12.12 of the DSU.

(23) (a) *India — Quantitative Restrictions on Imports of Agricultural, Textile and Industrial Products* complaint by Australia (WT/DS91/1). This request, dated 16 July 1997, raises the same issues in respect of India's quantitative restrictions on imports of agricultural, textile and industrial products as in the request by the US in DS90. On 23 March 1998, the two parties notified a mutually agreed solution.

(23) (b) *India — Quantitative Restrictions on Imports of Agricultural, Textile and Industrial Products*, complaint by Canada (WT/DS92/1). This request, dated 16 July 1997, raises the same issues in respect of India's quantitative restrictions on imports of agricultural, textile and industrial products as in the requests by the US (DS90) and Australia (DS91). On 25 March 1998, the two parties notified a mutually agreed solution.

(23) (c) *India — Quantitative Restrictions on Imports of Agricultural, Textile and Industrial Products*, complaint by Switzerland (WT/DS94/1). This request, dated 18 July 1997, raises the same issues in respect of India's quantitative restrictions on imports of agricultural, textile and industrial products as in the requests by the US (DS90), Australia (DS91), Canada (DS92), and New Zealand (DS93). However, Switzerland does not invoke the Agreement on Agriculture. On 23 February 1998, the two parties notified a mutually agreed solution.

(23) (d) *India — Quantitative Restrictions on Imports of Agricultural, Textile and Industrial Products*, complaint by the European Communities (WT/DS96/1). This request, dated 18 July 1997, raises the same issues in respect of India's quantitative

restrictions on imports of agricultural, textile and industrial products as in the requests by the US (DS90), Australia (DS91), Canada (DS92), New Zealand (DS93), and Switzerland (DS94). In addition, the EC is also alleging violations of Articles 2, 3 and 5 of the SPS Agreement. On 7 April 1998, the two parties notified a mutually agreed solution.

(23) (e) *India — Quantitative Restrictions on Imports of Agricultural, Textile and Industrial Products*, complaint by New Zealand (WT/DS93/1). This request, dated 16 July 1997, raises the same issues in respect of India's quantitative restrictions on imports of agricultural, textile and industrial products as in the requests by the US (DS90), Australia (DS91) and Canada (DS92). However, New Zealand makes an additional claim for nullification and impairment of benefits accruing to it under GATT 1994. In a letter dated 14 September 1998, but communicated to the Secretariat on 1 December 1998, the two parties notified a mutually agreed solution to this dispute.

(22) (a) *Philippines — Measures Affecting Pork and Poultry*, complaint by the United States (WT/DS74/1). This request, dated 1 April 1997, is in respect of the implementation by the Philippines of its tariff-rate quotas for pork and poultry. The US contends that the Philippines' implementation of these tariff-rate quotas, in particular the delays in permitting access to the in-quota quantities and the licensing system used to administer access to the in-quota quantities, appears to be inconsistent with the obligations of the Philippines under Articles III, X, and XI of GATT 1994, Article 4 of the Agreement on Agriculture, Articles 1 and 3 of the Agreement on Import Licensing Procedures, and Articles 2 and 5 of TRIMs. The US further contends that theses measures appear to nullify or impair benefits accruing to it directly or indirectly under cited agreements. On 12 March 1998, the parties communicated a mutually agreed solution to their dispute.

(22) (b) *Philippines — Measures Affecting Pork and Poultry* (WT/DS102/1), complaint by the United States. This request, dated 7 October 1997, is in respect of the same measures complained of by the US in DS74, but also includes Administrative Order No. 8, Series of 1997, which purports to amend the original measure

complained of in DS74. On 12 March 1998, the parties communicated a mutually agreed solution to their dispute.

(21) *United States — Measures Affecting Textiles and Apparel Products*, complaint by the European Communities (WT/DS85/1). This request, dated 23 May 1997, is in respect of changes to US rules of origin for textiles and apparel products. The EC alleges that the US has introduced changes to its rules of origin for textile and apparel products, which affect exports of EC fabrics, scarves and other flat textile products to the US. As a result, the EC alleges that EC products are no longer recognised in the US as being of EC origin and lose the free access to the US market that they had hitherto enjoyed. The EC contends that these changes in US rules of origin are in violation of the obligations of the US under Articles 2.4, 4.2 and 4.4 of the ATC, Article 4.2 of the Agreement on Rules of Origin, Article III of GATT 1994, and Article 2 of the TBT Agreement. On 11 February 1998, the two parties notified their mutually agreed solution.

(20) *Korea — Laws, Regulations and Practices in the Telecommunications Sector*, complaint by the European Communities (WT/DS40). This request for consultations, dated 9 May 1996, concerns the laws, regulations and practices in the telecommunications sector. The EC claims that the procurement practices of the Korean telecommunications sector (Korea Telecom and Dacom) discriminate against foreign suppliers. The EC also claims that the Korean government has favoured US suppliers under two bilateral telecommunications agreements between Korea and the US. Violations of GATT Articles I, III and XVII are alleged. On 22 October 1997, the parties notified the Secretariat of a mutually agreed solution.

(19) *Japan — Procurement of a Navigation Satellite*, complaint by the European Communities (WT/DS73/1). This request, dated 26 March 1997, is in respect of a procurement tender published by the Ministry of Transport (MoT) of Japan to purchase a multi-functional satellite for Air Traffic Management. The EC contends that the specifications in the tender were not neutral but referred explicitly to US specifications. This meant, the EC contends, that European bidders could effectively not participate in the tender.

The EC alleges inconsistency of this tender with Annex I of Appendix I of Japan's commitments under the Government Procurement Agreement (GPA). The EC also alleges violations of Articles VI(3) and XII(2) of the GPA. On 31 July 1997, the EC notified the Secretariat that a mutually agreed solution had been reached with Japan in this dispute. On 19 February 1998, the two parties communicated the text of their agreement to the DSB.

(18) *Hungary — Export Subsidies in Respect of Agricultural Products*, complaint by Argentina, Australia, Canada, New Zealand, Thailand and the United States (WT/DS35). This request, dated 27 March 1996, claims that Hungary violated the Agreement on Agriculture (Article 3.3 and Part V) by providing export subsidies in respect of agricultural products not specified in its Schedule, as well as by providing agricultural export subsidies in excess of its commitment levels. On 9 January 1997, Argentina, Australia, New Zealand and the United States requested the establishment of a panel. At its meeting on 25 February 1997 the DSB established a panel. Canada, Japan, Thailand and Uruguay reserved their third-party rights to the dispute. At the DSB meeting on 30 July 1997, Australia, on behalf of all the complainants, notified the DSB that the parties to the dispute had reached a mutually agreed solution, which required Hungary to seek a waiver of certain of its WTO obligations. Pending adoption of the waiver, the complaint was not formally withdrawn.

(17) *Turkey — Taxation of Foreign Film Revenues*, complaint by the United States (WT/DS43). This request for consultations, dated 12 June 1996, concerns Turkey's taxation of revenues generated from the showing of foreign films. Violation of GATT Article III is alleged. On 9 January 1997, the United States requested the establishment of a panel. At its meeting on 25 February 1997, the DSB established a panel. Canada reserved its third-party rights to the dispute. On 14 July 1997, both parties notified the DSB of a mutually agreed solution.

(16) *Pakistan — Patent Protection for Pharmaceutical and Agricultural Chemical Products*, complaint by the United States (WT/DS36). In its request for consultations dated 30 April 1996, the United States claimed that the absence in Pakistan of (i) either patent protection for pharmaceutical and agricultural chemical

products or a system to permit the filing of applications for patents on these products and (ii) a system to grant exclusive marketing rights in such products, violates TRIPS Agreement Articles 27, 65 and 70. On 4 July 1996, the United States requested the establishment of a panel. The DSB considered the request at its meeting on 16 July 1996, but did not establish a panel due to Pakistan's objection. At the DSB meeting on 25 February 1997, both parties informed the DSB that they had reached a mutually agreed solution to the dispute and that the terms of the agreement were being drawn up, and would be communicated to the DSB once finalized. On 28 February 1997, the terms of the agreement were communicated to the Secretariat.

(15) (a) *Japan — Measures Concerning Sound Recordings*, complaint by the United States (WT/DS28). This request, dated 9 February 1996, is the first WTO dispute settlement case involving the TRIPS Agreement. The United States claims that Japan's copyright regime for the protection of intellectual property in sound recordings is inconsistent with, inter alia, the TRIPS Agreement Article 14 (protection of performers, producers of phonograms and broadcasting organizations). On January 24 1997, both parties informed the DSB that they had reached a mutually satisfactory solution to the dispute.

(15) (b) *Japan — Measures Concerning Sound Recordings*, complaint by the European Communities (WT/DS42). This request for consultations, dated 24 May 1996, concerns the intellectual property protection of sound recordings under GATT Article XXII : 1. Violations of Articles 14.6 and 70.2 of the TRIPS Agreement are alleged. Earlier, the United States requested consultations with Japan on the same issue (WT/DS28), in which the EC joined. On 7 November 1997, both parties notified a mutually agreed solution.

(14) *Australia — Textiles, Clothing and Footwear Import Credit Scheme*, complaint by the United States (WT/DS57). This request, dated 7 October 1996, concerns a complaint by the United States against subsidies being granted and maintained by Australia on leather products under the TCF scheme. A violation of Article 3 of the SCM Agreement is alleged. The US is also invoking Article 30 of the SCM Agreement to the extent that it

incorporates by reference Article XXIII : 1 of GATT 1994. An official release from the USTR in Washington on 25 November 1996 indicates that the case has been settled.

(13) *United States — Anti-Dumping Investigation Regarding Imports of Fresh or Chilled Tomatoes from Mexico, complaint by Mexico* (WT/DS49). On 1 July 1996, Mexico requested consultations with the United States regarding the anti-dumping investigation on fresh and chilled tomatoes imported from Mexico under Article 17.3 of the Anti-dumping Agreement. Violations of GATT Articles VI and X as well as Articles 2, 3, 5, 6 and 7.1 of the Anti-dumping Agreement are alleged. Mexico claims this to be a case of urgency, where the expedited procedures under Articles 4.8 and 4.9 of the DSU are applicable. US Commerce Department official releases indicate that the case has been settled.

(12) *Portugal — Patent Protection under the Industrial Property Act*, complaint by the United States (WT/DS37). This request for consultations dated 30 April 1996, concerned Portugal's term of patent protection under its Industrial Property Act. The US claimed that the provisions in that Act with respect to existing patents were inconsistent with Portugal's obligations under the TRIPS Agreement. Violations under Articles 33, 65 and 70 were alleged. On 3 October 1996, both parties notified a mutually agreed solution to the DSB.

(11) *Poland — Import Regime for Automobiles*, complaint by India (WT/DS19). This request for consultations, dated 28 September 1995, concerns Poland's preferential treatment of the EC in its tariff scheme on automobiles. On 16 July 1996, both parties notified a mutually agreed solution to the DSB.

(10) *United States — Tariff Increases on Products from the European Communities*, complaint by the European Communities (WT/DS39). In its request for consultations, dated 17 April 1996, the EC claimed that the measures taken under the Presidential Proclamation No. 5759 of 24 December 1987 (retaliation against the "hormones" directive), which resulted in tariff increases on products from the European Communities, are inconsistent with GATT Articles I, II and XXIII, as well as DSU Articles 3, 22 and 23. On 19 June 1996, the EC requested the establishment of a

panel. In its request, the EC further claimed that the United States apparently failed to "ensure the conformity of its laws, regulations and administrative procedures with its obligations" under the WTO, with respect to the application of Section 301 of the 1974 Trade Act in this case (WTO Agreement Article XVI:4). The United States withdrew the measure on 15 July 1996, and the EC decided not to pursue its panel request, reserving its rights to reconvene, if necessary, a further meeting of the DSB at an early date.

(9) *European Communities — Trade Description of Scallops*, complaints by Canada (WT/DS7), Peru (WT/DS12) and Chile (WT/DS14). The complaint concerns a French Government Order laying down the official name and trade description of scallops. Complainants claim that this Order will reduce competitiveness on the French market as their product will no longer be able to be sold as "Coquille Saint-Jacques" although there is no difference between their scallops and French scallops in terms of colour, size, texture, appearance and use, *i.e.* it is claimed they are "like products". Violations of GATT Articles I and III and TBT Article 2 are alleged. A panel was established at the request of Canada on 19 July 1995. A joint panel was established on 11 October 1995 at the request of Peru and Chile on the same subject. The two panels have concluded their substantive work, but they suspended the proceedings pursuant to Article 12.12 of the DSU in May 1996 in view of the consultations held among the parties concerned toward a mutually agreed solution. The parties notified a mutually agreed solution to the DSB on 5 July 1996. Brief panel reports noting the settlement were circulated to Members on 5 August 1996 in accordance with the provisions of Article 12.7 of the DSU.

(8) *United States — Measures Affecting Imports of Women's and Girls' Wool Coats*, complaint by India (WT/DS32). In a communication dated 14 March 1996, India requested the establishment of a panel, claiming that the transitional safeguard measures on these textile products by the United States were inconsistent with ATC Articles 2, 6 and 8. A panel was established in the DSB meeting on 17 April 1996. However, on 25 April 1996, India requested "termination of further action in pursuance

of the decision taken by the DSB on 17 April 1996 to establish a panel" in light of the US removal of the safeguard measures on these products, which came into effect from 24 April 1996.

(7) *Korea — Measures Concerning Bottled Water*, complaint by Canada (WT/DS20). In this request, dated 8 November 1995, Canada claimed that Korean regulations on the shelf-life and physical treatment (disinfection) of bottled water were inconsistent with GATT Articles III and XI, SPS Articles 2 and 5 and TBT Article 2. At the DSB meeting on 24 April 1996, the parties to the dispute announced that they reached a settlement.

(6) *Venezuela — Anti-Dumping Investigation in Respect of Imports of Certain Oil Country Tubular Goods (OCTG)*, complaint by Mexico (WT/DS23), dated 5 December 1995. By a letter dated 6 May 1997, Mexico informed the Secretariat that Venezuela had terminated the anti-dumping investigation in this matter.

(5) (a) *European Communities — Duties on Imports of Cereals*, complaint by Canada (WT/DS9). Canada requested consultations with the EC on 10 July 1995 concerning EC regulations implementing some of the EC's Uruguay Round concessions on agriculture, specifically, regulations which impose a duty on wheat imports based on reference prices rather than transaction values, with the result that the duty-paid import price for Canadian wheat will be greater than the effective intervention price increased by 55% whenever the transaction value is greater than the representative price. A panel was established at the DSB meeting on 11 October 1995, but no panelists have been selected.

(5) (b) *European Communities — Duties on Imports of Grains*, complaint by the United States (WT/DS13). This request for consultations, dated 19 July 1995, has potentially broader product coverage than the case brought by Canada (WT/DS9, item 7(5)(a) below) but otherwise concerns much the same issues. On 28 September 1995, the US requested the establishment of a panel to be considered at the meeting of the DSB on 11 October 1995, but the EC objected to it. The US again requested the establishment of a panel to be considered at the meeting of the DSB on 3 December 1996, but later dropped the request at the meeting. On 13 February 1997 the US made a renewed request

for the establishment of a panel. At the DSB meeting on 20 March 1997, the US withdrew its request for a panel in this matter. On 26 March 1997, the US made a fresh request for the establishment of a panel. On 30 April 1997, the US informed the Secretariat that it was withdrawing its request for a panel in view of the fact that the EC had adopted regulations implementing an agreement reached on this matter.

(5) (c) *European Communities — Duties on Imports of Rice*, complaint by Thailand (WT/DS17). This request for consultations, dated 3 October 1995, covers more or less the same grounds as Canadian (WT/DS9) and the US (WT/DS13) complaints over the EC duties on grains (a) and 5(3) above). In addition, Thailand seems to have alleged that the EC has violated the most-favoured-nation requirement under GATT Article I in their preferential treatment of basmati rice from India and Pakistan. See also the Uruguayan complaint (WT/DS25).

(5) (d) *European Communities — Implementation of the Uruguay Round Commitments Concerning Rice*, complaint by Uruguay (WT/DS25). This request for consultations, dated 18 December 1995, seems similar to the claim by Thailand (WT/DS17).

(4) *Japan — Measures Affecting the Purchase of Telecommunications Equipment*, complaint by the European Communities (WT/DS15). This request for consultations, dated 18 August 1995, claims that a 1994 agreement reached between the United States and Japan concerning telecommunications equipment is inconsistent with GATT Articles I : 1, III : 4 and XVII : 1(c), and nullifies or impairs benefits accruing to the EC. The United States has joined in the consultations. Although there has been no official notification, the case appears to have been settled bilaterally.

(3) *United States — Imposition of Import Duties on Automobiles from Japan under Sections 301 and 304 of the Trade Act of 1974*, complaint by Japan (WT/DS6). On 19 July 1995, the parties notified settlement of this dispute. Japan had alleged that the import surcharges violated GATT Articles I and II.

(2) *Korea — Measures Concerning the Shelf-life of Products*,

complaint by the United States (WT/DS5). This request dated 3 May 1995, was in respect of requirements imposed by Korea on imports from the US which had the effect of restricting imports. The US alleged violations of Articles III and XI of GATT, Articles 2 and 5 of the SPS Agreement, Article 2 of the TBT Agreement, and Article 4 of the Agreement on Agriculture. The parties notified a mutually acceptable solution to this dispute on 31 July 1995.

(1) *Malaysia — Prohibition of Imports of Polyethylene and Polypropylene*, complaint by Singapore (WT/DS1). This, the first dispute under the WTO's dispute settlement procedures, was settled on 19 July 1995, with Singapore's withdrawal of the panel request.

Summary

Case titles in **bold** indicate those cases where the panel process has been completed;

Case titles in *italics* indicate those cases where settlement has been notified or is apparent;

Active panels are <u>underlined</u>.

Complaints by Developed Country Members (105 matters / 135 requests)
Respondent — developed
US, automobiles (DS6) **Japan, alcoholic beverages** (DS8, DS10, DS11) *Japan, telecom* (DS15) **Australia, salmon** (DS18) <u>Australia, salmon</u> (DS21) **EC, hormones** (DS26, DS48) *Japan, sound recordings* (DS28, DS42) **Canada, periodicals** (DS31) *Portugal, patent* (DS37) *US, Cuba (Helms Burton) Act* (DS38) *US, hormones retaliation* (DS39) **Japan, film** (DS44) Japan, distribution (DS45) *Australia, leather* (DS57) **EC, UK, Ireland, computers** (DS62, DS67, DS68) US, urea (DS63) Japan, pork (DS66) *EC, butter* (DS72) *Japan, procurement* (DS73) **Japan, agricultural products** (DS76) Belgium, telephone directories (DS80) Ireland, copyright (grant of rights) (DS82) Denmark,

intellectual property (enforcement) (DS83) US, textiles (DS85) *Sweden, intellectual property (enforcement)* (DS86) US, government procurement (DS88, DS95) US, poultry (DS100) Canada, subsidies (milk and cheese) (DS103) EC, subsidies (processed cheese) (DS104) **Australia, subsidies (auto leather)** (DS106, DS126) US, foreign sales corporations (tax treatment) (DS108) **Canada, dairy exports** (DS113) Canada, patent protection (pharmaceuticals) (DS114) Canada, film distribution (DS117) US, harbour tax (DS118) *Australia, anti-dumping measures (paper sheets)* (DS119) EC, Greece, intellectual property (DS124, DS125) Belgium, France, Greece, Ireland, Netherlands, subsidies (income tax measures) (DS127, DS128, DS129, DS130, DS131) Slovak Republic, dairy products (DS133) EC asbestos (DS135) US Anti-Dumping Act 1916 (DS136) EC wood conifers (DS137) US, countervailing duties (lead & steel) (DS138) Canada, auto industry (DS139, DS142) Slovak Republic, import duty (wheat) (DS143) US, cattle & swine (DS144) Argentina, countervailing duties (wheat gluten) (DS145), Japan, tariff quotas (leather) (DS147) Czech Republic, import duty (wheat) (DS148) US textiles (DS151) US sections 301-310 (DS152) EC patent protection (pharmaceuticals) (DS153) US, copyrights (DS160) US, Anti-Dumping Act 1916 (II) (DS162) US, import measures (bananas retaliation) (DS165) US, safeguard measures (DS166) US, countervailing duty (Cattle) (DS167) South Africa, anti-dumping (pharmaceuticals) (DS168) Canada, patent protection (DS170) EC & France, subsidies (FMS for Airbus) (DS172, 173) EC, trademark protection (DS174) US, Omnibus Act (Cuban rum trademarks) (DS176) US safeguard measure (NZ lamb) (DS177) US, safeguard measure (Australia lamb) (DS178) US, anti-dumping (steel) (DS184)

Respondents — developing

Korea, inspection of agricultural products (DS3, DS41) *Korea, shelf-life (DS5) Korea, bottled water* (DS20) *Pakistan, patent* (DS36) *Korea, telecom* (DS40) *Turkey, film tax* (DS43) Brazil, aircraft (DS46) **India, patent** (DS50) Brazil, automobiles (DS51, DS52, DS65, 81) Mexico, customs valuation (DS53) **Indonesia, automobiles** (DS54, DS55, DS59, DS64) Argentina, textiles (DS56) Philippines, pork and poultry (DS74, DS102) **Korea, alcoholic beverages** (DS75, DS84) Argentina, textiles (DS77) **India, patent** (DS79) Chile, alcoholic beverages (DS87) **India — quantitative restrictions** (DS90) *India, quantitative restrictions* (DS91, DS92, DS93, DS94, DS96) Korea, safeguard measure (dairy) (DS98) Mexico, anti-dumping (corn syrup) (DS101) Pakistan, hides, skins and leather (DS107) Chile, alcoholic beverages (DS109, DS110 only) Brazil, import payment terms (DS116) India, export commodities (DS120) Argentina, safeguard measures (footwear) (DS121) Thailand, anti-dumping duties (metal products) (DS122) Mexico, anti-dumping (corn syrup (DS132) India, auto (DS146) India, import restrictions (DS149) India, customs duties (DS150) Argentina, bovine hide and leather (DS155) Argentina, anti-dumping (drill bits) (DS157) EC Bananas II (DS158) Hungary, safeguard measure (steel) (DS159) Korea, beef imports (DS161, DS169) Korea, Government Procurement (DS163) Argentina, import measures (footwear), (DS164) Argentina, patent protection (DS171) India, investment (Motor Vehicles) (DS175) Brazil, import licensing (DS183)

Complaints by Developing Country Members (32 matters / 36 requests)
Respondent — developed
US, gasoline (DS2, DS4) *Poland, automobiles* (DS19) **US, underwear** (DS24) *US, wool coats* (DS32) **US, wool shirts** (DS33) *US, tomatoes* (DS49) **US, shrimp** (DS58, DS 61) **EC, poultry** (DS69) **Canada, aircraft** (DS70, DS71) US, brooms (DS78) *US, anti-dumping duties (CTVs)* (DS89) US, countervailing measures (salmon) (DS97) **US, anti-dumping (semiconductors)** (DS99) EC, bananas (DS105) US, tariff rate quota (groundnuts) (DS111), EC, import duties (rice) (DS134), EC, anti-dumping investigation (cotton fabrics) (DS140)

EC, anti-dumping duties (bed-linen) (DS141) EC, special & differential treatment (coffee) (DS154) South Africa, anti-dumping (pharmaceuticals) (DS168) US, anti-dumping measures (steel) (DS179)
Respondent — developing
Malaysia, polyethylene and polypropylene (DS1) **Brazil, coconut** (Philippines) (DS22) *Venezuela, OCTG* (DS23) **Turkey, textiles** (DS29, DS34, DS47) Brazil, coconut (Sri Lanka) (DS30) **Guatemala, cement** (DS60) Peru, countervailing duty investigation (buses) (DS112) Argentina, subsidies (footwear) (DS123) Guatemala, cement (DS156) Colombia, safeguard (polyester) (DS181) Ecuador, anti-dumping (cement) (DS182) Trinidad and Tobago, pasta (DS185)
Complaints by Both Developed and Developing Country Members (4 matters / 10 requests[1])
Respondent — developed
EC, scallops (DS7, DS12, DS14) *EC, grains* (DS9, DS13, DS17, DS25) EC, bananas (DS16, DS27) *Hungary, export subsidies* (DS35)

Total number of distinct matters : 144

Total number of consultation requests : 185[2]

1. This figure includes three requests made by developed country Members (DS7, DS9 and DS13). The total number of consultation requests made by developing country Member is 44. On the basis of distinct matters, the number is 36.

2. Three requests for the establishment of a panel (DS32, DS33 and DS181) were not preceded by requests for consultations under the DSU. Nonetheless, they are included in this figure since consultations were in fact held pursuant to the Agreement on Textiles and Clothing.

4

INTELLECTUAL PROPERTY RIGHTS

AN OVERVIEW OF THE AGREEMENT ON TRADE-RELATED ASPECTS OF INTELLECTUAL PROPERTY RIGHTS (TRIPS AGREEMENT)

Main Features of the TRIPS Agreement

The TRIPS Agreement, which came into effect on 1 January 1995, is to date the most comprehensive multilateral agreement on intellectual property. The areas of intellectual property that it covers are : copyright and related rights (*i.e.* the rights of performers, producers of sound recordings and broadcasting organizations); trademarks including service marks; geographical indications including appellations of origin; industrial designs; patents including the protection of new varieties of plants; the layout-designs of integrated circuits; and undisclosed information including trade secrets and test data.

The three main features of the Agreement are :

(i) **Standards.** In respect of each of the main areas of intellectual property covered by the TRIPS Agreement, the Agreement sets out the minimum standards of protection to be provided by each Member. Each of the main elements of protection is defined, namely the subject-matter to be protected, the rights to be conferred and permissible exceptions to those rights, and the minimum duration of protection. The Agreement sets these standards by requiring, first, that the substantive obligations of the main conventions of the WIPO, the Paris Convention for the Protection of Industrial Property (Paris Convention) and the Berne Convention for the Protection of Literary and Artistic Works (Berne Convention) in their most recent versions, must be complied with. With the exception of the provisions of the Berne Convention on moral rights, all the main substantive provisions of these conventions are incorporated by reference and thus become obligations under the TRIPS Agreement between TRIPS Member countries. The relevant provisions are to be found in Articles 2.1 and 9.1 of the TRIPS Agreement, which relate, respectively, to the Paris Convention and to the Berne Convention. Secondly, the TRIPS Agreement adds a substantial number of additional obligations on matters where the pre-existing conventions are silent or were seen as being inadequate. The TRIPS Agreement is thus sometimes referred to as a Berne and Paris-plus agreement.

(ii) **Enforcement.** The second main set of provisions deals with domestic procedures and remedies for the enforcement of intellectual property rights. The Agreement lays down certain general principles applicable to all IPR enforcement procedures. In addition, it contains provisions on civil and administrative procedures and remedies, provisional measures, special requirements related to border measures and criminal procedures, which specify, in a certain amount of detail, the procedures and remedies that must be available so that right holders can effectively enforce their rights.

(iii) **Dispute Settlement.** The Agreement makes disputes between WTO Members about the respect of the TRIPS obligations subject to the WTO's dispute settlement procedures.

In addition the Agreement provides for certain basic principles, such as national and most-favoured-nation treatment, and some general rules to ensure that procedural difficulties in acquiring or maintaining IPRs do not nullify the substantive benefits that should flow from the Agreement. The obligations under the Agreement will apply equally to all Member countries, but developing countries will have a longer period to phase them in. Special transition arrangements operate in the situation where a developing country does not presently provide product patent protection in the area of pharmaceuticals.

The TRIPS Agreement is a minimum standards agreement,

which allows Members to provide more extensive protection of intellectual property if they so wish. Members are left free to determine the appropriate method of implementing the provisions of the Agreement within their own legal system and practice.

Certain General Provisions

As in the main pre-existing intellectual property conventions, the basic obligation on each Member country is to accord the treatment in regard to the protection of intellectual property provided for under the Agreement to the persons of other Members. Article 1.3 defines who these persons are. These persons are referred to as "nationals" but include persons, natural or legal, who have a close attachment to other Members without necessarily being nationals. The criteria for determining which persons must thus benefit from the treatment provided for under the Agreement are those laid down for this purpose in the main pre-existing intellectual property conventions of WIPO, applied of course with respect to all WTO Members whether or not they are party to those conventions. These conventions are the Paris Convention, the Berne Convention, International Convention for the Protection of Performers, Producers of Phonograms and Broadcasting Organizations (Rome Convention), and the Treaty on Intellectual Property in Respect of Integrated Circuits (IPIC Treaty).

Articles 3, 4 and 5 include the fundamental rules on national and most-favoured-nation treatment of foreign nationals, which are common to all categories of intellectual property covered by the Agreement. These obligations cover not only the substantive standards of protection but also matters affecting the availability, acquisition, scope, maintenance and enforcement of intellectual property rights as well as those matters affecting the use of intellectual property rights specifically addressed in the Agreement. While the national treatment clause forbids discrimination between a Member's own nationals and the nationals of other Members, the most-favoured-nation treatment clause forbids discrimination between the nationals of other Members. In respect of the national treatment obligation, the exceptions allowed under the pre-existing intellectual property conventions of WIPO are also allowed under TRIPS. Where these exceptions allow material reciprocity, a consequential exception to MFN treatment is also permitted (*e.g.* comparison of terms for copyright protection in excess of the minimum term required by the TRIPS Agreement as provided under Article 7(8) of the Berne Convention as incorporated into the TRIPS Agreement). Certain other limited exceptions to the MFN obligation are also provided for.

The general goals of the TRIPS Agreement are contained in the Preamble of the Agreement, which reproduces the basic Uruguay Round negotiating objectives established in the TRIPS area by the 1986 Punta del Este Declaration and the 1988/89 Mid-Term Review. These objectives include the reduction of distortions and impediments to international trade, promotion of effective and adequate protection of intellectual property rights, and ensuring that measures and procedures to enforce intellectual property rights do not themselves become barriers to legitimate trade. These objectives should be read in conjunction with Article 7, entitled "Objectives", according to which the protection and enforcement of intellectual property rights should contribute to the promotion of technological innovation and to the transfer and dissemination of technology, to the mutual advantage of producers and users of technological knowledge and in a manner conducive to social and economic welfare, and to a balance of rights and obligations. Article 8, entitled "Principles", recognizes the rights of Members to adopt measures for public health and other public interest reasons and to prevent the abuse of intellectual property rights, provided that such measures are consistent with the provisions of the TRIPS Agreement.

Substantive Standards of Protection

Copyright

During the Uruguay Round negotiations, it was recognized that the Berne Convention already, for the most part, provided adequate basic standards of copyright protection. Thus it was agreed that the point of departure should be the existing level of protection under the latest Act, the Paris Act of 1971, of that Convention. The point of departure is expressed in Article 9.1 under which Members are obliged to comply with the substantive provisions of the Paris Act of 1971 of the Berne Convention, *i.e.*

Articles 1 through 21 of the Berne Convention (1971) and the Appendix thereto. However, Members do not have rights or obligations under the TRIPS Agreement in respect of the rights conferred under Article 6bis of that Convention, *i.e.* the moral rights (the right to claim authorship and to object to any derogatory action in relation to a work, which would be prejudicial to the author's honour or reputation), or of the rights derived therefrom. The provisions of the Berne Convention referred to deal with questions such as subject-matter to be protected, minimum term of protection, and rights to be conferred and permissible limitations to those rights. The Appendix allows developing countries, under certain conditions, to make some limitations to the right of translation and the right of reproduction.

In addition to requiring compliance with the basic standards of the Berne Convention, the TRIPS Agreement clarifies and adds certain specific points.

Article 9.2 confirms that copyright protection shall extend to expressions and not to ideas, procedures, methods of operation or mathematical concepts as such.

Article 10.1 provides that computer programs, whether in source or object code, shall be protected as literary works under the Berne Convention (1971). This provision confirms that computer programs must be protected under copyright and that those provisions of the Berne Convention that apply to literary works shall be applied also to them. It confirms further, that the form in which a program is, whether in source or object code, does not affect the protection. The obligation to protect computer programs as literary works means *e.g.* that only those limitations that are applicable to literary works may be applied to computer programs. It also confirms that the general term of protection of 50 years applies to computer programs. Possible shorter terms applicable to photographic works and works of applied art may not be applied.

Article 10.2 clarifies that databases and other compilations of data or other material shall be protected as such under copyright even where the databases include data that as such are not protected under copyright. Databases are eligible for copyright protection provided that they by reason of the selection or arrangement of their contents constitute intellectual creations. The provision also confirms that databases have to be protected regardless of which form they are in, whether machine readable or other form. Furthermore, the provision clarifies that such protection shall not extend to the data or material itself, and that it shall be without prejudice to any copyright subsisting in the data or material itself.

Article 11 provides that authors shall have in respect of at least computer programs and, in certain circumstances, of cinematographic works the right to authorize or to prohibit the commercial rental to the public of originals or copies of their copyright works. With respect to cinematographic works, the exclusive rental right is subject to the so-called impairment test : a Member is excepted from the obligation unless such rental has led to widespread copying of such works which is materially impairing the exclusive right of reproduction conferred in that Member on authors and their successors in title. In respect of computer programs, the obligation does not apply to rentals where the program itself is not the essential object of the rental.

According to the general rule contained in Article 7(1) of the Berne Convention as incorporated into the TRIPS Agreement, the term of protection shall be the life of the author and 50 years after his death. Paragraphs 2 through 4 of that Article specifically allow shorter terms in certain cases. These provisions are supplemented by Article 12 of the TRIPS Agreement, which provides that whenever the term of protection of a work, other than a photographic work or a work of applied art, is calculated on a basis other than the life of a natural person, such term shall be no less than 50years from the end of the calendar year of authorized publication, or, failing such authorized publication within 50 years from the making of the work, 50 years from the end of the calendar year of making.

Article 13 requires Members to confine limitations or exceptions to exclusive rights to certain special cases which do not conflict with a normal exploitation of the work and do not unreasonably prejudice the legitimate interests of the right holder. This is a horizontal provision that applies to all limitations and exceptions permitted under the provisions of the Berne Convention and the Appendix thereto as incorporated into the TRIPS Agreement. The application of these limitations is permitted also under the TRIPS Agreement, but the provision makes it clear that they must be applied in a manner that does not prejudice the legitimate interests of the right holder.

Related Rights

The provisions on protection of performers, producers of phonograms and broadcasting organizations are included in Article 14. According to Article 14.1, performers shall have the possibility of preventing the unauthorized fixation of their performance on a phonogram (*e.g.* the recording of a live musical performance). The fixation right covers only aural, not audiovisual fixations. Performers must also be in position to prevent the reproduction of such fixations. They shall also have the possibility of preventing the unauthorized broadcasting by wireless means and the communication to the public of their live performance.

In accordance with Article 14.2, Members have to grant producers of phonograms an exclusive reproduction right. In addition to this, they have to grant, in accordance with Article 14.4, an exclusive rental right at least to producers of phonograms. The provisions on rental rights apply also to any other right holders in phonograms as determined in national law. This right has the same scope as the rental right in respect of computer programs. Therefore it is not subject to the impairment test as in respect of cinematographic works. However, it is limited by a so-called grand-fathering clause, according to which a Member, which on 15 April 1994, *i.e.* the date of the signature of the Marrakesh Agreement, had in force a system of equitable remuneration of right holders in respect of the rental of phonograms, may maintain such system provided that the commercial rental of phonograms is not giving rise to the material impairment of the exclusive rights of reproduction of right holders.

Broadcasting organizations shall have, in accordance with Article 14.3, the right to prohibit the unauthorized fixation, the reproduction of fixations, and the rebroadcasting by wireless means of broadcasts, as well as the communication to the public of their television broadcasts. However, it is not necessary to grant such rights to broadcasting organizations, if owners of copyright in the subject-matter of broadcasts are provided with the possibility of preventing these acts, subject to the provisions of the Berne Convention.

The term of protection is at least 50 years for performers and producers of phonograms, and 20 years for broadcasting organizations (Article 14.5).

Article 14.6 provides that any Member may, in relation to the protection of performers, producers of phonograms and broadcasting organizations, provide for conditions, limitations, exceptions and reservations to the extent permitted by the Rome Convention.

Trademarks

The basic rule contained in Article 15 is that any sign, or any combination of signs, capable of distinguishing the goods and services of one undertaking from those of other undertakings, must be eligible for registration as a trademark, provided that it is visually perceptible. Such signs, in particular words including personal names, letters, numerals, figurative elements and combinations of colours as well as any combination of such signs, must be eligible for registration as trademarks.

Where signs are not inherently capable of distinguishing the relevant goods or services, Member countries are allowed to require, as an additional condition for eligibility for registration as a trademark, that distinctiveness has been acquired through use. Members are free to determine whether to allow the registration of signs that are not visually perceptible (*e.g.* sound or smell marks).

Members may make registrability depend on use. However, actual use of a trademark shall not be permitted as a condition for filing an application for registration, and at least three years must have passed after that filing date before failure to realize an intent to use is allowed as the ground for refusing the application (Article 14.3).

The Agreement requires service marks to be protected in the same way as marks distinguishing goods (see *e.g.* Articles 15.1, 16.2 and 62.3).

The owner of a registered trademark must be granted the exclusive right to prevent all third parties not having the owner's consent from using in the course of trade identical or similar signs for goods or services which are identical or similar to those in respect of which the trademark is registered where such use would result in a likelihood of confusion. In case of the use of an identical sign for identical goods or services, a likelihood of confusion must be presumed (Article 16.1).

The TRIPS Agreement contains certain provisions on well-known marks, which supplement the protection required by Article 6bis of the Paris Convention, as incorporated by reference into the TRIPS Agreement, which obliges Members to refuse or to cancel the registration, and to prohibit the use of a mark conflicting with a mark which is well known. First, the provisions of that Article must be applied also to services. Second, it is required that knowledge in the relevant sector of the public acquired not only as a result of the use of the mark but also by other means, including as a result of its promotion, be taken into account. Furthermore, the protection of registered well-known marks must extend to goods or services which are not similar to those in respect of which the trademark has been registered, provided that its use would indicate a connection between those goods or services and the owner of the registered trademark, and the interests of the owner are likely to be damaged by such use (Articles 16.2 and 3).

Members may provide limited exceptions to the rights conferred by a trademark, such as fair use of descriptive terms, provided that such exceptions take account of the legitimate interests of the owner of the trademark and of third parties (Article 17).

Initial registration, and each renewal of registration, of a trademark shall be for a term of no less than seven years. The registration of a trademark shall be renewable indefinitely (Article 18).

Cancellation of a mark on the grounds of non-use cannot take place before three years of uninterrupted non-use has elapsed unless valid reasons based on the existence of obstacles to such use are shown by the trademark owner. Circumstances arising independently of the will of the owner of the trademark, such as import restrictions or other government restrictions, shall be recognized as valid reasons of non-use. Use of a trademark by another person, when subject to the control of its owner, must be recognized as use of the trademark for the purpose of maintaining the registration (Article 19).

It is further required that use of the trademark in the course of trade shall not be unjustifiably encumbered by special requirements, such as use with another trademark, use in a special form, or use in a manner detrimental to its capability to distinguish the goods or services (Article 20).

Negotiations, Implementation and TRIPS Council Work

The TRIPS Council, which oversees the operation and implementation of the TRIPS Agreement has been discussing a number of issues which could lead to changes to the agreement.

These include issues related to geographical indications, intellectual property protection for biotechnological inventions and plant varieties and the possibility that one country could take legal action under the TRIPS Agreement even if the agreement has not specifically been violated ("non-violation" cases).

In addition, 2000 sees two major developments in TRIPS : developing countries (excluding the least developed) have to conform with the TRIPS Agreement on 1 January 2000, and the TRIPS Council is due to review the agreement's implementation — although a "review" does not necessarily lead to renegotiation or any other action.

These issues have been discussed or are due to be handled in the TRIPS Council. However, members also raised them in the WTO General Council's preparations for the Seattle Ministerial Conference. There were a number of proposals for the Seattle meeting to mandate negotiations or other work on these subjects after Seattle. Some members saw some of them as "implementation" issues to be settled in advance.

Geographical Indications

Simply put, geographical indications are place names (or words associated with a place) used to identify products (for example, "Champagne", "Tequila" or "Roquefort") which have a particular quality, reputation or other characteristic because they come from that place. The TRIPS Agreement provides a higher level of protection for geographical indications for wines and spirits (*i.e.*, subject to a number of exceptions, they have to be protected even if misuse would not cause the public to be misled).

Information that members have supplied during a fact-finding exercise shows that countries employ a wide variety of legal means to protect geographical indications : ranging from specific geographical indications laws to trademark law, consumer protection law, or common law. The TRIPS Agreement and current TRIPS work in the WTO takes account of that diversity.

The agreement calls for negotiations on two aspects of geographical indication protection, although it does not say when these should take place :

* the creation of a multilateral system for notifying and registering geographical indications for wines (the 1996 Singapore Ministerial Conference also called for preliminary work on "spirits") (Article 23.4)
* increasing protection for individual geographical indications. (Article 24)

Proposals for a system for notifying and registering geographical indications for wines (and spirits) have already been submitted to the TRIPS Council and discussions are due to continue in 2000. In all cases, participation in the system would be voluntary. One group of proposals sees the system as a database : members would report the geographical indications that they protect, and other members would take the information into account when they provide their own protection. Another group includes obligations — subject to certain conditions — for WTO members to protect the names listed in the register.

A number of countries have proposed extending the higher level of protection beyond wines and spirits to other products, including handicrafts, agricultural products and other beverages. Some members oppose the extension.

Industrial Designs

Article 25.1 of the TRIPS Agreement obliges Members to

provide for the protection of independently created industrial designs that are new or original. Members may provide that designs are not new or original if they do not significantly differ from known designs or combinations of known design features. Members may provide that such protection shall not extend to designs dictated essentially by technical or functional considerations.

Article 25.2 contains a special provision aimed at taking into account the short life cycle and sheer number of new designs in the textile sector : requirements for securing protection of such designs, in particular in regard to any cost, examination or publication, must not unreasonably impair the opportunity to seek and obtain such protection. Members are free to meet this obligation through industrial design law or through copyright law.

Article 26.1 requires Members to grant the owner of a protected industrial design the right to prevent third parties not having the owner's consent from making, selling or importing articles bearing or embodying a design which is a copy, or substantially a copy, of the protected design, when such acts are undertaken for commercial purposes.

Article 26.2 allows Members to provide limited exceptions to the protection of industrial designs, provided that such exceptions do not unreasonably conflict with the normal exploitation of protected industrial designs and do not unreasonably prejudice the legitimate interests of the owner of the protected design, taking account of the legitimate interests of third parties.

The duration of protection available shall amount to at least 10 years (Article 26.3). The wording "amount to" allows the term to be divided into, for example, two periods of five years.

Patents

The TRIPS Agreement requires Member countries to make patents available for any inventions, whether products or processes, in all fields of technology without discrimination, subject to the normal tests of novelty, inventiveness and industrial applicability. It is also required that patents be available and patent rights enjoyable without discrimination as to the place of invention and whether products are imported or locally produced (Article 27.1).

There are three permissible exceptions to the basic rule on patentability. One is for inventions contrary to ordre public or morality; this explicitly includes inventions dangerous to human, animal or plant life or health or seriously prejudicial to the environment. The use of this exception is subject to the condition that the commercial exploitation of the invention must also be prevented and this prevention must be necessary for the protection of ordre public or morality (Article 27.2).

The second exception is that Members may exclude from patentability diagnostic, therapeutic and surgical methods for the treatment of humans or animals (Article 27.3(a)).

The third is that Members may exclude plants and animals other than micro-organisms and essentially biological processes for the production of plants or animals other than non-biological and microbiological processes. However, any country excluding plant varieties from patent protection must provide an effective sui generis system of protection. Moreover, the whole provision is subject to review four years after entry into force of the Agreement (Article 27.3(b)).

The exclusive rights that must be conferred by a product patent are the ones of making, using, offering for sale, selling, and importing for these purposes. Process patent protection must give rights not only over use of the process but also over products obtained direcıly by the process. Patent owners shall also have the right to assign, or transfer by succession, the patent and to conclude licensing contracts (Article 28).

Members may provide limited exceptions to the exclusive rights conferred by a patent, provided that such exceptions do not unreasonably conflict with a normal exploitation of the patent and do not unreasonably prejudice the legitimate interests of the patent owner, taking account of the legitimate interests of third parties (Article 30).

The term of protection available shall not end before the expiration of a period of 20 years counted from the filing date (Article 33).

Members shall require that an applicant for a patent shall disclose the invention in a manner sufficiently clear and complete for the invention to be carried out by a person skilled in the art and may require the applicant to indicate the best mode for carrying out the invention known to the inventor at the filing date or, where priority is claimed, at the priority date of the application (Article 29.1).

If the subject-matter of a patent is a process for obtaining a product, the judicial authorities shall have the authority to order the defendant to prove that the process to obtain an identical product is different from the patented process, where certain conditions indicating a likelihood that the protected process was used are met (Article 34).

Compulsory licensing and government use without the authorization of the right holder are allowed, but are made subject to conditions aimed at protecting the legitimate interests of the right holder. The conditions are mainly contained in Article 31. These include the obligation, as a general rule, to grant such licences only if an unsuccessful attempt has been made to acquire a voluntary licence on reasonable terms and conditions within a reasonable period of time; the requirement to pay adequate remuneration in the circumstances of each case, taking into account the economic value of the licence; and a requirement that decisions be subject to judicial or other independent review by a distinct higher authority. Certain of these conditions are relaxed where compulsory licences are employed to remedy practices that have been established as anticompetitive by a legal process. These conditions should be read together with the related provisions of Article 27.1, which require that patent rights shall be enjoyable without discrimination as to the field of technology, and whether products are imported or locally produced.

Layout-designs of Integrated Circuits

Article 35 of the TRIPS Agreement requires Member countries to protect the layout-designs of integrated circuits in accordance with the provisions of the IPIC Treaty (the Treaty on Intellectual Property in Respect of Integrated Circuits), negotiated under the auspices of WIPO in 1989. These provisions deal with, inter alia, the definitions of "integrated circuit" and "layout-design (topography)", requirements for protection, exclusive rights, and limitations, as well as exploitation, registration and disclosure. An "integrated circuit" means a product, in its final form or an intermediate form, in which the elements, at least one of which is an active element, and some or all of the interconnections are integrally formed in and/or on a piece of material and which is intended to perform an electronic function. A "layout-design (topography)" is defined as the three-dimensional disposition, however expressed, of the elements, at least one of which is an active element, and of some or all of the interconnections of an integrated circuit, or such a three-dimensional disposition prepared for an integrated circuit intended for manufacture. The obligation to protect layout-designs applies to such layout-designs that are original in the sense that they are the result of their creators' own intellectual effort and are not commonplace among creators of layout-designs and manufacturers of integrated circuits at the time of their creation. The exclusive rights include the right of reproduction and the right of importation, sale and other distribution for commercial purposes. Certain limitations to these rights are provided for.

In addition to requiring Member countries to protect the layout-designs of integrated circuits in accordance with the provisions of the IPIC Treaty, the TRIPS Agreement clarifies and/or builds on four points. These points relate to the term of protection (ten years instead of eight, Article 38), the applicability of the protection to articles containing infringing integrated circuits (last sub clause of Article 36) and the treatment of innocent infringers (Article 37.1). The conditions in Article 31 of the TRIPS Agreement apply mutatis mutandis to compulsory or non-voluntary licensing of a layout-design or to its use by or for the government without the authorization of the right holder, instead of the provisions of the IPIC Treaty on compulsory licensing (Article 37.2).

Plant Varieties : Article 27.3(b)

Article 27 of the TRIPS Agreement defines the types of inventions which have to be eligible for patent protection and those which can be exempt. These include both products and processes, and they cover all fields of technology. In general, inventions eligible for patenting must be **new**, involve an **inventive**

step (or be **non-obvious**) and be **capable of industrial application** (or be **useful**). Article 27 also lists inventions which governments do not have to make eligible for patent protection.

It is part (b) (*i.e.* Article 27.3(b)) which is under review — as required by the TRIPS Agreement — and is also the subject of proposals for Seattle.

Broadly speaking, Article 27.3(b) allows governments to exclude plants, animals and "essentially" biological processes (but micro-organisms, and non-biological and microbiological processes have to be eligible for patents). However, plant *varieties* have to be eligible either for patent protection or through a system created specifically for the purpose ("*sui generis*"), or a combination of the two. For example, countries could enact a plant varieties protection law based on a model of the International Union for the Protection of New Varieties of Plants (UPOV).

The review of Article 27.3(b) began in 1999 as required by the TRIPS Agreement. The topics raised include : the pros and cons of various types of protection (patents, UPOV, etc); how to handle moral and ethical issues (*e.g.* whether invented life forms should be eligible for protection); how to deal with traditional knowledge and the rights of the communities where genetic material originates; and whether there is a conflict between the TRIPS Agreement and the international Biodiversity Convention (CBD). Countries have expressed a range of opinions on all these subjects, and some are seeking clarification on issues such as the meaning of the term "micro-organism" and the difference between "biological" and "microbiological" processes.

Some developing countries want to make sure that the TRIPS Agreement takes account of more specific concerns such as allowing their farmers to continue to save and exchange seeds that they have harvested, and preventing anti-competitive practices which threaten developing countries' "food sovereignty".

Whether the subject stays under review in the TRIPS Council or becomes a negotiation topic remains to be seen.

Non-violation Cases (Article 64.2)

In principle, disputes in the WTO involve allegations that a country has violated an agreement or broken a commitment.

Under the goods (GATT) and services (GATS) agreements, countries can complain to the Dispute Settlement Body if they can show that they have been deprived of an expected benefit because of some governmental action (for example a new production subsidy on an item on which a tariff concession has been made) — even if it does not violate one of these agreements. The purpose of allowing these "non-violation" cases is to preserve the balance of market access opportunities struck during multilateral negotiations.

The TRIPS Agreement has a temporary ban on non-violation disputes (Article 64.2) — disputes can only be brought under the TRIPS Agreement if the accused country is specifically alleged to have violated a provision. Article 64.2 says non-violation complaints cannot be brought to the WTO dispute settlement procedure during the first five years of the WTO Agreement (*i.e.* 1995—99).

A number of countries want the ban to continue, at least until the implications have been more fully examined. They argue that TRIPS is unlike GATT and GATS because it sets minimum standards and not the rules for market access or schedules of commitments. At least one country says non-violation cases should be allowed in order to discourage members from engaging in "creative legislative activity" that would allow them to get around their TRIPS commitments.

Protection of Undisclosed Information

The TRIPS Agreement requires undisclosed information — trade secrets or know-how — to benefit from protection. According to Article 39.2, the protection must apply to information that is secret, that has commercial value because it is secret and that has been subject to reasonable steps to keep it secret. The Agreement does not require undisclosed information to be treated as a form of property, but it does require that a person lawfully in control of such information must have the possibility of preventing it from being disclosed to, acquired by, or used by others without his or her consent in a manner contrary to honest commercial practices. "Manner contrary to honest commercial practices" includes breach of contract, breach of confidence and inducement to breach, as well as the acquisition of undisclosed information by third parties who knew, or were grossly negligent in failing to know, that such practices were involved in the acquisition.

The Agreement also contains provisions on undisclosed test data and other data whose submission is required by governments as a condition of approving the marketing of pharmaceutical or agricultural chemical products which use new chemical entities. In such a situation the Member government concerned must protect the data against unfair commercial use. In addition, Members must protect such data against disclosure, except where necessary to protect the public, or unless steps are taken to ensure that the data are protected against unfair commercial use.

Control of Anti-competitive Practices in Contractual Licences

Article 40 of the TRIPS Agreement recognizes that some licensing practices or conditions pertaining to intellectual property rights which restrain competition may have adverse effects on trade and may impede the transfer and dissemination of technology (paragraph 1). Member countries may adopt, consistently with the other provisions of the Agreement, appropriate measures to prevent or control practices in the licensing of intellectual property rights which are abusive and anti-competitive (paragraph 2). The Agreement provides for a mechanism whereby a country seeking to take action against such practices involving the companies of another Member country can enter into consultations with that other Member and exchange publicly available non-confidential information of relevance to the matter in question and of other information available to that Member, subject to domestic law and to the conclusion of mutually satisfactory agreements concerning the safeguarding of its confidentiality by the requesting Member (paragraph 3). Similarly, a country whose companies are subject to such action in another Member can enter into consultations with that Member (paragraph 4).

Enforcement of Intellectual Property Rights

The provisions on enforcement are contained in Part III of the Agreement, which is divided into five Sections. The first Section lays down general obligations that all enforcement procedures must meet. These are notably aimed at ensuring their effectiveness and that certain basic principles of due process are met. The following Sections deal with civil and administrative procedures and remedies, provisional measures, special requirements related to border measures and criminal procedures. These provisions have two basic objectives : one is to ensure that effective means of enforcement are available to right holders; the second is to ensure that enforcement procedures are applied in such a manner as to avoid the creation of barriers to legitimate trade and to provide for safeguards against their abuse.

The Agreement makes a distinction between infringing activity in general, in respect of which civil judicial procedures and remedies must be available, and counterfeiting and piracy — the more blatant and egregious forms of infringing activity — in respect of which additional procedures and remedies must also be provided, namely border measures and criminal procedures. For this purpose, counterfeit goods are in essence defined as goods involving slavish copying of trademarks, and pirated goods as goods which violate a reproduction right under copyright or a related right.

General Obligations

The general obligations relating to enforcement are contained in Article 41. Paragraph1 requires that enforcement procedures must be such as to permit effective action against any act of infringement of intellectual property rights, and that the remedies available must be expeditious in order to prevent infringements and they must constitute a deterrent to further infringements. On the other hand, these procedures must be applied in such a manner as to avoid the creation of barriers to legitimate trade and to provide for safeguards against their abuse.

The following three paragraphs contain certain general principles, the aim of which is to guarantee due process. Paragraph 2 deals with enforcement procedures. Such procedures must be fair and equitable, and they may not be unnecessarily complicated or costly, or entail unreasonable time-limits or unwarranted delays. Paragraph 3 concerns decisions on the merits of a case. Such decisions shall preferably be in writing and reasoned, and they shall be made available at least to the parties to the proceeding without undue delay. Decisions on the merits of a case shall be based only on evidence in respect of which parties were offered the opportunity to be heard. Paragraph 4 requires that parties to a proceeding shall have an opportunity for review by a judicial authority of final administrative decisions and, subject to jurisdictional provisions in a Member's law concerning the importance of a case, of at least the legal aspects of initial judicial decisions on the merits of a case. However, there is no obligation to provide an opportunity for review of acquittals in criminal cases.

According to paragraph 5, it is understood that the provisions on enforcement do not create any obligation to put in place a judicial system for the enforcement of intellectual property rights distinct from that for the enforcement of law in general, nor does it affect the capacity of Members to enforce their law in general. In addition, it is stated that nothing in these provisions creates any obligation with respect to the distribution of resources as between enforcement of intellectual property rights and the enforcement of law in general. However, a number of countries have found it helpful to establish special enforcement units that pool together required experience needed to effectively fight against counterfeiting and piracy. Moreover, some countries have centralized certain types of intellectual property issues in one or a limited number of courts in order to ensure the availability of necessary expertise.

Civil and Administrative Procedures and Remedies

The second Section requires that civil judicial procedures must be available in respect of any activity infringing intellectual property rights covered by the Agreement. The provisions of the Section elaborate in more detail basic features that such procedures must provide for.

Article 42 contains certain principles aiming at ensuring due process. Defendants are entitled to written notice which is timely and contains sufficient details of the claims. Parties must be allowed to be represented by independent legal counsel, and procedures may not impose overly burdensome requirements concerning mandatory personal appearances. All parties are entitled to substantiate their claims and to present all relevant evidence, while confidential information must be identified and protected.

Article 43 deals with how the rules on evidence should be applied in certain situations. In a situation where evidence that is likely to be important for one party is in the possession of the opposing party, the court must be empowered, provided that certain conditions are met, to order the latter party to produce that evidence. In addition, courts may be authorized to make their decisions on the basis of information presented to them, if a party refuses without good reason access to evidence that is in his or her possession, subject to providing the parties an opportunity to be heard.

The Section contains provisions on injunctions, damages and other remedies. Article 44 requires that the courts be empowered to order injunctions, *i.e.* to order a party to desist from infringements, including the possibility to prevent imported infringing goods from entering into domestic distribution channels. Members are not obliged to provide that authority where a person has acted in good faith. Article 45 provides that the courts must be empowered to order an infringer, at least if he or she acted in bad faith, to pay the right holder adequate damages. They must also be authorized to order the infringer to pay the right holder's expenses. These expenses may include appropriate attorney's fees. In appropriate cases, the courts may be authorized to order recovery of profits and/or payment of pre-established damages even where the infringer acted in good faith.

In order to create an effective deterrent to infringement, Article 46 requires that the judicial authorities must have the authority to order infringing goods to be disposed of outside the channels of commerce, or, where constitutionally possible, destroyed. Similarly, it must be possible to dispose of materials and instruments predominantly used in the production of the infringing goods. In considering such requests, the courts must take into account proportionality between the seriousness of the infringement and the remedies ordered as well as the interests of third parties. In respect of counterfeit trademark goods, it is clarified that the simple removal of the trademark unlawfully affixed shall not be sufficient, other than in exceptional cases, to permit release of the goods into the channels of commerce.

The judicial authorities may be authorized to order the infringer to inform the right holder of the identity of third persons involved in the production and distribution of the infringing goods or services and of their channels of distribution (Article 47). This option is aimed at assisting the right holders to find the source of infringing goods and to take appropriate action against other persons in the distribution channels. This provision must be applied in a way that is in proportion to the seriousness of the infringement.

The Section contains certain safeguards against abuse of enforcement procedures. Article 48 provides that the judicial authorities must have the authority to order the applicant who has abused enforcement procedures to pay an adequate compensation to the defendant who has been wrongfully enjoined or restrained to cover both the injury suffered and expenses. Such expenses may include appropriate attorney's fees. Public authorities and officials are exempted from liability to appropriate remedial measures only where actions are taken or intended in good faith in the course of the administration of that law.

Article 49 provides that, to the extent that any civil remedy can be ordered as a result of administrative procedures on the merits of a case, such procedures shall conform to principles equivalent in substance to those set forth in the Section.

Provisional Measures

Article 41 requires that enforcement procedures must permit effective action against infringements and must include expeditious remedies. As these judicial procedures may take a fair amount of time, it is necessary for the judicial authorities to be empowered to provide provisional relief for the right holder in order to stop an alleged infringement immediately. The provisions on provisional measures are contained in Article 50. It requires each country to ensure that its judicial authorities have the authority to order prompt and effective provisional measures. Such measures must be available in respect of any intellectual property right. Provisional measures have to be available in two situations. One is where they are needed to prevent an infringement from occurring, and to prevent infringing goods from entering into the channels of commerce. This includes preventing imported infringing goods from being dispersed into domestic distribution channels immediately after customs clearance. The other situation is where such measures are needed to preserve relevant evidence in regard to the alleged infringement.

Effective use of provisional measures may require that action be taken without giving prior notice to the other side. Therefore, the judicial authorities must have the authority to adopt provisional measures *inaudita altera parte*, *i.e.* without prior hearing of the other side, where appropriate, in particular where any delay is likely to cause irreparable harm to the right holder, or where there is a demonstrable risk of evidence being destroyed (paragraph 2).

The courts may require the applicant to provide any reasonably available adequate evidence that the applicant is the right holder and that the applicant's right is being infringed or that such infringement is imminent (paragraph 3). The applicant may also be required to supply information necessary for the identification of the goods (paragraph 5). Where provisional measures have been adopted *inaudita altera parte*, the parties affected must be given notice, without delay after the execution of the measures at the latest. The defendant has a right to review with a view to deciding, within a reasonable period after the notification of the measures, whether these measures shall be modified, revoked or confirmed (paragraph 4).

The provisions on provisional measures contain certain safeguards against abuse of such measures. The judicial authority may require the applicant to provide a security or equivalent assurance sufficient to protect the defendant and to prevent abuse (paragraph 3). Provisional measures shall, upon request by the defendant, be revoked or otherwise cease to have effect, if the applicant fails to initiate proceedings leading to a decision on the merits of the case within a reasonable period to be determined by the judicial authority ordering the measures. In the absence of such a determination, this period may not exceed 20 working days or 31 calendar days, whichever is the longer (paragraph 6). Where the provisional measures are revoked or where they lapse due to any act or omission by the applicant, or where it is subsequently found that there has been no infringement or threat of infringement of an intellectual property right, the judicial authorities shall have the authority to order the applicant to provide the defendant appropriate compensation for any injury caused by these measures (paragraph 7).

The above principles apply also to administrative procedures to the extent that any provisional measure can be ordered as a result of such procedures (paragraph 8).

Special Requirements Related to Border Measures

The emphasis in the enforcement part of the TRIPS Agreement is on internal enforcement mechanisms, which, if effective, would enable infringing activity to be stopped at source, the point of production. Where possible, this is both a more efficient way of enforcing IPRs and less liable to give rise to risks of discrimination against imports than special border measures. However, the Agreement recognizes that such enforcement at source will not always be possible and that in any event not all countries are Members of the TRIPS Agreement. The Agreement therefore also recognizes the importance of border enforcement procedures that will enable right holders to obtain the cooperation of customs administrations so as to prevent the release of infringing imports into free circulation. The special requirements related to border measures are contained in Section 4 of the enforcement part of the Agreement.

According to Article 51 of the Agreement, the goods which must be subject to border enforcement procedures must include at least counterfeit trademark and pirated copyright goods that are being presented for importation (see footnote 14 to that Article for the precise definition of these terms). The Article leaves flexibility to Member governments on whether to include imports of goods which involve other infringements of IPRs. Members are also free to determine whether to apply these procedures to parallel imports. This is confirmed in footnote 13 to the Article, according to which it is understood that there shall be no obligation to apply such procedures to imports of goods put on the market in another country by or with the consent of the right holder. In accordance with Article 60, Members may exclude from the application of these procedures *de minimis* imports, *i.e.* small quantities of goods of a non-commercial nature contained in travellers' personal luggage or sent in small consignments. Article 51 leaves it to Members to decide whether to apply corresponding procedures to the suspension by customs authorities of infringing goods destined for exportation from their territories, or to goods in transit.

The basic mechanism required by the Agreement is that each Member must designate a "competent authority", which could be administrative or judicial in nature, to which applications by right holders for customs action shall be lodged (Article 51). The right holder lodging an application to the competent authority shall be required to provide adequate evidence of a *prima facie* infringement of his IPR and to supply a sufficiently detailed description of the goods to make them readily recognizable by the customs authorities. The competent authorities shall then inform the applicant whether the application has been accepted and, if so, for what period, and give the necessary directions to customs officers (Article 52). After this, it is the responsibility of the applicant to initiate proceedings leading to a decision on the merits of the case. The Agreement requires a system to be put in place under which action will be taken on the basis of an application from a right holder, but leaves it to Members to determine whether they require competent authorities to act upon their own initiative. Article 58 contains certain additional provisions applicable to such *ex officio* action.

The provisions on border measures require the taking of what are essentially provisional measures against imports of infringing goods. Many of the same types of safeguards against abuse as appear in Article 50 on provisional judicial measures are provided for. The competent authority may require the applicant to provide a security or equivalent assurance sufficient to protect the defendant and the competent authorities and to prevent abuse. However, such security or equivalent assurance may not be such as to unreasonably deter recourse to these procedures (Article 53.1). The importer and the applicant must be promptly notified of the detention of goods (Article 54). If the right holder fails to initiate proceedings leading to a decision on the merits of a case within ten working days, the goods shall normally be released (Article 55). Where goods involve the alleged infringement of industrial designs, patents, layout-designs or undisclosed information, the importer must be entitled to obtain their release on the posting of a security sufficient to protect the right holder from any infringement, even if proceedings leading to a decision on the merits have been initiated (Article 53.2). Once judicial proceedings on the merits of a case have been initiated, the judicial authority may continue the suspension of the release of goods in accordance with a provisional judicial measure. In that case, the provisions on provisional measures in Article 50 shall be applied. The applicant may be required to pay appropriate compensation to persons whose interests have been adversely affected by the wrongful detention of goods or through detention of goods released pursuant to the failure of the applicant to initiate in time proceedings leading to a decision on the merits of the case (Article 56).

The competent authorities must be able to give the right holder sufficient opportunity to have any goods detained by the customs authorities inspected in order to substantiate his or her claims. Where goods have been found infringing as a result of a decision on the merits, the Agreement leaves it to Members whether to enable the right holder to be informed of other persons in the distribution channel so that appropriate action could also be taken against them (Article 57).

In regard to remedies, the competent authorities must have the power to order the destruction or disposal outside the channels of commerce of infringing goods in such a manner as to avoid any harm to the right holder. The principles contained in Article 46 on civil remedies, such as the need for proportionality, apply also to border measures. In regard to counterfeit trademark goods, the authorities may not allow the re-exportation of the infringing goods in an unaltered state or subject them to a different customs procedure, other than in exceptional circumstances. These remedies are without prejudice to other rights of action open to the right holder, such as to obtain damages through civil litigation, and are also subject to the right of the defendant to seek review by a judicial authority (Article 59).

Criminal Procedures

The fifth and final section in the enforcement chapter of the TRIPS Agreement deals with criminal procedures. According to Article 61, provision must be made for these to be applied at least in cases of wilful trademark counterfeiting or copyright piracy on a commercial scale. The Agreement leaves it to Members to decide whether to provide for criminal procedures and penalties to be applied in other cases of infringement of intellectual property rights, in particular where they are committed wilfully and on a commercial scale.

Sanctions must include imprisonment and/or monetary fines sufficient to provide a deterrent, consistent with the level of penalties applied for crimes of a corresponding gravity. Criminal remedies in appropriate cases must also include seizure, forfeiture and destruction of the infringing goods and of materials and instruments used to produce them.

Other Provisions

Acquisition and Maintenance of Intellectual Property Rights and Related *Inter Partes* Procedures

On the whole, the Agreement does not deal in detail with procedural questions concerning acquisition and maintenance of intellectual property rights. Part IV of the Agreement contains some general rules on these matters, the purpose of which is to ensure that unnecessary procedural difficulties in acquiring or maintaining intellectual property rights are not employed to impair the protection required by the Agreement. According to paragraph 1 of Article 62, Members may require, as a condition of the acquisition or maintenance of rights related to trademarks, geographical indications, industrial designs, patents and layout-designs, compliance with reasonable procedures and formalities. Where the acquisition of an intellectual property right is subject to the right being granted or registered, the procedures must permit the granting or registration of the right within a reasonable period of time so as to avoid unwarranted curtailment of the period of protection (paragraph 2). Procedures concerning the acquisition or maintenance of intellectual property rights and, where a Member's law provides for such procedures, administrative revocation and interpartes procedures such as opposition, revocation and cancellation, must be governed by the general principles concerning decisions and review set out in paragraphs 2 and 3 of Article 41 of the Agreement (paragraph 4). Final administrative decisions in such procedures must generally be subject to review by a judicial or quasi-judicial authority (paragraph 5).

Transitional Arrangements

The TRIPS Agreement gives all WTO Members transitional periods so that they can meet their obligations under it. The transitional periods, which depend on the level of development of the country concerned, are contained in Articles 65 and 66.

Developed country Members have had to comply with all of the provisions of the TRIPS Agreement since 1 January 1996. However, all Members, even those availing themselves of the longer transitional periods, have had to comply with the national treatment and MFN treatment obligation as of 1 January 1996.

For developing countries, the general transitional period is five years, *i.e.* until 1 January 2000. A country whose economy is in transition, but which is not a developing country, may nonetheless delay application until the year 2000, if it meets three tests :

— it is in the process of transformation from a centrally-planned into a market, free enterprise economy;

— it is undertaking structural reform of its intellectual property system; and

— it faces special problems in the preparation and implementation of intellectual property laws and regulations.

For those countries on the United Nations list of least-developed countries, the transitional period is eleven years. The Agreement provides a possibility to extend the transitional period upon duly motivated request.

There are two important substantive obligations that have been effective from the entry into force of the TRIPS Agreement on 1 January 1995. One is the so-called "non-backsliding" clause in Article 65.5 which concerns changes made during the transitional period, and the other the so-called "mail-box" provision in Article 70.8 for filing patent applications for pharmaceutical and agricultural chemical products during the transitional period.

The "non-backsliding" clause in Article 65.5 forbids countries from using the transition period to reduce the level of protection of intellectual property in a way which would result in a lesser degree of consistency with the requirements of the Agreement.

Special transition rules apply in the situation where a developing country does not provide product patent protection in a given area of technology, especially to pharmaceutical or agricultural chemical inventions, on the general date of application of the Agreement for that Member, *i.e.* in the year 2000. According to Article 65.4, such a developing country may delay the application of the TRIPS obligations on product patents to that area of technology for an additional five years (*i.e.* to the year 2005). However, the Agreement includes additional transitional arrangements in the situation where a country does not provide, as of the date of entry into force of the WTO Agreement, patent protection for pharmaceutical and agricultural chemical products commensurate with the TRIPS provisions. In accordance with the "mail-box" provision contained in Article 70.8, the country concerned must provide, as from the date of entry into force of the WTO Agreement, a means by which patent applications for such inventions can be filed. These applications will not need to be examined for their patentability until the country starts applying product patent protection in that area, *i.e.* for a developing country, at the end of the ten-year transition period. However, at that time, the application must be examined by reference to the prior art as it existed at the time the application was made. If the application is successful, product patent protection would then have to be granted for the remainder of the patent term counted from the filing date of the application. If a product that has been the subject of such a patent application obtains marketing approval before the decision on the grant of the patent is taken, there is an obligation under Article 70.9 to grant exclusive marketing rights for a period of up to five years to tide over the gap. This is subject to a number of safeguards to ensure that the product concerned is a genuine invention : subsequent to the entry into force of the WTO

Agreement, a patent application must have been filed, a patent granted and marketing approval obtained in another Member for the product in question.

Protection of Existing Subject-matter

An important aspect of the transition arrangements under the TRIPS Agreement is the provisions relating to the treatment of subject-matter already existing at the time that a Member starts applying the provisions of the Agreement. As provided in Article 70.2, the rules of the TRIPS Agreement generally apply to subject-matter existing on the date of application of the Agreement for the Member in question and which is protected in that Member on the said date. In respect of copyright and most related rights, there are additional requirements. Articles 9.1, 14.6 and 70.2 of the TRIPS Agreement oblige WTO Members to comply with Article 18 of the Berne Convention, not only in respect of the rights of authors but also in respect of the rights of performers and producers of phonograms in phonograms. Article 18 of the Berne Convention as incorporated into the TRIPS Agreement includes the so-called rule of retroactivity, according to which the Agreement applies to all works which have not yet fallen into the public domain either in the country of origin or the country where protection is claimed through the expiry of the term of protection. The provisions of Article 18 allow some transitional flexibility where a country is, as a result, taking subject-matter out of the public domain and putting it under protection, in respect of the interests of persons who have in good faith already taken steps on the basis of the material being in the public domain.

Developing Countries' Compliance

On 1 January 2000, developing countries have to comply with the TRIPS Agreement. (Least-developed countries have until 1 January 2006.) Several developing countries are asking for more time in order to deal with the large legislative and administrative burden of complying.

Technology Transfer

The proposals for the Seattle meeting included strengthening technology transfer provisions in general (Articles 7 and 8), and tightening obligations for developed countries to provide incentives for their enterprises and institutions to transfer technology to least-developed countries (Article 66.2)

Pharmaceuticals

Some members are proposing that the World Health Organization's list of essential drugs be exempt from patentability. Alternatively, they say developing countries should be able to issue compulsory licences for these drugs (*i.e.* force the patent holder to license other manufacturers, subject to appropriate conditions such as fees) so that the drugs can be supplied at "reasonable" prices.

Review of the TRIPS Agreement

The review is required in 2000, under Article 71.1. The TRIPS Council is due to take this issue up at its first meeting in 2000 (currently scheduled to be held in March). What the review will involved depends on the outcome of the Ministerial Conference and informal consultations between members and the council's chairman.

Among the topics on the table for Ministerial Conference are : ensuring that the TRIPS Agreement responds effectively and neutrally to new technological development and practices; incorporating new trade-related intellectual property treaties adopted outside the WTO; and streamlining administrative aspects such as harmonizing some aspects of the way governments process patent applications. Many of these proposals come from developed countries.

5

SERVICES — RULES FOR GROWTH AND INVESTMENT

The General Agreement on Trade in Services (GATS) is the first ever set of multilateral, legally-enforceable rules covering international trade in services. It was negotiated in the Uruguay Round. Like the agreements on goods, GATS operates on three levels : the main text containing general principles and obligations; annexes dealing with rules for specific sectors; and individual countries' specific commitments to provide access to their markets. Unlike in goods, GATS has a fourth special element : lists showing where countries are temporarily not applying the "most-favoured-nation" principle of non-discrimination. These commitments — like tariff schedules under GATT — are an integral part of the agreement. So are the temporary withdrawals of most-favoured-nation treatment.

A WTO Council for Trade in Services oversees the operation of the agreement. Negotiations on commitments in four topics have taken place after the Uruguay Round. A full new services round will start no later than 2000.

The Framework : The GATS Articles

Basic principles

(i) **All services** are covered by GATS.

(ii) **Most-favoured-nation treatment** applies to all services, except the one-off temporary exemptions.

(iii) **National treatment** applies in the areas where commitments are made.

(iv) **Transparency** in regulations, inquiry points.

(v) **Regulations** have to be objective and reasonable.

(vi) **International payments :** normally unrestricted.

(vii) **Individual countries' commitments :** negotiated and bound.

(viii) **Progressive liberalization** : through further negotiations.

GATS's 29 articles cover all services sectors. They contain the general obligations that all members have to apply :

Total Coverage

The agreement covers all internationally-traded services. This includes all the different ways of providing an international service — GATS defines four :

- services supplied from one country to another (*e.g.* international telephone calls), officially known as "cross-border supply".
- consumers or firms making use of a service in another country (*e.g.* tourism), officially known as "consumption abroad".
- a foreign company setting up subsidiaries or branches to provide services in another country (*e.g.* foreign banks setting up operations in a country), officially "commercial presence".
- individuals travelling from their own country to supply services in another (*e.g.* fashion models or consultants), officially "presence of natural persons".

Most-favoured-nation (MFN) Treatment

Favour one, favour all. MFN means treating one's trading partners equally. Under GATS, if a country allows foreign competition in a sector, equal opportunities in that sector should be given to service providers from all other WTO members. (This applies even if the country has made no specific commitment to provide foreign companies access to its markets under the WTO.)

MFN applies to all services, but some special temporary exemptions have been allowed (see below).

What about National Treatment?

National treatment — equal treatment for foreigners and one's own nationals — is treated differently for services. For goods (GATT) and intellectual property (TRIPS) it is a general principle. In GATS it only applies where a country has made a specific commitment, and exemptions are allowed. (See below.)

Transparency

GATS says governments must publish all relevant laws and regulations. Within two years (by the end of 1997) they have to set up inquiry points within their bureaucracies. Foreign companies and governments can then use these inquiry points to obtain information about regulations in any service sector. And they have to notify the WTO of any changes in regulations that apply to the services that come under specific commitments.

Regulations : Objective and Reasonable

Since domestic regulations are the most significant means of exercising influence or control over services trade, the agreement says governments should regulate services reasonably, objectively and impartially. When a government makes any administrative decisions that affect a service, it should also provide an impartial means for reviewing the decision (for example a tribunal).

Recognition

When two (or more) governments have agreements recognizing each other's qualifications (for example, the licensing or certification of service suppliers), GATS says other members must also be given a chance to negotiate comparable pacts. The recognition of other countries' qualifications must not be discriminatory, and it must not amount to protectionism in disguise. These recognition agreements have to be notified to the WTO.

International Payments and Transfers

Once a government has made a commitment to open a service sector to foreign competition, it must not normally restrict money being transferred out of the country as payment for services supplied ("current transactions") in that sector. The only exception is when there are balance-of-payments difficulties, and even then the restrictions must be temporary and subject to other limits and conditions.

Specific Commitments

Individual countries' commitments to open markets in specific sectors — and how open those markets will be — are the outcome of negotiations. The commitments appear in "schedules" that list the sectors being opened, the extent of market access being given in those sectors (*e.g.* whether there are any restrictions on foreign ownership), and any limitations on national treatment (whether some rights granted to local companies will not be granted to foreign companies.)

These commitments are "bound" : like bound tariffs, they can only be modified or withdrawn after negotiations with affected countries — which would probably lead to compensation. Because "unbinding" is difficult, the commitments are virtually guaranteed conditions for foreign exporters and importers of services and investors in the sector to do business.

Progressive Liberalization

The Uruguay Round was only the beginning. GATS requires more negotiations, the first to begin within five years. The goal is to take the liberalization process further by increasing the level of commitments in schedules.

The Annexes : Services are not all the Same

International trade in goods is a relatively simple idea to grasp : a product is transported from one country to another. Trade in services is much more diverse. Telephone companies, banks, airlines and accountancy firms provide their services in quite different ways. The GATS annexes reflect some of the diversity.

Movement of Natural Persons

This annex deals with negotiations on individuals' rights to stay temporarily in a country for the purpose of providing a service. It specifies that the agreement does not apply to people seeking permanent employment or to conditions for obtaining citizenship, permanent residence or permanent employment.

Financial Services

Instability in the banking system affects the whole economy. The financial services annex says governments have the right to take prudential measures, such as those for the protection of investors, depositors and insurance policy holders, and to ensure the integrity and stability of the financial system. It also excludes from the agreement services provided when a government exercising its authority over the financial system, for example central banks' services. Negotiations on specific commitments in financial services continued after the end of the Uruguay Round and ended in late 1997.

Telecommunications

The telecommunications sector has a dual role : it is a distinct sector of economic activity; and it is an underlying means of supplying other economic activities (for example electronic money transfers). The annex says governments must ensure that foreign service suppliers are given access to the public telecommunications networks without discrimination. Negotiations on specific commitments in telecommunications resumed after the end of the Uruguay Round. This led to a new liberalization package agreed in February 1997.

Air Transport Services

Under this annex, traffic rights and directly related activities are excluded from GATS's coverage. They are handled by other bilateral agreements. However, the annex establishes that the GATS will apply to aircraft repair and maintenance services, marketing of air transport services and computer-reservation services.

Countries' Commitments : On Market-opening

Each country lists specific commitments on service sectors and on activities within those sectors. The commitments guarantee access to the country's market in the listed sectors, and they spell out any limitations on market access and national treatment.

As an example; if a government commits itself to allow foreign banks to operate in its domestic market, that is a market access commitment. And if the government limits the number of licences it will issue, then that is a market access limitation. If it also says foreign banks are only allowed one branch while domestic banks are allowed numerous branches, that is an exception to the national treatment principle.

Market Access

The lists of market access commitments (along with any limitations and exemptions from national treatment) are negotiated as multilateral packages, although bilateral bargaining sessions are needed to develop the packages. The commitments therefore contain the negotiated and guaranteed conditions for conducting international trade in services. If a recorded condition is to be changed for the worse, then the government has to give at least three months' notice and it has to negotiate compensation with affected countries. But the commitments can be improved at any time. They will be subject to further liberalization through the future negotiations already committed under GATS. The first of these must start no later than 2000.

National Treatment

National treatment means treating one's own nationals and foreigners equally. In services, it means that once a foreign company has been allowed to supply a service in one's country there should be no discrimination between the foreign and local companies.

Under GATS, a country only has to apply this principle when it has made a specific commitment to provide foreigners access to its services market. It does not have to apply national treatment in sectors where it has made no commitment. Even in the commitments, GATS does allow some limits on national treatment.

This contrasts with the way the national treatment principle is applied for goods — in that case, once a product has crossed a border and been cleared by customs it has to be given national treatment even if the importing country has not made any commitment under the WTO to bind the tariff rate.

MFN Exemptions : Temporary and One-off

WTO members have also made separate lists of exceptions to the MFN principle of non-discrimination. When GATS came into force, a number of countries already had preferential agreements in services that they had signed with trading partners, either bilaterally or in small groups. WTO members felt it was necessary to maintain these preferences temporarily. They gave themselves the right to continue giving more favourable treatment to particular countries in particular service activities by listing "MFN exemptions" alongside their first sets of commitments. In order to protect the general MFN principle, the exemptions could only be made once; nothing can be added to the lists. They will be reviewed after five years (in 2000), and will normally last no more than 10 years. The exemption lists are also part of the GATS agreement.

On-going Work : Even Before the Next Round

At the end of the Uruguay Round governments agreed to continue negotiations in four areas : basic telecommunications, maritime transport, movement of natural persons, and financial services. Some commitments in some of these sectors had been made in the Uruguay Round agreements. The objective of continuing with the negotiations was to improve the package.

Basic Telecommunications

This was an area where governments did not offer commitments during the Uruguay Round — essentially because the privatization of government monopolies was a complex issues in many countries. Sophisticated value-added telecommunications services, which are more commonly provided on a private basis, were, however, included in many of the original GATS schedules. The negotiations on basic telecommunications ended in February 1997 with new national commitments due to take effect from January 1998.

Maritime Transport

Maritime transport negotiations were originally scheduled to end in June 1996, but participants failed to agree on a package of commitments. The talks will resume with the new services round due to start no later than 2000. Some commitments are already included in some countries' schedules covering the three main areas in this sector : access to and use of port facilities; auxiliary services; and ocean transport.

Movement of Natural Persons

"Movement of natural persons" refers to the entry and temporary stay of persons for the purpose of providing a service. It does not relate to persons seeking permanent employment or permanent residence in a country. Some commitments are already included in the schedules but it was agreed that negotiations to improve commitments would take place in the six months after the WTO came into force. These only achieved modest results.

Financial Services

Financial services is another area where further negotiations were scheduled to improve on the commitments included in the initial Uruguay Round schedules. Officially the first set of talks ended in July 1995, but the governments decided that more could be achieved if further talks could be held. These latest negotiations ended in December 1997.

Other Issues

GATS identifies several more issues for future negotiation. One set of negotiations would create rules that are not yet included in GATS : rules dealing with subsidies, government procurement and safeguard measures.

Another set of negotiations would seek rules on the requirements foreign service providers have to meet in order to operate in a market. The objective is to prevent these requirements being used as unnecessary barriers to trade. The focus is on : qualification requirements and procedures, technical standards and licensing requirements.

As part of this task, a working party on professional services has been set up. It is tackling the accountancy sector first, a priority set by ministers, but eventually all professional services should be covered. The first result of these discussions emerged in May 1997 when the Services Council adopted new guidelines for countries to use when negotiating agreements to recognize each others' professional qualifications in accountancy. The guidelines are not binding.

6

THE AGREEMENT ON GOVERNMENT PROCUREMENT

Introduction

Procurement of products and services by government agencies for their own purposes represents an important share of total government expenditure and thus has a significant role in domestic economies. While ensuring best value for money will be secured through an open and non-discriminatory procurement regime, governments sometimes seek to achieve certain other domestic policy goals through their purchasing decisions, such as promotion of local industrial sectors or business groups. Measures to this effect may be either explicitly prescribed in national legislations, for example prohibitions against the purchase of foreign goods or services or from foreign suppliers, preference margins, set-asides and offsets, or in the form of less overt measures or practices which have the effect of denying foreign products, services and suppliers the opportunity to compete in domestic government procurement markets, including excessive use of selective tendering, non-open technical specification requirements and, in particular, lack of transparency in tendering procedures including contract awards. Such discriminatory government procurement procedures and practices can lead to distortions in international trade.

Government procurement has been effectively omitted from the scope of the multilateral trade rules under the WTO, in the areas of both goods and services. In the General Agreement on Tariffs and Trade, originally negotiated in 1947, government procurement was explicitly excluded from the key national treatment obligation. More recently, government procurement has been carved out of main commitments of the General Agreement on Trade in Services. Since it is estimated that government procurement typically represents 10-15% of GDP, this represents a considerable gap in the multilateral trading system.

A growing awareness of the trade-restrictive effects of discriminatory procurement policies and of the desirability of fulfilling these gaps in the trading system resulted in a first effort to bring government procurement under internationally agreed trade rules in the Tokyo Round of Trade Negotiations. As a result, the first Agreement on Government Procurement was signed in 1979 and entered into force in 1981. It was amended in 1987, with this amended version entering into force in 1988. In parallel with the Uruguay Round, Parties to the Agreement held negotiations to extend the scope and coverage of the Agreement. The Agreement on Government Procurement (1994) (GPA) was signed in Marrakesh on 15 April 1994 — at the same time as the Agreement Establishing the WTO. The new Agreement entered into force on 1 January 1996. The GPA is one of the "plurilateral" Agreements included in Annex 4 to the Agreement Establishing the WTO, signifying that not all WTO Members are bound by it.

According to the statistics collected under the Tokyo Round Agreement, that Agreement applied annually to a total value of contracts of around US$30 billion in 1990-94. Under the new Agreement, the value of procurement that is opened up to international competition is estimated to have increased by ten times, with the extension of rules to cover procurement of services as well as goods and to cover sub-central entities and public utilities as well.

Main Features

The GPA establishes an agreed framework of rights and obligations among its Parties with respect to their national laws, regulations, procedures and practices in the area of government procurement. The cornerstone of the rules in the Agreement is non-discrimination. In respect of the procurement covered by the Agreement, governments Parties to the Agreement are required to give the products, services and suppliers of any other Party to the Agreement treatment "no less favourable" than that they give to their domestic products, services and suppliers and not to discriminate among goods, services and suppliers of other Parties (Article III : 1). Furthermore, each Party is required to ensure that its entities do not treat a locally-established supplier less favourably than another locally-established supplier on the basis of degree of foreign affiliation or ownership and do not discriminate against a locally-established supplier on the basis of country of production of the good or service being supplied (Article III : 2). In order to ensure that the basic principle of non-discrimination is followed and that access to procurement is available to foreign products, services and suppliers, the Agreement lays heavy emphasis on procedures for providing transparency of laws, regulations, procedures and practices regarding government procurement.

Scope and Coverage

The Agreement does not apply to all government procurement of the Parties. The obligations under the Agreement apply to procurement :

— by the procuring entities that each Party has listed in its schedule in Annexes 1 to 3 of Appendix I, relating respectively to central government entities, sub-central government entities and other entities such as utilities;

— of goods; and

— all services and construction services that are specified in positive lists, found respectively, in Annexes 4 and 5 of Appendix I;

— in respect of procurement contracts above certain threshold values. Each Party indicates the levels of minimum thresholds that apply to the procurement of goods and services under Annexes 1, 2 and 3 entities (Article I : 4). [Table on thresholds]. The thresholds as expressed in national currencies of Parties to the Agreement for 1996/97 are available in documents GPA/W/12 and Addenda 1-7 WTO documents on-line.

The Agreement authorizes Parties to modify the mutually agreed coverage of Appendices I to IV, subject to the procedures for rectification and modification specified in Article XXIV : 6.

Since its signature in April 1994, the Agreement's scope has been expanded through the incorporation in it of the results of a series of bilateral agreements between individual Parties. A loose-leaf system for Appendices to the Agreement is designed to reflect the up-to-date status of the Appendices as such changes occur.

When reading the schedules in Appendix I to ascertain whether a particular procurement contract is covered by the Agreement, it is important to check not only whether the procuring entity is covered, the threshold level and, if the contract is for a service, whether that service is covered, but also the General Notes at the end of most Parties' schedules which provide for a number of exceptions. It should be noted that exceptions from the obligations of the Agreement are also allowed for developing countries in certain situations (Article V) and for non-economic reasons, for example to protect national security interests, public morals, order or safety, human, animal or plant life or health or intellectual property, etc. (Article XXIII).

The Agreement (Article IX : 11) requires that notices of invitation to participate in an intended procurement make it clear, either in the notice itself or in the publication in which it appears, whether the procurement in question is covered by the Agreement.

Tendering Procedures

The Agreement contains a number of detailed procedural obligations which procuring entities have to fulfil to ensure the effective application of its basic principles (Articles VII to XVI). The purpose of these procedural requirements is to guarantee that access to covered procurement is effectively open and that an equal opportunity is given to foreign supplies and suppliers in competing for government contracts.

The Agreement allows the use of open, selective and limited tendering procedures, provided they are consistent with the provisions laid out in Articles VII to XVI.

— Under open procedures all interested suppliers may submit a tender (Article VII : 3 (a)).

— Under selective tendering procedures only those suppliers invited to do so by the entity may submit a tender (Articles VII : 3 (b) and X). To ensure optimum effective international competition, purchasing entities are required to invite tenders from the maximum number of foreign suppliers. Safeguards to ensure that the procedures and conditions for qualification of suppliers do not discriminate against suppliers of other Parties are set out in Article VIII. For example, any conditions for participation in tendering procedures by suppliers shall be limited to those that are essential to ensure the firm's capability to fulfil the contract and shall not have a discriminatory effect. Once a year the entities using the selective tendering method are required to publish, in a publication indicated in Appendix III to the Agreement, their lists of qualified suppliers, and to specify the period of validity of those lists and the conditions that need to be met for inclusion of interested suppliers in the lists (Article IX : 9).

— Under limited tendering procedures the entity contacts the potential suppliers individually (Article VII : 3(c)). The Agreement closely circumscribes the situations in which this method can be used, for example in the absence of tenders in response to an open tender or selective tender or in cases of collusion, when the product or service can be supplied only by a particular supplier, or for reasons of extreme urgency brought about by events unforeseeable by the entity (Article XV).

Entities may hold negotiations with suppliers making tenders, provided this is indicated in the initial tender notice or it appears from the tender evaluation that no one tender is the most advantageous and subject to safeguards to ensure that such negotiations do not discriminate between suppliers (Article XIV).

The Agreement prescribes certain minimum deadlines that must be allowed for the preparation, submission and receipt of tenders to enable responsive tendering (Article XI : 2). These must be set long enough to allow all suppliers, domestic and foreign, to prepare and submit tenders before the closing of the tendering procedures. In general the minimum shall be 40 days from the date of publication of an invitation to tender. The minimum time-limits for receipt of tenders may be reduced to 25 or even 10 days in certain well-defined circumstances.

In the tender documentation the purchasing entity is required to give all necessary information related to the procurement in question to enable potential suppliers to submit responsive tenders, including information required to be published in tender notices and other important information, for example economic and technical requirements, financial guarantees and the criteria for awarding the contract and procedural information such as the closing date and time for receipt of tenders (Article XII).

The objective of the procedural rules for submission, receipt and opening of tenders is to ensure fairness, equity and transparency in the procurement process (Article XIII : 1-3). All tenders solicited under open and selective procedures by entities shall be received and opened under procedures and conditions guaranteeing the regularity of the openings.

Only tenders that conform to the essential requirements of the tender notice or documentation and are from a supplier which complies with the conditions for participation can be considered for award. Entities have the obligation to award contracts to the tenderer who has been determined to be fully capable of undertaking the contract and whose tender is either the lowest tender or the tender which is determined to be the most advantageous in terms of the specific evaluation criteria set forth in the notices or tender documentation. An entity that has received a tender abnormally lower than other tenders may enquire with the tenderer to ensure that it can comply with the conditions of participation and be capable of fulfilling the terms of the contract (Article XIII : 4).

The modes of transmission of data foreseen under the relevant provisions of the Agreement are telex, telegram, facsimile. The Agreement recognizes the fact that its provisions do not take into account the rapidly emerging use of information technology in government procurement. In order to ensure that it does not constitute an obstacle to technical progress in this area, the Agreement calls for regular consultations in the Committee regarding developments in information technology and, if necessary, negotiation of modifications to the Agreement itself (Article XXIV : 8).

Other Provisions for Open Procurement

The use of offsets — measures to encourage local development or improve the balance-of-payments accounts by means of domestic content, licensing of technology, investment requirements, counter-trade or similar requirements — are explicitly prohibited in the Agreement. Notwithstanding this, developing countries may negotiate, at the time of their accession, conditions for the use of offsets provided these are used only for the qualification to participate in the procurement process and not as criteria for awarding contracts (Article XVI).

The Agreement contains obligations on technical specifications in order to prevent entities from discriminating against and among foreign goods and suppliers through the technical characteristics of products and services that they specify (Article VI). Technical specifications shall be in terms of performance rather than design, and be based on international standards, where they exist, or otherwise on national technical regulations, recognized national standards, or building codes.

Prior Information

Prior to the actual tendering process, Parties are required to publish an invitation to participate in the form of a tender notice in a publicly accessible publication indicated in Appendix II to the Agreement. The purpose is to inform all interested suppliers about the procurement opportunity and the relevant aspects of the procurement in question. Entities at central government level in Annex 1 are required to use a notice of proposed procurement, whereas other entities in Annexes 2 and 3 may use a notice of planned procurement (Article IX).

Post-award Information and Publication

Information must also be provided, after the award of the contract, on the award decision in the form of a notice, giving information on such matters as the nature and quantity of the products and services in the contract award, the name and address of the winning tenderer, and the value of the winning award or the highest and the lowest offer taken into account in the award of the contract (Article XVIII : 1).

Moreover, in response to a request from a supplier from a Party to the Agreement, the procuring entity must provide prompt and pertinent information on : its procurement practices; an explanation of the reasons why a supplier's application to qualify was rejected; why its existing qualification to tender was brought to an end; and on the characteristics and relevant advantages of the tender selected (Article XVIII : 2). However, entities are entitled to withhold certain information on grounds of confidentiality (Article XVIII : 4). The Agreement provides for the protection of confidential information (Article XIX : 4). In addition, the government of an unsuccessful tenderer, Party to the Agreement, may seek such additional information on the contract award as is necessary to ensure that the procurement was made fairly and impartially (Article XIX : 2).

There is a general requirement to publish laws, regulations, judicial decisions, administrative rulings of general application and any procedures regarding government procurement covered by the Agreement. The relevant publications are listed in Appendix IV (Article XIX : 1). As a further element of transparency under the Agreement, each government must collect and provide to the other Parties, through the Committee, statistics on its procurement covered by the Agreement (Article XIX : 5).

Special Rules for Developing Countries

The Agreement recognizes the development, financial and trade needs of developing countries, in particular least-developed countries, and allows special and differential treatment in order to meet their specific development objectives (Article V : 1). Development objectives of developing countries should be taken into account in the negotiation of coverage of procurement by entities in developed and developing countries (Article V : 3-7). Article V also contains provisions on : technical assistance (Article V : 8-11); establishment of information centres giving information on procurement practices and procedures in developed countries (Article V : 11); special treatment for least-developed countries

(Article V : 12 and 13); and review of the application of Article V (Article V : 14 and 15).

Enforcement

Disputes between Parties under the Agreement are subject to the procedures of the WTO Understanding on Rules and Procedures Governing the Settlement of Disputes (DSU) (Article XXII : 1). Because of the plurilateral nature of the Agreement, Article XXII contains a number of special rules or procedures (Article XXII : 3, 5 and 6). Of particular interest is the provision disallowing so-called "cross-retaliation" — the suspension of concessions or other obligations under the GPA as a result of disputes arising under the other WTO Agreements as well as suspension of concessions or other obligations under any other WTO Agreement because of any dispute arising under the GPA (Article XXII : 7). Moreover, under the Agreement the DSB has the authority to authorize consultations among parties to the dispute regarding remedies when withdrawal of violating measures is not possible (Article XXII : 3).

As a new and unique feature of the enforcement procedures in the WTO system, Article XX of the GPA sets out mandatory requirements for the establishment of a domestic bid challenge system, giving suppliers believing that a procurement has been handled inconsistently with the requirements of the GPA a right of recourse to an independent domestic tribunal. Parties may confer the authority to hear challenges by suppliers on national courts or on an impartial and independent review body. In the event that a bid challenge is heard by a review body which does not have the status of a court of law, either its decisions must be subject to judicial review or it must follow the procedures/criteria laid down in detail in the Agreement (Article XX : 6(a)-(g)). The challenge body must have the authority to order the correction of a breach of the Agreement or compensation for the loss or damages suffered by a supplier, but this may be limited to costs for tender preparation or protest. Pending the outcome of the challenge, it must be able to order rapid interim measures, including the suspension of the procurement process, to correct breaches of the Agreement and to preserve commercial opportunities (Article XX : 7 (a)-(c)).

Transparency in Government Procurement

For the last two-and-a-half years the WTO has actively pursued a work programme on the subject of transparency in government procurement. This has been based on a mandate adopted by Ministers at the WTO Singapore Ministerial Conference held in December 1996 to : "establish a working group to conduct a study on transparency in government procurement practices, taking into account national policies, and, based on this study, to develop elements for inclusion in an appropriate agreement".

With the upcoming Ministerial Conference, this work is now entering a critical phase. There are a number of proposals regarding the way in which the WTO work in this area might be pursued in future. One option is the conclusion of a multilateral transparency agreement in the context of a new round, another being the continuation of the work in the Working Group Moreover, a number of WTO Members have tabled draft agreements and are engaged in intensive consultations with their WTO partners with a view to preparing an agreement on transparency in government procurement that could be adopted by Ministerial Conference.

The Singapore mandate reflects the heavy emphasis placed throughout the WTO system of rules and practices on transparency. Transparency is often referred to as one of the three fundamental principles of the WTO, the others being most-favoured-nation and national treatment. The role of transparency is perhaps of greatest importance in situations where the extent to which rules of general application determine trading conditions is limited and the scope for discretionary decision-making is greatest. Government procurement is a notable example. The GATT and now the WTO have for a long time had a plurilateral Agreement, presently with 26 Parties[1] out of the 135 WTO Members, with detailed requirements in respect of transparency in government procurement. The object of the transparency provisions in this Agreement is not only to ensure that adequate information on procurement opportunities is made available and that decisions are fairly taken, but also to

1. Canada, the EU and its Member States, Hong Kong, China, Israel, Japan Korea, Liechtenstein, Netherlands with respect to Aruba, Norway, Singapore, Switzerland, United States.

facilitate monitoring of the commitments made under that Agreement not to discriminate against suppliers and supplies from other Parties.

The focus of the multilateral work presently under way on transparency in government procurement is somewhat different. First, as indicated, this work is multilateral in nature and aimed at drawing up an agreement to which all 135 WTO Members will be parties. Second, the focus is on transparency as such, rather than on transparency as a vehicle for monitoring market-access commitments. It is understood among WTO Members that the work presently under way on transparency in government procurement does not seek to regulate the extent to which governments provide preferences to domestic supplies or suppliers, provided of course that such preferences are transparent. However, some Members have indicated that they would wish future negotiations to keep the door open also to addressing obstacles to market access on a multilateral basis.

The WTO Working Group on Transparency in Government Procurement, since its first meeting in May 1997, has met nine times. The Working Group initiated its work by hearing presentations from other intergovernmental organizations which have international instruments and activities relevant to transparency in government procurement, notably the United Nations Commission for International Trade Law (UNCITRAL) and the World Bank. It then considered a WTO comparative study of the transparency-related provisions in existing international instruments on government procurement procedures as well as in national practices. This covered the procedures under the plurilateral WTO Agreement on Government Procurement, the UNCITRAL Model Law and the World Bank Guidelines, as well as available material on national practices.

The next stage in the work of the Working Group was the systematic study of 12 issues that were identified as important in relation to transparency in government procurement. These are : definition and scope of government procurement; procurement methods; publication of information on national legislation and procedures; information on procurement opportunities, tendering and qualification procedures; time-periods; transparency of decisions on qualification; transparency of decisions on contract awards; domestic review procedures; other matters related to transparency; maintenance of records of proceedings; information technology; language; fight against bribery and corruption; information to be provided to other governments (notification); WTO dispute settlement procedures; and technical cooperation and special and differential treatment for developing countries. Written contributions on national practices, on issues meriting study and setting out ideas for action have been presented by many members to the Working Group.

The work has shown a high degree of common thinking on many of the issues referred to above. The main questions on which further work is required include the scope of the transactions that would be covered by a transparency agreement, the treatment of single tendering practices, which are inherently less transparent, domestic review or challenge procedures and the applicability of WTO procedures for settling disputes between governments concerning allegations of non-compliance with the rules of a transparency agreement.

7

TRADE IN AGRICULTURAL COMMODITIES

Introduction

Up to 1995, GATT rules were largely ineffective in disciplining agricultural trade. In particular, export subsidies came to dominate many areas of world agricultural trade, while the disciplines on import restrictions were often flouted. The 1986-1994 Uruguay Round went a long way towards changing all that.

The trade is now firmly within the multilateral trading system. The Agriculture Agreement, together with individual countries' commitments to reduce export subsidies, domestic support and import barriers on agricultural products make up a comprehensive programme for reforming agricultural trade.

Numberical Targets for Cutting Subsidies and Protection

The reductions in agricultural subsidies and protection agreed in the Uruguay Round

	Developed Countries 6 years : 1995-2000	Developing Countries 10 years : 1995-2004
Tariffs		
average cut for all agricultural products	-36%	-24%
minimum cut per product	-15%	-10%
Domestic support		
cuts in total ("AMS") support for the sector	-20%	-30%

Exports		
value of subsidies (outlays)	-36%	-24%
subsidized quantities	-21%	-14%

Notes : Least-developed countries do not have to make commitments to reduce tariffs or subsidies. The base level for tariff cuts was the bound rate before 1 January 1995; or, for unbound tariffs, the actual rate charged in September 1986 when the Uruguay Round began.

Only the figures for cutting export subsidies appear in the agreement. The other figures were targets used to calculate countries' legally binding "schedules" of commitments.

The reform programme struck a balance between agricultural trade liberalization and governments' desire to pursue legitimate agricultural policy goals, including non-trade concerns. The reform brought all agricultural products (as listed in the agreement) under multilateral disciplines, including "tariff bindings" — WTO members have bound themselves to maximum tariffs on nearly all agricultural products, while many industrial tariffs remain unbound.

New Rules and Commitments

The objective of the Agriculture Agreement is to reform trade in the sector and to make policies more market-oriented. This would improve predictability and security for importing and exporting countries alike.

The new rules and commitments apply to : (i) market access — various trade restrictions confronting imports, (ii) domestic support — subsidies and other programmes, including those that raise or guarantee farmgate prices and farmers' incomes and (iii) export subsidies and other methods used to make exports artificially competitive.

The agreement does allow governments to support their rural economies, but preferably through policies that cause less distortion to trade. It also allows some flexibility in the way.

What is 'distortion'?

The concept of 'distortion' is used a lot when agricultural trade is discussed. Essentially, trade is distorted if prices are higher or lower than normal, and if quantities produced, bought, and sold are also higher or lower than normal — *i.e.* than the levels that would usually exist in a competitive market.

For example, import barriers and domestic subsidies can raise crop prices on a country's internal market. The higher prices can encourage over-production, and if the surplus is to be sold on world markets, where prices are lower, then export subsidies have to be paid. When some countries subsidize and others do not, the result can be that the subsidizing countries are producing considerably more than they normally would.

Governments usually give three reasons for supporting and protecting their farmers, even if this distorts agricultural trade : (i) to make sure that enough food is produced to meet the country's needs, (ii) to shield farmers from the effects of the weather and swings in world prices, (iii) to preserve rural society.

But the policies have often been expensive, and they have encouraged gluts leading to export subsidy wars. Countries with less money for subsidies have suffered. In negotiations, some countries have argued that trying to meet any of these objectives is counter-productive. Others have attempted to find ways of meeting the objectives without distorting trade too much.

The package contained more. It ensured that quantities imported before the agreement took effect could continue to be imported, and it guaranteed that commitments are implemented. Developing countries do not have to cut their subsidies or lower their tariffs as much as developed countries, and they are given extra time to complete their obligations. Special provisions deal with the interests of countries that rely on imports for their food supplies, and the least developed economies.

"Peace" provisions within the agreement aim to reduce the likelihood of disputes or challenges on agricultural subsidies over a period of nine years.

Market Access : 'tariffs only', Please

The new rule for market access in agricultural products is "tariffs only". Before the Uruguay Round, some agricultural imports were restricted by quotas and other non-tariff measures. These have been replaced by tariffs that provide more-or-less equivalent levels of protection — if the previous policy meant domestic prices were 75% higher than world prices, then the new tariff could be around 75%. (Converting the quotas and other types of measures to tariffs in this way was called "tariffication".)

Some new quantities were charged duty rates that were not prohibitive. This was achieved by a system of "tariff-quotas" — lower tariff rates for specified quantities, higher (sometimes much higher) rates for quantities that exceed the quota.

A tariff-quota

This is what a tariff-quota might look like

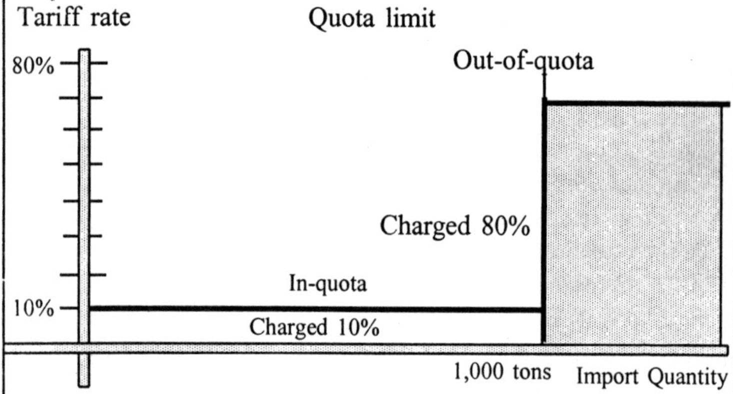

Imports entering under the tariff-quota (up to 1,000 tons) are charged 10%. Imports entering outside the tariff quota are charged 80%. Under the Uruguay Round agreement, the 1,000 tons would generally be based on actual imports in the base period or an agreed "minimum access" formula.

The newly committed tariffs and tariff quotas, covering all agricultural products, took effect in 1995. Uruguay Round participants agreed that developed countries would cut the tariffs (the higher out-of-quota rates in the case of tariff-quotas) by an average of 36%, in equal steps over six years. Developing countries would make 24% cuts over 10 years. Several developing countries also used the option of offering ceiling tariff rates in cases where duties were not "bound" (*i.e.* committed under GATT or WTO regulations) before the Uruguay Round. Least developed countries do not have to cut their tariffs. (These figures do not actually appear in the Agriculture Agreement. Participants used them to prepare their schedules — *i.e.* lists of commitments. It is the commitments listed in the schedules that are legally binding.)

For products whose non-tariff restrictions have been converted to tariffs, governments are allowed to take special emergency actions ("safeguards") in order to prevent swiftly falling prices or surges in imports from hurting their farmers. But the agreement specifies when and how those emergency actions can be introduced (for example, they cannot be used on imports within a tariff-quota). Four countries used "special treatment" provisions to restrict imports of particularly sensitive products (mainly rice) during the implementation period, but subject to strictly defined conditions, including minimum access for overseas suppliers. The four are: Japan, Rep of Korea, and the Philippines for rice; and Israel for sheepmeat, wholemilk powder and certain cheeses.

Market Access : Special Agricultural Safeguards

Safeguards are contingency restrictions on imports taken temporarily to deal with special circumstances such as a surge in imports. They normally come under the Safeguards Agreement, but the Agriculture Agreement has special provisions (Article 5) on safeguards.

The special safeguards provisions for agriculture differ from normal safeguards. In agriculture, unlike with normal safeguards:

* higher safeguards duties can be triggered automatically when import volumes rise above a certain level, or if prices fall below a certain level; and
* it is not necessary to demonstrate that serious injury is being caused to the domestic industry.

The special agricultural safeguard can only be used on products that were tariffied, but not on imports within the tariff quotas, and only if the government reserved the right to do so in its schedule of commitments on agriculture.

Proposals for the negotiations range from continuing with the provision in its current form, to its abolition, or its revision to prevent its use on products from developing countries. However, the right to use the special agricultural safeguard would lapse if there is no agreement in the negotiations after Seattle to continue the "reform process" initiated in the Uruguay Round.

Domestic Support

In WTO terminology, subsidies in general are identified by "boxes" which are given the colours of traffic lights: green (permitted), amber (slow down — *i.e.* be reduced), red (forbidden). In agriculture, things are, as usual, more complicated. The Agriculture Agreement has no red box, but there is a blue box for certain types of subsidies, and exemptions for developing countries (sometimes called an "S & D box").

The 'amber box'

For agriculture, all subsidies and other domestic support measures considered to distort production and trade (with some exceptions) fall into the amber box. The total value of these measures must be reduced.

The 'green box'

In order to qualify for the "green box", a subsidy must not distort trade, or at most cause minimal distortion. They have to be government-funded (not by charging consumers higher prices) and must not involve price support. They tend to be programmes that are not directed at particular products, and include direct income supports for farmers that are not related to (are "decoupled" from) production. "Green box" subsidies are therefore allowed without limits, provided they comply with relevant criteria (*for details, see Article 6 and Annex 2 of the Agriculture Agreement*).

Some countries say they would like to review the domestic subsidies listed in the green box because they believe that some of these, in certain circumstances, could have an influence on production or prices. Some others, including some major players advocating general agricultural trade liberalization, have said that the green box should not be changed because it is already satisfactory.

The 'blue box'

The blue box is an exemption from the general rule that all

subsidies linked to production must be reduced or kept within defined minimal ("de minimis") levels. It covers payments directly linked to acreage or animal numbers, but under schemes which also limit production by imposing production quotas or requiring farmers to set aside part of their land. Countries using these subsidies say they distort trade less than alternative amber box subsidies.

At the moment, the blue box is a permanent provision of the agreement. Some countries want it scrapped because the payments are only partly decoupled from production. Others say it is an important tool for supporting and reforming agriculture, and for achieving certain "non-trade" objectives.

Export Subsidies

Some countries are proposing the total elimination of export subsidies. Others reject the idea. In addition, some countries would like to examine the rules to prevent governments getting around ("circumventing") their commitments — including the use of state trading enterprises and subsidized export credits.

Who can Subsidize Exports?

The following 25 WTO members have export subsidy reduction commitments. Those without commitments cannot subsidize agricultural exports at all. Some among the 25 have decided to greatly reduce their subsidies or drop them completely.

Australia	Iceland	Romania
Brazil	Indonesia	Slovak Rep
Bulgaria	Israel	S. Africa
Canada	Mexico	Switzerland
Colombia	New Zealand	Turkey
Cyprus	Norway	United States
Czech Rep	Panama	Uruguay
European Union	Poland	Venezuela
Hungary		

Where the subsidies are listed, the agreement requires WTO members to cut both the amount of money they spend on export subsidies and the quantities of exports that receive subsidies. Taking averages for 1986-90 as the base level, developed countries have agreed to cut the value of export subsidies by 36% over the six years starting in 1995 (24% over 10 years for developing countries). Developed countries have also agreed to reduce the quantities of subsidized exports by 21% over the six years (14% over 10 years for developing countries). Least developed countries do not need to make any cuts.

During the six-year implementation period, developing countries are allowed under certain conditions to use subsidies to reduce the costs of marketing and transporting exports.

Developing Countries

Developing countries reflect a range of interests in the debate on agriculture, and the distinctions are not always clear.

Most members of the Cairns Group[1] — which favours much greater liberalization in agricultural trade — are developing countries. But like most WTO members, the Cairns Group would also like to see developing countries given "special and differential" treatment to take account of their needs.

Some countries say WTO arrangements should be more flexible so that developing countries can support and protect their agricultural and rural development and ensure the livelihoods of their large agrarian populations.

They argue, for example, that subsidies and protection are needed to ensure food security, to support small scale farming, to make up for a lack of capital, or to prevent the rural poor from migrating into already over-congested cities.

At the same time, some developing countries make a clear distinction between their needs and what they consider to be the desire of much richer countries to spend large amounts subsidizing agriculture at the expense of poorer countries.

Many developing countries complain that their exports still face high tariffs and other barriers in developed countries' markets

1. At present the Cairns Group includes Australia, Argentina, Brazil, Canada, Chile, Colombia, Fiji, Indonesia, Malaysia, New Zealand, Paraguay, the Phillippines, South Africa, Thailand and Uruguay.

and that their attempts to develop processing industries are hampered by tariff escalation (higher import duties on processed products compared to raw materials). They want to see substantial cuts in these barriers.

WTO statistics show that developing countries as a whole have seen a significant increase in agricultural exports. Agricultural trade rose globally by nearly $100bn between 1993 and 1998.[2] Of this, developing countries' exports rose by around $47bn — from $120bn to $167bn in the period. Their share of world agricultural exports increased from 40.1% to 42.4%. But within the group, some individual developing countries have seen their agricultural trade balance worsen — their imports have risen faster than their exports.

Decision on Net-food Importing Developing Countries

A number of developing countries which depend on imports for their food supply are also concerned about possible rises in world food prices as a result of reductions in richer countries' subsidies. Although they accepted that higher prices can benefit farmers and increase domestic production, they feel that their concerns about food imports need to be addressed more effectively.

The WTO agreements include a *Decision on the Possible Negative Effects of the Reform Programme on Least-Developed and Net-Food Importing Developing Countries*. As a result of this decision the Food Aid Convention was recently renegotiated and concluded in July 1999 in the International Grains Council. The WTO Committee on Agriculture also regularly reviews actions within the framework of the decision, in such areas as technical and financial assistance provided to least-developed and net-food importing countries to assist in improving their agricultural productivity and infrastructure.

'Non-trade' Concerns and 'Multifunctionality': Agriculture can Serve many Purposes

The Agriculture Agreement includes provisions for important "non-trade" concerns such as food security, the environment,

---

2. Excluding trade within the European Union.

structural adjustment (which can include rural development) and so on.

Most countries accept that agriculture is not only about producing food and fibre but also has other functions, including these non-trade objectives — although some dislike the buzzword "multifunctionality". The question debated in the WTO is whether "trade-distorting" subsidies, or subsidies outside the "green box", are needed in order to help agriculture perform its many roles.

Some countries say all the objectives can and should be achieved more effectively through "green box" subsidies which are targeted directly at these objectives. Examples include direct payments to producers, structural adjustment assistance, environmental programmes, and regional assistance programmes which do not stimulate agricultural production or affect prices. These countries say the onus is on the proponents of non-trade concerns and "multifunctionality" to show that the existing provisions, which were the subject of lengthy negotiations in the Uruguay Round, are inadequate for dealing with these concerns in targeted, non-trade distorting ways.

Other countries say the non-trade concerns are closely linked to production. They believe subsidies based on, or related to, production are needed for these purposes. For example, rice fields have to be promoted in order to prevent soil erosion, they say. A number of countries have produced studies to support their arguments, and these studies have also been debated.

Many exporting developing countries say multifunctionality is a form of special and differential treatment for rich countries. Several even argue that any economic activity — industry, services and so on — is equally multifunctional, and therefore if the WTO is to address this issue, it has to do so in all areas of the negotiations, not only agriculture. Some others say agriculture is special.

The Peace Clause

Article 13 ("due restraint") of the Agriculture Agreement protects countries using subsidies which comply with the agreement from being challenged under other WTO agreements. Without this "peace clause", countries would have greater freedom to take action against each others' subsidies, under the Subsidies and Countervailing Measures Agreement and other provisions. The peace clause is due to expire at the end of 2003.

Some countries want it extended so that they can enjoy some degree of "legal security", ensuring that they will not be challenged so long as they comply with their commitments under the Agriculture Agreement.

Others want it to lapse as part of their overall objective to see agriculture brought under general WTO disciplines, although they might be prepared to consider an extension, depending on what is agreed in other parts of the agriculture negotiation.

Fisheries and Forestry

The Agriculture Agreement does not include fishery and forestry products. Some WTO members would like to see specific disciplines negotiated for these products and have tabled proposals. In particular there are proposals for dealing with fisheries subsidies (both for fishing fleets and for fish farming) and their impact on fish stocks and the environment. The proposed rules and disciplines for forestry products would include the promotion of resource conservation and management, other environmental concerns, and disciplines on market access and export restrictions on logs. The proposals would almost certainly not come under the Agriculture Agreement.

Regulations for Animal and Plant Products: How Safe is Safe?

Problem: How do you ensure that your country's consumers are being supplied with food that is safe to eat — "safe" by the standards you consider appropriate? And at the same time, how can you ensure that strict health and safety regulations are not being used as an excuse for protecting domestic producers?

It allows countries to set their own standards. But it also says regulations must be based on science. They should be applied only to the extent necessary to protect human, animal or plant life or health. And they should not arbitrarily or unjustifiably discriminate between countries where identical or similar conditions prevail.

SANITARY AND PHYTOSANITARY (SPS) MEASURES

Sanitary and phytosanitary measures deal with food safety and animal and plant health standards. The WTO does not set the standards. The WTO's SPS Agreement encourages member countries to use standards set by international organizations. The SPS Agreement identifies three standard-setting organisations :

* the FAO-WHO Codex Alimentarius Commission —*for food safety*
* the International Office for Epizootics — *for animal health*
* the FAO's Secretariat of the International Plant Protection Convention — *for plant health*

It also says governments can agree to refer to any other international organizations or agreements whose membership is open to all WTO members.

The countries are also allowed to set their own standards. These standards can be higher than the internationally agreed ones, but the agreement says they should be based on scientific evidence, should not discriminate between countries, and should not be a disguised restriction to trade.

The provisions strike a balance between two equally important objectives: helping governments protect consumers, and animal and plant health against known dangers and potential hazards; and avoiding the use of health and safety regulations as protectionism in disguise.

The following issues are among those raised in the lead up to the ministerial conference. It remains to be seen whether they will be accepted for further work, or if they will be included in negotiations. These issues could be considered "implementation" of the existing agreement, or be studied by a working party without necessarily leading to negotiations to revise the SPS Agreement. Countries may decide they would prefer not to re-open the SPS Agreement.

Clarification of 'Vague' Provisions

A number of members, developing countries in particular,

say they want to see the wording of the agreement tightened, and some voluntary commitments turned into mandatory ones.

For example : Article 2 refers to equal treatment for countries "where identical or similar conditions prevail". Some developing countries complain that their products are not being given equal treatment because the "identical or similar conditions" are being overlooked. They would like the term to be clarified. Some countries would also like to see more developing countries included in agreements where governments recognize each others' SPS measures as equivalent, including inspection and certification procedures.

The SPS Agreement uses phrases such as "a reasonable" period of time in provisions on giving advance warning of new regulations, or on allowing developing countries an opportunity to adapt their exports to developed countries' higher standards.

Proposals range from : a simple call for the relevant time-period to be clarified, to specifying "at least 12 months" for developing countries to adapt to new regulations. Several countries want the whole of Article 10, which deals with special and differential treatment for developing countries, to be mandatory.

Some countries see the clarification as part of improving the implementation of the SPS Agreement. Others say it involves interpreting or modifying the agreement and therefore it should be included in the new negotiations. Some also say implementation issues have already been discussed in the SPS Committee during the review of the agreement's operation and implementation (which took place in 1998), and the committee should continue to be the forum for these issues.

Other Developing Countries' Concerns

In addition to seeking clarification on the above issues, a number of developing countries have expressed concern about their lack of resources for implementing the agreement. Among the burdens are :

* the obligation to keep fellow members informed, through the WTO's SPS Committee, about their regulations ("notification")

* monitoring new regulations in their export markets
* the difficulty of demonstrating sufficient scientific evidence to justify their own measures or challenge those of others

These countries are calling for both technical assistance, and more time to comply.

Risk and Precaution

The recent debate surrounding some food safety and animal health issues — including disputes in the WTO over the use of hormones in beef production and over regulations for salmon — raises the question of whether the SPS Agreement's preference for scientific evidence goes far enough in dealing with possible risks for consumers and producers.

A phrase that has emerged in the debate is the "precautionary principle", a kind of "safety first" approach to deal with scientific uncertainty. To some extent, Article 5.7[3] of the SPS Agreement addresses this, but some governments have said outside the WTO that they would like the principle strengthened.

Genetically Modified Organisms and Biotechnology

These issues possibly span several WTO agreements, including SPS, Agriculture, Intellectual Property (TRIPS) and Technical Barriers to Trade (TBT). They have also been discussed in the Trade and Environment Committee.

Among the proposals are suggestions for a new working party or "examination group" to be set up to consider how adequate and effective existing WTO rules are for dealing with genetically modified organisms, biotechnology and other new subjects.

---

3. Article 5, paragraph 7 of the SPS Agreement : "In cases where relevant scientific evidence is insufficient, a Member may provisionally adopt sanitary or phytosanitary measures on the basis of available pertinent information, including that from the relevant international organizations as well as from sanitary or phytosanitary measures applied by other Members. In such circumstances, Members shall seek to obtain the additional information necessary for a more objective assessment of risk and review the sanitary or phytosanitary measure accordingly within a reasonable period of time."

Article 20 and Beyond

Article 20 of the Agriculture Agreement says WTO members have to negotiate to continue the reform programme for agriculture.

Members generally accept that this should result in better market conditions, lower production distorting subsidies and reductions in export subsidies. However, there is no agreement about the depth of these reforms (how deep the cuts in subsidies and tariffs should go, and how far the quotas should be widened) or on how issues like some non-trade concerns should be addressed.

The forthcoming negotiations will be difficult but they will also contribute to further liberalization of agricultural trade. This will benefit those countries which can compete on quality and price rather than on the size of their subsidies. This is particularly the case for many developing countries whose economies depend on an increasingly diverse range of primary and processed agricultural products.

The Least Developed and Those Depending on Food Imports

Under the Agriculture Agreement, WTO members have to reduce their subsidized exports. But some countries have been highly dependent on supplies of cheap, subsidized food imported from the major industrialized nations. They include some of the poorest countries, and although their farming sectors might receive a boost from higher prices, they might need temporary assistance to make the necessary adjustments to deal with higher priced imports, and eventually to export. A special ministerial decision sets out objectives, and certain measures, for the provision of food aid and aid for agricultural development. It also refers to the possibility of assistance from the International Monetary Fund and the World Bank to finance commercial food imports.

World Trade in Agricultural Products, 1998

Value $bn	553
Annual change %	
1980-85	-2
1985-90	9
1990-98	4
1996	3
1997	-2
1998	-5
Share in world merchandise trade %	10.5
Share in world exports of primary products %	52.4

Source : *WTO Annual Report 1999*, table IV.3, includes intra-EU trade

Top 15 Agricultural Exporters and Importers, 1998

	Value $bn	Share in World %		Value $bn	Share in World %
Exporters			**Importers**		
United States	69.85	12.6	United States	62.40	10.6
France	41.06	7.4	Japan	56.59	9.6
Netherlands	34.74	6.3	Germany	48.89	8.3
Canada	30.02	5.4	United Kingdom	35.29	6.0
Germany	29.64	5.4	France	33.18	5.6
Belgium-Luxembourg	20.53	3.7	Italy	32.06	5.4
United Kingdom	19.49	3.5	Netherlands	21.22	3.6
Spain	17.47	3.2	Belgium-Luxembourg	20.45	3.5
Italy	17.08	3.1	Spain	18.12	3.1
Brazil	17.07	3.1	Russian Fed. [a]	14.50	2.5
Australia	14.97	2.7	Canada [b]	13.99	2.4
China	14.31	2.6	Hong Kong, China	12.70	-
Argentina	13.51	2.4	retained imports	6.92	1.2
Denmark	12.12	2.2	China	12.61	2.1
Thailand	11.46	2.1	Mexico [b]	9.57	1.6
			Korea, Rep. of	9.31	1.6
Above 15	363.30	65.7	Above 15	395.08	66.9

Source : *WTO Annual Report 1999 table IV.7*, includes intra-EU trade

a : Includes WTO Secretariat estimates. b : Imports are valued f.o.b.

Agricultural Products' Share in Trade, by Region, 1998

	Exports	Imports		Exports	Imports
Share in total merchandise trade, %			Share in primary products trade, %		
World	10.5	10.5	World	52.4	52.4
North America	11.1	6.6	North America	65.8	43.7
Latin America	23.8	10.8	Latin America	56.5	59.4
Western Europe	10.1	11.3	Western Europe	66.1	58.3
C./E. Europe/Baltic States/CIS	11.7	13.2	C./E. Europe/Baltic States/CIS	29.7	49.8
Africa	19.5	17.0	Africa	31.8	67.5
Middle East	4.3	13.1	Middle East	6.1	70.5
Asia	7.7	11.3	Asia	54.4	44.7

Source : WTO Annual Report 1999, table IV.5, includes intra-EU trade.

8

TRADE AND ENVIRONMENT

Background to WTO Work on Trade and Environment

When Trade Ministers approved the results of the Uruguay Round negotiations in Marrakesh in April 1994, they also took a Decision to begin a comprehensive work programme on trade and environment in the WTO. Their Decision ensured that the subject has been given and will continue to be given a high profile on the WTO agenda.

The issue of trade and environment was not included for negotiation in the Uruguay Round, but certain environmental concerns were nevertheless addressed in the results of the negotiations. The Preamble to the WTO Agreement includes direct references to the objective of sustainable development and to the need to protect and preserve the environment. The new Agreements on Technical Barriers to Trade and on Sanitary and Phytosanitary Measures take explicitly into account the use by governments of measures to protect human, animal and plant life and health and the environment. The Agreement on Agriculture exempts direct payments under environmental programmes from WTO Member's commitments to reduce domestic support for agricultural production, subject to certain conditions. The Agreement on Subsidies and Countervailing Measures treats as a non-actionable subsidy government assistance to industry covering up to 20 per cent of the cost of adapting existing facilities to new environmental legislation. And both the TRIPs and the Services Agreements contain environment-related provisions. More generally, and as was recognized in the results of the UN Conference on Environment and Development in 1992 (the "Earth Summit"), an open, equitable and non-discriminatory multilateral trading system has a key contribution to make to national and international efforts to better protect and conserve environmental resources and promote sustainable development.

The WTO Committee on Trade and Environment has brought environmental and sustainable development issues into the mainstream of WTO work. The Committee's first Report, which was submitted to the WTO Ministerial Conference in Singapore, notes that the WTO is interested in building a constructive relationship between trade and environmental concerns. Trade and environment are both important areas of policymaking and they should be mutually supportive in order to promote sustainable development. The multilateral trading system has the capacity to further integrate environmental considerations and enhance its contribution to the promotion of sustainable development without undermining its open, equitable and non-discriminatory character.

The Marrakesh Ministerial Decision on Trade and Environment

Trade Ministers in Marrakesh agreed to establish a WTO Committee on Trade and Environment (CTE) with a broad-based remit covering all areas of the multilateral trading system — goods, services and intellectual property. The CTE has been given both analytical and prescriptive functions : to identify the relationships between trade and environmental measures in order to promote sustainable development, and to make recommendations on whether any modifications to the provisions of the multilateral trading system are required.

Two important parameters have guided the CTE's work. One is that WTO competence for policy coordination in this area is limited to trade and those trade-related aspects of environmental policies which may result in significant trade effects for its Members. In other words, there is no intention that the WTO should become an environmental agency, nor that it should get involved in reviewing national environmental priorities, setting environmental standards or developing global policies on the environment; that will continue to be the task of national governments and of other intergovernmental organizations better suited to the task. The second parameter is that if problems of policy coordination to protect the environment and promote sustainable development are identified through the CTE's work, steps taken to resolve them must uphold and safeguard the principles of the multilateral trading system which governments spent seven years strengthening and improving through the Uruguay Round negotiations.

The CTE's work programme was set out initially in ten areas of work. A start on the work programme was made soon after the Marrakesh Ministerial meeting, under the authority of the WTO Preparatory Committee, and from 1 January 1995, with the coming into force of the WTO Agreement, the Committee on Trade and Environment was formally established to continue work in this area. The CTE process has been driven by proposals from individual WTO Members on issues of importance to them.

As directed by the Marrakesh Ministerial Decision, the CTE submitted a report on the progress on all items of its work programme to the 1996 Ministerial Conference in Singapore and the 1998 Ministerial Conference in Geneva. The CTE adopted its report for work undertaken in 1999, which will be submitted to the Ministerial Conference in Seattle.

Several WTO symposia have been held with representatives of civil society in recent years on the trade and environment interface. The most recent was the High-Level Symposium on Trade and Environment held in March 1999 at which more than 130 non-governmental and inter-governmental organizations participated. Participation also included senior-level representatives from trade, environment, and development ministries as well as other government agencies of WTO Members which deal with matters related to sustainable development. This meeting provided a forum for a useful exchange of views and information between the trade and environment communities.

A recent WTO Secretariat report argues that international economic integration and growth reinforce the need for sound environmental policies at the national and international levels. International cooperation is particularly important in addressing transboundary and global environmental challenges beyond the control of any individual nations. This would be true even if nations did not trade with one another.[1]

Important parameters

The Committee on Trade and Environment (CTE) has brought environmental and sustainable development issues into the mainstream of the WTO's work. There are several important parameters which have guided the CTE's work.

* The first parameter is that WTO competency for policy coordination in this area is limited to trade and those trade-related aspects of environmental policies which may result in significant trade effects for its Members. In other words, it is not intended that the WTO should become an environmental agency. Nor should it get involved in reviewing national environmental priorities, setting environmental standards or developing global policies on the environment. That will continue to be the task of national governments and of other intergovernmental organizations better suited to the task.
* The second parameter is that increased national coordination as well as multilateral cooperation is necessary to address environmental concerns.
* The third parameter is that secure market access opportunities are essential to help developing countries work towards sustainable development.

The contribution which the WTO could make to environmental protection was recognized at the United Nations Conference on Environment and Development (UNCED — the Earth Summit) in 1992, which stated that an open, equitable and non-discriminatory multilateral trading system has a key contribution to make to national and international efforts to better protect and conserve environmental resources and promote sustainable development.

---

1. The report, published in the *Special Studies* series of the WTO, is authored by Hakan Nordstrom of the Economic Research and Analysis Diivision of the WTO and Scott Vaughan, formerly with the United Nations Environmental Program (UNEP), and currently with the NAFTA Commission for Environmental Cooperation. See WTO Press Release No. 140, 8 October 1999.

Among the most important recommendations of the UNCED to the GATT at the time was to implement the results of the Uruguay Round.

In its first report in 1996, the CTE recognized that trade and environment are both important areas of policy-making and that they should be mutually supportive in order to promote sustainable development. The report noted that the multilateral trading system has the capacity to further integrate environmental considerations and enhance its contribution to the promotion of sustainable development without undermining its open, equitable and non-discriminatory character.

To raise awareness of the linkages between trade, environment and sustainable development and to enhance the diàlogue between policy makers from Ministries of both trade and environment in WTO Member Governments, the WTO Secretariat has organized a series of regional seminars on trade and environment for government officials from developing and least-developed countries and countries with economies in transition.

At its most recent meeting in October 1999, the CTE agreed to hold three meetings in 2000 and to continue to deepen the analysis of all items on the work programme based on the thematic clusters of market access and the linkages between the multilateral environment and trade agendas with the objective of fulfilling the mandate of the CTE.

The Relationship between the Provisions of the Multilateral Trading System and Trade Measures for Environmental Purposes, including those Pursuant to Multilateral Environmental Agreements

A range of provisions in the WTO can accommodate the use of trade-related measures needed for environmental purposes, including measures taken pursuant to multilateral environmental agreements (MEAs). Those that are cited regularly as being of key importance are the provisions relating to non-discrimination (MFN and national treatment) and to transparency. Beyond that, and subject to certain important conditions, the exceptions clauses contained in Article XX of the GATT allow a WTO Member legitimately to place its public health and safety and national environmental goals ahead of its general obligation not to raise trade restrictions or to apply discriminatory trade measures. These provisions have been a major focus of work of the CTE and will be kept under review in the future work programme.

Trade Measures Applied Pursuant to MEAs

One area of particular focus in the CTE's discussion has been the relationship between WTO provisions and trade measures applied pursuant to MEAs. It has been clear throughout the discussions on this issue in the GATT/WTO that the preferred approach for governments to take in tackling transboundary or global environmental problems is cooperative, multilateral action under an MEA. That was the approach endorsed by political leaders at the highest level in 1992 at the UNCED, and its appeal is quite evident from the point of view of the WTO which is dedicated to finding cooperative, multilateral solutions to problems in the area of trade. In the Report which the CTE has forwarded to the Ministerial Conference, WTO Members state that the WTO supports multilateral solutions to global and transboundary environmental problems and that unilateral actions in this context should be avoided.

While some MEAs contain trade provisions, the Report notes that trade restrictions are not the only nor necessarily the most effective policy instrument to use in MEAs, but that in certain cases they can play and important role. It also states that the WTO already provides broad and valuable scope for trade measures to be applied pursuant to MEAs in a WTO-consistent manner. To date, few MEAs contain trade provisions and no problem has arisen in the WTO over the use of trade measures applied pursuant to MEAs. A number of proposals have been put forward in the CTE to broaden the scope available under WTO provisions for the use of trade measures applied pursuant to MEAs, including some that would create an "environmental window" for the use of discriminatory trade measures against non-parties to MEAs, but these proposals have not attracted consensus support in the CTE.

As in the past few years, in June 1999 the CTE held an Information Session with Secretariats of MEAs relevant to the work of the CTE to discuss the trade-related developments in these agreements. At the June Session, presentations and papers were provided by the Convention on the International Trade in Endangered Species of Wild Fauna and Flora; the Montreal Protocol on Substances that Deplete the Ozone Layer; the United Nations Framework Convention on Climate Change; the Intergovernmental Forum on Forests; and the International Tropical Timber Organization. This meeting illustrated how trade-related measures function in MEAs and helped to deepen the understanding of the relationship between MEAs and the multilateral trading system.

Dispute Settlement

A related item concerns the appropriate forum for the settlement of potential disputes that may arise over the use of trade measures pursuant to MEAs; is it the WTO, or is it the dispute settlement mechanisms that exists in the MEAs themselves? There is general agreement that in the event a dispute arises between WTO Members who are each Parties to an MEA over the use of trade measures they are applying among themselves pursuant to the MEA, they should consider in the first instance trying to resolve it through the dispute settlement mechanisms available under the MEA. Were a dispute to arise with a non-party to an MEA, however, the WTO would provide the only possible forum for the settlement of the dispute.

In the Report, WTO Members note that better policy coordination between trade and environmental policy officials at the national level can help prevent situations from arising in which the use of trade measures applied pursuant to MEAs could become subject to disputes. Furthermore, they note that problems are unlikely to arise in the WTO over trade measures agreed and applied among Parties to an MEA. In the event of a dispute, however, WTO Members are confident that the WTO dispute settlement provisions would be able to tackle any problems which arise in this area, including in cases when resort to environmental expertise is needed.

Eco-labelling

Eco-labelling programmes are important environmental policy instruments. Eco-labelling was discussed extensively in the GATT, and that laid the basis in the CTE for a detailed examination of the issues involved. The key requirement from the WTO's point of view is that environmental measures that incorporate trade provisions or that affect trade significantly do not discriminate between home-produced goods and imports, nor between imports from or exports to different trading partners. Non-discrimination is the cornerstone of secure and predictable market access and undistorted competition : it guarantees consumer choice and it gives producers access to the full range of market opportunities. Subject to that requirement being met, WTO rules place essentially no constraints on the policy choices available to a country to protect its own environment against damage either from domestic production or from the consumption of domestically produced or imported products.

The CTE Report states that well-designed eco-labelling programmes can be effective instruments of environmental policy. It notes that in certain cases they have raised significant concerns about their possible trade effects. An important starting point for addressing some of those trade concerns is by ensuring adequate transparency in their preparation, adoption and application, including affording opportunities for participation in their preparation by interested parties from other countries. Further discussion is needed on how the use in eco-labelling programmes of criteria based on non-product-related processes and production methods should be treated under the rules of the WTO Agreement on Technical Barriers to Trade.

WTO Transparency Provisions

WTO transparency provisions fulfil an important role in ensuring the proper functioning of the multilateral trading system, in helping to prevent unnecessary trade restriction and distortion from occurring, in providing information about market opportunities and in helping to avoid trade disputes from arising. They can also provide a valuable first step in ensuring that trade and environment polices are developed and implemented in a mutually supportive way. Trade-related environmental measures should not be required to meet more onerous transparency requirements than other measures that affect trade. The CTE Report states that no modifications to

WTO rules are required to ensure adequate transparency for trade-related environmental measures. The WTO Secretariat will compile from the Central Registry of Notifications all notifications of trade-related environmental measures and collate these in a single database which can be accessed by WTO Members.

The Issue of the Export of Domestically Prohibited Goods

Concerns were raised by a number of developing country GATT Contracting Parties in the mid-1980s that certain hazardous or toxic products were being exported to them without them being fully informed about the environmental or public health dangers the products could pose. In the late-1980s a GATT Working Party examined ways of treating trade in goods which are severely restricted or banned for sale on the domestic market of the exporting country. A key consideration was that the importing country should be fully informed about the products it was receiving and have the right to reject them if it felt they would cause it environmental or public health problems.

In the period since the GATT Working Party ended its discussions, several MEAs have been negotiated to deal with problems of trade in environmentally hazardous products (*e.g.* the Basel Convention and London Guidelines). The WTO does not intend to duplicate work that has already been accomplished elsewhere in the area of domestically prohibited goods.

In the CTE Report, WTO Members agree to support the efforts of the specialized inter-governmental environmental organizations that are helping to resolve the problems which exist. However, they note that there may be a complementary role for the WTO to play in this area. As an initial step, the Secretariat will survey the information already available in the WTO on trade in domestically prohibited goods.

Trade Liberalization and Sustainable Development

Further liberalization of international trade flows, both in goods and services, has a key role to play in advancing economic policy objectives in Member countries. In that respect, WTO Member countries have already made an important contribution to sustainable development and better environmental protection worldwide through the conclusion of the Uruguay Round negotiations. This contribution will steadily increase as the results of the Round move towards full implementation. The UNCED also recognized an open, non-discriminatory trading system to be a prerequisite for effective action to protect the environment and to generate sustainable development. This is based on the perspective that countries, particularly developing countries, are dependent on trade as the main source of continued growth and prosperity.

The CTE is continuing to tackle this item of its work programme in the context of the built-in agenda for further trade liberalization initiatives contained in the results of the Uruguay Round negotiations. The CTE has noted that the removal of trade restrictions and distortions, in particular high tariffs, tariff escalation, export restrictions, subsidies and non-tariff barriers, has the potential to yield benefits for both the multilateral trading system and the environment. Discussions in 1999 included the sectors of agriculture and fisheries, energy, forestry, non-ferrous metals, textiles and clothing, leather and environmental services. The discussions highlighted areas where the removal of trade restrictions and distortions can be beneficial for the environment, trade and development, providing "win-win-win" opportunities.

Trade in Services and TRIPs

The Marrakesh Decision calls for the CTE to examine the role of the WTO in relation to the links between environmental measures and the new trade agreements reached in the Uruguay Round negotiations on services and intellectual property. Discussions on these two items of the work programme have broken new ground since there was very little understanding of how the rules of the trading system might affect or be affected by environmental policies in these areas.

With respect to the General Agreement on Trade in Services (GATS) and the environment, the Report notes that discussions in the CTE have not led to the identification of any measures that Members feel may be applied for environmental purposes to services trade which are not already adequately covered by GATS provisions, in particular in Article XIV (b).

In the case of intellectual property, WTO Members state in

the CTE Report that the Agreement on Trade-Related Aspects of Intellectual Property Rights (TRIPs) plays an essential role in facilitating access to and transfer of environmentally-sound technology and products. However, they have noted that further work will be required in this area, including on clarifying the relationship between the TRIPs Agreement and the Convention of Biological Diversity.

Further Work

WTO Members believe that work in the WTO on contributing to build a constructive relationship between trade, environment and sustainable development needs to continue. The CTE is continuing its work, reporting to the WTO General Council, with the same mandate and terms of reference which were given it by Ministers in Marrakesh in 1994.

9

TEXTILES AND CLOTHING

At the end of the Uruguay Round, developing countries considered the Agreement on Textiles and Clothing (ATC), which provides for the gradual dismantling of bilateral import quotas over a ten-year period, to have been a major result in their favour. Today — at the halfway point of ATC implementation — many developing countries are calling for a decision that would accelerate trade liberalization in this sector and redress what they consider to be an imbalance in the implementation of the Uruguay Round results.

Developing countries look at textiles and clothing — exports of which amounted to $331 billion last year representing 8.3% of world trade in manufactures — as one major manufacturing sector in which they have competitive advantage. They also believe that trade success in this area would be an important step up in the industrial development ladder.

In the old GATT, the Multifibre Arrangement (MFA) governed a large portion of the exports of textiles and clothing from developing countries, to the main developed countries. Under the MFA (1974-94), developed countries were able to establish quotas on textiles and clothing outside normal GATT rules.

The ATC requires members to liberalize trade in textiles and clothing in two ways. Members must progressively bring ("integrate") all textiles and clothing products under normal WTO rules in four steps (16% in the first stage beginning in 1995, a further 17 per cent at the second stage in 1998, a further 18 per cent in the third stage in 2003 and the remaining 49% in the final stage on 1 January 2005). Members that maintain quota restrictions (Canada, the European Union, Norway and the United States), must progressively enlarge the quotas by increasing the annual growth rates by a set percentage at each stage. When the products subject to quotas are integrated, the quotas are removed.

A special safeguard mechanism protects members from damaging surges in imports during this transitional period. A quasi-judicial body — the Textiles Monitoring Body (TMB) — supervises the implementation of the ATC, including the examination of disputes.

At the review of the first stage of integration and in the preparations for Seattle, developing country textile exporters have voiced serious concerns over what they view as lack of meaningful commercial benefits for them as the major importers have opted to integrate products of less export interest to developing countries with few quotas being removed. They have also criticized new restrictions imposed by a major importer through the use of the ATC safeguards as well as other measures taken by importing countries such as anti-dumping actions and changes in country-of-origin rules.

There is also the fear that with most of the quotas being kept for the final stage, the major importers might not be able to meet their obligations. A group of developing-country exporters[1] has suggested that in the current Ministerial Conference, Ministers secure liberalization of the sector by requiring major importers, among other things, to remove half of the existing quotas by the beginning of the year 2002.

The major importing members maintain that they have been observing scrupulously the requirements of the Agreement. In turn, they have criticized a lack of market-access improvements in other members in this sector as well as cases of quota circumvention through misdeclaration at customs of where the products come from.

1. The Internationi Textiles and Clothing Bureau : Argentina, Bangladesh, Brazil, China (observer in WTO), Colombia, Costa Rica, Egypt, El Salvador, Guatemala, Honduras, India, Indonesia, Korea, Macau, Maldives, Mexico, Pakistan, Paraguay, Peru, Sir Lanka, Thailand, uruguay and Hong Kong, China.

Leading Traders in Clothing, 1998 (US$ billions)

Exporters		Importers	
1. China	30.05	1. United States	55.72
2. Hong Kong, China	22.16	2. Germany	22.35
domestic exports	9.67		
re-exports	12.50		
3. Italy	14.74	3. Japan	14.72
4. United States	8.79	4. Hong Kong, China	14.30
		retained imports	1.80
		re-exports	12.50
5. Germany	7.68	5. United Kingdom	11.98
6. Turkey	7.06	6. France	11.64
7. Mexico	6.60	7. Italy	5.86
8. France	5.75	8. Belgium-Luxembourg	5.30
9. United Kingdom	4.92	9. Netherlands	5.27
10. Korea	4.65	10. Mexico	3.75

10

AGREEMENT ON FINANCIAL SERVICES

The World Trade Organization's negotiations on financial services concluded successfully on 12 December after 70 WTO Members reached a multilateral agreement to open their financial services sectors. The landmark agreement brings trade in this sector — worth trillions of dollars — under the WTO's multilateral rules on a permanent and full most-favoured-nation basis. The agreement covers more than 95 per cent of trade in banking, insurance, securities and financial information.

WTO Director-General Mr. Renato Ruggiero said the agreement came at a critical time. "With so much of the world facing economic turbulence, negotiators from all WTO Member states have shown once again the courage and commitment to pursue the policies of liberalization which are essential to economic stability, growth and development." He added that it is through the WTO's international rules, agreed by all WTO Members, "that businesses can best gain the certainty needed to plan their future international activities."

World banking assets amounted to some US$ 40 trillion in 1994 and foreign assets of deposit banks amounted to US$ 8.6 trillion in 1995. Whereas foreign exchange turnover in the world's major foreign markets amounted to US$ 1.2 trillion in 1995, outstanding futures and options in interest rates, currencies and stock market indices amounted to US$ 10 trillion.[1] According to

1. Estimates based on data from the International Monetary Fund and the Bank of International Settlements.

the OECD, gross insurance premiums in OECD countries exceeded US$ 2 trillion in 1995.

In all, 56 governments, counting the European Communities as one, made commitments during the negotiations to either maintain or expand the market access they currently offer foreign financial service suppliers.[2] The negotiations resumed in April 1997 and were chaired by Mr. Yoshio Okubo (Japan). The results of the negotiations build on previous multilateral negotiations held at the end of the Uruguay Round (1986-1993) and in July 1995 to open financial services markets. In all, 102 WTO Members now have multilateral commitments in this sector.

The results of the latest round of talks are part of a protocol which will be open for governments to accept until 29 January 1999. The agreement will enter into force on 1 March 1999 at the latest.

AGREEMENT ON FINANCIAL SERVICES

This landmark agreement comes at a critical time. With so much of the world facing economic turbulence, negotiators from all our members states have shown once again the courage and commitment to pursue the policies of liberalization which are essential to economic stability, growth and development.

Nations representing over 95% of the trade in banking, insurance, securities and financial information have brought financial services into the realm of international rules. It is through these international rules, agreed by all WTO members, that businesses can best gain the certainty needed to plan their future international activities.

A study by economists from the WTO Secretariat discusses

2. Australia; Bahrain; Bolivia; Brazil; Bulgaria; Canada; Chile; Colombia; Costa Rica; Cyprus; Czech Republic; the Dominican Republic; Ecuador; Egypt; El Salvador; the European Communities (15 members); Ghana; Honduras; Hong Kong, China; Hungary; Iceland; India; Indonesia; Israel; Jamaica; Japan; Kenya; Korea; Kuwait; Macau; Malaysia; Malta; Mauritius; Mexico; New Zealand; Nicaragua; Nigeria; Norway; Pakistan; Peru; Philippines; Poland; Romania; Senegal; Singapore; Slovak Republic; Slovenia; South Africa; Sri Lanka; Switzerland; Thailand; Tunisia; Turkey; the United States; Uruguay and Venezuela.

the benefits and challenges related to the liberalization of financial services trade in both developing and developed countries. The study highlights the importance of international competition in banking, securities and insurance markets while acknowledging the critical need for preserving prudential policies to safeguard financial systems for the benefit of investors and consumers.

The study, "Open Markets in Financial Services and the Role of the GATS" explains that trade liberalization in this sector will :

— enhance competition and improve sectoral efficiency, leading to lower costs, better quality, and more choice of financial services;

— improve financial intermediation and investment opportunities through better resource allocation across sectors, countries and time, and through better means of managing risks and absorbing shocks; and

— induce governments to improve macroeconomic management, domestic policy interventions in credit markets, and financial sector regulation and supervision.

Liberalization of financial services can have strong positive effects on income and growth. Developed and developing countries with open financial sectors have typically grown faster than those with closed regimes. The economic success of Hong Kong (China) and Singapore has been greatly facilitated by internationally-oriented financial service sectors. Many developing countries such as Argentina, Brazil, Ghana, Hungary, Indonesia, and Pakistan have become increasingly integrated in the world's financial markets.

The financial services sector has expanded rapidly in recent years. The study notes that employment increased by 25 to 50 per cent in a number of industrialized countries since 1970 and now represents 3 to 5 per cent of total employment. Value-added in the financial service sector has also grown considerably over the past 25 years and now reaches between 7 and 13 per cent of GDP in Hong Kong (China), Singapore, Switzerland, and the United States.

Financial service sector growth reflects the rise in international financial market activities. Lending and securities trading, and derivative markets have experienced rapid growth in the past 10 years, with many developing and transition economies also benefitting from improved international market access. Foreign ownership of banking assets, an indicator of commercial presence in this sector approaches 20 per cent in the United States, Argentina and Chile. Consequently, the study says, cross-border trade in financial services more than tripled between 1985 and 1995 and now exceeds US$ 50 billion for the most important trading countries. Data for the United States suggests that trade via commercial presence in foreign markets is even more important than cross-border trade.

The study identifies a number of challenges which must be met if countries are to reap the full benefits from trade liberalization in the financial services sector. It states that "macroeconomic stability, structural policies which minimize distortionary interventions in the financial sector and prudential regulation and supervision" must underpin the benefits of liberalization. The study notes that there is no universally applicable liberalization strategy and that the specific circumstances of each country should be taken into consideration.

The study stresses that maintaining the stability and security of the financial services system is of paramount importance. The authors point out that the General Agreement on Trade in Services (GATS) allows WTO Members to take prudential measures to protect investors and to ensure the integrity and stability of their domestic financial systems. It also permits the use of temporary non-discriminatory restrictions on balance-of-payments and transfers in the event of serious balance-of-payments and external financial difficulties. Moreover, the management of monetary and exchange rate policy falls outside the scope of the GATS.

In its overall assessment concerning the benefits of trade liberalization and the challenges for Member governments, the study states : "The benefits from participating in the multilateral negotiating process under the GATS, through market access and national treatment commitments, can accrue to countries without in any way compromising their ability to pursue sound macroeconomic and regulatory policies." Indeed, notes the study, "there are circumstances where forward commitment to liberalization may help to support the development of better macroeconomic and regulatory policies."

11

NEW ISSUES BEFORE WTO

TRADE AND LABOUR STANDARDS

For several years the issue of trade and core labour standards has been the subject of intense debate among and within some World Trade Organization member governments. Labour unions in the U.S. and other industrialised countries are concerned that free trade will lead to migration of jobs to the developing countries as transnational corporations shift production to countries where wages are low and trade unions lack the legal right to fight for better pay and working conditions.

Currently, labour standards are not subject to WTO rules and disciplines. But some WTO member governments in Europe and North America believe that the issue must be taken up by the WTO in some form if public confidence in the WTO and the global trading system is to be strengthened. These member governments argue that the rights such as: the freedom to bargain collectively, freedom of association, elimination of discrimination in the workplace and the elimination workplace abuse (including forced labour and certain types of child labour), are matters for consideration in the WTO. Several member governments have suggested that the issue be brought into the WTO through the formation of a working group to study the issue of trade and core labour standards. Bringing the matter to the WTO, these member governments believe, will provide incentives for WTO member governments to improve conditions for workers around the world.

This proposal is among the most controversial currently before the WTO. Most developing countries and many developed nations believe the issue of core labour standards does not belong in the WTO. These member governments see the issue of trade and labour standards as a guise for protectionism in developed-country markets. Developing-country officials have said that efforts to bring labour standards into the WTO represent a smokescreen for undermining the comparative advantage of lower-wage developing countries.

Many officials in developing countries argue that better working conditions and improved labour rights arise through economic growth. They say that if the issue of core labour standards became enforceable under WTO rules, any sanctions imposed against countries with lower labour standards would merely perpetuate poverty and delay improvements in workplace standards. The more developing countries are allowed to export, the more prosperous they will grow and this will automatically raise labour standards.

The issue of trade and labour standards has been with the WTO since its birth. At the Ministerial Conference of the General Agreement on Tariffs and Trade held in Marrakesh in April 1994 to sign the treaty that formed the WTO, nearly all ministers expressed a point of view on the issue. The Chairman of that conference concluded there was no consensus among member governments at the time, and thus no basis for agreement on the issue.

At the first WTO Ministerial Conference in Singapore in December 1996 the issue was taken up and addressed in the Ministerial Declaration. At Singapore, Ministers stated :

"We renew our commitment to the observance of internationally recognized core labour standards. The International Labour Organization (ILO) is the competent body to set and deal with these standards, and we affirm our support for its work in promoting them. We believe that economic growth and development fostered by increased trade and further trade liberalization contribute to the promotion of these standards. We reject the use of labour standards for protectionist purposes, and agree that the comparative advantage of countries, particularly low-wage developing countries, must in no way be put into question. In this regard, we note that the WTO and ILO Secretariats will continue their existing collaboration."

Since taking office in September 1999, WTO Director-General Mike Moore, has met twice with ILO Director-General Juan Somavia. Mr. Moore has said he looks forward to co-operating with Mr. Somavia and other officials from the ILO. He has also been clear that the WTO will be guided by Ministers on the issue of trade and core labour standards.

Existing collaboration between the WTO and the ILO includes participation by the WTO in meetings of ILO bodies, the exchange of documentation and informal cooperation between the ILO and WTO Secretariats.

Since the Singapore Ministerial Conference, the ILO has taken two significant steps in addressing the issue of workers' rights. In 1998, ILO member governments adopted the ILO Declaration on Fundamental Principles and Rights at Work and its Follow-up. Under this declaration, ILO member governments endorsed some basic principles which are included in the core ILO Conventions. (These conventions are the fundamental workplace rights including: freedom of association and recognition of the right to collective bargaining; elimination of all forms of forced labour; the effective abolition of child labour and the elimination of discrimination in hiring and employment practices.)

ILO Member Governments agreed to respect and promote these Core Conventions even if they have not ratified all of them. As a follow-up, the ILO will issue annual reports[1] in which ILO officials will obtain information from governments which have not ratified all of the conventions on any changes that may have taken place in national laws or regulations and which may impact these fundamental labour rights.

If countries like the U.S. are genuinely concerned about the welfare in Asia, Africa and Latin America, they should make a beginning by ensuring that their own TNCs adhere to ethical and

1. The Follow-Up to the ILO Declaration provides for two things : (1) annual reports, which will contain the sort of information described in the above paragraph and (2) the Global Report which is designed to provide, every four years, "a dynamic global picture relating to each category of fundamental principles and rights..." The purpose of the Global Report is to help provide assessment of the need for technical co-operation in improving labour standards.

equitable employment practices. Secondly, these countries should abandon their highly restrictive and protectionist approach towards the free flow of labour. The best way of improving labour standards would be to allow workers from the developing world free access to 'first world' labour markets. Just as capital should be free to go wherever rate of return is the highest, labour should be free to go wherever wages are the highest. Unless the United States is prepared to agree to free mobility of workers across international borders, its concern for labour rights is simply a humbug.

The demonstrators at Seattle claimed WTO promoted a form of globalisation where greedy multinationals maximised profits by shifting factories to poor countries. They pointed out that this took away jobs, investment and production unfairly from the west. They claimed, simultaneously, that the process impoverished and exploited poor countries.

Both these criticisms are absurd. If globalisation is robbing it of the jobs and production, how is it that the united states to-day has the lowest unemployment and highest growth rate for decades.

Most of the imports from the developing countries are labour-intensive and there is certainly a risk of barriers to such imports on the pretext of non-adoption of labour standards. The developing countries should strongly resist this and take the position that issues related to labour should be raised in the appropriate forum of the International Labour Organisation (ILO).

Child Labour

The ILO convention on elimination of the worst forms of child labour protects children under 18 from slavery and similar practices, prostitution and pornography, illicit activities such as drug production and trafficking, and work likely to harm the health, safety, or morals of children.

Ostensively referring to India, Mr. Clinton strongly criticised the practice of child abuse. He was categorical that the developing countries would have to agree to the setting up of a working group on trade and labour. The U.S. side even hinted at imposition of sanctions on the child labour issue. It threatened to take this step if the developing countries did not implement the ILO convention.

Mr. Clinton, in a rejoinder to the stand of India and some other developing countries on child labour, said : "To deny the importance of the issue of child labour in a global economy is to deny the dignity of work. The belief that honest labour fairly compensated gives meaning and structure to our lives. I hope we can affirm these values at this meeting."

The U.S. President observed : "The answer is not to just throw away the issue. The answer is to write the rules in such a way that people in our position, the wealthy countries, can not use this as an instrument of protectionism. We can find a way to do this."

Child labour is a fact of life in developing countries, as it was in western countries till quite recently. The United States abolished child labour only in 1938. The developing countries do not like child labour but it is an inescapable product of poverty.

International studies show that child labour drops sharply with the rise in country's income because the rise in parent's income enables them to send children to school. The best way to eliminate child labour is to implement trade and investment policies which raise incomes in the poor countries. A western law on garment or carpets made by children will not put these children into school. Instead it will push them in other industries where working conditions are worse or into prostitution.

INFORMATION TECHNOLOGY PRODUCTS

A WTO agreement is helping push the information technology revolution forward. Beginning in 2000, most of the world trade in information technology products (worth $680 billion last year for office and telecom equipment, a large part of which are IT products) will be completely free of tariffs under the WTO Information Technology Agreement (ITA), which has been reducing customs duties on IT products such as computers and telecom equipment since 1997, and benefiting offices and consumers across the globe through lower prices.

From the 29 participants that negotiated the ITA during

WTO's first Ministerial Conference in Singapore in December 1996, membership has now risen to 51 that account for 93% of world trade in IT products. The new participants include many developing countries, transition economies and even governments currently negotiating their WTO membership. At an IT symposium organized by the WTO Secretariat in July, several industry representatives attested to the dynamic role of information technology in promoting economic growth in developing countries.

Participation in the ITA means that the country must eliminate tariffs and all other duties and charges on covered IT imports from all WTO members by 1 January 2000. Some participants have been granted longer implementation periods for a few products. The agreement lists in two annexes the products covered, which can be grouped into the following six categories : computers, software, telecom equipment, semiconductors, semiconductor manufacturing equipment and scientific instruments.

Talks on expanding the product coverage (or "ITA II") began in 1997 when participants began proposing additional IT products for tariff elimination. Negotiations intensified in 1998 when some participants tabled a joint ITA II list. The talks, however, failed to produce an ITA II list acceptable to all participants. One point of contention was the proposed addition of certain electronic consumer goods that are also used with computer products.

Consultations among delegations on ITA II continued informally this year although there had been no formal discussions on this subject in the ITA Committee. Several participants — in the preparatory process for the Ministerial Conference — have proposed concluding an ITA II deal in Seattle.

The current ITA deals only with the elimination of tariffs and not with other trade barriers. At the IT symposium, industry representatives complained that different national safety standards and import licensing requirements have resulted in additional shipment costs — through delays and additional paperwork — that have reduced the benefits of ITA tariff cuts. In the ITA Committee, participants have agreed to examine non-tariff barriers.

Leading Traders in Office and Telecom Equipment, 1998
(US$ billions)

Exporters		Importers	
1. United States	113.89	1. United States	155.91
2. Japan	86.03	2. United Kingdom	47.44
3. Singapore	57.60	3. Germany	45.82
4. United Kingdom	43.25	4. Hong Kong, China	43.03
5. Chinese Taipei	38.44	5. Singapore	37.21
6. Hong Kong, China	36.63	6. Japan	36.55
7. Malaysia	34.61	7. Netherlands	31.73
8. Germany	34.21	8. France	30.93
9. Korea	31.82	9. Chinese Taipei	23.79
10. Netherlands	30.36	10. Canada	22.69

TRADE AND INVESTMENT

Since 1997, WTO members have been engaged in analysis and debate about the relationship between international trade and investment, and its implications for economic growth and development. In the Working Group on the Relationship between Trade and Investment, members have examined a range of international investment instruments and existing agreements, and have debated the possible pros and cons of negotiating a multilateral framework of investment rules in the WTO. UNCTAD has played an important role in this analytical process, particularly in helping WTO delegations better understand the development dimension of this subject.

In the preparatory process leading up to the Ministerial Conference, eight separate, and very similar, proposals have been tabled by 29 WTO members recommending that a decision be taken by Ministers in Seattle to begin negotiating a WTO agreement on foreign direct investment (FDI).

These members have made it clear that the agreement they are proposing to negotiate in the WTO bears no relationship to the OECD's Multilateral Agreement on Investment — in the

WTO, negotiations would start from a blank sheet of paper. Their proposals have attracted support from a number of other WTO members, both developed and developing.

At the same time, some other WTO members — developed and developing — have made it clear that they are opposed to a negotiation on this subject in the WTO, at least for the time being. They prefer to continue with the analysis and debate that was begun in 1997.

The key elements of the proposals tabled so far are that :

- Negotiations would cover FDI only;
- Development provisions would be central to the framework of rules and disciplines, which otherwise would be based on similar WTO principles such as transparency and non-discrimination;
- The ability of host governments to regulate the activity of investors should be respected;
- Trade-distorting and investment-distorting policies and practices should be addressed, through suitable disciplines;
- Commitments on access to investment opportunities in host countries should be negotiated "bottom-up" (similar to the approach used in the General Agreement on Trade in Services); and
- WTO dispute settlement rules should apply, but only to government-to-government disputes.

The question of how to treat investors' responsibilities, and investment protection, has also been placed on the table for consideration in a negotiation, if one is launched.

TRADE AND COMPETITION POLICY

As government barriers to trade and investment have been reduced, there have been increasing concerns that the gains from such liberalization may be thwarted by private anti-competitive practices. There is also a growing realization that mutually supportive trade and competition policies can contribute to sound economic development, and that effective competition policies help to ensure that the benefits of liberalization and market-based reforms flow through to all citizens.

Approximately 80 WTO Member countries, including some 50 developing and transition countries, have adopted competition laws, also known as "antitrust" or "anti-monopoly" laws. Typically, these laws provide remedies to deal with a range of anti-competitive practices, including price fixing and other cartel arrangements, abuses of a dominant position or monopolization, mergers that limit competition, and agreements between suppliers and distributors ("vertical agreements") that foreclose markets to new competitors. The concept of competition "policy" includes competition laws in addition to other measures aimed at promoting competition in the national economy, such as sectoral regulations and privatization policies.

The WTO Working Group on the Interaction between Trade and Competition Policy (WGTCP) was established at the Singapore Ministerial Conference in December 1996 to consider issues raised by Members relating to the interaction of these two policy fields. Since its initial meeting in July 1997, the Group has examined a wide range of such issues. The approximately 125 submissions received by the Working Group from Members thus far attest to the keen interest that has been shown by Members in the subject.

In 1997 and 1998, the work of the WTO Working Group was organized around a Checklist of Issues Suggested For Study which was developed at the first meeting of the Group. In particular, the work focused on the following main elements of the Checklist :

- The relationship between the objectives, principles, concepts, scope and instruments of trade and competition policy; and their relationship to development and economic growth.
- Stocktaking and analysis of existing instruments, standards and activities regarding trade and competition policy, including of experience with their application.
- The interaction between trade and competition policy,

including consideration of the following sub-elements :

* the impact of anti-competitive practices of enterprises and associations on international trade;
* the impact of state monopolies, exclusive rights and regulatory policies on competition and international trade;
* the relationship between the trade-related aspects of intellectual property rights and competition policy;
* the relationship between investment and competition policy;
* the impact of trade policy on competition.

A detailed Report on the Group's deliberations on the above matters was issued in December 1998. The Report documents views expressed by Members regarding matters such as the mutually supportive relationship between trade liberalization and competition policy, the categories of anti-competitive practices that can impact adversely on international trade and investment and the potential contributions of competition policies to economic development. In addition, since 1997 the WTO has organized, in cooperation with UNCTAD and the World Bank, four Symposia on issues related to the work of the Working Group.

Pursuant to a decision by the General Council of the WTO, the Working Group examined in 1999 three further topics :

(i) the relevance of the fundamental WTO principles of national treatment, transparency, and most-favoured-nation treatment to competition policy and vice versa;

(ii) approaches to promoting cooperation and communication among Members, including in the field of technical cooperation; and

(iii) the contribution of competition policy to achieving the objectives of the WTO, including the promotion of international trade.

While the relevance of WTO principles to competition policy and the need for enhanced cooperation among Members in addressing anti-competitive practices were affirmed by a number of Members, views differed as to the need for action at the level of the WTO to enhance the relevance of competition policy to the multilateral trading system. In particular, while a number of Members expressed support for the development of a multilateral framework on competition policy in the WTO, to support the implementation of effective competition policies by Member countries and reduce the potential for conflicts in this area, others questioned the desirability of such a framework and favoured bilateral and/or regional approaches to cooperation in this field.

The question of the desirability of developing a multilateral framework on competition policy will now be taken up at the Ministerial Conference. In the preparations for the Conference, a number of Members have renewed the call for a WTO framework to support the implementation of effective national competition policies by Members and enhance the overall contribution of competition policy to the multilateral trading system while other Members have expressed continuing objections to negotiations on this matter.

TRADE FACILITATION

The issue of trade facilitation brings the WTO right to the customs' gate. Traders from both developing and developed countries have long pointed to the vast amount of red tape that still exists in moving goods across borders. Documentation requirements often lack transparency and are vastly duplicative in many places, a problem often compounded by a lack of cooperation between traders and official agencies. Despite advances in information technology, automatic data submission is still not commonplace.

UNCTAD estimates that the average customs transaction involves 20-30 different parties, 40 documents, 200 data elements (30 of which are repeated at least 30 times) and the re-keying of 60-70% of all data at least once. With the lowering of tariffs across the globe, the cost of complying with customs formalities has been reported to exceed in many instances the cost of duties to be paid. In the modern business environment of just-in-time production and delivery, traders need fast and predictable release of goods. An APEC study estimated that trade facilitation programs would generate gains of about 0.26 percent of real GDP to APEC, almost double the expected gains from tariff liberalization, and that the savings in import prices would be between 1-2% of import prices for developing countries in the region.

Analysts point out that the reason why many small and medium size enterprises — who as a whole account in many economies for up to 60% of GDP creation — are not active players in international trade, has more to do with red tape rather than tariff barriers. The administrative barriers for enterprises who do not regularly ship large quantities are often simply too high to make foreign markets appear attractive.

For developing country economies, inefficiencies in areas such as customs and transport can be roadblocks to the integration into the global economy and may severely impair export competitiveness or inflow of foreign direct investment. Trade facilitation will not only benefit importers and consumers who face higher prices caused by the red tape in their own import administration, but exporters as well. Developing country exporters are increasingly interested in removing administrative barriers in other developing countries, which today account for 40% of their trade in manufactured goods.

WTO rules comprise a variety of provisions that aim to enhance transparency and set minimum procedural standards in aspects of trade administration, such as Articles VIII and X of the GATT 1994, and the Agreements on Import Licensing, Technical Barriers to Trade, or SPS. Yet the WTO has no specific provisions on customs and border-crossing procedures, except in the Agreement on Customs Valuation. Article VIII of the GATT 1994 merely recognizes the need for minimizing the incidence and complexity of import and export formalities and related documentation requirements.

Trade facilitation was added to the WTO agenda at the Singapore Ministerial Conference in 1996, when Ministers requested the Council for Trade in Goods to undertake a work programme to assess the scope for WTO rules concerning the simplification of trade procedures.

In the Goods Council, delegations agree that simplification of trade procedures can result in considerable savings in time, money and human resources that would benefit each and every economy. Some delegations have emphasized that automation and the use of information technology would not only cut down on paperwork but also increase the efficiency of customs administrations. One member reported that its introduction of an automated customs clearance system had reduced clearance times for sea cargo from an average of 26.1 hours to 5.6 hours, and for air cargo from 2.3 to 0.7 hours. Another member reported that allowing importers to fill in customs papers electronically had reduced the completion time of all information requirements to within 15-30 minutes.

A number of delegations favour a WTO agreement on trade facilitation aimed at reducing administrative barriers on import and export transactions in order to expedite the passage and release of goods. They say such an agreement would back up customs reform and modernization efforts of members and ensure that the same principles are applied all over the world. The EC, US, Korea and Switzerland have in fact proposed the launching of negotiations towards such an agreement.

While agreeing on the benefits of trade facilitation, a number of other delegations question the need for a binding WTO agreement in this area subject to dispute-settlement rules. They say that such an agreement will add further to implementation burdens of developing countries, which lack resources to modernize customs facilities. Instead, they have called for a comprehensive technical assistance programme in trade facilitation, and encourage ongoing work in this area in various WTO bodies — such as the completion of the harmonisation negotiations in rules of origin — and in other international organizations, such as the World Customs Organization.

ELECTRONIC COMMERCE

The growing importance of electronic commerce in global trade led the Members of the WTO to adopt a declaration on global electronic commerce on 20 May 1998 at their second Ministerial Conference in Geneva, Switzerland. The declaration directed the General Council of the WTO to establish a comprehensive work programme to examine all trade-related issues arising from electronic commerce, and to present a report on the progress of the work programme at the third Ministerial Conference of the WTO.

The declaration setting up the work programme included the statement that "Members will continue their current practice of not imposing customs duties on electronic commerce". A work programme on electronic commerce was adopted by the General Council on 25 September 1998 under which issues related to electronic commerce would be examined by the Council for Trade in Services, the Council for Trade in Goods, the Council for TRIPS and the Committee on Trade and Development.

Each of these bodies produced a report for the General Council at the end of July 1999. The following is a summary of the main points which emerge from the reports to the General Council :

- WTO Members Governments identified three types of transactions on the Internet :
  - * Transactions for a service which is completed entirely on the Internet from selection to purchase and delivery.
  - * Transactions involving "distribution services" in which a product, whether a good or a service, is selected and purchased on-line but delivered by conventional means.
  - * Transactions involving the telecommunication transport function, including provision of Internet services.
- The general view of Member Governments of the WTO is that the vast majority of transactions on the Internet are services which are covered by the General Agreement on Trade in Services (GATS).
- WTO Member Governments hold the general view that the GATS does not distinguish between technological means of delivery.
- The general view of Member Governments is that all

the provisions of the GATS apply to trade in services through electronic means.

- There is a disagreement on the classification of a small number of products made available on the Internet, as to whether or not they are services or goods. This disagreement is on products such as books and software. Whereas a printed book delivered through conventional means is classified as a good, there are Member Governments of the WTO who hold the view that the digital version of the text of such a book is a service which should be covered by the GATS. Other Member Governments hold the view that such a product remains a good which is subject to customs duties and other provisions of the GATT Agreement. There are also those who think that such a product constitutes a third category of products which are neither goods nor services and for which special provisions need to be devised.
- Questions are raised about how the Telecommunications annex of the GATS should relate to access to and use of Internet access services. Many Internet service providers (ISPs) and services may benefit from the Annex provisions ensuring fair and reasonable access to the leased circuits they obtain from pubic telecom operators. But some Member Governments wonder if, or to what extent, ISPs themselves should be obliged by the Annex to offer such access to others.

12

THE WTO AGREEMENTS AND DEVELOPING COUNTRIES

Introduction

The agreements that emerged from the 1986-94 Uruguay Round — the WTO's agreements — are now five years old and a new round of negotiations has been launched. However, five years after the agreements took effect, developing countries still experience difficulties with their implementation.

On the one hand, developing countries lack the financial and human resources to fulfil their commitments such as the complex requirements of the intellectual property (TRIPS) agreement. On the other hand, they say developed countries have failed to implement the agreements in a way that would benefit developing countries' trade.

Special and differential (S&D) provisions are included in all the WTO agreements. There are two broad categories :

(a) more flexible terms within specified time limits : for example, longer transition periods, smaller commitments (for example the commitments on agriculture); and

(b) clauses which say in broad terms that developed countries should help developing countries in specific areas (such as technology transfer under intellectual property protection) but without defining exactly what action is needed.

In other words, the provisions are designed both to help developing countries implement the agreements and to accentuate the benefits they might enjoy. However, five years later, developing countries feel that these provisions have not served their purpose. They argue that the more specific S&D provisions of category (a) are usually insufficient and that the broader requirements of category (b) are too vague and often ignored.

For this reason, the issue of implementation promises to be prominent in the present round of negotiations. Developing countries are eager to see the Ministerial Declaration include language to correct perceived oversights in the Uruguay Round texts. Indeed, many developing countries argue that they are owed this redressal of the Uruguay Round's results before a new round can start. To cite Senior Vice President and Chief Economist of the World Bank "As developing countries take steps to open their economies and expand their exports, in too many sectors they find themselves confronting significant trade barriers — leaving them, in effect, with neither aid nor trade. They quickly run up against dumping duties, when no economist would say they are really engaged in dumping, or they face protected or restricted markets in their areas of natural comparative advantage, like agriculture or textiles."

Compliance with Uruguay Round Requirements

In their proposals to the General Council, developing countries have identified several difficulties they face in implementing the WTO agreements. Most frequently mentioned are the following :

Intellectual Property

All developing countries, except the least developed, have to implement the Trade-Related Aspects of Intellectual Property Rights (TRIPS) Agreement by 1 January 2000. (Least-developed countries have until 1 January 2006.) For most, this means amended or new intellectual property legislation and new or more effective means of enforcement.

Many developing countries argue that five years is not enough for such a radical change and have proposed that this transition period be extended. Some say that the five year implementation period granted to them was chosen haphazardly rather than on the basis of their level of development. These countries say they should be allowed to apply different degrees of intellectual property protection, depending on the level of development.

Others envisage the inclusion in the TRIPS Agreement of additional commitments, for example in relation to the transfer of technology and the protection of geographical indications.

Trade-related Investment Measures

The Trade-Related Investment Measures (TRIMS) Agreement deals with policies that are considered inconsistent with GATT. An illustrative list includes such measures as minimum local content and trade balancing requirements. Developing countries have to eliminate inconsistent measures by 1 January 2000, least-developed countries by 1 January 2002.

Again, developing countries say there is too little time for too many changes. They would also like to retain the flexibility to choose investment promotion policies that they consider necessary to fulfil their developmental needs, including some of those listed as inconsistent with GATT.

Furthermore, some developing countries say they missed the boat : they were unable to notify some of their investment measures in time (they had to do this immediately) and they cannot now apply these measures.

Sanitary and Phytosanitary Measures and Technical Barriers to Trade

Sanitary and phytosanitary (SPS) measures deal with animal and plant health and safety, and food safety. The Technical Barriers to Trade (TBT) Agreement deals with other technical standards. Both agreements say that members have to take into account the special needs of developing countries when they prepare these regulations. However, developing countries feel they are excluded from the creation of international standards and are often expected to comply with standards that go beyond their technical ability or financial capacity.

Environment

The environmental lobby from the west has been raising its voice against the damage to the environment by poor countries in their efforts to increase their exports. They point out that the increase in exports has been at the cost of environmental degradation.

Developing countries like India have strongly opposed the inclusion of environmental standards in the agenda of WTO because it is viewed as a tool by the rich countries to create non-tariff barriers to trade.

The rich countries remain the world's biggest polluters in terms of the chemicals and gases they release into the atmosphere and the garbage they throw out every day.

The rich countries have enforced strict environmental protection standards on their own industries as a result of which many multinational corporations have had to shift their production bases to poorer countries which do not have such high environmental standards. Many industries like leather tanning have been banned in the rich countries because of their polluting effect on the environment through the discharge of effluents. NGOs from developing countries have been protesting against this aspect of globalisation in which the rich countries are transferring their polluting industries to the poor.

Improved Market Access for Developing Countries' Exports

Developing countries say market access has not met expectations for their exports in two areas : agriculture and textiles. They recognize that the letter of the agreements has not been violated, but they feel that the spirit of these agreements has not been honoured.

Agriculture

Developing countries' complaints focus on some extremely high tariffs, tariff escalation (higher tariffs on processed goods than on raw materials, which penalizes processing in exporting countries), the difficulties in gaining access to markets through tariff quotas and the trade-distorting effects of subsidies. They are calling for lower barriers on agricultural goods that they export.

Textiles and Clothing

The WTO's Agreement on Textiles and Clothing does two things. Over a 10-year period, it integrates the sector into GATT rules, and as part of that process it phases out quotas. Developing countries complain that although 33 per cent of trade has been integrated as committed, only a few quotas have actually been removed. They add that what little market access has resulted from the implementation of the agreement has been cancelled out by measures taken by the importing countries, such as transitional safeguards, anti-dumping actions and discriminatory rules of origin.

The provisions relating to special and differential treatment of developing countries, which have largely consisted of longer transition periods and technical assistance, are inadequate and insufficient. In fact, such meagre palliatives do not address the needs and aspirations of developing countries which the multilateral system must address.

The WTO discipline should allow sufficient freedom and flexibility to the developing countries to persue their development strategies and must make a distinction between developed and developing countries where such a distinction is warranted. The Human Development Report 1999 has very well documented the increasing inequality between countries even in this decade. For instance by the late 1990s, a fifth of world's people living in the highest income countries had 82 per cent of the world export market while the bottom fifth, just one per cent. Steps need to be taken to close these widening gaps. World Bank economist J. Michael Finger has calculated that import restrictions by developed nations reduce their national incomes by about twice the amount they received in foreign aid.

Possible Outcome from Present Round of Negotiations

Several developing countries have submitted specific wish-lists to the WTO General Council. These include :

- the creation of a working group to look at implementation issues
- converting all S&D provisions into concrete commitments
- tighter restrictions on the use of anti-dumping measures
- allowing developing countries more flexibility in applying food, animal and plant health and safety (SPS) measures to their products

- enabling developing countries to participate more in bodies which set food safety and technical standards
- speeding up the integration of textiles and clothing products into GATT rules
- allowing developing countries more time and greater flexibility to implement the agreements on investment measures (TRIMs) and intellectual property (TRIPS)
- allowing developing countries greater flexibility to subsidize agriculture
- tighter restrictions in the use of subsidies by developed countries in agriculture

LEAST-DEVELOPED COUNTRIES

The elimination of all barriers to imports from the least-developed countries (LDCs) is among the top priorities outlined for the present round of negotiations by World Trade Organization Director-General Mike Moore.

Since his first day in office, 1 September 1999, Mr. Moore has called on WTO member governments to do away with tariffs and quotas on products from the LDCs.

"Taken together, least-developed countries constitute only half of one percent of world trade. Removing barriers to trade from these countries poses no serious threat to anyone, but it does provide some of the poorest people on earth with the gift of opportunity that is vital to their future growth and development," Mr. Moore said.

Mr. Moore would like to see Ministers agree to eliminate barriers to LDC products as an opening move of importance at the Conference, which may launch a new round of trade negotiations which are expected to last several years.

The notion of removing barriers to imports from LDCs was previously introduced by former WTO Director-General Renato Ruggiero in July 1996 at the Group of Eight Summit in Lyon, France. In December of that year Ministers from Member Governments agreed at the first WTO Ministerial Conference in Singapore to adopt a Comprehensive and Integrated Plan of Action for LDCs.

One result of that initiative was a high-level meeting for LDCs in Geneva in October 1997. At that meeting, Canada, Egypt, the European Union, Mauritius, Switzerland, Turkey and the United States provided formal notification of their intention to improve access to their markets for the LDC imports. The meeting also led to the creation of the Integrated Framework for Trade-Related Technical Assistance for the LDCs.

For the first time, the Secretariats of the WTO, UNCTAD, the World Bank, the International Monetary Fund, the United Nations Development Programme and the International Trade Centre, combined forces to begin efforts aimed at bringing the LDCs in from the sidelines of the multilateral trading system. The idea of the Integrated Framework is to provide a needs-driven, coordinated response to the problems that LDCs have faced in taking full advantage of the global trading system.

To date, more than 40 LDC countries have submitted needs assessments and the six agencies have responded with co-ordinated responses for action. These needs range from addressing insufficient capacity for producing competitive products, to improvements in transportation and telecommunications infrastructure, to assistance in establishing the legal and institutional framework to better comply with WTO rules and obligations and maximize benefits that arise from participating in the global trading system.

While the Integrated Framework has brought the issue of LDC marginalization from the trading system to the attention of all WTO member governments, many such governments believe that the process requires a fresh political commitment if it is adequately to address the LDC concerns.

In December 1998, Amb. Iftekhar Ahmed Chowdhury of Bangladesh, speaking on behalf of the 29 LDC governments which are members of the WTO, proposed a Comprehensive New Plan of Action as a means of injecting momentum into efforts to assist the LDCs. In this proposal, Amb. Chowdhury called for the improvement of certain WTO agreements including the agreement on Trade-Related Aspects of Intellectual Property Rights (TRIPS) and for easier LDC access to the Dispute Settlement System.

He also called on Ministers in Seattle to :

- follow through on commitments made at the second WTO Ministerial Conference in Geneva in 1998 to "continue to improve market-access conditions for products exported by the Least Developed Countries on as broad and liberal a basis as possible";
- accelerate accession procedures for LDC candidates for WTO membership;
- push for reductions in the LDC debt burden;
- work with other organizations to improve supply-side capacity in LDCs.

Several WTO member governments have proposed improving market access for LDCs as part of their list of proposals for the present round of negotiations, including the European Union. Other member governments, including the United States, have taken steps to unilaterally reduce barriers to imports from these countries.

Mr. Moore has welcomed these efforts and called on Ministers to agree in Seattle to expand upon these and other programmes of support for the poorest countries. The Director-General is also seeking to have the WTO's core budget for technical assistance expanded from SF 716,000 to SF 10 million over the next three years so that developing countries, and particularly the LDCs, can more effectively participate in the new negotiations. Currently, about 90% of WTO technical assistance activity is paid for through trust funds donated by member governments.

While acknowledging that trade and the WTO alone cannot provide all the answers to the deep economic difficulties of least developed countries, Mr. Moore said through closer coherence with other international organizations, including the five partner organizations of the Integrated Framework, the international community can and must make an important contribution to raising living standards of families in the world's poorest countries.

13

FAILURE OF SEATTLE CONFERENCE

The formal opening of the WTO Ministerial Conference was delayed as thousands of labour and environment activists took to streets and blocked all arterial roads leading to the convention centre despite heavy security. This was to protest the WTO's failure to address to these issues. President Clinton pandered to his trade unions and NGOs at the expense of MNCs. The U.S. presidential race is on, and Clinton wanted to get labour and NGO support for Al Gore, the leading Democratic candidate.

The process was dominated by the United States, European Union and Japan. A majority of the WTO members comprising developing countries of Africa, Latin America and the Caribbeans bitterly complained of their being excluded from the process of discussion as 25 or so powerful countries monopolised the deliberations.

The chairperson of the conference, Ms. Charlene Barshefsky, who is also U.S. Trade Representative, virtually hijacked the process of negotiations at the Seattle meet and her strongarm tactics invited volatile reactions from many of the Trade Ministers participating in the discussions. In fact she was quite candid in admitting that she was constantly in touch with the White House during the day and before taking the decision to suspend the conference, she had spoken to the U.S. President. She told a press conference that the 135 nation-members were chasing too many complex issues in too short a time.

Never in the history of this global body had there been so may walkouts from meetings. A majority of the members came out with a statement, expressing their profound disagreement, anger and disappointment with the Seattle process.

Earlier there were charges of contrived consensus against the WTO leadership, but never before had the developing countries shown such solidarity against the lack of transparency in the deliberations and changes in the draft document. Trade Ministers of Latin America and Caribbean countries said that so long as the conditions of transparency, openness and participation of all members were not ensured, they would not join hands to provide consensus.

The joint statement of these members even said that they were concerned that the working groups set up by the WTO had ended up as an exercise in pretence rather than transparency. In fact the target of all dissidence and protests at the WTO meet was Ms. Barshefsky, who conducted the proceedings like a bully, caring little for the views of the Asian, African and Latin American countries.

The U.S. strategy all through had been to keep the member countries divided. The U.S. President divided the developing countries by announcing a special package for the least developed countries. But despite its success in delinking the least developed countries from the general group of developing countries, it overshot its limits at the Seattle meet. This was obvious from the open opposition by a large number of Asian and African countries.

The U.S. side was ready with the draft declaration and the Trade Ministers were categorically told by Ms. Barshefsky to finalise the draft before afternoon. But since the developing countries from Asia, Africa and Latin America had not been consulted at all, there was a revolt and statements were made announcing that they would not be a party to the consensus.

Despite all prodding by the U.S. Trade Representative after this sudden development, the 'contrived' consensus was not achieved. On all the major issues covered by the five working groups, there were several drafts making it difficult to prepare a common document. Soon after she gave up attempts and allowed other senior ministers to undertake the task of evolving a consensus on the draft declaration.

The situation, by then, was completely out of control. By

evening it was obvious that the meeting would end in a deadlock. It was then decided to suspend the negotiations without issuing any common declaration.

The result of the suspension of the WTO talks is that the so-called decision on the setting up of the working group to discuss the possibility of a group on trade, globalisation and labour standards now stands frozen.

Sharp division among the developed countries was an equally important factor for the collapse of the Seattle talks. The European Union was reluctant to cut down on its heavy export subsidy to farmers. But the American and CAIRNS group (eighteen farm exporting countries including Argentina, Uruguay, Australia, Canada, etc.) have been advocating for greater access to the EU market. The United States itself is guilty; it provides a per capita annual subsidy of $ 30,000 to its farmers.

The United States is interested in lower tariff and non-tariff barriers in such areas as services, telecommunications, and agricultural biotechnology. In addition, it seeks an extension of the present moratorium on Internet taxation. In fact, agriculture was a major controversial subject even in the Uruguay round, which led to the creation of WTO. Unless the developed countries appreciably reduce their subsidies, developing countries cannot have much hope of gaining from global agriculture trade.

The political compulsions of a presidential election coming up this year are an important reason for the U.S. insistence on core labour standards being included in the WTO discussions.

India and many other developing countries believe that labour standards are better handled by International Labour Organisation (ILO), issues of child labour by UNICEF, and environmental factors by the UN Environmental Programme (UNEP). They are, after all, entities specially set up to tackle those specific problems. India rejected even EU-Japan proposal for a study group outside WTO.

Echoing the long-standing complaints of the Third World, the World Bank president, James Wolfensohn, said at Seattle : "It makes no sense to urge poor countries to reform their economies, to urge them to compete and pay their way in the world, while denying them the means to compete."

14

DOHA ROUND OF TRADE NEGOTIATIONS

As many of us are aware, the Doha Round journey has neither been smooth nor easy. In Doha, in 2001, we celebrated joyful moments, when the Round was launched; we experienced the difficult moments at Cancun, Mexico in 2003, when many feared that the multilateral trading system had lost its sense of direction. In July 2004, after many sleepless nights, Members agreed on the July Framework and in Hong Kong, the following year, a ray of hope again appeared in front of us. But July 2006 and thereafter we had to face up to the "suspension" and again the negotiations were thrown to the bottom of the valley. Fortunately, Members still have not lost confidence and are back into full negotiation mode again.

The Present Scenario

Today the Doha Round is at the crossroads : the path towards success or the slow move towards a deep freeze.

WTO Members had pledged to conclude these negotiations by the end of the year 2007, ahead of the start of the intense political process in the US in 2008, which will be followed by changes in the European Parliament and in the European Commission in 2009. But if this is to be achieved, key progress in agriculture subsidies and tariffs on agriculture and industrial tariffs is immediately required.

Director-General Pascal Lamy, in his report to the General Council, on 27 July 2007 said that meetings between 2006 to May 2007 pointed to the negotiators' "high level of commitment to concluding the Round". He also noted "some significant differences" but stated that "convergence is within our reach if you are all reaay to show the necessary will and flexibility to close the gaps".

Delegations of Member Countries returned to the process to engage in an intensive negotiation from 3 September 2007, starting with agriculture.

Negotiations continued in Geneva in an attempt to close the gaps in WTO Members' positions in relation to the negotiating texts on agriculture and Non-Agricultural Market Access (NAMA). Intensive TRIPS (intellectual property rights) and services negotiations were also conducted in October 2007. A draft services negotiating text was expected to be ready by December 2007.

The key to a breakthrough remained the three core issues of agricultural market access, agricultural domestic support and NAMA. Greater certainty from the EU and other importers on the market-access outcome on a product-by-product basis, combined with movement by the US on domestic support and a more realistic position from key developing countries on NAMA, was essential if progress was to be made before the end of the year 2007.

Agriculture discussions resumed in early October 2007, with an intensive three-week period of senior officials, G12, Cairns Group and technical meetings to review the Agriculture.

Progress on market access continues to lag that in other "pillars". Throughout the consultations, the Agriculture Chair, Crawford Falconer, urged Members to find their own compromises ahead of his preparation of a revised text.

Discussions on the draft negotiating text continued throughout October 2007, with most developing countries arguing that the draft text should be changed to impose lesser reductions on them. The NAMA-11 group (including India, Brazil and South Africa) was particularly vocal in seeking more concessions for developing countries. Developed countries stressed the need for cuts to developing country tariffs to be large enough to generate new trade flows. Meanwhile, various countries submitted proposals addressing specific concerns held by recently-acceded Members, small and vulnerable economies, and countries within customs unions.

Following the last round of plurilateral (collective) services negotiations in Geneva in September 2007, WTO Members' attention turned to the development of a services text.

In October, the Chair of the negotiating group on services commenced consultations with the Members with a view to securing agreement on the basic elements of such a text. Australia is still working hard to achieve commercially meaningful result on services. It is believed to be the opportune time for Members to give serious consideration to what is required to ensure that the services outcome will be commensurate with what it finally agreed on agriculture and NAMA.

According to a recent report published in *The Economic Times,* India will lose out in services sector in case the WTO's Doha Round of trade negotiations fails, as per a paper brought out by the Finance Ministry. The paper further added that the country could be a major beneficiary from greater market access in services unlike other developing nations.

India is Asia's third largest economy with a size of nearly one trillion dollars. Services contribute about 61 per cent of GDP and the sector is growing at a double-digit rate. A clear plan for services highlighting the potential gains for India in terms of growth, employment and exports can possibly give a new direction to the country's strategy in WTO negotiations. The paper entitled "Strategy for India's Service Sector: Broad Contours", published in the newspaper asserted that our future strategies should depend on our assessment of the export potential in the near and medium term in different services, the likely increase in market access in different services as a result of WTO negotiations which can benefit India and the likely impact on India's growth.

Citing the example of India and Brazil becoming very close coalition partners despite having different economic interests, the paper pointed out that future negotiations would need realistic strategic alliances which can fetch good dividends.

In fact, we have to be more forthcoming in future negotiations and set our own agenda and make others to react instead of reacting ourselves as we have been doing for quite some time.

The three principal stakeholder interests for India in Doha have been services, manufacturing and agriculture. It seems that the domestic battle over Doha is between the industrial and poor farmer lobbies on the one hand and the services lobby on the other.

There is a hint of criticism of how India sets its trade negotiation agenda, in that India tends to react defensively instead of being proactive in its demands. This marks a failure of domestic trade politics in identifying Indian interests.

The leaders of India, Brazil and South Africa noted that WTO Doha Round of trade negotiations is entering a critical stage. These negotiations are now in a genuine multilateral process, with draft modalities texts for agriculture and industrial goods that provide a good basis for negotiations. They reaffirmed their commitment to carry out negotiations towards an outcome that is fair and acceptable to all.

The leaders reiterated the importance of the development dimension of the Round and welcomed the strengthened engagement, solidarity, and cooperation among developing countries in that process.

The leaders underlined that agriculture remains the key to the conclusion of the Round. To truly deliver on the development benefits of the Round, they called for the removal of long-standing distortions and restrictions in international agricultural trade such as subsidies and trade barriers that affect the agricultural exports of and domestic production in developing countries. They also asserted that developed countries must agree to substantial and effective cuts in the latter's trade distorting support, with new disciplines that prevent box shifting and commit to real and new trade flows in agriculture. They underscored that meaningful and operable special and differential treatment, which includes development instruments of Special Products and the Special Safeguard Mechanism are vital to address the concerns of developing countries having a large population of subsistence and low-income farmers.

The leaders emphasized that any progress towards achieving the above goals is a development imperative and should not be linked with meeting the disproportionate demands by developed countries in the NAMA and services negotiations. They asserted that developing countries have been constructive and willing to negotiate in all areas, and urged others to act with the same disposition.

The leaders recalled their commitment to making a contribution to market opening in the Doha Round in agriculture, NAMA, and services that will create new trade flows. They also committed to ensure that the process of the negotiations is not held hostage to "who goes first". They reaffirmed their conviction that all Members must "move together" to arrive at a balanced and fair outcome of the negotiations.

The leaders stated that through constant dialogue, reciprocal flexibility, non-dogmatic approach and good faith efforts, full modalities in the agriculture and industrial goods negotiations could be achieved before the year-end, together with equivalent results in other areas. They reiterated their commitment to achieving such a positive outcome within this framework.

The leaders underscored the importance of incorporating the development dimension in international discussions concerning intellectual property. They emphasised that intellectual property is not an end in itself, but one of the instruments to encourage innovation for technological, industrial and economic and social development. They also recalled that it is fundamental to preserve policy spaces necessary for ensuring access to knowledge, promoting public goals in the fields of health and culture, and a sustainable environment.

The leaders reaffirmed the need to reach a solution for the problem raised by the granting of intellectual property rights on biological resources and/or associated traditional knowledge, without due compliance with relevant provisions of the Convention on Biological Diversity such as the granting of erroneous patents or the registration of undue trademarks. In this regard, they recalled the presentation in the WTO of the proposal co-sponsored, among others, by the three IBSA countries to amend the TRIPS Agreement by introducing a mandatory requirement for the disclosure of origin, prior informed consent, and also fair and equitable benefit sharing of biological resources and/or associated traditional knowledge used in inventions for which applications for intellectual property rights are filed.

If WTO members do not energise the negotiations soon, governments will be forced to confront the unpleasant reality of failure. This will mean throwing overboard the very significant package of trade opening and rule making that is available and stripping the global economy of one of its most powerful and enduring sources of strength and stability.

It will also mean failure to address remaining inequities in the multilateral trading system. It has been expressed by several developing countries that failure to conclude the Round would deprive them of outcomes that would benefit development — from the reduction of agricultural distortions — to the duty-free, quota-free package for the least developed countries' exports and "aid for trade." Improving trade opportunities for developing countries, eliminating trade restrictions that continue to penalize their exports and handicap their economic growth, is thus at the heart of today's international agenda to promote political stability, development and alleviate poverty.

Three issues are at the forefront of the discussions : agricultural subsidies, agricultural tariffs and industrial tariffs. Work is also ongoing on trade in services to prepare the improved offers that each country should table in order to be ready for negotiations on the specifics of further market opening.

Furthermore, there is work in the areas of anti-dumping, subsidies — including fisheries subsidies, trade facilitation or trade and environment, with development being like a red thread through all of them.

In respect of agricultural subsidies negotiations, the ball is very much in the court of the United States. Unless the US offers deeper cuts in its agricultural subsidies beyond its current proposal, the other countries will not follow suit.

What is pending the final conclusion of the Round is the elimination, by 2013, of the most damaging type of subsidies — the agricultural export subsidies. According to the agreement already on the table, a substantial part thereof should be gone by 2010.

On agricultural market access, it is mainly for the European Union and the G10 (including countries like Japan and Korea) to agree on greater cuts in tariffs and enhanced access to their internal markets, beyond their current positions. On this part of the negotiations, India and the G33 must also make a contribution. They need to ensure that the special protection, which has been already secured for their most sensitive agricultural products, does not negate the overall objective of providing increased market access opportunities as agreed when the Round was launched in 2001.

As far as industrial tariffs are concerned — this is the area we commonly call NAMA or non-agricultural market access — the expectation is to see large developing countries, amongst which some of the members of the G20, like Brazil, India and Argentina, to agree on cuts in their import tariffs. Again, the necessary flexibility will be considered for some products, but the idea is that industrial tariffs are cut automatically, according to a new technology called the Swiss-formula, which cuts more on the high tariffs and less in the lower ones.

The Doha Development Agenda has been the biggest challenge for the WTO since its creation in 1995. It is a challenge to achieve what was started in the Uruguay Round : a more level playing field in areas of particular interests to developing countries, such as agriculture. It is a challenge because it touches the edge of some of its Members' most entrenched interests. It will therefore take a great deal of political courage and commitment to conclude this Round successfully.

It is to be remembered that at Hong Kong, in December 2005, WTO Ministers had agreed to establish modalities for agriculture and non-agricultural market access (NAMA) by April 30, 2006, submit the draft schedules by July 31, 2006 and conclude the negotiations across all areas of the Doha Round by the end of

2006. In respect of services, all Members were to file their revised offers by July 31, 2006 and submit the draft schedules by October 31, 2006. These deadlines were unfortunately missed despite intensive negotiations.

The intensive discussions through January to July 2006 had focused mainly on the triangular issues of Domestic Support, Agricultural Market Access (AMA), and NAMA. At the informal meeting of the Trade Negotiations Committee (TNC) held on July 24, 2006, the Director General, WTO, who is its Chairman, reported that "it remained clear that the gaps remain too wide", and recommended that the only course of action would be to suspend the negotiations across the Round as a whole to allow serious reflection by participants. In the light of the impasse, particularly in agriculture, and ruling out the possibility of finishing the Round by the end of 2006, Members agreed to suspend the negotiations across all areas of the Doha Work Programme, and to resume them when the negotiating environment was right. For India, the suspension of the Round has been a disappointment. It was an avoidable delay in the delivery of the development promises of the Round.

A strong WTO reflects the widespread desire to operate in a fairer and more open multilateral trading system which provides a stable anchor to world economies as they become more intertwined. It is the belief that international trade can play a major role in growth and poverty alleviation and all our peoples can benefit from the increased opportunities and welfare gains that the multilateral trading system generates.

The decision by WTO Members in 2001 to designate the Doha Round a "Development Round" was a recognition that there remain, in today's multilateral trading system, rules, disciplines and imbalances that penalise developing countries, and that these must be corrected. The objective, therefore, is to improve the multilateral disciplines and the commitments by all Members of the WTO in such a way that they establish a more level playing field and provide developing countries with better conditions to enable them to reap the benefits of opening trade.

The pertinent question is : If the Doha Round is good for all of us, why is it so difficult to conclude? The reasons are crystal clear :

Firstly, this is a very ambitious Round on several fronts. The scope of the negotiations is much larger and deeper than in any previous Round. The method of negotiation is also much more ambitious. In previous Rounds, there were no formulae agreed for tariff reductions; people worked with averages so it was possible to hide products from tariff cuts with the resulting tariff peaks. Now with one formula it may be fairer but it is also much more difficult because it hurts in addressing tariff peaks in both developed and developing countries, on products such as textile and clothing or automobiles.

Secondly, this is a "Development Round", which aims at addressing the remaining unfair rules in the trade system, in particular developed countries' trade distorting subsidies in agriculture. At the same time, the Round allows for the protection of developing countries' specific sensitivities in agriculture, in particular through its provisions on sensitive products, special products or the special safeguard mechanism.

Thirdly, the actors now are different from previous Rounds. Developing countries are much more active in this Round, which is a good sign of their deeper commitment. There are now several groups of them, such as G20, G33, NAMA 11 or the LDC Group, depending on interests, sensitive sectors and strategy. This is specially true in agriculture which is at the core of the Round. We don't work with the QUAD anymore. We have a new G4 : US, EC, India, and Brazil, and G6 with Australia and Japan.

Furthermore, the large number of Members and the diversity of topics coupled with the WTO's traditional bottom-up approach and single undertaking nature of the negotiating agenda — where nothing is agreed until everything is agreed — makes it more challenging to reach consensus.

The WTO is a small governance system where we already have a few elements in place. We have a multilateral system that recognizes different values, including a consensus on the benefits resulting from market opening while respecting sustainable development. We also have other values such as the need to respect religious diversity or the right to protect the environment. In WTO it is now clearly recognized that in some circumstances non-trade values can supersede trade considerations.

The main mission of the WTO is to open markets and regulate world trade for the benefit of all people. To perform this task four main channels are made use of : first, provide a forum where Members negotiate international agreements which are then adopted; second, we have monitoring and surveillance mechanisms — including peer reviews — of Members' actions; third, we have a strong mechanism of adjudication and enforcement of Members' obligations; finally, we have a mandate to ensure coherence with some other international organizations.

The basic value underpinning the WTO is that market opening is good. The multilateral trading system helps to increase economic efficiency, and it can also help reduce corruption and bad government. Trade has played an increasing role in the world economy over the past few decades as illustrated by the fact that the growth of real trade exceeded that of world output. The ratio of world exports of goods and services to GDP rose from 13.5 per cent in 1970 to 32 per cent in 2005 and all major geographic regions recorded an excess of trade over output growth.

The impression has also arisen that in the multilateral trading system, the system has evolved to the disadvantage of a certain part of the WTO Membership — that comprising the developing countries. This bias would not be sustainable in the long run and it is therefore necessary to correct it if we want the multilateral trading system to thrive.

The challenge of market opening and globalisation for developing countries calls for enhanced international action. A fundamental aspect of the Doha Round is to correct some of the remaining imbalances in the current trade rules in favour of developing countries and to improve rules that will provide all Members and, in particular, developing country Members, with authentic market opportunities.

A number of the substantive rules of the WTO do perpetuate some bias against developing countries. This is the case of the agriculture sector, which today holds the key to unlocking the rest of the Doha Agenda. How can agriculture, which represents less than 8 per cent of world trade keeps the entire Doha Round agenda off track? Simply because food production remains a very sensitive sector for rich and poor countries alike. And since the current Round is one of development and moreover, more than 70 per cent of the world's poor live in rural areas, there is no way the Doha Development Agenda can continue if the existing agriculture bias in favour of rich countries is not properly addressed. Reforming agriculture rules is necessary to ensure sustainable development.

This is the reason why, in the Doha mandate, all WTO Members agreed in 2001 that : "...the long-term objective is to establish a fair and market-oriented trading system through a programme of fundamental reform encompassing strengthened rules and specific commitments on support and protection in order to correct and prevent restrictions and distortions in world agricultural markets."[1]

Similar bias exists with regard to the remaining tariff peaks and high tariffs applied by developed countries on sectors such as textiles and clothing, where a large number of developing countries have a comparative advantage. The new rules on market access for non-agricultural products would address these peaks to benefit exports from developing countries. These are just some of the examples.

Doha Round is therefore crucial for both developed and developing countries as a fundamental tool to control and harness globalisation and to ensure sustainable development. Concluding the Doha Round is therefore understandably difficult. It is the most ambitious attempt that governments have made to open trade multilaterally — because of its scope, including agriculture, and because of the number of countries that are negotiating and will share the results.

In agriculture, in order to rebalance the multilateral trading system in favour of developing countries, this Round has thus to deliver "effective cuts" in trade-distorting agriculture subsidies in developed countries. It will also deliver the elimination of the most damaging type of subsidies — export subsidies by 2013. It also has to deliver improved market access, including on South-South trade, through the reduction of tariffs and removal of quantitative restrictions, especially on products where developing countries have a comparative advantage. At the same time, WTO members have recognised the right of developing countries to protect a number of special products on criteria of food security, livelihood security and rural development and to use a special safeguard mechanism to protect against import surges. Although all this has already been agreed, the question that matters is "how much" reduction.

On cotton, rich countries have already agreed to eliminate all export subsidies; they have also agreed to make deeper and faster reductions in trade-distorting domestic subsidies for cotton than for the remainder of agricultural products.

For the poorest countries, there is already agreement to provide duty-free and quota-free access to 97 per cent of all LDC products on a lasting basis, with a view to eventually extending this treatment to 100 per cent of their products.

There is also agreement to open services markets, an area of growing importance for many developing countries and with a huge growth potential as India itself attests. There is agreement to curb fishery subsidies which contribute to the depletion of our oceans, to facilitate customs procedures, to introduce greater transparency in anti-dumping procedures and to foster trade in environmentally friendly goods and services.

All these are areas where a country like India which is progressively and steadily integrating into the world economy stands to gain from this Round.

Member countries are now working at three different levels. First, political leaders in many countries have expressed their support and full engagement to conclude this Round. In addition to the clear ASEAN determination as expressed in Cebu, we saw the engagement of US President Bush, German Chancellor Merkel, President Lula, PM Manmohan Singh, PM Abe and many other heads of States in Asia and Africa. Second, trade ministers in key countries are doing shuttle diplomacy, testing numbers, looking into specifics, and trying to reach convergence. Third, senior officials and experts are also discussing in the different negotiating groups in Geneva.

As already mentioned, three issues are at the forefront of the discussions at the moment : agricultural subsidies, agricultural tariffs and industrial tariffs. All parties need to make a greater contribution, starting with agriculture. The United States has to accept cuts in its subsidies beyond its current offer. The EU and the G10 (including countries like Japan and Korea) have to agree to greater cuts in agriculture tariffs beyond their current positions. India and the G33 also have to make a contribution. They need to ensure that the special protection they have already secured for their most sensitive agricultural products does not negate the overall objective of providing more market access. If we are to reach a result, all Members have to move. No one through this Round should be asked to undertake disproportionate commitments. Each country will have to make its contribution, with bigger players contributing more than smaller and weaker ones.

This Round aims to significantly reduce the trade-distorting domestic support that is extended to agriculture. In general, the most distorting forms of support are those that are directly linked to production, and which distort the market signals to farmers. They can encourage them to oversupply particular products, leading to massive surpluses and the depression of international prices. This, however, does not imply that the WTO is somehow trying to curtail farmers' safety nets. Governments can continue to support their farmers. However, they must simply refrain from doing so in a manner that is linked to production. Decoupled income support to farmers, along with other governmental measures to promote food security, to protect the environment, to provide regional assistance are certainly allowed under the Agreement on Agriculture's "Green Box".

The Doha Round also calls for a substantial improvement in market access for agriculture products, with the highest tariffs being cut the most. This area provides for a number of safety nets for farmers. It allows WTO Members to nominate, quote, unquote, "Sensitive Products". While these are products for which a substantial improvement in market access is also required, the Doha Round allows such access to take place through a *softer approach* than the general formula, through a combination of tariff cuts and quotas.

Likewise, with open trade and modernised multilateral trade rules, many developing countries would face severe capacity constraints which would prevent them from being able to benefit from this. Furthermore, adjustment costs for many of them are often simply too high. Aid for Trade, which is also, a part of the Doha Agenda aims at complementing the trade negotiations, by providing development assistance to help these countries unlock their full trade and growth potential.

Aid for Trade is all about helping the private sector — entrepreneurs, traders, investors — to seize export opportunities. Above all, it is about greater international cooperation and coherence — between the WTO, the World Bank, the IMF, and the UN at the global level, and between trade, finance and development ministries at the national level — because it is at the ground level that policy coherence must begin.

The world faces the prospect of 400 preferential trade agreements by 2010 and the challenge of ensuring that they contribute to the health of world trade. It is a matter of fact that bilateral trade agreements cannot replace multilateral rules. The conclusion of preferential trade agreements can create an incentive for even further discrimination, which eventually will hurt all trading partners. Countries outside an agreement will try to conclude agreements with one of those that are inside to avoid exclusion. This has been called the "domino effect" or "bandwagon effect" and is the reason for much of the regional trade agreement activity seen in Asia recently. In other words, the consequence is that the preferences obtained through forming a preferential agreement against competitors tend to be shortlived. The more agreements one has, the less meaningful the preferences would be.

Besides, bilateral agreements cannot solve systemic issues such as rules of origin, anti-dumping, agricultural and fisheries subsidies. These issues simply cannot be handled at the bilateral level. Take for instance, negotiations to eliminate or reduce trade-distorting agricultural subsidies, or fisheries subsidies. There is no such thing as a "bilateral" farmer or fisherman, or a "bilateral" chicken and a "multilateral" farmer or chicken or fish. Subsidies are given to farmers for all their poultry production. The same is true for rules on anti-dumping.

The proliferation of regional trade agreements can greatly complicate the trading environment, creating a web of incoherent rules. For instance, take rules of origin : an increasing number of WTO Members are party to ten or more regional trade agreements, most of which for a given Member, contain agreement-specific rules of origin which are necessary to ensure that the preferences go to one's partner and not to others. This complicates the production processes of business which may be obliged to tailor their products for different preferential markets in order to satisfy rules of origin. It also complicates life for customs officials who are obliged to assess the same product differently depending on its origin, thus compromising the transparency of the trading regime.

The WTO imposes three types of substantive conditions for regional agreements to be WTO consistent. First, with respect to the overall impact of the regional trade agreement vis-à-vis other Members : there is the obligation not to raise barriers to trade with third parties. This is quantifiable in terms of tariffs, but less easy to measure in terms of other trade regulations such as standards or rules of origin. Secondly, with reference to what we call the "external requirement". A free trade agreement cannot lead to higher import duties for its members while a customs union must harmonise the external trade policies of its members and compensate affected non-members accordingly. Thirdly, on the "internal dimension" of regional trade agreements, tariffs and other restrictive regulations of commerce must be phased out "substantially" from all trade. Again, the tariff component can be quantified, but it is harder to determine in the case of other restrictive trade regulations as there is no agreed definition of the term.

It is therefore clear that the WTO authorizes regional trade agreements, the operation of which should not lead to situations where the non-party would "pay the price" of internal preferences.

In order to ensure coherence, regional agreements are to be "promptly" notified to the WTO and reviewed by its peers before the regional trade agreement is implemented. To put it simply, the WTO favours a strong multilateral trading system, complemented — not substituted — by a new generation of regional trade agreements.

India's Regional Trading Arrangements

Turning to India, the country has signed free trade agreements with Sri Lanka, Bhutan, Singapore and is involved in the South Asia Free Trade Agreement (SAFTA). India is also negotiating with ASEAN countries, besides Chile, Mauritius, MERCOSUR, SACU and Thailand. More recently, proposals for free trade agreements with Korea, China, Malaysia and some other countries have been tabled. Compared with US or the EC, India did not have as many FTAs, but it seems that India is quickly catching up.

India views Regional Trading Arrangements (RTAs) as 'building blocks' towards the overall objective of trade liberalization complementing the multilateral trading system. In the past, India had adopted a very cautious and guarded approach to regionalism. Recognizing that RTAs would continue to feature prominently in world trade, India engaged with its trading partners/blocs with the intention of expanding its export market and began concluding in principle agreements and moving in some cases even towards Comprehensive Economic Cooperation Agreements (CECAs) which covers Free Trade Agreement (FTA) in goods, services, investments and identified areas of economic cooperation. Framework agreements have already been entered into with a number of trading partners with specific road maps to be followed and specified time frames by which the negotiations are to be completed. Joint Study Groups have also been set up for examining feasibility of CECA between India-Japan, India-Brazil-South Africa and India-Russia. The reports are at various stages of completion. India and European Commission have also set up a High Level Trade Group (HLTG) as mandated by the India-EU Summit held in New Delhi on September 7, 2005. The mandate on the HLTG is to explore ways and means to increase bilateral economic flows including the possible launching of negotiations on a comprehensive trade and investment agreement.

An overview of the trade deal in Hong Kong and Singapore would help assess India's stand on issues of subsidies and regional trade agreements.

HONG KONG MINISTERIAL CONFERENCE

Ministers from the WTO's 149 member governments had approved a declaration in July 2004 in Hong Kong that laid down 2013 as deadline for eliminating of agriculture export subsidies with a substantial part in the first half of the implementation period. Developing countries without Aggregate Measurement of Support (AMS), such as India, will be exempted from reductions in *de minimis* and the overall cut in trade-distorting domestic support, consisting of AMS, the "Blue Box" and *de minimis*, that is entitlement to provide "Amber Box" subsidies up to 10 per cent of value. The other provisions included herein are duty-free, quota-free market access for all LDCs' products to all developed countries. Developing countries declaring themselves to be in a position to do so to also provide such access, though flexibility in coverage and in the phase in of their commitments is provided. It is to be noted here that the three heaviest subsidisers, namely the EC, the US and Japan will attract the highest levels of cuts in their trade-distorting domestic support entitlements.

In cotton, export subsidies to be eliminated by developed countries in 2006 and trade-distorting domestic subsidies to be reduced more ambitiously and over a shorter period of time. Developing countries like India will continue to have the right to provide marketing and transport subsides on exports for 5 years beyond the end date for elimination of all forms of export subsidies.

Trade Deal in Hong Kong

The trade deal in Hong Kong has made a few small symbolic steps to help move the process of trade negotiations forward, but has sidestepped a final deal on the big issues of opening up trade in agriculture, services, and industrial products. Instead, it has agreed largely to the symbolic date for the ending of one type of agricultural subsidies, export subsidies, which make up less than 2 per cent of total subsidies by 2013.

In addition, it has offered some help to poor countries, by agreeing to a plan to grant tariff-free access to goods from the world's 49 poorest countries, which make up less than 1 per cent of all trade. Cotton farmers in West Africa will get some extra help as well. However, no final trade deal has been made yet.

Beneficiaries and Losers of Trade Deal

If we get a final trade deal, the big winners are likely to be big agricultural exporters like Brazil, Argentina, Australia and Canada which will be able to sell more goods abroad. Besides, the very poorest countries will also gain from the extra aid they have been promised and more access to rich country markets. Consumers in rich countries, especially the European Union, might also have cheaper food prices.

Moreover, businesses and consumers in developing countries could also gain from more efficient services in banking, shipping and telecommunications, while China will gain from being able to export more manufactured goods.

While other developing countries like Pakistan might lose out if the least developed countries get preferential treatment over rich country markets. The poor farmers in those countries might be hit if the more efficient producers like Brazil are able to sell more into their markets. Workers in protected industries in countries like India could also be hit by increased imports. However, the unskilled workers in rich countries might have relatively poorer chances of getting good jobs if there is shift towards service sector employment. It is to be remembered that the commitment to open up service markets stays in the draft, despite complaints from some developing states.

Reactions on Draft

Talks have failed as no agreement on a firm date for ending farm export subsidies could be reached. The US and developing states wanted a 2010 deadline, but the European Union has rejected this. The European Union stuck to its intransigent position on the end date of 2013 for the elimination of export subsidies and the developing countries gave up their demand for an earlier end date despite the initial collective efforts of the G110.

The protests came as delegates studied the text of the draft agreement, which has been condemned by some developing countries for not addressing their concerns.

Many feel they are being pressed too hard to allow foreign competition in service industries. While some are also likely to be disappointed by the lack of progress on a plan to give duty-free and quota-free access to exports for the world's least-developed states.

Some African countries have been seeking the elimination of subsidies for rich-country cotton farmers. The draft stops short of that, suggesting instead that they should be cut further and more quickly than for other farm products. But the draft text asked rich states to scrap export subsidies for cotton by 2006, to help West African producers. However, the European Union has none and the US is already in the process of eliminating its main cotton export supports. African cotton producers say that huge US subsidies distort trade but the US says it will only agree to a deal on cotton as part of wider settlement on agriculture.

The European Union says that all food aid should be given in cash and that US grain shipments to developing countries distort the market. The US believes food aid in kind is vital in famine relief.

Pitiful "Concessions"

The gross inadequacy of the so-called "concessions" can be understood from the fact that export subsidies comprise less than 2 per cent of the total farm subsidies in the developed world. There has been no concrete commitment on reduction of domestic support other than export subsidies. The European Union can continue to subsidise agriculture to the tune of 55 billion euros per year. The European Union budget adopted recently ensures that nothing can be touched in the agriculture budget till at least 2013. The US budget reconciliation process and the final vote in the Congress is set to extend the domestic support to agriculture and the counter-cyclical support to commodities upto around 2011.

The US refused to give duty-free access to exports from the LDCs for 99.9 per cent of product lines and finally the agreement has been on 97 per cent, which would enable the US and Japan to deny market access to the LDCs in several product lines like rice and textiles. Much of the Aid for Trade for LDCs, which is being showcased by the developed countries as a "development package", is disguised under conditional loan packages that are contingent upon further opening up of their markets.

India stands to gain almost nothing from the so-called "concessions" offered by the developed countries. Whatever little benefit in terms of enhanced market access would accrue to developing countries would be cornered by agri-exporters like Brazil, Argentina, etc. India's proactive support to the Annex C of the Ministerial Text (on Services), which was opposed by a large number of developing countries with the G90 submitting an alternative draft, was most unfortunate. This reflected lack of commitment on India's part to the unity of the developing nations. The supposed gains in terms of Mode 1 and Mode 4 liberalisation that might accrue to India, which would only benefit some sections of the corporate sector like the BPO industry and a small segment of the skilled professionals, do not justify compromising the interests of the overwhelming majority of our population.

India's complicity in pushing the final agreement along with Brazil, the leading country of the G20, reflects poorly on their ability to provide leadership to the developing countries. It is noteworthy that Cuba and Venezuela categorically expressed their reservations on the texts on NAMA and services in the concluding session of the Ministerial Conference.

Disturbing Deal on Services

The most dangerous aspect of the Hong Kong deal is the agreement on services (Annex C of the Ministerial Text) that seeks to subvert the basic structure of the General Agreement on Trade in Services (GATS), where countries are hitherto allowed to make voluntary commitments to liberalise their services sector in accordance with the level of their economic development and national requirements. Para 7 of Annex C emphasises request-offer negotiations on a 'plurilateral basis', which would undermine that flexibility. Though these 'plurilateral negotiations' (in a specific sector or Mode) are seemingly envisaged as part of the 'request-offer' approach. The way the text is worded in Para 7(b) makes it clear that those who receive such a request "shall enter" into plurilateral negotiations on such requests "so organised" as to facilitate participation by all members. In effect, any individual developing country receiving such 'plurilateral' requests will find it very difficult to resist them. Given the situation, it is quite possible that developing countries like India would be soon forced into sectoral and government procurement negotiations through offers made by the developed countries for across-the-board opening up of services sectors.

While the government has already launched its propaganda on the supposed gains accruing to India following further liberalisation in Mode 1 and Mode 4, in terms of more outsourcing and more H1B visas, it is silent on the agreed "objectives" with regard to Mode 3, i.e. "commercial presence" category of service providers, which is a euphemism for FDI in a huge range of services — from banking and insurance — to health and education. Major concessions on the part of developing countries have been made here which would only benefit the MNCs based in the developed world. On Mode 3, the agreed "objectives" are "commitments on enhanced levels of foreign equity participation; removal or substantial reduction of economic needs test; commitments allowing greater flexibility on the types of legal entity permitted." The objectives of the multilateral investment regime and government procurement, which developed countries had pushed earlier on from the Singapore Conference in 1997 (hence the name Singapore issues) and given up in the aftermath of Cancun after strong resistance from the developing countries, have made a re-entry through the backdoor in the services text in Hong Kong, this time with the active support and collaboration of India. The gains of Cancun have thus been frittered away.

By agreeing to the objective of securing "commitments on enhanced levels of foreign equity participation" under Mode 3, India has paved the way for greater liberalisation of the services sector in future. Besides the threat of commercialisation of social services like higher education and health facilities (which have already figured in India's offer list), this would also come into conflict with India's domestic regulations in terms of the FDI caps in financial services like Banking, Insurance, etc. GATS clauses of progressive liberalisation will also ensure that foreign service providers have to be given the same regulatory treatment as domestic ones. This will severely compromise the ability of developing countries to regulate foreign service providers.

Developing Countries to Slash Agricultural Tariff

India's prime interest in agriculture was to ensure the protection of our small and marginal farmers from the onslaught of artificially low priced imports or threat thereof. The proposals for agricultural tariff cuts, which are already on the table, are quite ambitious and the G20 has already committed itself to undertake cuts to the extent of two-thirds the level of the cuts applicable to developed countries. Moreover, India has 100 per cent tariff lines bound in agriculture with the difference in the applied level and the bound level not very marked in many lines. In this context, the systemic problem faced by our small and marginal farmers practicing subsistence agriculture will only get aggravated as a result of the impending tariff cuts that have been agreed. It is being claimed by the government that the right to designate a number of agricultural product lines as Special Products based upon the considerations of food and livelihood security and Special Safeguard Mechanism based on import quantity and price triggers, which have been mentioned in the Ministerial Text, adequately addresses the concerns of our farmers. The claim is questionable since the nature as well as the extent of protection under Special Products remains restricted and the Special Safeguard Mechanism, admittedly, is a measure to deal with an emergency and is of "a temporary nature". In the light of the insignificant reductions in domestic farm subsidies by the developed countries therefore, tariff reduction commitments by the developing countries seem to be totally unjustifiable.

Lacking Full Reciprocity

Developing countries have also agreed on the Swiss formula for tariff cuts under NAMA. Although the coefficients will be negotiated later, it is unlikely that the developed countries will agree upon sufficiently large coefficients for the formula that would ensure adequate policy space for developing countries in future to facilitate development of different sectors of their industries. The ritual references to "less than full reciprocity" and "special and differential treatment" in the Ministerial Text fail to conceal the fact that the flexibilities provided by the July Framework (Para 8) regarding the nature of the tariff reduction formula, product overage, extent of binding and depth of cuts have been done away with. Moreover, no concrete commitment has been obtained in the Ministerial Text for the removal of the non-tariff barriers by the developed countries, which is their principal mode of protection, despite the developing countries making such major concessions on industrial tariff cuts.

The fact of the matter is that the developing countries have committed themselves to cuts in both agriculture and industrial tariffs, without getting anything substantial in return from the developed countries. India has facilitated the adoption of this bad deal in the backdrop of an acute crisis faced by Indian agriculture. The opportunity to fundamentally rework the iniquitous Agreement on Agriculture and protecting domestic policy space vis-à-vis industrial protection by the developing countries, which could have been achieved by galvanizing the unity of the G110, has unfortunately been lost.

Agri-exports and India's Stand on Agricultural Issues in WTO

India's total exports of agricultural and allied products including plantations at US $10.5 billion in 2005-06 constitute 10.2 per cent of its export share. Developed country markets continued to account for nearly 35 per cent of India's agri-exports. However, its contribution to national economy is significant in terms of sustaining livelihood of a significant proportion of the population, including a large number of producers and landless agricultural labourers (characterized as low-income and resource-poor). This section of population lacks skills and is not covered under any safety nets which are essential for ensuring a minimal cross-sector labour mobility. Like India, most developing countries are in a similar situation in sharp contrast to the reality of the agriculture sector in developed countries. Apart from a number of agricultural crops, a number of other products, including livestock products, are produced in hilly/mountainous or other disadvantaged regions, or by tribal communities and women. India, and other developing countries have, therefore, been insisting that special and differential treatment for developing countries must be integral to all aspects, including the negotiated outcome, on agriculture under the Doha Round in the WTO.

Mitigating the risks facing the low-income, resource-poor and subsistence farmers associated with price declines, price volatility and predatory competition and other market imperfections, including the huge amounts of production and trade-distorting subsidies provided by some developed countries to their agriculture sector, remains paramount. Therefore, along with other developing countries, particularly its alliance partners in the G20 and G33, India has been emphasizing that the Doha agricultural outcome must include at its core :

- Removal of distorting subsidies and protection by developed countries to level the playing field; and
- Appropriate provisions designed to safeguard food and/or livelihood security, and to meet the rural development needs in developing countries.

Apart from appropriate policy flexibilities to enable developing country governments to help the low-income and vulnerable producers absorb or insure themselves against risks, India has also taken the stand that governments must also be able to foster stable and remunerative prices for domestic producers in order to increase productivity and gradually move away from dependence on low-productivity agriculture. To these ends, meaningful and effective instruments (Special Products and the Special Safeguard Mechanism) are important for developing countries like India. At Hong Kong, it has been agreed that Special Products and the

Special Safeguard Mechanism shall be an integral part of the modalities and the outcome of negotiations in agriculture. Moreover, developing countries shall have the right to self-designate an appropriate number of Special Products, guided by indicators based on the three fundamental criteria of food security, livelihood security and rural development needs. These designated products will attract more flexible treatment. Developing country Members will also have the right to recourse to a Special Safeguard Mechanism based on import quantity and price triggers, with precise arrangements to be further defined.

TRIPS Review Not Considered

The developed countries have been able to extract the maximum advantage possible out of the TRIPS agreement. Therefore they are not interested in a Review of the TRIPS Agreement. However, it was in India's interest to bring to the table issues related to TRIPS that should be considered for review and for necessary amendments. Specifically, they pertain to issues such as patent period, patenting of life forms, the possibility of having special provisions for sectors related to health and food security. This is well within the mandate of the TRIPS agreement, where a mandated review of the agreement is long overdue. Many developing countries have already called for such a review.

It is also surprising that India did not oppose the decision of the WTO (announced on December 6) to amend the TRIPS Agreement based on a mechanism that has failed to prove it can increase access to medicines. The so-called "August 30th decision" which was designed in 2003 — in the aftermath of the Doha Declaration on Public Health and Access to Medicines — to allow production and export of generic medicines to countries without manufacturing capability, is widely acknowledged to be cumbersome and inefficient. Till date there is not a single instance where the mechanism has been used, and not one patient has benefited from its use despite the fact that newer medicines, such as second-line AIDS drugs, are priced out of reach of poor patients. India should have argued for delaying of the amendment and exploring the possibility of an improved mechanism for supply of patented drugs at affordable prices to countries without manufacturing capabilities. The amendment has made permanent a burdensome drug-by-drug, country-by-country decision-making process, which does not take into account the fact that economies of scale are needed to attract interest from manufacturers of medicines. Without the pull of a viable market for generic pharmaceutical products, manufacturers are not likely to want to take part in the production-for-export system on a large scale. The draft text, however, is also explicit that the cuts must come also in indirect subsidies to farm products like export credits, state trading enterprises and food aid.

Unlike Brazil and Australia which are efficient exporters of agricultural goods, India's interests have always been dictated by the need to safeguard millions of small farmers who operate majority of farm holdings in the countryside. India may be a fast expanding and prospective economic power, yet, it remains a very closed economy with some of the highest agricultural tariffs in the world.

Citing food security concerns, India thus can be exempted from making any reduction commitments in terms of domestic support and the obligation to provide any minimum market access in agricultural goods. The agreement also protects countries like India from unfair competition from imports. India can raise duties on farm produce because of a surge in imports or because the import price was too low. Unlike India, Brazil as a major farm exporter will benefit from greater access to the US and European Union market.

While India has defensive interests in agriculture, its edge is mainly in services. Unlike many developing countries, it has, in fact, taken offensive positions in this area as it has export interests in information technology (IT). The country also seeks greater access to European Union and US in terms of the movement of natural persons or what is termed as Mode 4 in cross-border supply of services. Indications are that there was only limited movement on this matter at the Hong Kong Ministerial Conference. If this route is blocked due to opposition by the US and European Union, it will affect India's ability to offer in agriculture and industrial tariffs.

From India's point of view, services present a different picture than agriculture and industrial tariffs. As an emerging global power in IT and business services, the country, in fact, is a demandeur in the WTO talks as it seeks more liberal commitments on the part of its trading partners for cross-border supply of services, including the movement of natural persons to developed countries or what is termed as Mode 4 for the supply of services. The last thing it needs at this juncture is pressure to be a tad defensive in an area where it can afford to be more aggressive.

Unfortunately, this is indeed what the prevalent mindset dictates. The left, for instance, has asked the UPA government to withdraw its binding commitment to allow foreign universities to open their branches in India that was made at the WTO negotiations in services in August 2005 as it would foster "cultural insensitivity", among other things. India then had offered to take extensive commitments in a number of new services such as architecture, tourism, life insurance, recreation, culture and sports and education. This sort of pressure to roll back will weaken India's hand at the services talks — post-Hong Kong.

The question arises as to why educational services cannot be opened up? The left's argument regarding "cultural insensitivity" underscores its concerns that the curriculum of foreign varsities might have a viewpoint different from, say, a nationalist position on India's struggle for independence or Kashmir. The fees charged by foreign universities are also expected to be exorbitant and would only intensify the prevalent "urban elitist bias" in higher education. These concerns surfaced after the union cabinet approved India's negotiating position and the Indian delegation then extended a binding commitment in August 2005.

In sharp contrast, the interest of the European Union and US is more in establishing a commercial presence in developing countries. Thus if a lawyer or insurance company from the European Union or US establishes an office in India, this sort of service is supplied through commercial presence. Accordingly, this Mode 3 of supply is accompanied by requests for more liberal policies on foreign direct investment in sectors like insurance. These developed countries are lukewarm to demands for a more liberal regime for the movement of natural persons because of the high unemployment in their economies.

Naturally, there is scope for aggressive give and take in such negotiations, including the possibility of making cross-sectoral concessions in agriculture and industrial tariffs. While the focus so far has been on agriculture, the talks on services also have a bearing on the successful conclusion to the Doha round. Unfortunately, however, only 64 members have presented initial offers on services, if the European Union is counted as one country, as on June 20, 2005. Only 15 members have presented revised offers.

WTO AND DEVELOPING COUNTRIES

In an unprecedented show of unity all the developing country groupings, for the first time in the World Trade Organisation (WTO), held a Ministerial Meeting in Hong Kong during the Sixth Ministerial Conference where the G20, the G33, the African-Caribbean-Pacific (ACP) countries, the Least Developed Countries (LDCs), the Africa Group and the Small Economies came together on a single platform and decided to better coordinate their efforts in order to develop a common approach to issues of common interest. The coming together was not mere posturing, but a genuine reflection of developing countries' resolve to take multilateral trade negotiations forward in a manner that would ensure that global trade was not only open but also equitable and fair.

In a joint statement reiterating their shared interest in the development dimension of the Doha Round and their expectations of the comprehensive development outcome, the Ministers of all the developing countries agreed as follows :

1. The Round must result in the removal of the distortions that inhibit the export growth of developing countries and the provision of adequate policy space to ensure their sustainable socio-economic development. To this end, they agreed that developed countries must eliminate export support measures by 2010 while addressing specific needs of LDCs and also substantially reduce trade distorting domestic support.

2. Market access for products of export interest from developing countries in developed country markets must improve substantially and concerns of preferences of receiving countries must be addressed.
3. Emphasizing the importance of special & differential (S&D) treatment in all the three pillars of agriculture negotiations, they stressed the role of Special Products (SPs) and Special Safeguard Mechanism (SSM) as a means of addressing the food security, rural development and livelihood means of developing countries in the area of agricultural market access.
4. They reaffirmed their support for LDC demands for duty-free and quota-free (DFQF) market access and called for a concrete outcome in Hong Kong on this issue.
5. They stressed the need for a commitment at Hong Kong to address the issue of cotton ambitiously, expeditiously and specifically.
6. The specific measures should be adopted to address trade-related issues raised by the small, vulnerable economies.
7. Vowing to intensify the dialogue while recognizing the diversity of their situations and perceptions, they reiterated their commitment to a successful conclusion of the Doha Round by the end of 2006. This however, as already stated, has not materialised as yet.

The unprecedented alliance among a large number of developing and least developed countries having diverse interests is the most significant developments so far in the Hong Kong Ministerial Conference.

WTO AND INDIA

In agriculture, the July 2004 Framework, *inter alia*, agreed to incorporate two specific instruments of Special Products and Special Safeguard Mechanism in order to protect poor farmers in developing countries. Incrementally, the Hong Kong Declaration agreed that developing countries shall have the right to self-determination of which products constitute Special Products. Similarly, in respect of the Special Safeguard Mechanism, even though the tariff reductions have as yet not been defined, it has been now agreed through concerted efforts by India, that both volume and price triggers shall be available to developing countries to address an import surge or a dip in prices which typically result in lowering of incomes of farmers. These are definite gains for India, whichever angle they may be viewed from.

A foremost objective of Government in the agriculture negotiations has been to safeguard the food and livelihood security and rural development needs of India's poor farmers. To this end, the Government has managed to secure that developmental assistance will get incorporated into the "Green Box" and subsidies provided though *de minimis* provisions remain unimpeded.

The Hong Kong Declaration has secured a commitment from heavy export subsidizers such as the European Communities to eliminate the substantial part of export subsidies half way through the Doha Round, and not at its fag end. At the same time, developing country export subsidies related to marketing and transport can continue for 5 years beyond the end date of all export subsidies.

On domestic support, the US has offered to cut its overall trade-distorting support by 53 per cent, and the European Union its support by 70 per cent. Nevertheless, India and the G20 have continued to press for not only substantial cuts in the levels of "Amber Box" and overall trade-distorting support, including the "Blue Box", but have also been insisting that stringent criteria must guide developed country domestic support programmes. At Hong Kong, developing countries have been able to secure that the highest levels of cuts will be applied on the three heaviest subsidizers, namely the European Union, US and Japan, who together account for around US $ 250 billion of the annual domestic subsidies out of the global total of around US $ 350 billion.

In industrial products, all proposals, including the Argentina-Brazil-India (ABI) proposal entailing multiple coefficients based on each country's tariff average, remain on the table. Furthermore, all aspects of special and differential treatment for developing countries, including less than full reciprocity, and flexibilities to address sensitive sectors, remain entrenched in the Declaration. Through paragraph 24 it has now been agreed that a high level of ambition must be our objective in tariff reductions in products of export interest to developing countries both in agriculture and in industrial products. This provides us with a valuable route to secure market access opportunities, particularly in sectors where developed countries have continued to maintain tariff peaks and tariff escalations.

The interests of Indian farmers have been fully protected in the Hong Kong Ministerial Agreement. India has been able to secure agreement that WTO will not come in the way of Domestic Support given to farmers in developing countries like India, which has a preponderance of small farmers. Therefore, all the programmes of the government aimed at benefiting farmers will not be subject to any WTO discipline. Secondly, there is also an agreement that developing countries will be able to declare an appropriate number of Special Products on a self-selection basis. These are agricultural products of concern to developing countries which would be outside the ambit of tariff reduction. This will help our farmers in protecting their important crops from unfair international competition. Thirdly, we will also have a Special Safeguard Mechanism which means that we will be able to raise import duties on agricultural products if there is a surge in their imports or there is a fall in their prices. Our farmers would not have to worry about their income levels falling due to unfair competition from subsidized imports. And finally, agreement has been reached on complete elimination of Export subsidies on all agricultural products by developed countries. This will not only help in protecting our farmers from unfair competition in the domestic market, but also open up new opportunities for export of agricultural products.

Regarding domestic industry, the interests of Indian industry have been fully protected in the Hong Kong Ministerial Agreement. Preservation of adequate negotiating space was a goal and has been ensured for the future. The provision to promote our export interests too have been strengthened. A clear instruction to focus on reduction of tariffs, especially tariff peaks and tariff escalation, on products of export interest to developing countries has been included in the Declaration. The concept of less than full reciprocity in reduction commitments by developing countries has been firmly reiterated and incorporated in the paragraph relating to the formula. It has been ensured that flexibilities for developing countries will be included in the final package. This reinforces the paragraph 8 provisions of the July Framework Agreement allowing exemption of a specific number of tariff lines from formula cuts. The Ministerial Declaration calls for a Swiss Formula with coefficients that preserves all the proposals on the table, including the one submitted by Argentina, Brazil and India (ABI), which envisages a multilple coefficient Swiss Formula based on each country's tariff average.

In services, the policy space essential for developing countries including India has been fully preserved; the primacy of the Request-Offer process has been maintained and the architecture of the General Agreement on Trade in Services (GATS) remains intact. In view of the fact that the flexibility for developing countries has been fully preserved, each member including India can decide on the level of commitments that they would take commensurate with their levels of development and national policy objectives. In other words, there is no compulsion on developing countries to open up service sectors. Market access in services areas of export interest to India like Mode 4 categories of contractual service suppliers and independent professionals of developing countries has been assured, while commitments at the existing levels in respect of cross-border supply (Modes 1 & 2) which include business process outsourcing (BPO) and e-enabled services have been secured. Regarding the issue of Trade Related Intellectual Property Rights (TRIPS) Convention on Bio-Diversity (CBD) which was taken up strongly by India during the Hong Kong deliberations, it has been decided to further intensify discussions in the two areas of interest to India and other developing countries, namely Geographical Indications and Biological Diversity. "In TRIPS and CBD, this should enable us, by the end of the Doha Round, to create a balance between private intellectual property rights and rights of communities over genetic material and traditional knowledge. The benefit from an extension of the higher level of protection for geographical indications to products of interest to developing countries would increase the welfare of farmers and artisans, by enabling them to get better price realization, and more markets, for agri-products and handicrafts, like Darjeeling tea, Basmati rice, Alphonso mangoes, Pochampalli silk and other such items."[2]

India Firm on End Date for Removal for Agri Export Subsidies by Developed Countries and Flexibility for Developing Countries to Protect Domestic Industries

The Government of India is firm on the issues of interest to it in the key sectors of Agriculture and NAMA. It advocates for the elimination of all forms of export subsidies in the agriculture sector. Such subsidies kept the prices of agricultural products in the international market at artificially low levels and adversely impacted on the interests of poor farmers in developing countries like India who were not able to get remunerative returns for their produce. The Government has further stressed that there would be no movement as far as India was concerned in the area of industrial tariffs (i.e., non-agricultural market access — NAMA) either, without the flexibilities in tariff reduction commitments that were required to protect domestic industries in India.

In order to safeguard the interests of Indian agriculture, the G20 — of which India is a founder member — has also sought elimination of all forms of export subsidies by a credible end date. On NAMA or industrial tariff negotiations, the Government of India has already made clear during the Hong Kong Ministerial Conference that it would not be possible for India to move forward in the negotiations without the flexibilities that developing countries needed to protect their domestic industries such as offering less than the formula reduction or making no reduction at all on a specified number of tariff lines covering their sensitive items/sectors. This is absolutely vital for countries like India in order to be able to safeguard the interests of small and medium enterprises which provide livelihood to millions of industrial workers.

While arguing for elimination of all forms of agricultural export subsidies by the developed countries in general and cotton subsidies in particular, India cited the case of Chhindwara as an example where the heavy subsidies given by developed countries were adversely impacting farmers including those dependent on cotton and pushing them to the margins of impoverishment.

India has expressed its full support for putting the African initiative on cotton on priority in the WTO negotiations, saying : "In other countries too where cotton is a major crop, such as India, this phenomenon has caused large scale loss of livelihoods, leading to thousands of farmers becoming indebted and even committing suicide. It is not merely an economic or commercial issue — but an urgent and serious human imperative that should be addressed effectively, expeditiously, and with all honesty".

ISSUE OF TRIPS AND CBD

India raised the issue of Trade Related Intellectual Property Rights (TRIPS) Agreement and Convention on Bio-Diversity (CBD) at the Hong Kong Ministerial Conference of the World Trade Organisation (WTO) during a meeting with the Facilitator Mr. Walker, Minister of Chile, on "Other Issues" which included TRIPS and environment-related matters. It has been stated that harmonizing the WTO TRIPS Agreement with CBD was vital for preventing bio-piracy and the rich traditional knowledge of developing countries.

Describing the imbalance in the TRIPS Agreement between private intellectual property rights (IPRs) and the intellectual heritage of indigenous communities as part of the unfinished agenda of development inherited from the Uruguay Round, it was pointed out at the plenary session : "There is growing popular discontent among developing countries over bio-piracy and the misappropriation of their traditional knowledge for commercial gain. The Hong Kong Ministerial Conference must pave the way for the launch of negotiations on the issues pertaining to the relationship between the TRIPS Agreement and the Convention on Bio-Diversity".

On the issue of trade in environmental goods and services, India has opposed the "list approach" for seeking tariff reduction on environmental goods as it is not beneficial for developing countries. The "list approach" focuses only on goods and is, in fact, seen as a back door method to bring in NAMA. India has submitted an alternate approach called "environmental project approach" proposing that all environmental goods and services in the project should get tariff concessions.

Amendment in TRIPS and CBD

India along with a number of other developing countries, rich in biodiversity, has proposed an amendment in the TRIPS Agreement to address prevention of bio-piracy and check misappropriation of traditional knowledge. This amendment would pave the way for an international legally binding regime. This is an implementation issue under Para 109 in pursuance of Para 12 of the Doha Ministerial Declaration.

India believes that to prevent bio-piracy of genetic resources and misappropriation of traditional knowledge, the TRIPS Agreement needs to be amended, and three elements, "Disclosure of Country of Origin", "Prior Informed Consent", and "Benefit Sharing" arrangement — together called "Disclosure Requirements", can be incorporated in the TRIPS Agreement.

TRADE RULES MUST BENEFIT THOSE WHO NEED IT MOST

The Doha Round of multilateral trade negotiations should not perpetuate the inequities of global trade. The ambition of developed countries cannot and must not trample on the aspirations of four-fifths of humanity. In the name of completion, if the content of this round only perpetuates the inequities of global trade, then such round would not serve its purpose.

The Doha mandate was to correct the *development deficit* left by the Uruguay Round. Negotiations in Hong Kong would have failed if they did not contribute towards creating a rule-based world order, which not only makes trade free, but also fair.

There would not be any agricultural agreement without Special Products and Special Safeguard Mechanism which were needed to ensure the livelihood and food security of millions of farmers and if effectively applied, could be the bedrock of any agricultural outcome of the Doha Round. The agriculture was structurally the most flawed sector of international trade. It was in agriculture that many developing countries had natural comparative advantage, but they were shut out from world markets by a complex edifice of protection built on high tariff walls, domestic and export subsidies, and an intricate maze of non-tariff barriers. In many developing countries, including India, hundreds of millions of low-income and subsistence farmers eked out a precarious livelihood from agriculture. Unless the playing field is completely leveled, they cannot enter the arena of international competition. Our farmers are quite willing to deal with trade flows — but not with an avalanche of subsidy flows from developed countries.

Regarding industrial tariffs or non-agricultural market access (NAMA), it may be pointed out that market access was not about tariffs alone, as non-tariff barriers such as abuse of both anti-dumping and technical standards hindered market access for developing countries. It is of no use having zero duty levels on aeroplanes, while maintaining a 30 per cent duty on leather handbags! India's traditional industries such as textiles, clothing, leather products, footwear and a range of other medium technology products, involve livelihood of hundreds of millions of industrial workers of small and medium enterprises in developing countries.

Similarly, access to overseas markets in services could be a powerful instrument to banish poverty in developing countries by giving stimulus to economic growth. This is why the liberalization of professional services trade in Modes 1 & 4 needs to figure high on the development agenda. It is also, of course, a paramount need of businesses everywhere in a globalised economy. The services negotiations need a clear direction, without undermining the flexibilities available to developing countries under the GATS framework.

ROADMAP FOR ELIMINATION OF TRADE DISTORTING FARM SUBSIDIES BY DEVELOPED COUNTRIES

The developed countries should come forward with a roadmap for total elimination of trade distorting agricultural subsidies which depress international prices of agricultural produce, thereby hurting farmers in developing countries like India. The real challenge before trade negotiators was the paradox of "one dollar per day versus one billion dollars per day". The vast majority of the poor in developing countries were subsisting on one US dollar per day or less as against agricultural subsidies as high as US $ 1 billion per day in developed countries.

The WTO must address the issues of the least developed countries (LDCs), vulnerable economies, small states and provide a level playing field for all. In agriculture, if we are to correct the existing structural flaws, export subsidies must go on a date to be negotiated. On domestic support, there must be a roadmap for reduction and eventual elimination. Agricultural tariff is the only defensive mechanism available to the developing countries to guard against subsidized imports. For example, tariff on cotton in India is only 10 per cent whereas the US subsidy for cotton is over 42 per cent. India is not against trade flows but against subsidy flows.

Regarding the question on non-agricultural market access (NAMA) or industrial tariffs, what was important was not the formula but what it actually translated into in real terms. Criticising the latest NAMA proposal put forward by the European Union (EU) at the G4 meeting, India pointed out that the European Union proposal for Swiss coefficient of 10 for both developed and developing countries would translate into industrial tariff reduction of 77 per cent for India while the European Union would reduce only by 24 per cent! It described this as special & differential (S&D) treatment in reverse and rejected the proposal outright as unacceptable. India demanded that the European Union must come forward with specific proposals for reducing its tariffs, before developing countries were asked to reduce by even two-thirds of that, in keeping with the principle of proportionality implicit in the S&D provisions for developing countries in WTO agreements. Market access for India in NAMA means elimination of tariff peaks and tariff escalation in developed country markets, end to abuse of anti-dumping laws and removal of non-tariff barriers (NTBs) all of which adversely affected trade flows from developing countries. Market access is not an issue of tariffs alone.

Conclusion

The Doha Round aims at working towards a global trade agreement that would liberalise markets, primarily agriculture, manufacturing and services, to reduce poverty and promote development. The trade talks are designed to help increase trade and develop the economies of poorer countries.

Despite the fact that agriculture accounts for only about eight per cent of world trade, it is the key to any deal because of its importance for developing countries. The deal has to give developing countries the same flexibility in opening up their fledgling industries, which its counterpart, that is, rich nations expect in politically sensitive farm sectors.

Indeed, today reaching agreement on subsidies depends on additional concessions from the US equivalent to less than a week's worth of transatlantic trade. It depends on an additional handful of percentage reduction in the highest agriculture tariffs by the EU and Japan. It depends on an additional handful of percentage reduction in the highest industrial tariffs by emerging economies such as Brazil and India. All this needs to be done, not by tomorrow, but over a transition period of several years to leave space for a smooth adjustment.

NOTES

1. Doha Mandate on Agriculture, Doha Round of WTO Multilateral Trade Negotiations, Doha, Qatar, November 2001.
2. Trade Related Intellectual Property Rights (TRIPS) Convention on Bio-Diversity (CBD) WTO Ministerial Conference, Hong Kong, China, December 2005.

APPENDICES

Appendix-I

DEVELOPING COUNTRIES IN WORLD TRADE

This chapter provides an overview of major trends in the participation of developing countries in world trade over the past two decades, followed by a brief examination of some of the key factors that were associated with trends for different groups of developing countries — in particular, the sharply different trade performance of most developing countries in Asia (very positive) and that of a number of the poorest developing countries (very disappointing).

I. MAJOR TRENDS IN DEVELOPING COUNTRIES' TRADE PERFORMANCE

The Changing Structure of World Trade

Over the past two decades developments in the three broad product categories of world merchandise trade have differed sharply. While the value of exports of mining products (mainly fuels) and agricultural products rose between four and five times, those of manufactured goods increased nine times (Chart 1.A). Most of these differences in long-term developments can be attributed to volume rather than price changes. On a volume basis, manufactured exports more than tripled, in contrast to gains of 70 per cent and 25 per cent, respectively, for agricultural products and mining products (Chart 2.A). Nominal prices for mining products as a group in 1994 stood about 314 times above their level in 1973, while those of manufactures and agricultural products were up 2.8 and 2.2 times, respectively (Chart 2.B).[1]

After fluctuating in the range of 55 to 60 per cent between 1973 and 1985, the share of manufactures in merchandise trade had increased sharply to around 78 per cent by 1995 (Chart l.B). The remaining 22 per cent is divided about equally between agriculture and mining. Agricultural products experienced a slow but steady erosion of their share over the two decades, from more than 20 per cent of world trade in 1973 to somewhat more than 11 per cent in 1995. The share of mining products — heavily influenced by oil prices — peaked in 1980 and dropped sharply thereafter. In 1995, the share of mining products in world merchandise trade was around 11 per cent, compared with 17 per cent in 1973 and 28 per cent in 1980.

Trade Performance of the Aggregate of Developing Countries

Taking into account the very large share of primary products in developing countries' exports in the 1970s (more than three-quarters), it is not surprising that the share of developing countries (as a group) in world merchandise trade peaked in the same year as the share of mining products did, namely 1980 (Table 1). Following the historical peak share of 28 per cent that year, the share of the developing countries in world merchandise trade declined in line with oil prices over the first half of the 1980s. Once oil prices bottomed out in 1986, the share of the

TABLE 1

Share of Developing Countries in World Merchandise Exports, 1973-1995

(Percentage based on value figures)

	1973	**1980**	**1985**	**1990**	**1995p**
Agricultural products	27	28	29	25	26½
Mining products	55	64	49½	50	47½
Fuels	*68½*	*72*	*54’A*	*60*	*57*
Manufactures	7	10	13	15½	20
Total merchandise	**19**	**28**	**23**	**21½**	**22½**

Notes : (1) In this table, China is not included in developing country group.

(2) 1995 figures are provisional.

developing countries started to rise again, largely due to their growing share of world trade in manufactured goods.

CHART 1

World Merchandise Exports by Major Product Group : Value Developments, 1973-95

A. Values (Billion dollars)

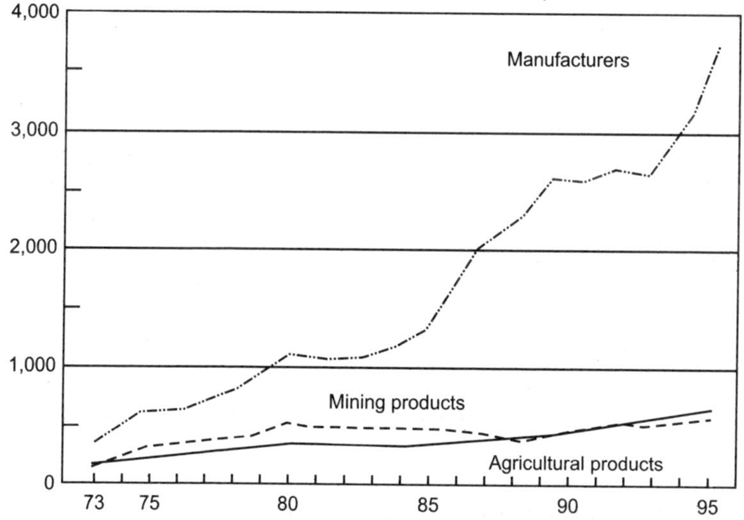

B. Shares (percentage)

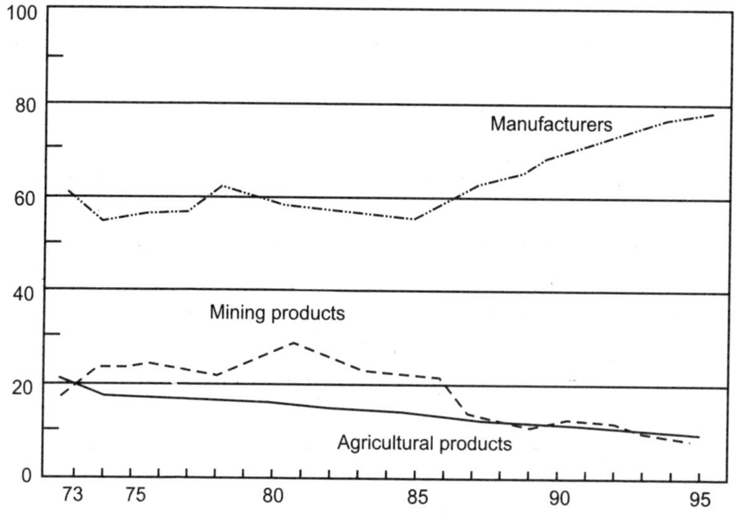

CHART 2

World Merchandise Exports by Major Product Group : Value Price Developments, 1973-94

A. Volume Indices, 1973=100

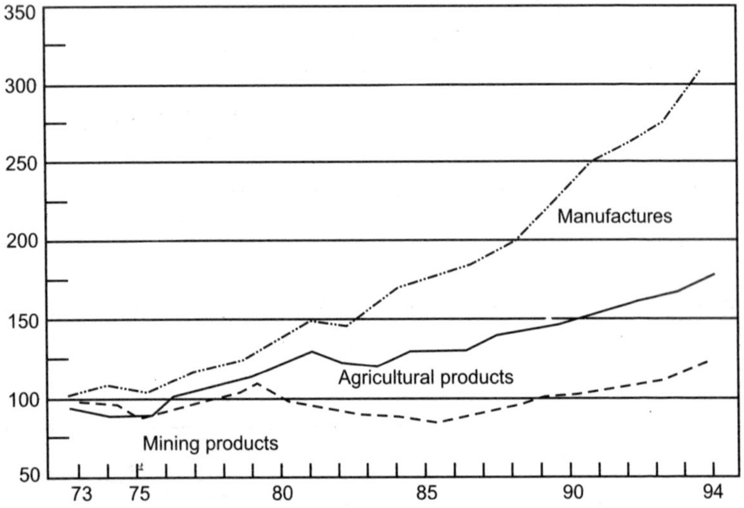

B. Price (unit value), Indices 1973=100

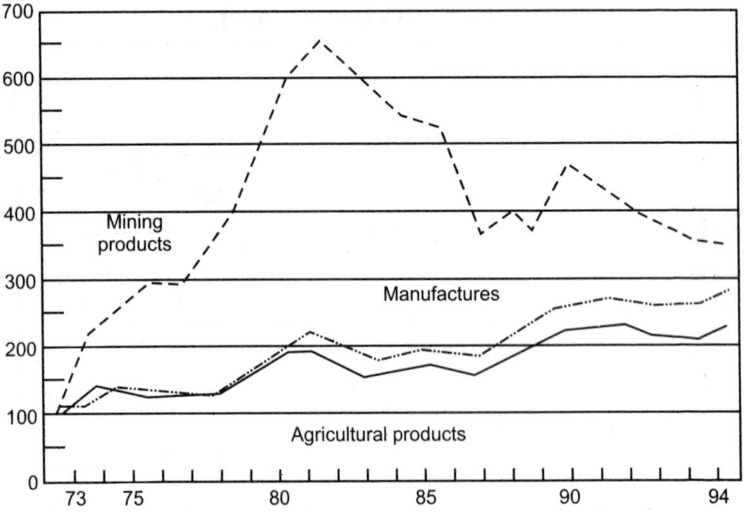

As is evident from Table 2, the product composition of developing countries' merchandise exports has changed dramatically in the past decade; particularly as regards manufactures (close to a doubling of the share to nearly two-thirds) and mining products (a decline in the share of more than half to less than one-quarter). The strong gains in manufactures brought the share of developing countries in world exports of manufactures to 20 per cent last year, double the 1980 share and nearly triple the 1973 share.

TABLE 2

Product Structure of Developing Countries Merchandise Exports, 1973-95

(Percentage based on value figures)

	1973	1980	1985	1990[a]	1995
Agricultural products	30	15	17½	14½	14
Mining Products	47½	65	47	34	22½
Fuels	*39½*	*61*	*43½*	*29½*	*19*
Manufactures	22	19	34½	50½	62½
Total merchandise[b]	**100**	**100**	**100**	**100**	**100**

a : Break in time series can affect comparison between 1985 and 1990.

b : Including unspecified products.

Notes : (1) In this table, China is not included in developing country group.

(2) 1995 figures are provisional.

Trade Performance of Developing Countries by Region

Trends in their respective shares in world merchandise trade over the past decade varied among the regions. While the developing countries in each of the major regions recorded export growth, as can be seen from Chart 3, the developing countries in Asia increased their market share dramatically, while Latin America's share stagnated and those of Africa and the Middle East declined. As a result, the shares of Africa and the Middle East in world merchandise trade are now below that of China.

There is a relatively close link between this trade performance and the share of manufactures in the merchandise exports of the

CHART 3

Developing Countries Merchandise Exports, 1985-95 (Billion dollars and percentage)

A. Values

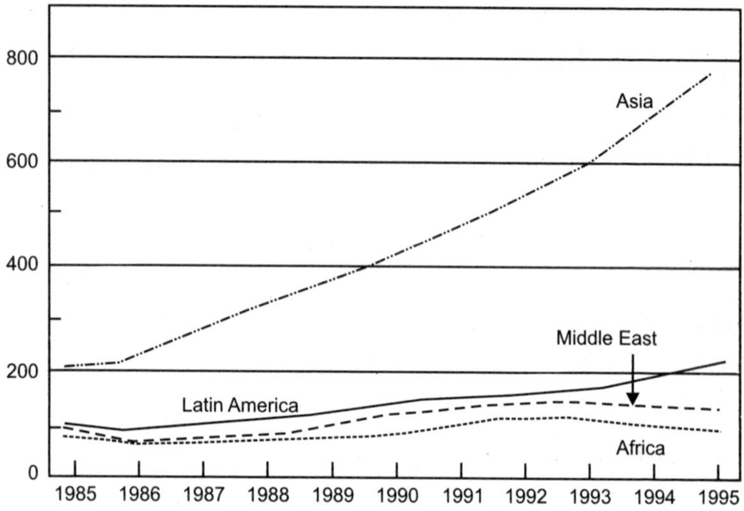

B. Shares of Selected Regions in World Merchandise Exports

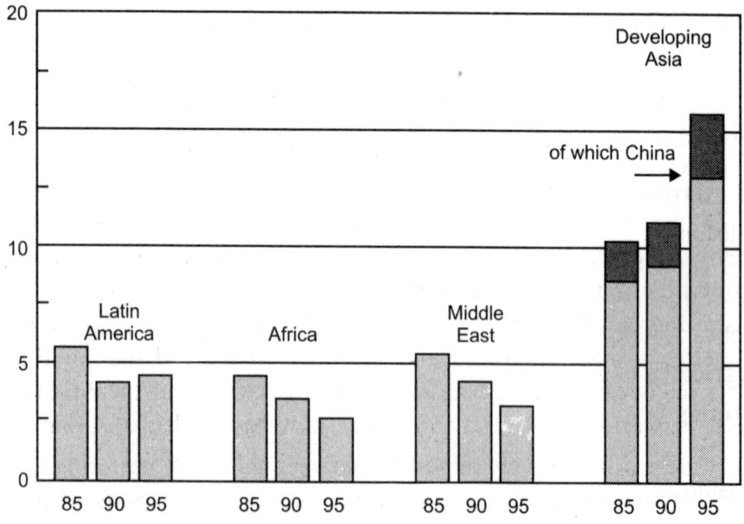

respective regions. Figures in Table 3 for developing Asia (excluding China), China, and the group of "other developing countries" reveal a highly different product structure of merchandise exports. While manufactures account for more than 80 per cent of total merchandise exports for China and other developing countries in Asia, the corresponding share for the group of "other developing countries" is less than half that figure. Developing Asia and China have high shares not only in manufactures but also in many of the fastest growing product categories, such as office and telecom equipment, clothing and other consumer goods (such as footwear and toys). In 1994, the group of "other developing countries" exported more mining products than manufactured goods, and the share of agricultural products in their exports was also noticeably higher than for developing Asia and China.

TABLE 3

Global Trade and the Product Structure of Selected Developing Areas, 1985-94

	World Exports : Annual Growth Rate 1985-94	Product Structure of Exports in 1994		
		Developing Asia*	China	Other Developing Countries
Manufactures	**5.8**	**81.2**	**82.0**	**38.3**
of which :				
- Office and telecom equipment	12.3	26.2	8.2	3.2
- Clothing	7.6	8.3	18.7	4.5
- Other consumer goods	6.7	10.7	24.2	4.0
Agricultural products	**1.8**	**10.4**	**12.2**	**18.4**
Mining products	**-2.6**	**7.3**	**5.3**	**42.1**
Fuels	-8.1	5.8	3.4	36.6
Total merchandise	**2.8**	**100.0**	**100.0**	**100.0**

*Excluding China.

Another factor which distinguishes developing Asia and China on one hand, and all other developing countries combined on the other, is their respective participation in the globalization process. Data on the evolution of trade-to-GDP ratios, and on inflows of foreign direct investment (FDI), are useful, albeit rough, indicators of the extent of integration into the global economy. As regards the ratio of trade in goods and services to GDP, the contrast between developing Asia (including China) and other developing countries is evident in Chart 4. For the Asian developing countries a dramatic doubling in their

CHART 4

Ratio of Trade in Goods and Services to GDP for Developing Areas, 1974-94

(Based on constant 1987 prices and exchange rates)

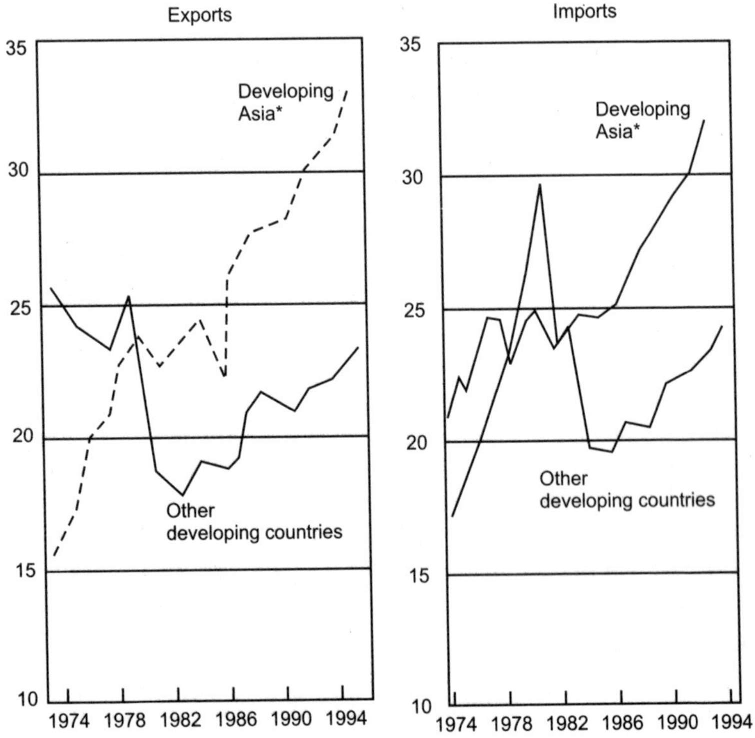

* Includes China.

trade-to-GDP ratio can be observed for the 1974 to 1994 period; if China is excluded from developing Asia, the trade-to-GDP ratio is significantly higher; however, the trend increase in the ratio is very similar. The "other developing countries" as a group, in contrast, have trade-to-GDP ratios in 1994 which are — despite the recovery since 1986 — not much different from the 1974 levels.[2]

Along with a more favourable trade performance over the past decade, the developing countries in Asia also recorded a much stronger investment performance. Most South East Asian countries reported ratios of domestic fixed investment to GDP of around 30 per cent during the 1985-1994 period, while those of Latin America and Africa fluctuated around 20 per cent. At the same time, the former countries were more open and attractive to foreign direct investment. As is evident from Chart 5, developing Asia and China attracted most of the FDI flows to developing countries. Inflows into China alone are estimated to be roughly equivalent to the FDI inflows to Latin America, while Africa and

CHART 5

Cumulative FDI Inflows into Selected Developing Regions, 1988-94

(Billion dollars)

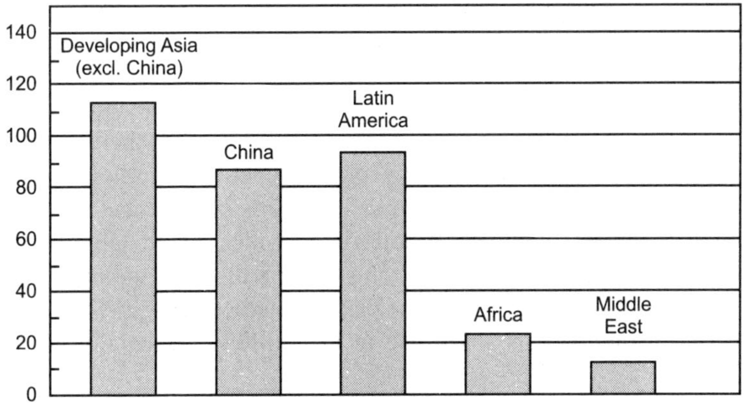

Source : IMF, Balance of Payments Yearbook, 1995

the Middle East attracted only very small shares of the FDI flows to developing countries.

A Closer Look at the Strong and Weak Trade Performances

In order to examine trade performances on a more disaggregated level, two partially overlapping comparisons are developed briefly below (a third comparison is given in Box 1 on page 306). The first involves comparing a group of countries that recorded above average export growth during 1985-94, with a group of countries that recorded negative export growth over that same period (see Annex for the composition of the two groups).

Among the 25 countries that recorded above average growth of merchandise exports during 1985-94, 15 reported "steady" above average growth (that is, for both the sub-periods 1985-90 and 1990-94). A large majority of these steady strong performers — 12 out of 15 countries — export mainly manufactures (the share of manufactures in their respective merchandise exports ranged from 70 to 97 per cent in 1994). Half of the remaining ten strong (but not "steady" exporters) also export principally manufactured goods. As regards the 35 countries whose exports in 1994 were below the 1985 level, only four export principally manufactures. A review of those four traders reveals that very particular factors explain their presence among the poor performers.[3]

Although the comparison between the poor and strong performers indicates a correlation between the share of manufactures in total merchandise exports and the growth of total merchandise exports, there are at least two important examples where strong export growth coincided with a moderate share of manufactures in total merchandise trade. In the case of Viet Nam, the high and steady export growth (from a very low level of exports in 1985) is linked not only to the rapid rise in exports of manufactures, but also to the development of oil fields which led to significant exports of crude oil, and to strong exports of food (mainly rice). The rise in exports of crude oil and manufactured goods can be partly attributed to a sharp rise in FDI inflows, especially in the 1990s.

Chile is another country with a strong export performance and a very low share of manufactures (traditionally defined) in total exports (17 per cent). The success of Chile is linked to the successful diversification into "new" (sometimes highly processed) agricultural products and an above average performance for its largest single export product, namely copper. Even though all copper exporters benefited from the fact that copper prices increased faster than the prices of other commodities, Chile increased its share in global copper output from 16 per cent in 1985 to 26 per cent in 1993 (while at the same time, the share of copper in Chile's total merchandise exports declined from 47 to 38 per cent). Other dynamic exports included fish, shell fish, fruits, wine and wood pulp. Important elements in the export expansion of both copper and agricultural products were the wide ranging liberalization and privatization programs and the associated inflow of FDI, which gives Chile one of the largest stocks of FDI per capita in Latin America.

Much of the concern about "marginalization" centres on the group of least developed countries (LLDCs). The source of this concern is readily apparent from the figures in Table 4, as is the motivation behind the search for lessons in the experience of East Asian economies. Low trade-to-GDP ratios, low investment and small shares of manufacturing in GDP and exports, are common traits of the "typical" LLDCs.[4] It should be added that Bangladesh — by far the largest country among the LLDCs — is a partial exception. With a high share of manufactures in its total merchandise exports (83 per cent in 1994), it figured among those traders which expanded their exports faster than world trade through 1985-94.

The wide range of experience among developing countries is also examined in a recent World Bank report, using some of the same variables mentioned above (such as the share of manufactures in exports).[5] Box 1 reproduces the principal conclusions of that analysis, the latter two of which anticipate points made later in this chapter.

TABLE 4

Comparison of Trade Performance and Other Selected Indicators for Different Groups of Developing Countries, 1980-94

	All Developing Countries[a]	Least Developed Countries	Six East Asian Traders[b]
1	2	3	4
Merchandise exports:			
value	3.2	1.4	11.5
Annual percentage change	8.7	1.3	12.0
1980-90			
1990-94			
Merchandise exports:			
volume	3.7	0.6	9.8
Annual percentage change	9.0	3.8	10.6
1980-90			
1990-94			
Merchandise exports	260	28	2,700
Per capita ($)			
1994			
Merchandise exports	24	9	—
Share in GDP (%)			
1993			
Exports of manufactures	59	21	85
Share in merchandise exports (%) 1992			
Manufacturing output	21	11	—
Share in GDP (%)	23	9	—
1980			
1990			

1	2	3	4
Gross fixed investment	26	16	—
Share in GDP (%)	26	15	—
1980			
1990			

a : Developing country figures include China.

b : WTO Secretariat estimates. The six traders are Chinese Taipei, Hong Kong, Republic of Korea, Malaysia, Singapore and Thailand. Hong Kong re-exports are excluded.

Source : UNCTAD, *Handbook of International Trade and Development Statistics,* 1994; and *The Least Developed Countries, 1996 Report,* Annex II, Basic Data on the Least Developed Countries.

Box 1

Disparities in Global Integration

Reproduced from Chapter 2 of *Global Economic Prospects and the Developing Countries,* World Bank, April 1996

Developing countries as a group have participated extensively in the acceleration of global integration, although some have done much better than others....This chapter reviews developing countries' widely varying experience with integration over the past ten years and explores the causes and implications of the large disparities. ... The analysis draws four main conclusions :

* Changes in integration were highly differentiated. Many developing countries became less integrated with the world economy over the past decade, and a large divide separates the least from the most integrated. It is striking, for example, that the ratio of trade to GDP fell in forty-four of ninety-three developing countries over the past ten years, while the ratio of FDI to GDP fell in more than a third.

* Countries with the highest levels of integration tended to exhibit the fastest output growth, as did countries that made the greatest advances in integration. Many low-income countries are among the least integrated, however, and some became even more

(*Contd...*)

marginalized during this period, experiencing both falling incomes and reduced integration. But other low-income countries — including some of the largest — were among the fastest integrators.

* Sound policies play an important role in determining both growth and the speed of integration. Policy reforms designed to increase an economy's growth and stability are likely to influence a country's speed of integration, both directly and through their effect on growth. Reforms that promote stable macro-economic conditions, realistic exchange rates, and open trade and investment regimes are also important for growth and integration.

* Improvements in the external environment and modest reforms in many lagging integrators suggest that their growth rates may show some improvement in the next decade. But if current policies and trends persist, many developing countries can expect to fall further behind OECD countries in per capita GDP.

TABLE 5

Speed of Integration of Developing Countries, Early 1980s to Early 1990s

(Number of countries)

Ranking	East Asia	South Asia	Latin America and the Caribbean	Middle East and North Africa	Sub-Saharan Africa	Europe and Central Asia
Fast integrators	6	3	5	2	2	5
Moderate integrators		2	5	4	10	2
Weak integrators	3	—	9	2	10	—
Slow integrators	—	—	2	5	14	2
Total	9	5	21	13	36	9

Source : World Bank Staff Estimates.

Note : To summarize integration trends, the analysis... uses a speed of integration index derived from changes between the early 1980s and early 1990s in four of the indicators discussed above : the ratio of real trade to GDP, the ratio of FDI to GDP, Institutional Investor credit ratings, and the share of manufactures in exports. The speed of integration index is the simple average of changes in the four indicators over the period expressed as standardized scores.

On the basis of this index, developing countries are grouped in four categories ranging from "fast integrators" (those with the highest index values) to "slow integrators" (those with the lowest; Table 5). This classification is not intended to derive a precise categorization of individual countries but rather to develop evidence about the factors that might account for large differences in the speed of integration among groups of countries, and the consequences of this for performance.

Commercial Services

It appears that the share of developing countries in world exports and imports of commercial services increased between 1987 and 1994 (however, the share remains somewhat below the share of developing countries in world merchandise trade).[6] This is entirely due to the performance of the Asian developing countries, as other regions reported a stagnating or declining share in world services trade. As regards the three major categories of commercial services — transport, travel and other business services — the available data suggest that the developing countries as a group have increased their market shares in all three categories since 1987.

II. FACTORS UNDERLYING THE VARIED TRADE PERFORMANCES OF DEVELOPING COUNTRIES

For ease of exposition, this part is divided into "external factors" and "domestic factors". The discussion is limited to certain key factors in each category (any attempt at a complete listing would be well beyond the scope of this overview chapter). A third section briefly highlights the fact that factors in one category often interact in important ways, both with one another and with factors in the other category.

(1) External Factors

Access to Foreign Markets

Although the average level of tariff protection on non-agricultural imports into the industrial countries is relatively low — once the Uruguay Round reductions are fully implemented they will average 3.8 per cent — import barriers represent a serious obstacle in specific sectors.[7] Agriculture has been highly protected and exports frequently subsidized, and special provisions permitting discriminatory quotas on textiles and clothing, in place since the beginning of the 1960s, were expanded with the introduction of the Multifibre Arrangement (MFA) in 1974. In the area of manufactures more generally, there was a proliferation of so-called "grey area" measures (VERs, OMAs and so forth) from the late 1960s until the beginning of the Uruguay Round, with an above-average incidence on labour-intensive exports from developing countries.[8] More recently, anti-dumping actions and countervailing duties have increasingly been used to restrict imports.[9]

There are post-Uruguay Round tariff peaks for some products of critical interest to developing countries, including textiles, clothing, and fish and fish products. As a result, the average reduction in tariffs for industrial country imports from developing countries other than the LLDCs (37 per cent) is lower than the average reduction in applied tariffs for imports from all countries (40 per cent), while the average reduction on imports from LLDCs was even smaller (25 per cent). On the other hand, it should be noted that the below-average reductions in tariffs on textiles and clothing do not take into account the increase in market access that will result from the phase-out of MFA-related restrictions. At the same time, an important feature of the tariff commitments made by the developed countries in the Uruguay Round is a substantial increase in *bound* duty-free treatment. Once the agreed tariff reductions have been fully implemented, the proportion of merchandise imports entering duty-free will increase from just over 10 to almost 40 per cent for the United States, from almost 24 to almost 38 per cent for the European Union, and from 35 to 71 per cent for Japan.

While the MFA was a major distortion of world trade which affected many developing countries' participation in world trade in textiles and clothing, individual countries have been affected in very different ways by the MFA, depending on their comparative advantage in these products. On the one hand, there are the exporters of textiles and clothing which currently have a strong comparative advantage and whose market access has been tightly restricted, and which therefore will benefit from the Uruguay Round agreement to abolish MFA-related restrictions.[10] On the other hand, two groups of exporters may suffer transitional adjustment costs as a result of its abolition. These are, first, those countries with large quotas based on a previous comparative advantage that has been eroded by rising real wages and/or the emergence of even lower-cost suppliers among the newcomers (in those cases in which existing quotas are not fully utilized, much of the transitional adjustment to the reduced competitiveness presumably has already occurred); and second, those that may have been induced by MFA restrictions on other suppliers to enter the production of textiles and clothing without possessing a true comparative advantage in the production of these goods.

Developing countries, in particular the LLDCs, are concerned about the erosion of the margins of preference they enjoyed under the GSP and Lomé Convention. The tariff reductions agreed to in the Tokyo Round (an average cut of one-third in industrial country tariffs on manufactures) reduced preference margins, which in turn are being further reduced as the tariff reductions agreed to in the Uruguay Round (a further 40 per cent reduction) are implemented.[11] The impact of preference erosion, of course, depends in part on the rate of utilization of the preferences. As studies by the UNCTAD and others have pointed out, the utilization of existing preferential arrangements — and thus their trade promoting effects — have been limited for various reasons.

Half of the European Union's imports from Africa are petroleum and other fuels that enter under MFN rates bound at zero, and three-quarters of the imports of industrial products enter duty free or under very low MFN tariffs.[12] In the case of GSP, there are limits on product coverage and limits on the extent of duty free entry. Restrictive rules of origin and an implicit lack of permanence are characteristics of virtually all preference schemes. At the same time, the impact of the Uruguay Round on Lomé Convention preference margins on agricultural products such as sugar, cut flowers, vegetables and fruits, and beef, may also be relatively limited. Moreover, for agricultural products the initial level of preferences granted was higher and rules of origin are less of a problem than for manufactured products, so that the rate of utilization of preferences granted for agricultural products is generally higher than for manufactured products.

The bias in the structure of many developing countries' exports towards unprocessed products has often been related to the structure of tariffs and other trade barriers in major markets, in particular their tendency to increase or "escalate" with the level of a product's processing. Substantial reductions in tariff escalation in developed country markets was a major objective of developing countries in the Uruguay Round, and this goal was to a degree achieved. In Canada, there will now be little or no tariff escalation affecting paper, rubber, zinc, and tin. In the European Union, the same holds true for paper and tin, while the absolute level of escalation for tobacco products has been greatly reduced. The extent of tariff escalation for U.S. imports will be eliminated or greatly reduced for several products, including paper, jute, nickel, lead, and tobacco. Nevertheless, tariff escalation continues to be a feature of developed country tariff structures whose reduction or elimination will no doubt remain an important developing country goal.[13]

The LLDCs in particular have also been concerned by the growing importance of free trade areas and customs unions in recent years, which now cover virtually all their major export markets, including Europe and North America. Since most of the major regional trading arrangements do not include LLDCs, they are concerned that these arrangements will result in a loss of preferences vis-a-vis third countries and, more generally, increase their degree of marginalization. While the LLDCs and other third countries might benefit from the trade-creating effects of the regional arrangements — and from the stimulus to growth and thus import demand in the member countries — they might incur costs as a consequence of the trade-diverting effects (and perhaps also investment diversion). While the importance of the trade-diverting effects is difficult to assess, there are reasons to think that actual diversion effects on overall LLDC exports will be limited. Most LLDC exports do not directly compete with members' mutual trade, even if there might be some exceptions such as clothing for Bangladesh and various agricultural products. The tariff reductions and bindings agreed to in the Uruguay Round agreement will ensure that the degree of discrimination against third countries is reduced.[14]

An additional concern that has been raised by developing countries over past decades has been the implications of anticompetitive practices by private enterprises in restricting the market access of developing countries to industrialized countries. For example, a recent UNCTAD Report drew attention to the need to ensure that trade obligations and concerns are not frustrated by private anti-competitive practices and that there is a convergence in the objectives and the application of national competition policies to prohibit cartel and collusive tendering as "most national competition policies still do not apply to restrictive business practices which solely attract foreign markets.[15]

Keeping the "Market Access" Factor in Perspective

The aspects of market access described above are relevant to any explanation of the export performance of developing countries as a group over the past two decades. On the other hand, they are less helpful in explaining why many developing countries have been much less successful than others in expanding their exports over that period. In some industrial country markets, such as that of the United States, nearly all developing countries have confronted essentially the same import barriers. In others, such as the European Union, many of the countries in Africa or among the LLDCs with a below average export record actually had more liberal market access for a wide range of products — for example via Lome Convention preferences — than did the countries which recorded above average expansions of exports.

Capital Inflows

Although not directly related to exports in the first instance, the growing constraints on foreign aid and the difficulties in attracting increased foreign private financing and investment are affecting the growth prospects of countries lagging behind in global integration.

The figures in Table 6 document the well-known trend for official development aid to represent a much smaller share, and private capital inflows a much larger share, of capital flows to developing countries (export credits are also down sharply from the 1989 level). In just eight years, there has been nearly a complete reversal of the respective shares of official development finance and private capital inflows.

Recent capital flows into developing Asia and Latin America have been largely private direct investment and portfolio flows to private sector borrowers rather than official flows and commercial bank lending to public sector borrowers; in Africa, in contrast, aggregate net capital inflows are still largely official flows.[16]

TABLE 6

Capital Flows into Developing Countries from OECD Countries, 1986-94

(Billions of U.S. dollars, and percentage shares in parentheses)

	1986	1989	1994[1]
Official development finance[2]	50.1 (66.9)	60.9 (52.7)	70.2 (38.2)
Of which : ODA	38.5 (51.5)	48.8 (42.2)	59.7 (32.5)
Total export credits	-0.6 (-0.8)	9.4 (8.1)	3.2 (1.7)
Private flows	25.3 (33.8)	45.3 (39.2)	110.4 (60.1)
Of which : Direct investment	10.7 (14.3)	26.5 (22.9)	47.0 (25.6)
Total net resource flows	74.8 (100.0)	115.6 (100.0)	183.8 (100.0)

1. Provisional.
2. The concept of Official Development Finance embraces the resource receipts measure of Official Development Assistance (ODA) together with non-concessional disbursements for development purposes from multilateral institutions and other official bilateral flows for development purposes (including refinancing loans) which have too low a grant element to qualify as ODA.

Source : OECD (1996a).

With limited access to private capital, official development assistance continues to be by far the leading source of external financing for the poorest countries. For the 1988-94 period, flows of official development assistance represented 98 per cent of the net financial flows to the LLDCs.[17]

World foreign direct investment flows (FDI), measured in current dollars, declined in the early 1980s after the cyclical peak in 1979-80. By 1984-85, annual FDI flows had recovered to the previous peak level. Thereafter, a sharp rise in FDI flows could be observed in the second half of the 1980s, and in 1989-90 the flows were about four times larger than the average FDI flows of 1980-85. This record level of FDI flows was not maintained, and markedly lower FDI flows were reported for the years 1991 to 1993. Averaging global FDI outflows and inflows, it is estimated that in 1994, FDI flows were roughly at the same nominal level as in the previous peak 1989-90. Preliminary data for 1995, indicate a new surge in FDI flows with an increase exceeding 40 per cent.[18]

For analytical purposes it is worthwhile to relate global FDI flows to other global indicators which experience similar cyclical and price factors. The available data for the three times series — global FDI, world merchandise trade and gross fixed investment of OECD countries — indicate that global FDI flows did not grow faster than world merchandise trade or OECD fixed investment during the 1980-85 period, but expanded considerably faster in the second half of the 1980s. For the 1990-94 period, FDI flows lagged behind both gross fixed investment and world merchandise trade. In 1995, FDI flows again expanded significantly faster than world merchandise trade (40 per cent versus 19 per cent).

The share of the developing countries in world FDI inflows, which decreased between the first half of the 1980s and the second half of the 1980s, increased from 15 to about 35 per cent between 1990 and 1994. China played a major role in this increase, but other developing countries, in particular in Asia and Latin America, have also benefited from a sharp increase in FDI. At the same time, FDI flows to the developing countries are highly concentrated. In 1994, China accounted for about 40 per cent of all FDI inflows into the developing countries and another nine countries for another 40 per cent.[19]

A noteworthy development is that a large part of this increase can be attributed to a sharp rise in FDI outflows from Hong Kong. Estimates, based on partner statistics, indicate that Hong Kong FDI outflows rose from $2.2 billion in 1990 to $21 billion in 1994, accounting for more than two-thirds of all developing countries' outflows.

Most of the OECD FDI outflows go to other developed countries. As can be seen from the FDI stock data, 75 to 80 per cent of the outward stock of OECD countries is in other OECD countries. This high ratio is not surprising as the share of intra-OECD exports in total OECD exports in 1994 was also nearly 75 per cent. Both trade and investment data reflect the strong integration within the OECD area.

The composition of capital inflows has also differed dramatically across regions. While FDI comprised over 40 per cent of net capital flows to Asia during 1989-94, the majority of flows into Latin American countries have been portfolio investment, with FDI accounting for little more than a quarter of capital flows to that region.[20] Anticipating the discussion of "domestic factors" in the next section, it is evident that in some Latin American countries, high real interest rates attracted large portfolio investments and contributed to the rise in FDI inflows. In the aftermath of the Mexican Peso crisis, the importance of more stable, longer-term oriented capital inflows in the form of FDI became apparent again. The benefits of FDI inflows linked to a policy of broadly-based economic liberalization and privatization programmes are perhaps less spectacular in the short-run, but improve the longer-term growth perspective. Portfolio flows have also been a major factor in the Middle East and Europe, including in Egypt and Turkey, while FDI into that region has been minimal. In Africa, the dominant type of inflow is official flows.

Once again anticipating the discussion of "domestic factors", according to the World Bank East and South Asia are expected to continue to grow at a slightly reduced but still relatively rapid pace due to, among other things, increasing intra-regional trade, strong domestic demand and large inflows of foreign capital.[21] In Latin America and the Caribbean, growth will be sluggish as macroeconomic adjustments in Mexico and Brazil continue to work themselves out. Similarly, the recent boom in FDI inflows to Europe and Central Asia are forecast to consolidate the positive growth performance in these transition economies, although conditions remain difficult in several Central Asian and Caucasus republics. Prospects for the LLDCs are less sanguine, particularly for those in Africa. The forecast for world commodity prices is for continued decline, albeit a gradual one, following the rebound in 1994-95. This points to further terms of trade declines for these countries and further weakening of their growth prospects and ability to attract foreign investment.

More generally, Africa's poor performance in attracting capital flows can be explained by the region's difficulties in improving economic policies, its lower overall economic performance, its persistent debt problems and — as a crucial economy-wide reflection of these factors, worth bearing in mind in devising new approaches — the greater uncertainty facing investors, domestic as well as foreign. According to the IMF, "some African countries — the CFA franc zone countries, Kenya and Uganda, for example — have recently attracted private capital flows, as policy reform efforts have gathered strength and structural adjustment measures have helped to maintain gains in competitiveness resulting from more appropriate exchange rate policies".[22]

Other External Factors

As the world economy becomes increasingly integrated, external influences have an ever-greater impact on countries' own domestic economies. Due to their typically smaller size and less diversified economic structure, many developing countries are more strongly affected by, and more vulnerable to, changes in the international environment than the industrial countries. Indeed, over the past several decades developing economies have experienced to varying degrees the impacts of, among other things, fluctuations in world interest rates on their outstanding debts, and cyclical changes in industrial country demand for their exports. Over 1984-93, the IMF estimates that these effects, together with the previously mentioned relative decline in primary commodity prices, combined to reduce the average growth rate of those developing countries with the lowest growth performance by three-quarters of one percentage point.[23]

Finally, mention should be made of a factor that straddles the external/domestic distinction, namely the debt burden of the LLDCs. The level of the LLDCs' stock of external debt is estimated to have been $126.7 billion in 1993, while the ratio of the total debt to GNP was 70 per cent in the same year.[24] The situation is even worse for African LLDCs, where the external debt amounted to $96.7 billion in 1993, with a ratio of total debt to GNP of 130 per cent.

There is an emerging consensus on the need to address the LLDCs' debt burden by new methods and approaches. In particular, an IMF-World Bank debt initiative under consideration recognizes the need to bring the levels of LLDC debt to a point of sustainability. The plan entails the participation of other international financial institutions, and the Paris Club of official creditors, and other bilateral creditors to reduce to sustainable levels the external debt burden of a number of countries pursuing sound economic policies.[25]

(2) Domestic Factors

There is little doubt that for many of the developing countries whose export performance in the past decade has been disappointing, the primary problem is an inadequate domestic supply response rather than a lack of export opportunities. In the past decade, about one-third of the countries in the LLDC group have been afflicted by acute civil strife and political instability which have severely retarded development efforts.[26] The economies of the LLDCs have been hampered by a number of structural factors, including macroeconomic imbalance, lack of human and physical capital, poorly developed infrastructure, and poorly functioning institutions.[27]

Trade Policies and Participation in the WTO

Domestic protection is one of the main sources of distortions between domestic and international prices, which cause countries to use their scarce resources less efficiently. Very high levels of protection in particular can seriously impair both export performance and domestic growth. Protection reduces the profitability of exporting relative to serving the domestic market ("a tax on imports is a tax on exports"), blunts incentives to adopt world-class standards of product quality and production efficiency, and, particularly when the size of the domestic market is not in itself a sufficient attraction, can negatively affect the country's attractiveness to foreign investors.[28] There are still large differences between developing countries in the extent of liberalization undertaken and the levels of existing protection. Tariffs in South Asia, averaging around 45 per cent in the early 1990s remain very high, with substantial peaks and restrictions in consumer goods. African countries, in general, have been more successful in reducing quantitative restrictions than tariffs which are still in the 25-30 per cent range, showing little change from the second half of the 1980s. In contrast, average tariffs in East Asia (excluding China) are in the 10-20 per cent range and non-tariff measures have been cut back although many such measures remain. Protection in Latin America has also been dramatically reduced with average applied tariffs now in the 10-20 per cent range and few remaining non-tariff measures.

The disciplines accepted by all WTO developing countries in the Uruguay Round increased significantly through their tariff bindings, acceptance of all the Multilateral Trade Agreements, including more intensified disciplines covering domestic policy measures such as subsidization, and new multilateral commitments in the areas of services and intellectual property rights.[29] Commitments in their goods and services schedules also help lock-in reforms in the trade regime, thereby adding to the credibility of the reforms in the eyes of foreign and domestic investors.[30] At the same time, provisions in various agreements grant differential and more favourable treatment (principally longer implementation periods) to developing countries, and in some cases to countries in transition to a market economy.

As a result, the developing countries, and in particular the LLDCs, are faced with the challenge of organizing themselves to effectively participate in the multilateral trading system. Among the prerequisites for a more effective integration into the international trading system, and thus into the global economy, are the need (i) to seize the trading opportunities arising from the rules, concessions and commitments by trading partners; (ii) to effectively exercise their trading rights in export markets; (iii) to fully implement their trade obligations, turning them into a way of enhancing the stability and transparency of their trade regimes, and to devise and execute development policies within the framework of these obligations, and (iv) to define and pursue their trade and development interests in trade negotiations, ensuring that their concerns are fully reflected in the future international trade agenda. Many developing countries — and especially the LLDCs — have found themselves poorly equipped in terms of institutional infrastructure and human and financial resources available to meet these challenges. A major effort is required on their part with respect to institution building and the upgrading and specialization of human resources and improved forms of information collection and management.[31]

With respect to the administration of their trade regimes and to their participation in WTO work and activities, the developing countries need to expand their human resources and institutional infrastructure. International organizations as well as donor governments are presently assisting developing countries and countries in transition to more actively participate in the international trading system. These organizations and donors should collaborate to coordinate and focus their assistance on institution building, training and information management, keeping in mind the potential for improvements in these areas to play an important role in helping the LLDCs to reverse the trend toward marginalization.

Export Concentration

In most of the least developed and other low-income countries, primary products — incorporating low levels of processing — continue to account for the bulk of both national production and exports. Given the changing structure of world trade described at the beginning of this chapter, it is not surprising that most of the countries that have participated little or not at all in global integration are primary commodity-dependent countries with relatively small and highly inefficient manufacturing sectors. As a result, these countries are especially vulnerable to external (or domestic) shocks and are generally viewed as having limited growth prospects.

In their assessment of the future trends of African economies, Goldin et al. (1993) note that,

> Agriculture remains the foundation of Africa's economic development, and its weakness underlies the poor overall performance. Over the last 20 years the growth in agricultural production trailed behind population growth by almost a percentage point per year. The result was increasing dependence on food imports and declining food exports (down an average of 3 per cent per year) and a loss of up to 50 per cent of Africa's market shares abroad. Despite this, dependence on agricultural exports has grown : more than 75 per cent of the export revenue for 14 Sub-Saharan nations comes from agriculture, and

six countries rely on agriculture for over 90 per cent of their export earnings.

Moreover, it should be added that Sub-Saharan countries have generally failed to diversify into non-traditional commodities, such as horticultural products, fruits, and vegetables, whereas OECD countries' imports of such products have increased much faster than imports of traditional unprocessed products.[32]

That being said, it is also true that a recent World Bank study calls into question the conventional wisdom that "commodity dependence" is always bad for economic growth.[33] The authors conclude,

> ... that problems often associated with commodity-dependence do not arise because of commodity-dependence per-se and that they can be alleviated through appropriate policies. ... In other words, ... countries can be both commodity dependent and have high export and income growth.
>
> An examination of the components of successful commodity sectors in various countries strongly suggests that it is the initiatives and innovative actions of the private sector that make these commodity sectors dynamic and vibrant. Such successful cases are found in the coffee sector in Uganda, the gold mines in Ghana, and the cut-flower industry in Colombia. Transfers of foreign capital and technology that have played important roles in developing new commodity and processing industries in a number of countries are best achieved when the private sector takes the initiative.
>
> ... important roles for governments to play .... include eliminating price controls and state monopolies, promoting research and development, developing infrastructure in transportation and communication, enticing foreign capital and technology transfers, and establishing a legal system for the use of innovative financial instruments (p. 40).

Macroeconomic Policies

Countries which recorded above average export growth and ability to attract FDI reported median inflation rates of 7-11 percentage points below those in the less successful performers in the 1984-93 period. They also reported real exchange rate volatility only a quarter that in the less successful group. The less successful groups, moreover, tended to have higher budget deficits, to have more volatile deficits over time, and to shrink their deficits at a slower rate (those in the poorest performing group actually expanded their deficits during the 1980s).[34]

Macroeconomic instability is not the only way large fiscal deficits adversely affect the pace of a country's integration into the global economy. In particular, when they are externally financed, fiscal deficits tend to appreciate the real exchange rate via inflows of capital (the same effect occurs via inflation when the deficits are financed by domestic monetary expansions). A real appreciation in turn affects trade by favouring the non-traded sector over the traded sector, deterring exporters and foreign investors, and encouraging capital flight at the first hint of a devaluation. Equally, if not more seriously, in many instances, persistent fiscal imbalances are the underlying cause of low rates of national saving and investment.

TABLE 7

Developing Countries : Budgetary and Economic Indicators in Africa and Developing Asia[a]

(Annual averages, in per cent of GDP, unless otherwise noted)

	Africa		Asia	
	1983-89	1990-95	1983-89	1990-95
Central Government fiscal balance	-4.8	-5.3	-3.4	-2.3
Private saving	16.5	16.8	26.4	33.1
Private investment	13.5	13.5	15.0	20.1
External debt	59.5	86.5	25.8	26.2
Real GDP (annual percentage change)	2.6	1.8	7.7	8.0
Consumer prices (annual percentage change)	16.0	26.6	7.9	9.2

a : Figures for developing Asia include China.
Source : IMF (1996).

Between 1983-89 and 1990-95, the average fiscal deficit for the Africa region widened, while for the developing countries as a group it declined. As the IMF (1996, p. 64) notes :

> While some of [the African] countries have managed to make modest progress in reducing fiscal deficits, in part because of external debt rescheduling agreements in the late 1980s and early 1990s, ... most of the adjustment has been in the form of lower capital expenditure ... for Africa as a whole, the ratio of current government expenditure to GDP increased by over 2 percentage points in the 1990-1995 period, while the ratio of capital expenditure to GDP was marginally lower than in the mid-1980s. The average fiscal deficit declined in 1995 to just under 4 per cent of GDP, but for most African countries the fiscal situation remains fragile, with many countries still heavily dependent on grants to finance large fiscal imbalances.

Infrastructure. The experience of different countries' reform efforts suggest that stable macroeconomic policies, structural reforms, and outward-oriented trade and investment regimes go a long way to provide economic stability and thereby lower the risk premium attached to investment in LLDCs — a precondition to attracting foreign investors.[35] In those countries which have persisted in economic reforms, the positive results are beginning to become apparent. In particular, reforms designed to strengthen the financial sector appear to be an essential first step. Particularly for the LLDCs, financial market regulation and supervision can pave the way for subsequent liberalization of capital movements, which are necessary to promote growth and improve resource allocation.[36] Then, a reform program aiming towards full capital account convertibility can begin with the liberalization of trade-related investment and FDI flows, allowing LLDCs to achieve many of the benefits of foreign capital while minimizing the risks of capital flow reversals or similar problems.

The largely successful adjustment program undertaken by Uganda since 1986 provides a case in point. Faced with an infrastructure devastated by civil war, an enormous and growing debt burden, a fixed and overvalued exchange rate, and declining coffee prices (virtually its only remaining export), Uganda enacted the Economic Recovery Program and has since staged an impressive turnaround in growth, savings and investment, and inflation.[37] The components of the program included fiscal stabilization through tax reform, tight monetary and credit policies to increasingly shift domestic credit towards the private sector, and financial reforms such as the creation of a government securities market and the strengthening of banks and central bank operations to improve the monetary policy transmission mechanism. Foreign exchange and price liberalization took place in steps, the public sector has been downsized and many former state-owned enterprises are being privatized. While the reforms continue and the gains are being consolidated, the benefits to Uganda from political and economic stability, as well as enhanced credibility amongst the international investment community, are readily apparent.

Most LLDCs have implemented financial sector reforms as part of broader policy-reform programmes. As UNCTAD (1996a, p. XII) notes,

> Financial liberalization in [LLDCs] has mainly comprised the reduction or removal of allocative controls over interest rates and lending, the introduction of market-based techniques of monetary control and the easing of entry restrictions on private capital.... The impact [of these reforms] on the efficiency of resource allocation has been limited, however, largely because of problems relating to macroeconomic instability.... Large government budget deficits in several [LLDCs] have forced nominal interest rates to very high levels and crowded the private sector out of credit markets.

In some LLDCs, financial markets are still dominated by government banks which do not behave as efficient, commercially oriented, financial intermediaries. Effective institutional solutions to these problems have not yet been devised in most LLDCs.

Other Domestic Factors

Inadequate and inefficient road/rail/air transport facilities, storage facilities and telecommunications have also acted to limit the supply-side response of developing countries, with the problems being especially serious in the LLDCs. To take one important example, high transport costs are a serious impediment to African exports.[38] Recent analysis suggests that, in some instances, freight costs outweigh the impact of tariffs. Freight costs for African exports to the United States generally are considerably higher than on similar goods originating in other countries, and there can be little doubt that these charges reduce incentives for new investment in export-oriented production, for example, in the further processing for export of groundnuts and copra.[39]

Institutions. At the institutional level, many developing countries, particularly LLDCs, lack a transparent legal and regulatory frameworks, including company and bankruptcy laws and investment codes. Moreover, UNCTAD (1996, p. III) notes that,

> ... the private-enterprise sector, which is the key agent of development, is not well developed in most LLDCs and its growth is constrained by shortages of capital and of entrepreneurial, managerial, technical and marketing skills. Technological capacities in many industries in LLDCs are rudimentary, which together with the low levels of educational attainment of the workforce, is a major impediment to raising productivity.

Despite export opportunities, many small and medium-sized export enterprises — especially in the LLDCs — are critically constrained by the lack of pre- and post-shipment credit facilities and, by the lack of business information and market intelligence.

Trade promotion. Efforts to enhance export performance will require not only technical assistance aimed at strengthening the institutional infrastructure for trade and trade policy, but also initiatives aimed at enhancing the outward orientation of the private sector. Enterprise-oriented technical cooperation programmes can underpin efforts to, improve international marketing and business development, especially in the LLDCs, by focusing on product and market development, trade finance, export quality management, export packaging, and training in international purchasing and supply management. Under the right conditions, the pay-off to such efforts can be even higher when special attention is given to the needs of small and medium size enterprises, again especially in the LLDCs.

(3) Interaction among the External and Domestic Factors

In reality, the many external and domestic factors that determine a country's export performance — and more generally the pace of its integration into the global economy — do not operate independently. There is a complex interaction, both positive and negative; a factor in one category can interact with others in the category, and developments in external factors can improve or worsen the effects of domestic factors and vice versa.

To take just one example from a virtually unlimited list of positive and negative interactions, inflows of FDI, by bringing resources which are in short supply in the host country — including capital, technology, and such intangible resources as organizational, managerial and marketing skills — can assist national efforts to restructure the economy and make it more competitive. As a financial inflow, it can help with balance-of-payments problems and/or make possible increased imports of capital equipment. It also can improve market access for the host country's exports of goods and services, through the multinational corporation's (MNCs) intra-firm exports (that is, exports from host-country affiliates to either the parent firm or affiliates in other countries) and arm's length exports to international markets serviced by the MNC.

NOTES

1. Relative price comparisons depend importantly on the reference period, in particular for mining products. In the 1950's and 1960's the prices of mining products declined relative to those of the other two product categories. The same holds true if the observation period is limited to 1985-95, during which prices for minerals actually fell in nominal terms, while those of agricultural products and manufacturers rose by 40 per cent and 60 per cent, respectively.
2. The sharp rise of imports to GDP in the "other developing countries" in the period 1974 to 1981 was linked to the terms of trade gains of the oil exporting countries. The sharp contraction in imports from 1982 onwards

is the combined result of the decline of oil (and other primary commodity) prices and the debt crisis.

3. Those factors are: (a) the high share of manufactures in the case of Niger is due solely to uranium which is classified under chemicals (not a typical labour intensive manufactured product); (b) in the case of the Dominican Republic, the poor performance in national exports is more than offset by the sharp rise in exports of manufacturers from processing zones (which the Dominican Republic excludes from statistics on national exports); if exports from processing zones are included, the Dominican Republic would rank among those exporters with steady above average growth; (c) in the case of Barbados, merchandise exports are of declining importance due to the shift to the services (tourism) industry (in the 1990s, Barbados exported four times more services than merchandise); and (d) in Haiti's case, civil strife combined with a partial trade embargo produced a collapse of merchandise exports.
4. Many of the LLDCs are in Africa. Commenting on the disappointing economic growth in Africa, Sachs (1996) observes "Africa's growth rates are not huge mysteries. The evidence on cross-country growth suggests that Africa's chronically low growth can be explained by standard economic variables linked to identifiable (and remediable) policies. Remedies that have worked in East Asia can also work, with suitable modification, in Africa. Where they have been tried — in Mauritius, to some extent in Botswana and (very recently) Uganda — the result has been growth at East Asian rates. ... Fortunately, the geographical [15 of 53 countries are landlocked] and resource conditions play only a modest role in Africa's growth shortfall. The lion's share can be attributed to the lack of openness, lack of market incentives and lack of national saving."
5. World Bank (1996).
6. Problems with the available data on trade in commercial services — including incomplete coverage, and frequent revisions in definitions and coverage — preclude a detailed analysis by region or country, especially of trends over time.
7. See, for example, GATT 1994, in particular Tables II.2 and II.3 on pre- and post-Uruguay Round tariff levels. In the mid-1960s, the OECD countries' average tariff on imports of manufactures from developing countries was 17 per cent. Today, developing countries as a group face OECD tariffs of under 4 per cent when account is taken of tariff preferences. See World Bank (1996).
8. See GATT (1993).

9. The number of anti-dumping actions reported to the GATT Secretariat has fluctuated widely over the last decade, with a steady rise since 1990. However, the impact of anti-dumping cannot be judged only from the number of cases in which duties are actually imposed. Often the threat of a formal anti-dumping duty and the resulting loss of customers because of the uncertainty created by the investigation process has induced threatened exporters to reduce their exports or to increase their prices.
10. As is well known, the integration process resulting in a phase-out of MFA restrictions is subject to a ten-year transition period, with much of the liberalization occurring in the final two steps (on 1 January 2002 and 1 January 2005). Moreover, there have been criticisms of the degree of liberalization thus far (see the July 1996 submission by Pakistan to the General Council, on behalf of ten developing countries; G/L/92).
11. On a trade-weighted basis, the Uruguay Round resulted in an estimated overall loss of preference margins for all LLDC products covered by preferences of about 8 percentage points for Canada, 3 points in the EU and Japan, and 2 points in the United States. See UNCTAD (1996).
12. When the MFN tariff is low, exporters may find it cheaper to pay the MFN duty than to complete the paperwork, related to rules of origin, required to qualify for the preferential tariff.
13. For details on post-Uruguay Round tariff escalation, see GATT (1994). According to the World Bank the importance of tariff escalation in explaining this bias in developing countries' exports should not be exaggerated (World Bank, 1996). When estimating the magnitude of tariff escalation faced by developing countries, account needs to be taken of the GSP and the Lome Convention preferences. Results derived from a study of the structure of European Union tariffs applied to primary commodities exported from Sub-Saharan Africa show that because of tariff preferences, tariffs have not been a major general constraint to the further processing and export of African commodities, (reference?). The World Bank points to two other explanations for the bias. First, some commodity processing operations involve highly capital intensive and mechanized operations that are typically the comparative advantage of middle- and high-income countries. Second, various other market entry barriers such as international transport costs which have been found to escalate with processing, can work against further processing in some developing countries.
14. See UNCTAD (1996a).
15. See UNCTAD (1996b).
16. OECD (1996a).
17. UNCTAD (1996a).

18. It is generally acknowledged that international statistics on FDI are of poor quality. Despite efforts to harmonize balance-of-payments' statistics, the concepts and methods applied by the national statistical agencies continue to differ widely — even among the major OECD countries — which impairs severely the comparability between countries and the quality of the information for any regional or global aggregate.

    One major distortion in the FDI statistics is the treatment of re-invested earnings which is not — as recommended — always included in FDI flows. In the case of the United States, re-invested earnings often account for more than half of FDI outflows in a given year. It is therefore no surprise that reported values on bilateral investment flows can differ widely depending on which source is used, and that global estimates for FDI outflows and inflows can differ markedly although, in principle, both should be identical.

19. The ten economies with the largest FDI inflows in 1994 are (in descending order), China, Singapore, Malaysia, Hong Kong, Brazil, Peru, Indonesia, Nigeria, Chile and Colombia. See IMF (1996c).
20. This paragraph draws on IMF (1995b).
21. This paragraph draws on World Bank (1996).
22. See IMF (1995b).
23. See IMF (1994).
24. See UNCTAD (1996a).
25. See IMF (1996b), pp. 229-34.The suggested criteria for sustainability are a debt-service ratio (debt-service payments as a per cent of export earnings) in the range of 20-25 per cent, and a present value of all claims on the country not exceeding 200-250 per cent of export earnings. Other criteria that come with the plan are "vulnerability factors". These include the country's reserve position, its vulnerability to shocks, its dependence on a single or small number of commodity exports, and the impact of debt service on its fiscal position.
26. See UNCTAD (1996a).
27. Institutions and their rules have a very strong bearing on an economy's efficiency and growth prospects, a point which is made very forcefully and convincingly by North (1990).
28. For an explanation, backed up by empirical analysis, of how a country's own import barriers inevitably end up reducing its exports, see Clements and Sjaastad (1985).
29. This and the three subsequent paragraphs draw heavily on UNCTAD/WTO (1996).

30. However, there is still scope for policy reversals as many developing countries have bound their tariffs at "ceiling" levels, often well above the applied rates. For example, most Latin American Members of the WTO have bound their post-Uruguay industrial tariffs at rates ranging between 25 and 45 per cent. This matters because ceiling bindings, even if they give some certainty on tariff levels for the future, confer less stability than tariffs bound at applied rates.
31. Strengthening institutional infrastructure will require intensified training programmes involving academic and research institutes and 'on-the-job training". An essential element of a strengthened institutional infrastructure is an improved capacity to cope with increasing information and data and improved access to and use of information technology and the design of effective, user friendly trade data and information networks. This could involve developing countries pooling their resources to set up or strengthen sub-regional or regional institutions to support their participation in trade negotiations and in the trading system in general.
32. See World Bank (1996) and OECD (1996c).
33. See Yabuki and Akiyama (1996).
34. See World Bank (1996).
35. See IMF (1995a).
36. See IMF (1995b).
37. Uganda's experience with economic reform is more fully detailed in WTO (1995). See also IMF (1995b).
38. See World Bank (1996).
39. Using estimates of the effective rates of protection corresponding to the transport costs, the World Bank study shows that freight costs contribute to a bias in the structure of Africa's exports away from processed products. For example, in the case of animal and vegetable oils, the effective rate of protection associated with transport costs is estimated at 56 per cent, which is more than 5 times higher than the corresponding nominal rate of protection. The other important conclusion of the World Bank study is that there are more policy options for reducing transport costs than is generally recognized. These options include measures aimed at achieving economies of scale and other cost reductions in transport services. Many developing country governments have adopted anti-competitive cargo reservation schemes in the hope of achieving objectives such as the development of national, fleets. These reservation schemes have been largely unsuccessful in promoting national lines, but their anti-competitive effects have resulted in markedly higher freight rates (World Bank 1996).

REFERENCES

Clements, K.W. and L. Sjaastad (1985), *How Protection Taxes Exporters,* Thames Essays No. 39. Gower for the Trade Policy Research Centre.

GATT (1994), "The Results of the Uruguay Round of Multilateral Trade Negotiations", mimeo., November.

Goldin, I., O. Knudsen, and D. van der Mensbrugghe (1993), *Trade Liberalization : Global Economic Implications,* OECD and The World Bank.

IMF (1994), *World Economic Outlook,* May.

IMF (1995a), *World Economic Outlook,* May.

IMF (1995b), *World Economic Outlook,* October.

IMF (1996a), *World Economic Outlook,* May.

IMF (1996b), *IMF Survey,* 15 July.

Martin, W. and L.A. Winters (1995), *The Uruguay Round — Widening and Deepening the World Trading System,* The World Bank.

North, D.C. (1990), *Institutions, Institutional Change and Economic Performance,* Cambridge University Press.

OECD (1996a), *Development Assistance Committee 1995 Report.*

OECD (1996b), "Recent Trends on Foreign Direct Investment", *Financial Market Trends 64,* June.

OECD (1996c), *The Uruguay Round and Processed Agricultural Products,* mimeo., June.

Sachs, J. (1996), "It can be done", *The Economist,* 29 June.

UNCTAD (1995), *World Investment Report.*

UNCTAD (1996a), *The Least Developed Countries* : 1996 Report, with annexes.

UNCTAD (1996b), "Report of the Secretary-General of UNCTAD to the Ninth Session of the Conference", 2 January (TD/366).

UNCTAD and WTO (1996), "Strengthening the Participation of Developing Countries in World Trade and the Multilateral Trading System", mimeo.

World Bank (1996), *Global Economic Prospects and the Developing Countries.*

WTO (1995), *Trade Policy Review : Uganda,* Vol. I.

Yabuki, N. and T. Akiyama (1996), "Is Commodity-Dependence Pessimism Justified?" Policy Research Working Paper 1600, World Bank.

ANNEX

TWO GROUPS OF DEVELOPING ECONOMIES

(A) A selection of twenty-five economies whose merchandise exports expanded more rapidly than world exports during 1985-94, listed in descending order of the percentage increase in exports (an asterisk indicates those economies which recorded above average export growth in both sub-periods, 1985-90 and 1990-94)[a] :

Thailand*	Chile*	Sri Lanka
Viet Nam*	Chinese Taipei*	Colombia
Hong Kong*	Philippines*	Costa Rica
China*	India*	Nepal
Singapore*	Israel*	Mexico
Malaysia*	Pakistan*	Syria
Malta*	Tunisia*	Indonesia
Korea, Rep. of*	Bangladesh	
Mauritius	Botswana	

a Twelve economies with above average export growth are not included in the list because (i) the 1985 figure was very small (less than $50 million) and/or the 1985 figure was more than 25 per cent below the 1980 figure (which suggests that merchandise exports were unusually low in 1985).

(B) Thirty-five economies whose merchandise exports in 1994 were below the 1985 level, listed in increasing order of the percentage decline in exports (Guinea had the smallest decline, and so on) :

Guinea	Qatar	Mongolia
Burundi	Brunei Darussalam	Barbados
Suriname	Kiribati	Zaire
Grenada	Nigeria	Liberia
Trinidad and Tobago	Netherlands Antilles	Haiti
Cote d'lvoire	Libyan Arab	Rwanda
Sierra Leone	Jamahiriya	Afganistan
Congo	Comoros	Samoa
Dominican Republic	St. Vincent and the	Cuba
Niger	Grenadines	Iraq
Togo	Cape Verde	
Gambia	Algeria	
Vanuatu	Sao Tome and Principe	

Appendix-II

TEXT OF PROPOSALS CIRCULATED BY INDIA

PROPOSAL REGARDING THE AGREEMENT ON AGRICULTURE

Concrete and operational provisions for the special and differential treatment of the developing countries should be defined taking into account their different levels of economic development, the role of agriculture in their economy with a large rural population, the need for food security and the vulnerability of the agricultural sector in developing countries. Trade distorting support being provided by some developed countries has a negative effect on trade in a number of agricultural products of interest to developing countries. Similarly, export subsidies have continued to distort world agriculture for too long and it is imperative that use of such export subsidies is eliminated.

Issues

Article 20 of the Agreement on Agriculture provides for negotiations for continuing the reform process in the agriculture sector. Article 20 of the Agreement also specifically stipulates that these negotiations should be based on the experience of implementing the provisions of the Agreement, and in particular, should take into account the non-trade concerns and the implementation of special and differential provisions for developing-country Members. Obviously, therefore, an important aspect of these negotiations is that they should address the concerns and shortcomings which the Members, particularly the developing-country members, have faced in the implementation of the Agreement since its adoption.

As a background to the concerns that we have on implementation, we would like to state that a number of developing countries like India have predominantly agrarian economies, where a very large percentage of the population is dependent on agriculture for their livelihood. India is one such example where nearly two thirds of the population is dependent on this sector. While the main concern of such countries, over the years, has been to ensure food sufficiency for their populations, they have at the same time also sought to find stable markets for their products. Inspite of the fact that the preamble to the Agreement specifically mandated developed countries to provide greater opportunity and access to the agricultural products of interest to developing countries, this special and differential treatment in the area of market access has not been forthcoming.

In fact a number of studies have shown that the post-Uruguay Round base tariffs of a number of sensitive commodities in many industrialised countries are higher than the actual tariff equivalents of all border measures which existed in 1986-88. Even the minimum market access sought to be provided through the use of tariff quotas has not been effective, since the administration of Tariff Rate Quotas (TRQs) continues to be unsatisfactory, specially for new suppliers. TRQs, therefore, need to be abolished totally.

Trade-distorting support being provided by some developed countries has had a disproportionately negative effect on trade in a number of agricultural products which developing countries export. In fact, domestic support is an area where the playing field is definitely not even, since developed countries who had notified base AMS (Aggregate Measurement of Support) levels can, and have, continued to provide large scale trade-distorting domestic support. The effective reduction in the level of support being provided in the so-called "amber box" has been insignificant. Moreover, since AMS reductions have been based on aggregates, countries have been able to shift support amongst different products, thereby being able to provide support to sensitive products despite their AMS reduction commitments. There is also a noticeable and alarming shift of support being provided by some developed countries from the "amber box" to the "green box". It is, therefore, imperative that all support, whether in the amber, blue or green box, is brought down to a common percentage of present production value, rather than being reduced from former support levels. Apart from creating a level playing field, such an approach would have added advantage that it would considerably simplify notification requirements.

Similarly export subsidies have continued to distort world agriculture trade for too long. It is, therefore, imperative that the use of export subsidies is eliminated, and a suitable time-frame determined for the phase-out of these subsidies, so that their trade distorting effect is gradually eliminated. It would also be important to address issues related to circumvention and roll-over of export subsidies during the negotiations.

Some aspects of the green box measures may also need to be reviewed in order to provide a certain degree of flexibility to developing countries. For instance, the restrictions on public holdings for food security purposes and domestic aid do not appear to be entirely realistic since at times it is neither possible nor practical to insist on a hard and fast criterion for eligibility for distributing subsidised food grains, particularly in view of the geographical spread of the vulnerable sections of society. It would, therefore, be appropriate to revisit the "Green Box" to include programmes that are more responsive to the requirements of developing countries.

In our view, the only way that these concerns can be met is by providing a certain degree of flexibility to developing countries by appropriately modifying the provisions of the Agreement on Agriculture, particularly as far as domestic support and green box measures are concerned. For instance, it would be important to recognise that in times to come the 10 per cent de minimis level presently allowed under the AMS may not be sufficient for developing countries to give the kind of support they would need to provide to alleviate poverty and sustain rural employment. Moreover, specific guidelines would need to be formulated on how to compensate for excessive rate of inflation and depreciation of currency — problems which developing countries face while calculating their AMS.

Proposals

Concrete and operational provisions for the special and differential treatment of developing countries shall be defined, taking into account the experience of developing countries in adapting to the present reform process, their differing level of economic development, the role of agriculture in their economies with a large rural population, the need for food security, as well as the vulnerability of the agricultural sector in developing countries.

Sum of all domestic support (whether in the green, blue or amber box) provided by developed countries should not exceed an appropriate proportion of the total value of agricultural production. Developing countries should be provided additional flexibility as a special and differential provision.

If in the calculation of the AMS, domestic support prices are lower than the external reference price (so as to ensure access of poor households to basic foodstuff) thereby resulting in negative product-specific support, then Members should be allowed to increase their non-product specific support by an equivalent amount. Also suitable methodology should be adopted for taking into account the high levels of inflation while making the domestic support notification.

Tariff-rate quotas should be abolished forthwith. However, if they are to be continued for a short transition period, then the administration of TRQs must be clearly laid down so as to provide trading opportunities to all Members in an equitable manner and discipline discriminatory and non-transparent TRQ allotment.

Programmes that are responsive to the requirements of developing countries, including any/all measures aimed at ensuring food security, particularly in the context of large agrarian economies, should be included in the green box.

A time-bound but comprehensive elimination of all export subsidies being provided by developed countries. Export subsidies should only be permitted as an S&D provision for developing countries.

Any tariff reducing proposal/formula used during the negotiations should provide a certain flexibility to predominantly agrarian countries in so that they can protect the livelihood of rural populations from possible surges of imports.

PROPOSAL REGARDING THE AGREEMENT ON SANITARY AND PHYTOSANITARY MEASURES

Means have to found to ensure participation of developing countries in the development of standards by international standard setting bodies. Standards are often being adopted without taking into account the problems and constraints that developing countries face.

Issues

Arbitrary and restrictive sanitary and phytosanitary (SPS) measures continue to represent a major obstacle to international trade of agricultural products. Developing-country exports are usually affected in two ways. Firstly, because the SPS measures are often developed in a non-transparent manner and developing countries invariably do not get adequate opportunity to respond to the proposed measures. Secondly, the Agreement provides that in order to ensure that the adoption of a new SPS regulation does not cause barriers to trade, there should be a reasonable interval between its publication and its entry into force. It further provides that "longer time-frames for compliance" be provided for developing countries. The basic purpose of these provisions is to provide sufficient time to producers in developing countries to adopt their products to the requirements of new regulations. In practice, compliance of these provisions by countries introducing new measures has been largely non-existent. Though the SPS Agreement provides that countries base their SPS measures on international standards, guidelines and recommendations, the participation of developing countries in the international standardisation activities has been limited and ineffective. A number of international standards are thus being developed without the participation of developing countries. As a result, standards are often being adopted without taking into account the problems and constraints that developing countries face. Means have, therefore, to be found to ensure participation of developing countries in the development of standards by international standard-setting bodies.

Solution to some of these issues, which the experience of standardisation activities raise, as well as those arising from ineffective participation of developing countries in these bodies could perhaps be found by reviewing the definition of an international standard. International standards could be distinguished according to the purpose for which they are being adopted *i.e.* whether for use on a voluntary or a mandatory basis. Guidelines and recommendations, in the context of the Agreement could be developed and adopted in the international standard setting bodies by majority. These guidelines or recommendations would be voluntary in nature. However, any international standards which would form a basis for a universal SPS measure should only be adopted by consensus. Moreover, in the formulation of such mandatory standards, an agreed minimum number of countries from different regions must have participated in the technical work throughout the process relating to its adoption.

Proposals

Even though Article 10 : 1 of the SPS Agreement provides that in the preparation and application of SPS measures, Members shall take into account the special needs of the developing countries, this has rarely been done. Article 10 : 1, therefore, needs to be translated into mandatory provisions.

Similarly, Article 10 : 2 which provides for longer time-frames for compliance on products of interest to developing-country Members has only been followed in the breach. This provision should be modified to make it mandatory/obligatory for developed countries to provide longer time-frames for compliance of new SPS measures for products from developing countries.

If a SPS measure is found to create a problem for several developing countries, then the country which has adopted it should be obliged to reconsider it. If, after reviewing its implications, it still reconfirms the measure, then it should provide the necessary technical cooperation to the affected countries.

The participation of developing countries in the international standard development process is extremely limited and ineffective. International standardising bodies must ensure the presence of countries at different levels of development and from different geographical regions, throughout different phases of standard setting. It must be ensured that in the formulation of standards the specific conditions prevailing in developing countries are taken into account. The international standard setting organisations, which are all observers in the SPS Committee, should, at the very minimum, be urged to accept the obligation to periodically report to the SPS Committee in this regard.

Paragraph 2 of Annex B of the Agreement stipulates that Members shall allow a reasonable interval between publication of a sanitary or phytosanitary regulation and its entry into force in order to allow producers, particularly in developing countries, to adapt their products and methods of production to the new requirements. This has rarely been done. The provisions of this paragraph should therefore be made mandatory and what constitutes a "reasonable interval" should be specified.

Though Article 4 of the SPS Agreement encourages equivalency, this principle has more often than not been interpreted as meaning "sameness". Equivalency may be the best option for developing countries until their participation in international standard setting bodies becomes satisfactory. This provision, therefore, must be suitably clarified so as to ensure that equivalence agreements are entered upon, particularly with developing countries.

Though the SPS Agreement encourages Members to enter in (MRAs), so far developing countries have not been included in such agreements. It is suggested that (i) MRAs are developed in a transparent way; (ii) they should be open to parties that may wish to join them at a later stage; and (iii) they should contain Rules of Origin which allow all products which pass the conformity assessment procedures to benefit from the MRA.

The definition of an international standard, guideline and recommendation (paragraph 3 of Annex A) needs to be revised so that a differentiation is introduced between mandatory international standards and a voluntary international guideline/recommendation.

Article 12:7 provides for a review of the operation and implementation of the Agreement three years after the date of entry into force of the Agreement and thereafter as the need arises. It is important that a decision is taken to the effect that this review is carried out once every two years.

PROPOSAL ON IPR ISSUES

The TRIPS Agreement should be reviewed to consider ways and means to operationalise the objectives and principles relating to transfer and dissemination of technology to developing countries.

The TRIPS (Trade Related Intellectual Property Rights) Agreement has as its preambular objective a desire to ensure that measures and procedures to enforce intellectual property rights (IPR's) do not themselves become barriers to legitimate trade. Further, one of its objectives is to contribute to the transfer and dissemination of technology. It has, amongst its principles, the promotion of public interest in sectors of vital importance to the socio-economic and technological development of its Members. At the same time, the Agreement recognises intellectual property rights as private rights. Finally, the Agreement encourages adjustments aimed at higher levels of protection of intellectual property rights. With these objectives, principles and provisions in view, India would like to initiate a discussion on some of the issues that have been of great concern to WTO Members, including many developing countries. These issues are by no means exhaustive, nor do they represent the entirety of Members' concerns on intellectual property rights. They are intended to initiate discussions on issues related to IPRs so that the objectives of the WTO Agreement such as raising standards of living, ensuring full employment, increasing trade and promoting sustainable development are achieved.

Proposal 1 – Transfer of Technology

This proposal aims at a more effective implementation of the provisions relating to transfer of technology.

Article 7 of the TRIPS Agreement states :

"The protection and enforcement of intellectual property rights should contribute to the promotion of technological innovation and to the transfer and dissemination of technology to the mutual advantage of producers and users of technological knowledge and in a manner conducive to social and economic welfare, and to a balance of rights and obligations".

Article 8.2 states :

"Appropriate measures, provided they are consistent with the provisions of the Agreement, may be needed to prevent the abuse of intellectual property rights by right holders or the resort to practices which unreasonably restrain trade or adversely affect the international transfer of technology."

India believes that Articles 7 and 8.2 are overarching provisions that should qualify other provisions of the Agreement that are meant to protect intellectual property rights. Technology has become one of the most important determinants for economic development. Emerging patterns of technology generation and transfer have been researched intensively. A recent analysis of the mode of technology transfers suggests a reversal of the growing popularity of arm's length licensing in the 1970s and mid-1980s to intra-firm transfers since the mid-1980s. For example, 80 per cent of transfers by US corporations and 95 per cent by German corporations in 1995 were made on internal basis compared to 69 per cent and 92 per cent respectively in 1985. This is only one example of the changing pattern of technology transfers provided here to highlight the need to address in the WTO issues such as transfer, dissemination and innovation.

One of the important objectives of the WTO Agreement, as mentioned in its preamble, is the need for positive efforts designed to ensure that developing countries secure a share in the growth in international trade commensurate with the needs of their economic development. However, the TRIPS Agreement in its current form might tempt IPR holders to charge exorbitant and commercially unviable prices for transfer or dissemination of technologies held through such IPRs. It is important, therefore, to build disciplines for effective transfer of technology at fair and reasonable costs to developing countries so as to harmonise the objectives of the WTO Agreement and the TRIPS Agreement.

Similarly, Article 40 recognises that licensing practices or conditions pertaining to IPRs could restrain competition and have adverse effects on trade and may impede the transfer and dissemination of technology. It provides Members with certain rights to ensure that this does not happen. Further, of more importance to developing and least developed countries, Article 67 obliges developed country Members to provide, on request and on mutually agreed terms and conditions, technical and financial cooperation in their favour. Since developing countries are still availing transition periods under the Agreement, awareness and capacity to seek such co-operation may be lacking. Again, Article 66.2 obliges developed country Members to provide incentives to enterprises and institutions in their territories for the purpose of promoting and encouraging technology transfer to least developed countries. There has been little effort to implement this provision, raising doubts about the effectiveness of the Agreement to facilitate technology transfers.

One proposal on technology transfers has already been made in the Committee on Trade and Environment (CTE). In that Committee, India has proposed that owners of environmentally sound technology and products should sell such technologies and products at fair and most favourable terms and conditions upon demand to any interested party which has an obligation to adopt these under national law of another country or under international law. Similar concerns regarding the need for the transfer of technology have been expressed with respect to electronics commerce also. Concerns have also been raised on the need for transfer of technology in a commercially viable manner for ensuring positive outcomes for developing countries through the increasing linkage between trade and investment.

Transfer of technology at fair and most favourable terms has been highlighted in all discussions and debates on sustainable development. The Rio Declaration of 1992 as well as most of the multilateral environmental agreements emphasises the need for such technology transfers. The preamble of the WTO Agreement affirms the objective of sustainable development in a manner consistent with the respective needs and concerns of Members at different levels of development. Thus, an obligation is cast upon the WTO to bring about easy access to and wide dissemination of technology relevant for sustainable development.

Facilitating the access to developing countries of technologies selected by them as appropriate to their requirements constitutes one of the key elements in accelerating the pace of their economic and social development. Such access is generally the result of licences and technology transfer agreements. Prospective technology seekers in developing countries face serious difficulties in their commercial dealings with technology holders in the developed countries. These difficulties are basically of three kinds : those which arise from the imperfections of the market for technology; those attributable to the relative lack of experience and skill of enterprises and institutions in developing countries in concluding adequate legal arrangements for the acquisition of technology; and those government practices, both legislative and administrative, in both developed and developing countries, which influence the implementation of national policies and procedures designed to encourage the flow of technology to, and its acquisition by, developing countries. These difficulties may have to be addressed specifically in order to fully implement TRIPS provisions relating to transfer and dissemination of technology, particularly in the light of Articles 7, 8, 40, 66.2 and 67. Some of these difficulties may be overcome by suitable safeguards in the domestic IPR laws of developing countries, particularly those arising out of the provisions of Articles 30, 31 and 40. Since developing countries have transition periods available under Article 65, these laws may still be in the formulation stage. In addition, the transfer and dissemination needs of the developing countries have to be seen from the point of view of the capacity of those in need of accessing technologies, particularly where the cost of technology may be prohibitive due to economies of scale and other reasons. In such cases, in order to implement the related provisions of the TRIPS Agreement, commercially viable mechanisms need to be found. This could be studied in the WTO, particularly in the light of the need for effective implementation of Articles 7, 8, 40, 66.2 and 67.

The high cost of technology makes it difficult for the smaller, poorer developing countries to acquire appropriate technology on commercial terms. Such countries may be able to acquire appropriate technology critically needed for their development only through government to government negotiations and with the financial assistance provided by government and other institutions in developed countries or inter-governmental organisations. For those enterprises and institutions in developing countries, which will not have the benefit of external financing, the acquisition of appropriate technology on international commercial terms will impose a burden on the local economy unless the price of the technology can be brought within manageable limits.

The denial of dual-use technologies, even on a commercial basis, to developing countries is another aspect that leads to widening of the technology gap between developed and developing countries. Under this guise a variety of technologies and products are being denied to developing countries which could otherwise have helped to accelerate their growth process. This issue needs to be carefully examined and seriously dealt with as a trade distorting and restrictive measure.

It is, therefore, proposed that the TRIPS Agreement may be reviewed to consider ways and means to operationalise the objective and principles in respect of transfer and dissemination of technology to developing countries, particularly the least developed amongst them.

Proposal 2 – Biodiversity

The scope of this proposal is limited to harmonisation of the approaches to the utilisation of living resources found in the TRIPS Agreement on the one hand and the UN Convention on Biological Diversity (CBD) on the other. It does not address issues which are likely to come up in the built-in agenda with regard to Article 27.3 (b) or Article 71. It does not address issues relating to patenting of plants and animals or to the issue of benefit sharing in commercial exploitation of ex situ materials. The above issues are being and will be engaging the attention of the international community in WTO and other fora and separate proposals would surely be presented there.

The preamble of the TRIPS Agreement recognises IPRs to be private rights. Article 27.3 incorporates specific obligations on the issue of patenting life forms to the extent that it obliges Members to provide product patents for micro-organisms and for non-biological and microbiological processes. In addition, Article 27.3 (b) stipulates that all Members shall provide for the protection of plant varieties, either by patents or by an effective sui generis system or by a combination thereof.

CBD, on the other hand, in its preamble, categorically reaffirms that nation states have sovereign rights over their own biological resources, recognises the desirability of sharing equitably the benefits arising from the use of these resources as well as traditional knowledge, innovations and practices relevant to the conservation of biological diversity and its sustainable use, and acknowledges that special provisions are required to meet the needs of developing countries.

These two international agreements are intrinsically linked with one another. It is important to study the relationship between the provisions of the CBD and those of the TRIPS Agreement and suggest reconciliation of any contradictions therein within the overall objective of conservation of biological resources with sustainable development. CBD unambiguously states that the authority to determine access to genetic resources rests with national governments and is subject to national legislation. It also states that access, where granted, shall be on mutually agreed terms and shall be subject to the prior informed consent of the resource provider. It also enjoins the international community to respect, preserve and maintain knowledge innovations and practices of indigenous and local communities and encourages sharing of benefits arising from their utilisation. The conference of parties of CBD has initiated a work programme to give effect to these provisions.

Sustainable development being an objective of the WTO also, it becomes incumbent upon us to examine ways and means to harmonise the approaches to utilisation of living resources in the CBD and in the TRIPS Agreement. In implementing their obligations under the CBD, Members would exercise sovereign rights over their biological resources. In order that this does not impede innovation, intellectual property rights may have to be integrated into such an exercise. At the same time, the right of holders of traditional knowledge to share benefits arising out of such innovation cannot be over-emphasised. This could be possible if commercial exploitation of such innovations is encouraged only on the condition that the innovators share the benefits through material transfer agreements/transfer of information agreements. A material transfer agreement would be necessary where the inventor wishes to use the biological material and a transfer of information agreement would be necessary where the inventor bases himself on indigenous or traditional knowledge. Such an obligation could be incorporated through inclusion of provisions in Article 29 of the TRIPS Agreement requiring a clear mention of the biological source material and the country of origin. Article 29 deals with conditions on patent applicants. This part of the patent application should be open to full public scrutiny on filing of the application. This would permit countries with possible opposition claims to examine the application and state their claims well in time. At the same time domestic laws on biodiversity could ensure that the prior informed consent of the country of origin and the knowledge holder of the biological raw material meant for usage in a patentable invention would enable the signing of material transfer agreements or transfer of information agreements, as the case may be. Such a provision in the domestic law should be considered compatible with the TRIPS Agreement. The suggestion basically asks for further transparency in the form of additional information in patent applications, and an approach which allows a harmonious construction of the two international agreements.

Proposal 3 – Higher Level of Protection for Geographical Indications of Goods

Section 3 of Part II of the TRIPS Agreement deals with geographical indications. Article 23 therein provides for additional protection for geographical indications for wines and spirits even where the true origin of goods is indicated or the geographical indications is used in translation or accompanied by expressions such as "kind", 'type', 'imitation' or the like. Such additional protection is not available to goods other than wines and spirits.

It is an anomaly that the higher level of protection is available only for — wines and spirits. It is proposed that such higher level of protection should be available for goods other than wines and spirits also. This would be helpful for products of export interest like basmati rice, Darjeeling tea, alphonso mangoes, Kolhapuri slippers in the case of India. It is India's belief that there are other Members of the WTO who would be interested in higher level of protection to products of export interest to them like Bulgarian yoghurt, Czech Pilsen beer, many agricultural products of the European Union, Hungarian Szatmar plums and so on. There is a need to expedite work already initiated in the TRIPS Council in this regard, under Article 24, so that benefits arising out of the TRIPS Agreement in this area are spread out wider.

PROPOSAL REGARDING EXTENSION OF PROTECTION OF GEOGRAPHICAL INDICATIONS

(Agreement on TRIPS)

Higher level of protection should be available for goods other than wines and spirits also. This would be helpful of products of export interest to India and other countries in the case of items like Basmati Rice, Darjeeling tea etc.

Introduction

The protection of geographical indications is an industrial property measure which makes it possible to protect all products, whether man-made or natural, that are distinguished by their quality, reputation or the other characteristics essentially attributable to their geographical origin.

Section 3 (Articles 22-24) of the WTO Agreement on Trade-Related Aspects of Intellectual Property Rights (TRIPS) regulates all matters relating to this important means of protection.

Article 23 grants additional protection exclusively for wines and spirits.

Proposal

On different occasions, in the context of the Council for TRIPS, certain WTO Members have expressed interest in having the above mentioned protection extended to cover other products of special importance to them. In this connection, the above-mentioned countries request that the said additional protection be extended to products other than wines and spirits.

PROPOSAL REGARDING THE AGREEMENT ON TRADE-RELATED INVESTMENT MEASURES

There is a need to review provisions in the Agreement on TRIMS which come in the way of acceleration of economic growth in developing countries and deny these countries the means to maintain balance of payments stability.

Issues

Measures taken by governments to impose conditions to encourage and direct investment according to certain national priorities are considered as "trade-related investment measures — TRIMs". The Agreement on TRIMs prohibits five types of such measures as they are considered to be inconsistent with GATT rules on "national treatment" and the rules against use of "quantitative restrictions". Important among these are "domestic content" and "export performance" requirements. The developing countries have a transitional period of five years, that is up to 1 January, 2000 to eliminate TRIMs covered by the Agreement, provided they have notified them to WTO when the Agreement became operational.

However, the domestic content is an extremely useful and necessary tool from the point of view of developing countries. Such a requirement is often necessary for (i) encouraging domestic economic activities in raw material and intermediate input sectors; (ii) upgradation of input production; (iii) prevention of wastage of foreign exchange in the import of raw material and intermediate inputs; (iv) ensuring linkages of FDI (Foreign Direct Investment) with domestic economic activities; (v) encouraging indigenisation in case of FDI; and (vi) acting in several other ways as an important instrument in the development process. Similarly, developing countries also find export performance requirement to be useful and necessary from the point of view of balanced economic growth and national development.

In the light of the above, there is, therefore, a need to review these provisions in the Agreement, as they come in the way of accelerating economic growth in developing countries and deny these countries the means to maintain balance-of-payments stability. In particular, the transition period mentioned in Article 5 paragraph 2 needs to be extended and developing countries be provided another opportunity to notify existing TRIMs measures.

Proposals

The Agreement poses problems both with respect to the limited transition period available for removing TRIMS and the denial of freedom to countries to channelise investments in such a manner that fulfils their developmental needs. There is, therefore, a need to review provisions in the Agreement relating to local-content requirements as the existing provisions come in the way of accelerating the industrialisation process in developing countries and deny these countries the means to maintain balance-of-payments stability. With a view to ensuring that these instruments may be maintained by developing countries till such time that their developmental needs demand, the transition period mentioned in Article 5 paragraph 2 needs to be extended.

Article 5:3 which recognises the importance of taking account of the development, financial and trade needs of developing countries while dealing with trade related investment measures, has remained inoperative and ineffectual. The provisions of this Article must, therefore, be suitably amended and made mandatory.

The TRIMs Agreement should be modified to provide developing countries another opportunity to notify existing TRIMs measures which they would be then allowed to maintain till the end of the revised transition period.

Developing countries should be exempted from the disciplines on the application of domestic-content requirement by providing for an enabling provision in Article 2 or Article 4 to this effect.

PROPOSAL REGARDING SERVICES — GATS

The importance of the Mode 4 of the General Agreement on Services (GATS) *i.e.* movement of natural persons, for developing countries is obvious and yet commitments made by the developed countries in this area are far from satisfactory. Commitments undertaken by the developed countries being modest, there is a need to make substantially higher commitments in this area if the balance of benefits under GATS is to be preserved.

Issues

Articles IV and XIX:2 of the General Agreement on Trade in Services (GATS) provide for S&D (Special & Differential) treatment for developing countries. But the actual history of implementation since the conclusion of the Uruguay Round Agreement does not evidence the extension of such treatment to the developing countries. Also, the importance of Mode 4 for developing countries is obvious; and yet commitments made by the developed countries in this area were far from satisfactory. An assessment by the Council for Trade in Services (CTS) under Article XIX is mandatory before embarking on negotiating guidelines for the new round of negotiations. Such an assessment must be carried out by CTS in collaboration with UNCTAD who have already commenced such work. Until such an assessment is complete, both in overall terms and sector-wise, it is very difficult to conclude that developing countries have gained from the GATS so far.

Proposals

Mode 4 commitments undertaken by developed countries being modest, there is a need for making substantially higher commitments in this area if the balance of benefits under GATS is to be preserved. Higher levels of commitments can be achieved on the basis of the following : rules that are transparent, no additional tariff/tax or other regulatory restrictions on the nationals of foreign countries that do not apply to one's own nationals, no quantitative limits on temporary movement of natural persons, fees/charges applicable for providing social security nets should not apply to temporary movement of natural persons, no non-tariff barriers and no regulatory restrictions on the movement of natural persons.

At least in sectors of interest to developing countries, the Economic Needs Test would not apply; where it would apply exceptionally, it would be based on transparent and objective criteria.

Need to list those sectors where visas would be issued automatically for temporary movement of natural persons; also certain occupations to be exempt from the work permit/residency requirement for short periods of trade-related presence.

In modes other than Mode 4, developing countries to be given S&D treatment as outlined in Articles IV and IX of GATS.

Any future negotiations in GATS to be guided by the same architecture based on positive list, request and offer approach, no prior exclusion of any mode and by the principles outlined in Article IX for developing countries. For Mode 4, a new list of occupations using the ILO International Standard Classification of Occupations could be established. It is also incumbent on the CTS to establish modalities for treatment of autonomous liberalisation undertaken by Members since the Uruguay Round. And finally, Article IV to be given real meaning in any new commitments by developed countries. Also, a monitoring mechanism to be set up for tracking implementation of Article IV of the GATS Agreement.

Appendix-III

WTO HONG KONG DRAFT MINISTERIAL DECLARATION, 2005

(Hong Kong, 13-18 December 2005)

DOHA WORK PROGRAMME

Revision

1. We reaffirm the Declarations and Decisions we adopted at Doha, as well as the Decision adopted by the General Council on 1 August 2004, and our full commitment to give effect to them. We renew our resolve to complete the Doha Work Programme fully and to conclude the negotiations launched at Doha successfully in 2006.

2. We emphasize the central importance of the development dimension in every aspect of the Doha Work Programme and recommit ourselves to making it a meaningful reality, in terms both of the results of the negotiations on market access and rule-making and of the specific development-related issues set out below.

3. In pursuance of these objectives, we agree as follows :

Agriculture Negotiations

4. We reaffirm our commitment to the mandate on agriculture as set out in paragraph 13 of the Doha Ministerial Declaration and to the Framework adopted by the General Council on 1 August 2004. We take note of the report by the Chairman of the Special Session on his own responsibility (TN/AG/21, contained in Annex A). We welcome the progress made by the Special Session of the Committee on Agriculture since 2004 and recorded therein.

5. On domestic support, there will be three bands for reductions in Final Bound Total AMS and in the overall cut in trade-distorting domestic support, with higher linear cuts in higher bands. In both cases, the Member with the highest level of permitted support will be in the top band, the two Members with the second and third highest levels of support will be in the middle band and all other Members, including all developing country Members, will be in the bottom band. In addition, developed country Members in the lower bands with high relative levels of Final Bound Total AMS will make an additional effort in AMS reduction. We also note that there has been some convergence concerning the reductions in Final Bound Total AMS, the overall cut in trade-distorting domestic support and in both product-specific and non product-specific *de minimis* limits. Disciplines will be developed to achieve effective cuts in trade-distorting domestic support consistent with the Framework. The overall reduction in trade-distorting domestic support will still need to be made even if the sum of the reductions in Final Bound Total AMS, *de minimis* and Blue Box payments would otherwise be less than that overall reduction. Developing country Members with no AMS commitments will be exempt from reductions in *de minimis* and the overall cut in trade-distorting domestic support. Green Box criteria will be reviewed in line with paragraph 16 of the Framework, *inter alia*, to ensure that programmes of developing country Members that cause not more than minimal trade-distortion are effectively covered.

6. We agree to ensure the parallel elimination of all forms of export subsidies and disciplines on all export measures with equivalent effect to be completed by the end of 2013. This will be achieved in a progressive and parallel manner, to be specified in the modalities, so that a substantial part is realized by the end of the first half of the implementation period. We note emerging convergence on some elements of disciplines with respect to export credits, export credit guarantees or insurance programmes with repayment periods of 180 days and below. We agree that such programmes should be self-financing, reflecting market consistency, and that the period should be of a sufficiently short duration so as not to effectively circumvent real commercially-oriented

discipline. As a means of ensuring that trade-distorting practices of STEs are eliminated, disciplines relating to exporting STEs will extend to the future use of monopoly powers so that such powers cannot be exercised in any way that would circumvent the direct disciplines on STEs on export subsidies, government financing and the underwriting of losses. On food aid, we reconfirm our commitment to maintain an adequate level and to take into account the interests of food aid recipient countries. To this end, a "safe box" for bona fide food aid will be provided to ensure that there is no unintended impediment to dealing with emergency situations. Beyond that, we will ensure elimination of commercial displacement. To this end, we will agree effective disciplines on in-kind food aid, monetization and re-exports so that there can be no loophole for continuing export subsidization. The disciplines on export credits, export credit guarantees or insurance programmes, exporting state trading enterprises and food aid will be completed by 30 April 2006 as part of the modalities, including appropriate provision in favour of least-developed and net food-importing developing countries as provided for in paragraph 4 of the Marrakesh Decision. The date above for the elimination of all forms of export subsidies, together with the agreed progressivity and parallelism, will be confirmed only upon the completion of the modalities. Developing country Members will continue to benefit from the provisions of Article 9.4 of the Agreement on Agriculture for five years after the end-date for elimination of all forms of export subsidies.

7. On market access, we note the progress made on *ad valorem* equivalents. We adopt four bands for structuring tariff cuts, recognizing that we need now to agree on the relevant thresholds — including those applicable for developing country Members. We recognize the need to agree on treatment of sensitive products, taking into account all the elements involved. We also note that there have been some recent movements on the designation and treatment of Special Products and elements of the Special Safeguard Mechanism. Developing country Members will have the flexibility to self-designate an appropriate number of tariff lines as Special Products guided by indicators based on the criteria of food security, livelihood security and rural development.

Developing country Members will also have the right to have recourse to a Special Safeguard Mechanism based on import quantity and price triggers, with precise arrangements to be further defined. Special Products and the Special Safeguard Mechanism shall be an integral part of the modalities and the outcome of negotiations in agriculture.

8. On other elements of special and differential treatment, we note in particular the consensus that exists in the Framework on several issues in all three pillars of domestic support, export competition and market access and that some progress has been made on other special and differential treatment issues.

9. We reaffirm that nothing we have agreed here compromises the agreement already reflected in the Framework on other issues including tropical products and products of particular importance to the diversification of production from the growing of illicit narcotic crops, long-standing preferences and preference erosion.

10. However, we recognize that much remains to be done in order to establish modalities and to conclude the negotiations. Therefore, we agree to intensify work on all outstanding issues to fulfil the Doha objectives, in particular, we are resolved to establish modalities no later than 30 April 2006 and to submit comprehensive draft Schedules based on these modalities no later than 31 July 2006.

Cotton

11. We recall the mandate given by the Members in the Decision adopted by the General Council on 1 August 2004 to address cotton ambitiously, expeditiously and specifically, within the agriculture negotiations in relation to all trade-distorting policies affecting the sector in all three pillars of market access, domestic support and export competition, as specified in the Doha text and the July 2004 Framework text. We note the work already undertaken in the Sub-Committee on Cotton and the proposals made with regard to this matter. Without prejudice to Members' current WTO rights and obligations, including those flowing from actions taken by the Dispute Settlement Body, we reaffirm our commitment to ensure having an explicit decision on cotton within the agriculture negotiations and through the

Sub-Committee on Cotton ambitiously, expeditiously and specifically as follows :

- All forms of export subsidies for cotton will be eliminated by developed countries in 2006.
- On market access, developed countries will give duty and quota free access for cotton exports from least-developed countries (LDCs) from the commencement of the implementation period.

  [It is recognized that the objective is that, as an outcome for the negotiations, trade distorting domestic subsidies for cotton production should be reduced more ambitiously than under whatever general formula is agreed and that it should be implemented over a shorter period of time than generally applicable. We will commit ourselves to give priority in the negotiations to reach such an outcome.]

12. With regard to the development assistance aspects of cotton, we welcome the Consultative Framework process initiated by the Director-General to implement the decisions on these aspects pursuant to paragraph 1.b of the Decision adopted by the General Council on 1 August 2004. We take note of his Periodic Reports and the positive evolution of development assistance noted therein. We urge the Director-General to further intensify his consultative efforts with bilateral donors and with multilateral and regional institutions, with emphasis on improved coherence, coordination and enhanced implementation and to explore the possibility of establishing through such institutions a mechanism to deal with income declines in the cotton sector. Noting the importance of achieving enhanced efficiency and competitiveness in the cotton producing process, we urge the development community to further scale up its cotton-specific assistance and to support the efforts of the Director-General. In this context, we urge Members to promote and support South-South cooperation, including transfer of technology. We welcome the domestic reform efforts by African cotton producers aimed at enhancing productivity and efficiency, and encourage them to deepen this process. We reaffirm the complementarity of the trade policy and

development assistance aspects of cotton. We invite the Director-General to furnish a third Periodic Report to our next Session with updates, at appropriate intervals in the meantime, to the General Council, while keeping the Sub-Committee on Cotton fully informed of progress. Finally, as regards follow up and monitoring, we request the Director-General to set up an appropriate follow-up and monitoring mechanism.

NAMA Negotiations

13. We reaffirm our commitment to the mandate for negotiations on market access for non-agricultural products as set out in paragraph 16 of the Doha Ministerial Declaration. We also reaffirm all the elements of the NAMA Framework adopted by the General Council on 1 August 2004. We take note of the report by the Chairman of the Negotiating Group on Market Access on his own responsibility (TN/MA/16, contained in Annex B). We welcome the progress made by the Negotiating Group on Market Access since 2004 and recorded therein.

14. We adopt a Swiss Formula with coefficients at levels which shall *inter alia* :

— Reduce or as appropriate eliminate tariffs, including the reduction or elimination of tariff peaks, high tariffs and tariff escalation, in particular on products of export interest to developing countries; and

— Take fully into account the special needs and interests of developing countries, including through less than full reciprocity in reduction commitments.

We instruct the Negotiating Group to finalize its structure and details as soon as possible.

15. We reaffirm the importance of special and differential treatment and less than full reciprocity in reduction commitments, including paragraph 8 of the NAMA Framework, as integral parts of the modalities. We instruct the Negotiating Group to finalize its details as soon as possible.

16. In furtherance of paragraph 7 of the NAMA Framework, we recognize that Members are pursuing sectoral initiatives. To this end, we instruct the Negotiating Group to review proposals

with a view to identifying those which could garner sufficient participation to be realized. Participation should be on a non-mandatory basis.

17. For the purpose of the second indent of paragraph 5 of the NAMA Framework, we adopt a non-linear mark-up approach to establish base rates for commencing tariff reductions. We instruct the Negotiating Group to finalize its details as soon as possible.

18. We take note of the progress made to convert non *ad valorem* duties to *ad valorem* equivalents on the basis of an agreed methodology as contained in JOB(05)/166/Rev.1.

19. We take note of the level of common understanding reached on the issue of product coverage and direct the Negotiating Group to resolve differences on the limited issues that remain as quickly as possible.

20. As a supplement to paragraph 16 of the NAMA Framework, we recognize the challenges that may be faced by non-reciprocal preference beneficiary Members as a consequence of the MFN liberalization that will result from these negotiations. We instruct the Negotiating Group to intensify work on the assessment of the scope of the problem with a view to finding possible solutions.

21. We note the concerns raised by small, vulnerable economies, and instruct the Negotiating Group to establish ways to provide flexibilities for these Members without creating a sub-category of WTO Members.

22. We note that the Negotiating Group has made progress in the identification, categorization and examination of notified NTBs. We also take note that Members are developing bilateral, vertical and horizontal approaches to the NTB negotiations, and that some of the NTBs are being addressed in other fora including other Negotiating Groups. We recognize the need for specific negotiating proposals and encourage participants to make such submissions as quickly as possible.

23. However, we recognize that much remains to be done in order to establish modalities and to conclude the negotiations. Therefore, we agree to intensify work on all outstanding issues to fulfil the Doha objectives, in particular, we are resolved to

establish modalities no later than 30 April 2006 and to submit comprehensive draft Schedules based on these modalities not later than 31 July 2006.

Balance between Agriculture and NAMA

24. We recognize that it is important to advance the development objectives of this Round through enhanced market access for developing countries in both Agriculture and NAMA. To that end, we instruct our negotiators to ensure that there is a comparably high level of ambition in market access for Agriculture and NAMA. This ambition is to be achieved in a balanced and proportionate manner consistent with the principle of special and differential treatment.

Services Negotiations

25. The negotiations on trade in services shall proceed to their conclusion with a view to promoting the economic growth of all trading partners and the development of developing and least-developed countries, and with due respect for the right of Members to regulate. In this regard, we recall and reaffirm the objectives and principles stipulated in the GATS, the Doha Ministerial Declaration, the Guidelines and Procedures for the Negotiations on Trade in Services adopted by the Special Session of the Council for Trade in Services on 28 March 2001 and the Modalities for the Special Treatment for Least-Developed Country Members in the Negotiations on Trade in Services adopted on 3 September 2003, as well as Annex C of the Decision adopted by the General Council on 1 August 2004.

26. We urge all Members to participate actively in these negotiations towards achieving a progressively higher level of liberalization of trade in services, with appropriate flexibility for individual developing countries as provided for in Article XIX of the GATS. Negotiations shall have regard to the size of economies of individual Members, both overall and in individual sectors. We recognize the particular economic situation of LDCs, including the difficulties they face, and acknowledge that they are not expected to undertake new commitments.

27. We are determined to intensify the negotiations in accordance with the above principles and the Objectives, Approaches

and Timelines set out in Annex C to this document with a view to expanding the sectoral and modal coverage of commitments and improving their quality. In this regard, particular attention will be given to sectors and modes of supply of export interest to developing countries.

Rules Negotiations

28. We recall the mandates in paragraphs 28 and 29 of the Doha Ministerial Declaration and reaffirm our commitment to the negotiations on rules, as we set forth in Annex D to this document.

TRIPS Negotiations

29. We take note of the report of the Chairman of the Special Session of the Council for TRIPS setting out the progress in the negotiations on the establishment of a multilateral system of notification and registration of geographical indications for wines and spirits, as mandated in Article 23.4 of the TRIPS Agreement and paragraph 18 of the Doha Ministerial Declaration, contained in document TN/IP/14, and agree to intensify these negotiations in order to complete them within the overall time-frame for the conclusion of the negotiations that were foreseen in the Doha Ministerial Declaration.

Environment Negotiations

30. We reaffirm the mandate in paragraph 31 of the Doha Ministerial Declaration aimed at enhancing the mutual supportiveness of trade and environment and welcome the significant work undertaken in the Committee on Trade and Environment (CTE) in Special Session. We instruct Members to intensify the negotiations, without prejudging their outcome, on all parts of paragraph 31 to fulfil the mandate.

31. We recognize the progress in the work under paragraph 31(i) based on Members' submissions on the relationship between existing WTO rules and specific trade obligations set out in multilateral environmental agreements (MEAs). We further recognize the work undertaken under paragraph 31(ii) towards developing effective procedures for regular information exchange between

MEA Secretariats and the relevant WTO committees, and criteria for the granting of observer status.

32. We recognize that recently more work has been carried out under paragraph 31(iii) through numerous submissions by Members and discussions in the CTE in Special Session, including technical discussions, which were also held in informal information exchange sessions without prejudice to Members' positions. We instruct Members to complete the work expeditiously under paragraph 31(iii).

Trade Facilitation Negotiations

33. We recall and reaffirm the mandate and modalities for negotiations on Trade Facilitation contained in Annex D of the Decision adopted by the General Council on 1 August 2004. We note with appreciation the report of the Negotiating Group, attached in Annex E to this document, and the comments made by our delegations on that report as reflected in document TN/TF/M/11. We endorse the recommendations contained in paragraphs 3, 4, 5, 6 and 7 of the report.

DSU Negotiations

34. We take note of the progress made in the Dispute Settlement Understanding negotiations as reflected in the report by the Chairman of the Special Session of the Dispute Settlement Body to the Trade Negotiations Committee (TNC) and direct the Special Session to continue to work towards a rapid conclusion of the negotiations.

S&D Treatment

35. We reaffirm that provisions for special and differential (S&D) treatment are an integral part of the WTO Agreements. We renew our determination to fulfil the mandate contained in paragraph 44 of the Doha Ministerial Declaration and in the Decision adopted by the General Council on 1 August 2004, that all S&D treatment provisions be reviewed with a view to strengthening them and making them more precise, effective and operational.

36. We take note of the work done on the Agreement-specific proposals, especially the five LDC proposals. We agree

to adopt the decisions contained in Annex F to this document. However, we also recognize that substantial work still remains to be done. We commit ourselves to address the development interests and concerns of developing countries, especially the LDCs, in the multilateral trading system, and we recommit ourselves to complete the task we set ourselves at Doha. We accordingly instruct the Committee on Trade and Development in Special Session to expeditiously complete the review of all the outstanding Agreement-specific proposals and report to the General Council, with clear recommendations for a decision, by December 2006.

37. We are concerned at the lack of progress on the Category II proposals that had been referred to other WTO bodies and negotiating groups. We instruct these bodies to expeditiously complete the consideration of these proposals and report periodically to the General Council, with the objective of ensuring that clear recommendations for a decision are made no later than December 2006. We also instruct the Special Session to continue to coordinate its efforts with these bodies, so as to ensure that this work is completed on time.

38. We further instruct the Special Session, within the parameters of the Doha mandate, to resume work on all other outstanding issues, including on the cross-cutting issues, the monitoring mechanism, and the incorporation of S&D treatment into the architecture of WTO rules, and report on a regular basis to the General Council.

Implementation

39. We reiterate the instruction in the Decision adopted by the General Council on 1 August 2004 to the TNC, negotiating bodies and other WTO bodies concerned to redouble their efforts to find appropriate solutions as a priority to outstanding implementation-related issues. We take note of the work undertaken by the Director-General in his consultative process on all outstanding implementation issues under paragraph 12(b) of the Doha Ministerial Declaration, including on issues related to the extension of the protection of geographical indications provided for in Article 23 of the TRIPS Agreement to products other than

wines and spirits and those related to the relationship between the TRIPS Agreement and the Convention on Biological Diversity. We request the Director-General, without prejudice to the positions of Members, to intensify his consultative process on all outstanding implementation issues under paragraph 12(b), if need be by appointing Chairpersons of concerned WTO bodies as his Friends and/or by holding dedicated consultations. The Director-General shall report to each regular meeting of the TNC and the General Council. The Council shall review progress and take any appropriate action no later than 31 July 2006.

TRIPS & Public Health

40. We reaffirm the importance we attach to the General Council Decision of 30 August 2003 on the Implementation of Paragraph 6 of the Doha Declaration on the TRIPS Agreement and Public Health, and to an amendment to the TRIPS Agreement replacing its provisions. In this regard, we welcome the work that has taken place in the Council for TRIPS and the Decision of the General Council of 6 December 2005 on an Amendment of the TRIPS Agreement.

Small Economies

41. We reaffirm our commitment to the Work Programme on Small Economies and urge Members to adopt specific measures that would facilitate the fuller integration of small, vulnerable economies into the multilateral trading system, without creating a sub-category of WTO Members. We take note of the report of the Committee on Trade and Development in Dedicated Session on the Work Programme on Small Economies to the General Council and agree to the recommendations on future work. We instruct the Committee on Trade and Development, under the overall responsibility of the General Council, to continue the work in the Dedicated Session and to monitor progress of the small economies' proposals in the negotiating and other bodies, with the aim of providing responses to the trade-related issues of small economies as soon as possible but no later than 31 December 2006. We instruct the General Council to report on progress and action taken, together with any further recommendations as appropriate, to our next Session.

Trade, Debt & Finance

42. We take note of the report transmitted by the General Council on the work undertaken and progress made in the examination of the relationship between trade, debt and finance and on the consideration of any possible recommendations on steps that might be taken within the mandate and competence of the WTO as provided in paragraph 36 of the Doha Ministerial Declaration and agree that, building on the work carried out to date, this work shall continue on the basis of the Doha mandate. We instruct the General Council to report further to our next Session.

Trade & Transfer of Technology

43. We take note of the report transmitted by the General Council on the work undertaken and progress made in the examination of the relationship between trade and transfer of technology and on the consideration of any possible recommendations on steps that might be taken within the mandate of the WTO to increase flows of technology to developing countries. Recognizing the relevance of the relationship between trade and transfer of technology to the development dimension of the Doha Work Programme and building on the work carried out to date, we agree that this work shall continue on the basis of the mandate contained in paragraph 37 of the Doha Ministerial Declaration. We instruct the General Council to report further to our next Session.

Doha Paragraph 19

44. We take note of the work undertaken by the Council for TRIPS pursuant to paragraph 19 of the Doha Ministerial Declaration and agree that this work shall continue on the basis of paragraph 19 of the Doha Ministerial Declaration and the progress made in the Council for TRIPS to date. The General Council shall report on its work in this regard to our next Session.

TRIPS Non-violation and Situation Complaints

45. We take note of the work done by the Council for Trade-Related Aspects of Intellectual Property Rights pursuant to paragraph 11.1 of the Doha Decision on Implementation-Related

Issues and Concerns and paragraph 1.h of the Decision adopted by the General Council on 1 August 2004, and direct it to continue its examination of the scope and modalities for complaints of the types provided for under subparagraphs 1(b) and 1(c) of Article XXIII of GATT 1994 and make recommendations to our next Session. It is agreed that, in the meantime, Members will not initiate such complaints under the TRIPS Agreement.

E-Commerce

46. We take note of the reports from the General Council and subsidiary bodies on the Work Programme on Electronic Commerce, and that the examination of issues under the Work Programme is not yet complete. We agree to reinvigorate that work, including the development-related issues under the Work Programme and discussions on the trade treatment, *inter alia*, of electronically delivered software. We agree to maintain the current institutional arrangements for the Work Programme. We declare that Members will maintain their current practice of not imposing customs duties on electronic transmissions until our next Session.

LDCs

47. We reaffirm our commitment to effectively and meaningfully integrate LDCs into the multilateral trading system and shall continue to implement the WTO Work Programme for LDCs adopted in February 2002. We acknowledge the seriousness of the concerns and interests of the LDCs in the negotiations as expressed in the Livingstone Declaration, adopted by their Ministers in June 2005. We take note that issues of interest to LDCs are being addressed in all areas of negotiations and we welcome the progress made since the Doha Ministerial Declaration as reflected in the Decision adopted by the General Council on 1 August 2004. Building upon the commitment in the Doha Ministerial Declaration, developed-country Members, and developing-country Members declaring themselves in a position to do so, agree to implement duty-free and quota-free market access for products originating from LDCs as provided for in Annex F to this document. Furthermore, in accordance with our commitment in the Doha Ministerial Declaration, Members shall take additional measures to provide effective market access, both

at the border and otherwise, including simplified and transparent rules of origin so as to facilitate exports from LDCs. In the services negotiations, Members shall implement the LDC modalities and give priority to the sectors and modes of supply of export interest to LDCs, particularly with regard to movement of service providers under Mode 4. We agree to facilitate and accelerate negotiations with acceding LDCs based on the accession guidelines adopted by the General Council in December 2002. We commit to continue giving our attention and priority to concluding the ongoing accession proceedings as rapidly as possible. We welcome the Decision by the TRIPS Council to extend the transition period under Article 66.1 of the TRIPS Agreement. We reaffirm our commitment to enhance effective trade-related technical assistance and capacity building to LDCs on a priority basis in helping to overcome their limited human and institutional trade-related capacity to enable LDCs to maximize the benefits resulting from the Doha Development Agenda (DDA).

Integrated Framework

48. We continue to attach high priority to the effective implementation of the Integrated Framework (IF) and reiterate our endorsement of the IF as a viable instrument for LDCs' trade development, building on its principles of country ownership and partnership. We highlight the importance of contributing to reducing their supply side constraints. We reaffirm our commitment made at Doha, and recognize the urgent need to make the IF more effective and timely in addressing the trade-related development needs of LDCs.

49. In this regard, we are encouraged by the endorsement by the Development Committee of the World Bank and International Monetary Fund (IMF) at its autumn 2005 meeting of an enhanced IF. We welcome the establishment of a Task Force by the Integrated Framework Working Group as endorsed by the IF Steering Committee (IFSC) as well as an agreement on the three elements which together constitute an enhanced IF. The Task Force, composed of donor and LDC members, will provide recommendations to the IFSC by April 2006. The enhanced IF shall enter into force no later than 31 December 2006.

50. We agree that the Task Force, in line with its Mandate and based on the three elements agreed to, shall provide recommendations on how the implementation of the IF can be improved, *inter alia*, by considering ways to :

1. provide increased, predictable, and additional funding on a multi-year basis;
2. strengthen the IF in-country, including through mainstreaming trade into national development plans and poverty reduction strategies; more effective follow-up to diagnostic trade integration studies and implementation of action matrices; and achieving greater and more effective coordination amongst donors and IF stakeholders, including beneficiaries;
3. improve the IF decision-making and management structure to ensure an effective and timely delivery of the increased financial resources and programmes.

51. We welcome the increased commitment already expressed by some Members in the run-up to, and during, this Session. We urge other development partners to significantly increase their contribution to the IF Trust Fund. We also urge the six IF core agencies to continue to cooperate closely in the implementation of the IF, to increase their investments in this initiative and to intensify their assistance in trade-related infrastructure, private sector development and institution building to help LDCs expand and diversify their export base.

Technical Cooperation

52. We note with appreciation the substantial increase in trade-related technical assistance since our Fourth Session, which reflects the enhanced commitment of Members to address the increased demand for technical assistance, through both bilateral and multilateral programmes. We note the progress made in the current approach to planning and implementation of WTO's programmes, as embodied in the Technical Assistance and Training Plans adopted by Members, as well as the improved quality of those programmes. We note that a strategic review of WTO's technical assistance is to be carried out by Members, and expect that in future planning and implementation of training and

technical assistance, the conclusions and recommendations of the review will be taken into account, as appropriate.

53. We reaffirm the priorities established in paragraph 38 of the Doha Ministerial Declaration for the delivery of technical assistance and urge the Director-General to ensure that programmes focus accordingly on the needs of beneficiary countries and reflect the priorities and mandates adopted by Members. We endorse the application of appropriate needs assessment mechanisms and support the efforts to enhance ownership by beneficiaries, in order to ensure the sustainability of trade-related capacity building. We invite the Director-General to reinforce the partnerships and coordination with other agencies and regional bodies in the design and implementation of technical assistance programmes, so that all dimensions of trade-related capacity building are addressed, in a manner coherent with the programmes of other providers. In particular, we encourage all Members to cooperate with the International Trade Centre, which complements WTO work by providing a platform for business to interact with trade negotiators, and practical advice for small and medium-sized enterprises (SMEs) to benefit from the multilateral trading system. In this connection, we note the role of the Joint Integrated Technical Assistance Programme (JITAP) in building the capacity of participating countries.

54. In order to continue progress in the effective and timely delivery of trade-related capacity building, in line with the priority Members attach to it, the relevant structures of the Secretariat should be strengthened and its resources enhanced. We reaffirm our commitment to ensure secure and adequate levels of funding for trade-related capacity building, including in the Doha Development Agenda Global Trust Fund, to conclude the Doha Work Programme and implement its results.

Commodity Issues

55. We recognize the dependence of several developing and least-developed countries on the export of commodities and the problems they face because of the adverse impact of the long-term decline and sharp fluctuation in the prices of these commodities. We take note of the work undertaken in the

Committee on Trade and Development on commodity issues, and instruct the Committee, within its mandate, to intensify its work in cooperation with other relevant international organizations and report regularly to the General Council with possible recommendations. We agree that the particular trade-related concerns of developing and least-developed countries related to commodities shall also be addressed in the course of the agriculture and NAMA negotiations. We further acknowledge that these countries may need support and technical assistance to overcome the particular problems they face, and urge Members and relevant international organizations to consider favourably requests by these countries for support and assistance.

Coherence

56. We welcome the Director-General's actions to strengthen the WTO's cooperation with the IMF and the World Bank in the context of the WTO's Marrakesh mandate on Coherence, and invite him to continue to work closely with the General Council in this area. We value the General Council meetings that are held with the participation of the heads of the IMF and the World Bank to advance our Coherence mandate. We agree to continue building on that experience and expand the debate on international trade and development policymaking and inter-agency cooperation with the participation of relevant UN agencies. In that regard, we note the discussions taking place in the Working Group on Trade, Debt and Finance on, *inter alia*, the issue of Coherence, and look forward to any possible recommendations it may make on steps that might be taken within the mandate and competence of the WTO on this issue.

Aid for Trade

57. We welcome the discussions of Finance and Development Ministers in various fora, including the Development Committee of the World Bank and IMF, that have taken place this year on expanding Aid for Trade. Aid for Trade should aim to help developing countries, particularly LDCs, to build the supply-side capacity and trade-related infrastructure that they need to assist them to implement and benefit from WTO Agreements and more broadly to expand their trade. Aid for Trade cannot be a

substitute for the development benefits that will result from a successful conclusion to the DDA, particularly on market access. However, it can be a valuable complement to the DDA. We invite the Director-General to create a task force that shall provide recommendations on how to operationalize Aid for Trade. The Task Force will provide recommendations to the General Council by July 2006 on how Aid for Trade might contribute most effectively to the development dimension of the DDA. We also invite the Director-General to consult with Members as well as with the IMF and World Bank, relevant international organisations and the regional development banks with a view to reporting to the General Council on appropriate mechanisms to secure additional financial resources for Aid for Trade, where appropriate through grants and concessional loans.

Recently-acceded Members

58. We recognize the special situation of recently-acceded Members who have undertaken extensive market access commitments at the time of accession. This situation will be taken into account in the negotiations.

Accessions

59. We reaffirm our strong commitment to making the WTO truly global in scope and membership. We welcome those new Members who have completed their accession processes since our last Session, namely Nepal, Cambodia and Saudi Arabia. We note with satisfaction that Tonga has completed its accession negotiations to the WTO. These accessions further strengthen the rules-based multilateral trading system. We continue to attach priority to the 29 ongoing accessions with a view to concluding them as rapidly and smoothly as possible. We stress the importance of facilitating and accelerating the accession negotiations of least-developed countries, taking due account of the guidelines on LDC accession adopted by the General Council in December 2002.

ANNEX A

Agriculture

Report by the Chairman of the Special Session of the Committee on Agriculture to the TNC

1. The present report has been prepared on my own responsibility. I have done so in response to the direction of Members as expressed at the informal Special Session of the Committee on Agriculture on 11 November 2005. At that meeting, following the informal Heads of Delegation meeting the preceding day, Members made it crystal clear that they sought from me at this point an objective factual summary of where the negotiations have reached at this time. It was clear from that meeting that Members did not expect or desire anything that purported to be more than that. In particular, it was clear that, following the decision at the Heads of Delegation meeting that full modalities will not be achieved at Hong Kong, Members did not want anything that suggested implicit or explicit agreement where it did not exist.

2. This is not, of course, the kind of paper that I would have chosen or preferred to have prepared at this point. Ideally, my task should have been to work with Members to generate a draft text of modalities. But this text reflects the reality of the present situation. There will be — because there must be if we are to conclude these negotiations — such a draft text in the future. I look at this now as a task postponed, but the precise timing of this is in the hands of Members.

3. As for this paper, it is precisely what it is described to be. No more, no less. It is the Chairman's report and, as such, it goes from me to the TNC. It is not anything more than my personal report — in particular, it is not in any sense an agreed text of Members. It does not, therefore, in any way prejudge or prejudice the positions of Members on any matter within it or outside of it. And, it certainly does not bind Members in any way. It should go without saying that the agreed basis of our work is, and shall remain, the Doha Mandate itself and the Framework in the Decision adopted by the General Council on 1 August 2004.

4. As to the character of the paper, I have endeavoured to reflect what I discerned as the wishes of Members when they directed me to prepare this paper. I have tried to capture as clearly as I can such conditional progress and convergence as has developed in the post-July 2004 period. In doing so, I have not tried to brush under the carpet divergences that remain, and the paper tries to be just as clear on those points. Of course, it is a summary report. As such, it cannot — and does not — recapitulate each and every detail on each and every issue. But I took from Members' comments that they would prefer a paper which could 'orient' further discussion.

5. In that regard, I hope that anyone reading this paper would be able to get a pretty clear idea of what it is that remains to be done. Members made it clear that it was not my task as Chair to prescribe what is to be done next in a programmatic way. My task was to register where we are now, but I confess to having done so with an eye to genuinely clarifying where key convergences exist or key divergences remain, rather than obscuring or overcomplicating matters.

6. My own sense, when I review this myself, is the compelling urgency of seizing the moment and driving the process to a conclusion as rapidly as possible. We have made — particularly since August of this year — genuine and material progress. Indeed, it has come at a relatively rapid pace. It is also clear to me that it has been the product of a genuinely negotiating process. In other words, it has been a case of making proposals and counterproposals. That is why the matters covered in this report have an essentially conditional character. As I see it, the reality is that we have yet to find that last bridge to agreement that we need to secure modalities. But it would be a grave error, in my view, to imagine that we can take much time to find that bridge. As Chair, I am convinced that we must maintain momentum. You don't close divergences by taking time off to have a cup of tea. If you do so, you will find that everyone has moved backwards in the meantime. That, it seems to me, is a profound risk to our process. I would like to believe that this report at least underlines to us that there is indeed something real and important still within our grasp and we ought not to risk

losing it. Our overriding challenge and responsibility is to meet the development objective of the Doha Development Agenda. To meet this challenge and achieve this goal, we must act decisively and with real urgency.

7. The future life of this paper, if any, is a matter entirely in the hands of TNC Members to decide. This, as I see it, is the proper safeguard of the integrity of what has come to be described as a "bottom-up" process.

Domestic Support

8. There has been very considerable potential convergence, albeit on a manifestly conditional basis.

Overall Cut

— There is a working hypothesis of three bands for overall cuts by developed countries. There is a strongly convergent working hypothesis that the thresholds for the three bands be US$ billion 0-10; 10-60; >60. On this basis, the European Communities would be in the top band, the United States and Japan in the second band, and all other developed countries at least in the third band. For developing countries, there is a view that either developing countries are assigned to the relevant integrated band (the bottom) or that there is a separate band for them.[1]

— Based on post-July 2005 proposals, there has been an undeniably significant convergence on the range of cuts. Of course, this has been conditional. But subject to that feature, a great deal of progress has been made since the bare bones of the July 2004 Framework. The following matrix provides a snapshot :

Bands	Thresholds (US$ billion)	Cuts
1	0-10	31%-70%
2	10-60	53%-75%
3	>60	70%-80%

De Minimis

— On product-specific *de minimis* and non-product-specific *de minimis*, there is a zone of engagement for cuts between 50% and 80% for developed countries.

— As regards developing countries, there are still divergences to be bridged. In addition to the exemption specifically provided for in the Framework, there is a view that, for all developing countries, there should be no cut in *de minimis* at all. Alternatively, at least for those with no AMS, there should be no cut and, in any case, any cut for those with an AMS should be less than 2/3 of the cut for developed countries.

Blue Box

9. There is important and significant convergence on moving beyond (*i.e.* further constraining) Blue Box programme payments envisaged in the July 2004 Framework. However, the technique for achieving this remains to be determined. One proposal is to shrink the current 5% ceiling to 2.5%.[2] Another proposal rejects this in favour of additional criteria disciplining the so-called "new" Blue Box only. Others favour a combination of both, including additional disciplines on the "old" Blue Box.

AMS

— There is a working hypothesis of three bands for developed countries.

— There is close (but not full) convergence on the thresholds for those bands. There appears to be convergence that the top tier should be US$25 billion and above. There is some remaining divergence over the ceiling for the bottom band : between US$12 billion and 15 billion.

— There has been an undeniably significant convergence on the range of cuts. Of course, this has been conditional. But, that understood, a great deal of progress has been made since the bare bones of the July 2004 Framework. The following matrix[3] provides a snapshot :

Bands	Thresholds (US$ billion)	Cuts
1	0 -12/15	37-60%
2	12/15-25	60-70%
3	>25	70-83%

— There is therefore working hypothesis agreement that the European Communities should be in the top tier, and the United States in the second tier. However, while the basis for Japan's placement as between these two tiers has been narrowed, it remains to be finally resolved.

— For developed countries in the bottom band, with a relatively high level of AMS relative to total value of agriculture production, there is emerging consensus that their band-related reduction should be complemented with an additional effort.

— What is needed now is a further step to bridge the remaining gap in positions — particularly as regards the United States and the European Communities, it being understood that this is not a matter to be resolved in isolation from the other elements in this pillar and beyond.

— On the base period for product-specific caps, certain proposals (such as for 1995-2000 and 1999-2001) are on the table. This needs to be resolved appropriately, including the manner in which special and differential treatment should be applied.

Green Box

10. The review and clarification commitment has not resulted in any discernible convergence on operational outcomes. There is, on the one side, a firm rejection of anything that is seen as departing from the existing disciplines while there is, on the other, an enduring sense that more could be done to review the Green Box without undermining ongoing reform. Beyond that there is, however, some tangible openness to finding appropriate ways to ensure that the Green Box is more "development friendly" *i.e.* better tailored to meet the realities of developing country agriculture but in a way that respects the fundamental requirement of at most minimal trade distortion.

Export Competition

End Date

11. While concrete proposals[4] have been made on the issue of an end date for elimination of all forms of export subsidies,

there is at this stage no convergence. There are suggestions for the principle of front-loading or accelerated elimination for specific products, including particularly cotton.

Export Credits

12. Convergence has been achieved on a number of elements of disciplines with respect to export credits, export credit guarantee or insurance programmes with repayment periods of 180 days and below. However, a number of critical issues remain.[5]

Exporting State Trading Enterprises

13. There has been material convergence on rules to address trade-distorting practices identified in the July 2004 Framework text, although there are still major differences regarding the scope of practices to be covered by the new disciplines. Fundamentally opposing positions remain, however, on the issue of the future use of monopoly powers. There have been concrete drafting proposals on such matters as definition of entities and practices to be addressed as well as transparency. But there has been no genuine convergence in such areas.

Food Aid

14. There is consensus among Members that the WTO shall not stand in the way of the provision of genuine food aid. There is also consensus that what is to be eliminated is commercial displacement. There have been detailed and intensive discussions, some of which have even been text-based, but not to a point where a consolidated draft text could be developed. This has been precluded by Members clinging to fundamentally disparate conceptual premises. There are proposals that in the disciplines a distinction should be made between at least two types of food aid : emergency food aid and food aid to address other situations. However, there is not yet a common understanding where emergency food aid ends and other food aid begins, reflecting concerns that this distinction should not become a means to create a loophole in disciplines. A fundamental sticking point is whether, except in exceptional, genuine emergency situations, Members should (albeit gradually) move towards untied, in-cash

food aid only, as some Members propose but other Members strongly oppose.[6]

Special and Differential Treatment

15. Framework provisions for special and differential treatment, including with respect to the monopoly status of state trading enterprises in developing countries and an extended lifetime for Article 9.4, have been uncontroversial, but details remain to be established.

Special Circumstances

16. Work on the criteria and consultation procedures to govern any ad hoc temporary financing arrangements relating to exports to developing countries in exceptional circumstances is not much developed.

Market Access

Tiered Formula

— We have progressed on *ad valorem* equivalents.[7] This has successfully created a basis for allocating items into bands for the tiered formula.

— We have a working hypothesis of four bands for structuring tariff cuts.

— There has been very considerable convergence on adopting a linear-based approach for cuts within those bands. Members have, of course, by no means formally abandoned positions that are even more divergent.[8] We need now to narrow the extent of divergence that remains. This will include whether or not to include any "pivot" in any band.

— Members have made strong efforts to promote convergence on the size of actual cuts to be undertaken within those bands. But, even though genuine efforts have been made to move from formal positions (which of course remain), major gaps are yet to be bridged. Somewhat greater convergence has been achieved as regards the thresholds for the bands. Substantial movement is clearly essential to progress.[9]

— Some Members continue to reject completely the concept of a tariff cap. Others have proposed[10] a cap between 75-100%.

Sensitive Products

— Members have been prepared to make concrete — albeit conditional — proposals on the number of sensitive products. But, in a situation where proposals extend from as little as 1% to as much as 15% of tariff lines, further bridging this difference is essential to progress.

— The fundamental divergence over the basic approach to treatment of sensitive products needs to be resolved.[11] Beyond that, there needs to be convergence on the consequential extent of liberalisation for such products.

Special and Differential Treatment

— Just as for developed countries, there is a working hypothesis of four bands for developing countries. There is no disagreement on lesser cuts within the bands. A certain body of opinion is open to considering cuts of two-thirds of the amount of the cuts for developed countries as a plausible zone in which to search more intensively for convergence.[12] But significant disagreement on that remains, and divergence is, if anything, somewhat more marked on the connected issue of higher thresholds for developing countries.[13]

— Some Members continue to reject completely the concept of a tariff cap for developing countries. Others have proposed[14] a cap at 150%.

— For sensitive products, there is no disagreement that there should be greater flexibility for developing countries, but the extent of this needs to be further defined.[15]

Special Products

— Regarding *designation* of special products, there has been a clear divergence between those Members which consider that, prior to establishment of schedules, a list of non-exhaustive and illustrative criteria-based indicators should be established and those Members which are looking for a list which would act as a filter or screen for the selection of such products. Latterly, it has been proposed (but not yet discussed with Members as a whole) that a developing country Member should have the right to designate at least 20 per cent of its agricultural tariff lines as Special Products, and be further entitled to designate an SP where, for that product, an AMS has been notified and exports have taken place. This issue needs to be resolved as part of modalities so that there is assurance of the basis upon which Members may designate special products.

— Some moves toward convergence on *treatment* of Special Products have been made recently. Some Members had considered that special products should be fully exempt from any new market access commitments whatsoever and have automatic access to the SSM. Others had argued there should be some degree of market opening for these products, albeit reflecting more flexible treatment than for other products. In the presence of this fundamental divergence, it had clearly been impossible to undertake any definition of what such flexibility would be. Genuine convergence is obviously urgently needed. There is now a new proposal for a tripartite categorization of Special Products involving limited tariff cuts for at least a proportion of such products which remains to be fully discussed. It remains to be seen whether this discussion can help move us forward.

Special Safeguard Mechanism

— There is agreement that there would be a special safeguard mechanism and that it should be tailored to the particular circumstances and needs of developing countries. There is no material disagreement with the view that it should have a quantity trigger. Nor is there disagreement with the view that it should at least be capable of addressing effectively what might be described as import "surges". Divergence remains over whether, or if so how, situations that are lesser than "surge" are to be dealt with. There is, however, agreement that any remedy should be of a temporary nature. There remains strong divergence however on whether, or if so how, a special safeguard should be "price-based" to deal specifically with price effects.

— There is some discernible openness, albeit at varying levels, to at least consider coverage of products that are likely to undergo significant liberalisation effects, and/or are already bound at low levels and/or are special products. Beyond that, however, there remains a fundamental divergence between those considering all products should be eligible for such a mechanism and those opposing such a blanket approach.

Other Elements

17. There has been no further material convergence on the matters covered by paragraphs 35 and 37 of the July 2004 Framework text. The same may be said for paragraph 36 on tariff escalation, albeit that there is full agreement on the need for this to be done, and a genuine recognition of the particular importance of this for commodities exporters. Certain concrete proposals have been made on paragraph 38 (SSG) and met with opposition from some Members.

18. Concrete proposals have been made and discussed on how to implement paragraph 43 of the July 2004 Framework on tropical and diversification products. But there remains divergence over the precise interpretation of this section of the July Framework[16] and no common approach has been established.

19. The importance of long-standing preferences pursuant to paragraph 44 of the July 2004 Framework is fully recognised and concrete proposals regarding preference erosion have been made and discussed.[17] There seems not to be inherent difficulty with a role for capacity building. However, while there is some degree of support, *e.g.* longer implementation periods for at least certain products in order to facilitate adjustment, there is far from convergence on even this. Some argue it is not sufficient or certainly not in all cases, while others that it is not warranted at all.

Least-Developed Countries

20. There is no questioning of the terms of paragraph 45 of the July Framework agreement, which exempts least-developed countries from any reduction requirement. The stipulation that "developed Members, and developing country Members in a position to do so, should provide duty-free and quota-free market access for products originating from least-developed countries" is not at this point concretely operational for all Members. At this stage, several Members have made undertakings. Proposals for this to be bound remain on the table.[18]

Cotton

21. While there is genuine recognition of the problem to be addressed and concrete proposals have been made, Members remain at this point short of concrete and specific achievement that would be needed to meet the July Framework direction to address this matter ambitiously, expeditiously and specifically. There is no disagreement with the view that all forms of export subsidies are to be eliminated for cotton although the timing and speed remains to be specified. Proposals to eliminate them immediately or from day one of the implementation period are not at this point shared by all Members. In the case of trade distorting support, proponents seek full elimination with "front-loaded" implementation.[19] There is a view that the extent to which this can occur, and its timing, can only be determined in the context of an overall agreement. Another view is that there could be at least substantial and front-loaded reduction on cotton specifically from day one of implementation, with the major implementation achieved within twelve months, and the remainder to be completed within a period shorter than the overall implementation period for agriculture.[20]

Recently-Acceded Members

22. Concrete proposals have been made and discussed, but no specific flexibility provisions have commanded consensus.

Monitoring and Surveillance

23. A proposal has been made but there is no material advance at this point.

Other Issues

24. On paragraph 49 (sectoral initiatives, differential export taxes, GIs) certain positions and proposals have been tabled and/ or referred to. They are issues that remain of interest but not agreed.

25. At this point, proposals on paragraph 50 have not advanced materially.

26. In the case of small and vulnerable economies, a concrete proposal has been made recently. It has not yet been subject to consultation.

27. There is openness to the particular concerns of commodity-dependent developing and least-developed countries facing long-term decline and/or sharp fluctuations in prices. There is, at this point (where, overall, precise modalities are still pending), support for the view that such modalities should eventually be capable of addressing effectively key areas for them.[21]

ANNEX B

Market Access for Non-Agricultural Products

Report by the Chairman of the Negotiating Group on Market Access to the TNC

A. INTRODUCTION

1. A Chairman's commentary of the state of play of the NAMA negotiations was prepared in July 2005 and circulated in document JOB(05)/147 and Add.1 (hereinafter referred to as the "Chairman's commentary"). The current report, made on my responsibility, reflects the state of play of the NAMA negotiations at this juncture of the Doha Development Agenda, and supplements that commentary.

2. With an eye on the forthcoming Ministerial, Section B of this report attempts to highlight those areas of convergence and divergence on the elements of Annex B of Decision adopted by the General Council on 1 August 2004, (hereinafter referred to as the "NAMA framework"), and to provide some guidance as to what may be a possible future course of action with respect to

some of the elements. Section C of the report provides some final remarks about possible action by Ministers at Hong Kong.

3. In preparing this report, use has been made of documents provided by Members (as listed in TN/MA/S/16/Rev.2) as well as the discussions in the open-ended sessions of the Group, plurilateral meetings and bilateral contacts, as long as they were not in the nature of confessionals.

B. SUMMARY OF THE STATE OF PLAY

4. Full modalities must have detailed language and, where required, final numbers on all elements of the NAMA framework. Such an agreement should also contain a detailed work plan concerning the process after the establishment of full modalities for the purpose of the submission, verification and annexation of Doha Schedules to a legal instrument. While acknowledging that progress has been made since the adoption of the NAMA framework, the establishment of full modalities is, at present, a difficult prospect given the lack of agreement on a number of elements in the NAMA framework including the formula, paragraph 8 flexibilities and unbound tariffs.

5. Regarding the structure of this section, generally Members recognize that the issues identified in the preceding paragraph are the three elements of the NAMA framework on which solutions are required as a matter of priority, and that there is a need to address them in an interlinked fashion. So, this report will commence with these three subjects before moving on to the other elements of the NAMA framework in the order in which they are presented therein.

Formula (paragraph 4 of the NAMA framework)

6. On the non-linear formula, there has been movement since the adoption of the NAMA framework. There is a more common understanding of the shape of the formula that Members are willing to adopt in these negotiations. In fact, Members have been focusing on a Swiss formula. During the past few months, much time and effort has been spent examining the impact of such a formula from both a defensive and offensive angle. In terms of the specifics of that formula, there are basically two

variations on the table : a formula with a limited number of negotiated coefficients and a formula where the value of each country's coefficient would be based essentially on the tariff average of bound rates of that Member, resulting in multiple coefficients.

7. In order to move beyond a debate on the merits of the two options (and in recognition of the fact that what matters in the final analysis is the level of the coefficient) more recently Members have engaged in a discussion of numbers. Such a debate has been particularly helpful, especially as it demonstrated in a quantifiable manner to what extent the benchmarks established in paragraph 16 of the Doha Ministerial Declaration would be achieved. While it is evident that one of the characteristics of such a formula is to address tariff peaks, tariff escalation and high tariffs (as it brings down high tariffs more than low tariffs), one benchmark which has been the subject of differences of opinion has been that of "less than full reciprocity in reduction commitments" and how it should be measured. Some developing Members are of the view that this means less than average percentage cuts, *i.e.*, as translated through a higher coefficient in the formula, than those undertaken by developed country Members. However, the latter have indicated that there are other measurements of less than full reciprocity in reduction commitments including the final rates after the formula cut which in their markets would be less than in developing country markets. Also, in their view, such a measurement of less than full reciprocity in reduction commitments has to take into account not only the additional effort made by them in all areas but also of paragraph 8 flexibilities and the fact that several developing Members and the LDCs would be exempt from formula cuts.

8. Other objectives put forward by developed Members and some developing Members as being part of the Doha NAMA mandate are : harmonization of tariffs between Members; cuts into applied rates; and improvement of South-South trade. However, these objectives have been challenged by other developing Members who believe that, on the contrary, they are not part of that mandate.

9. During the informal discussions, many Members engaged in an exchange on the basis of an approach with two coefficients. In the context of such debates, the coefficients which were mentioned for developed Members fell generally within the range of 5 to 10, and for developing Members within the range of 15 to 30, although some developing Members did propose lower coefficients for developed Members and higher coefficients for developing Members. In addition, a developing country coefficient of 10 was also put forward by some developed Members. However, while this discussion of numbers is a positive development, the inescapable reality is that the range of coefficients is wide and reflects the divergence that exists as to Members' expectations regarding the contributions that their trading partners should be making.

Flexibilities for Developing Members Subject to a Formula (paragraph 8 of the NAMA framework)

10. A central issue concerning the paragraph 8 flexibilities has been the question of linkage or non-linkage between these flexibilities and the coefficient in the formula. A view was expressed that the flexibilities currently provided for in paragraph 8 are equivalent to 4-5 additional points to the coefficient in the formula, and as a result there was need to take this aspect into account in the developing country coefficient. In response, the argument has been made by many developing Members that those flexibilities are a stand alone provision as reflected in the language of that provision, and should not be linked to the coefficient. Otherwise, this would amount to re-opening the NAMA framework. Some of those Members have also expressed the view that the numbers currently within square brackets are the minimum required for their sensitive tariff lines, and have expressed concern about the conditions attached to the use of such flexibilities, such as the capping of the import value. In response, the point has been made by developed Members that they are not seeking to remove the flexibilities under paragraph 8, and therefore are not re-opening the NAMA framework. They further point out that the numbers in paragraph 8 are within square brackets precisely to reflect the fact that they are not fixed and may need to be adjusted downwards depending on the level

of the coefficient. In addition, the need for more transparency and predictability with regard to the tariff lines which would be covered by paragraph 8 flexibilities has been raised by some of these Members. Some developing Members have also advanced the idea that there should be the option for those developing Members not wanting to use paragraph 8 flexibilities to have recourse to a higher coefficient in the formula in the interest of having a balanced outcome.

Unbound Tariff Lines (paragraph 5, indent two of the NAMA framework)

11. There has been progress on the discussion of unbound tariff lines. There is an understanding that full bindings would be a desirable objective of the NAMA negotiations, and a growing sense that unbound tariff lines should be subject to formula cuts provided there is a pragmatic solution for those lines with low applied rates. However, some Members have stressed that their unbound tariff lines with high applied rates are also sensitive and due consideration should be given to those lines. There now appears to be a willingness among several Members to move forward on the basis of a non-linear mark-up approach to establish base rates, and in the case of some of these Members, provided that such an approach yields an equitable result. A non-linear mark-up approach envisages the addition of a certain number of percentage points to the applied rate of the unbound tariff line in order to establish the base rate on which the formula is to be applied. There are two variations of such an approach. In one case, a constant number of percentage points are added to the applied rate in order to establish the base rate. The other variation consists of having a different number of percentage points depending on the level of the applied rate. In other words, the lower the applied rate the higher the mark-up and the higher the applied rate, the lower the mark-up. There is also one proposal on the table of a target average approach where an average is established through the use of a formula, with the unbound tariff lines expected to have final bindings around that average.

12. On a practical level, in their discussions on unbound tariff lines, Members have been referring mostly to the constant

mark-up methodology to establish base rates. In the context of such discussions, the number for the mark-up has ranged from 5 to 30 percentage points. Once again the gap between the two figures is wide, but Members have displayed willingness to be flexible.

Other Elements of the Formula (paragraph 5 of the NAMA framework)

13. Concerning product coverage (indent 1), Members have made good progress to establish a list of non-agricultural products as reflected in document JOB(05)/226/Rev.2. The main issue is whether the outcome of this exercise should be an agreed list or guidelines. It would appear that several Members are in favour of the former outcome, however, some have expressed their preference for the latter. In any event, there are only a limited number of items (17) on which differences exist and Members should try and resolve these differences as quickly as possible.

14. On *ad valorem* equivalents (indent 5), agreement was reached to convert non *ad valorem* duties to *ad valorem* equivalents on the basis of the methodology contained in JOB(05)/166/Rev.1 and to bind them in *ad valorem* terms. To date, four Members have submitted their preliminary AVE calculations, but there are many more due. Those Members would need to submit this information as quickly as possible so as to allow sufficient time for the multilateral verification process.

15. The subject of how credit is to be given for autonomous liberalization (indent 4) by developing countries provided that the tariff lines are bound on an MFN basis in the WTO since the conclusion of the Uruguay Round has not been discussed in detail since the adoption of the NAMA framework. However, this issue may be more usefully taken up once there is a clearer picture of the formula.

16. All the other elements of the formula such as tariff cuts commencing from bound rates after full implementation of current commitments (indent 2), the base year (indent 3), the nomenclature (indent 6) and reference period for import data (indent 7) have not been discussed any further since July 2004,

as they were acceptable to Members as currently reflected in the NAMA framework.

Other Flexibilities for Developing Members

Members with low binding coverage (paragraph 6 of the NAMA framework)

17. A submission by a group of developing Members, covered under paragraph 6 provisions, was made in June 2005. The paper proposed that Members falling under this paragraph should be encouraged to substantially increase their binding coverage, and bind tariff lines at a level consistent with their individual development, trade, fiscal and strategic needs. A preliminary discussion of this proposal revealed that there were concerns about this proposal re-opening this paragraph by seeking to enhance the flexibilities contained therein. Further discussion of this proposal is required. However, it appears that the issue of concern to some of the paragraph 6 Members is not related so much to the full binding coverage, but rather to the average level at which these Members would be required to bind their tariffs.

Flexibilities for LDCs (paragraph 9 of the NAMA framework)

18. There appears to be a common understanding that LDCs will be the judge of the extent and level of the bindings that they make. At the same time, Members have indicated that this substantial increase of the binding commitments which LDCs are expected to undertake should be done with a good faith effort. In this regard, some yardsticks for this effort were mentioned including the coverage and level of bindings made in the Uruguay Round by other LDCs as well as the more recently acceded LDCs.

Small, Vulnerable Economies

19. A paper was submitted recently by a group of Members which proposes *inter alia* lesser and linear cuts to Members identified by a criterion using trade share. While some developing and developed Members were sympathetic to the situation of such Members, concerns were expressed with respect to the threshold used to establish eligibility, and also the treatment envisaged.

Other developing Members expressed serious reservations about this proposal which in their view appeared to be creating a new category of developing Members, and to be further diluting the ambition of the NAMA negotiations. The sponsors of this proposal stressed that the small, vulnerable economies had characteristics which warranted special treatment.

20. This is an issue on which there is a serious divergence of opinion among developing Members. This subject will need to be debated further. Discussions may be facilitated through additional statistical analysis.

Sectorals (paragraph 7 of the NAMA framework)

21. It appears that good progress is being made on the sectoral tariff component of the NAMA negotiations. Work which is taking place in an informal Member-driven process has focused on *inter alia* identification of sectors, product coverage, participation, end rates and adequate provisions of flexibilities for developing countries. Besides the sectorals based on a critical mass approach identified in the Chairman's commentary — bicycles, chemicals, electronics/electrical equipment, fish, footwear, forest products, gems and jewellery, pharmaceuticals and medical equipment, raw materials and sporting goods — I understand that work is ongoing on other sectors namely apparel, auto/auto parts and textiles.

22. While this component of the NAMA negotiations is recognized in the NAMA framework to be a key element to delivering on the objectives of paragraph 16 of the Doha NAMA mandate, some developing Members have questioned the rationale of engaging in sectoral negotiations before having the formula finalized. Many have also reiterated their view that sectorals are voluntary in nature. The point has also been made by other developing Members that sectorals harm smaller developing Members due to an erosion of their preferences. However, the proponents of such initiatives have argued that sectorals are another key element of the NAMA negotiations and an important modality for delivering on the elimination of duties as mandated in paragraph 16 of the Doha Ministerial Declaration. In addition, they have pointed out that some of the sectorals were initiated by

developing Members. Moreover, such initiatives require substantive work and were time-consuming to prepare. Concerning preference erosion, this was a cross-cutting issue.

23. Members will need to begin considering time-lines for the finalization of such work, and the submission of the outcomes which will be applied on an MFN basis.

Market Access for LDCs (paragraph 10 of the NAMA framework)

24. In the discussions on this subject, it was noted that the Committee on Trade and Development in Special Session is examining the question of duty-free and quota-free access for non-agricultural products originating from LDCs. Consequently, there is recognition by Members that the discussions in that Committee would most probably have an impact on this element of the NAMA framework, and would need to be factored in at the appropriate time.

Newly Acceded Members (paragraph 11 of the NAMA framework)

25. Members recognize the extensive market access commitments made by the NAMs at the time of their accession. From the discussions held on this subject, it was clarified that those NAMs which are developing Members have access to paragraph 8 flexibilities. As special provisions for tariff reductions for the NAMs, some Members are willing to consider longer implementation periods than those to be provided to developing Members. Other proposals such as a higher coefficient and "grace periods" for the NAMs were also put forward, but a number of Members have objected to these ideas. There has also been a submission by four low-income economies in transition who have requested to be exempt from formula cuts in light of their substantive contributions at the time of their WTO accession and the current difficult state of their economies. While some Members showed sympathy for the situation of these Members, they expressed the view that other solutions may be more appropriate. Some developing Members also expressed concern about this proposal creating a differentiation between Members. Further discussion is required on these issues.

NTBs (paragraph 14 of the NAMA framework)

26. Since adoption of the July 2004 framework, Members have been focusing their attention on non-tariff barriers in recognition of the fact that they are an integral and equally important part of the NAMA negotiations. Some Members claim that they constitute a greater barrier to their exports than tariffs. The Group has spent a considerable amount of time identifying, categorizing and examining the notified NTBs. Members are using bilateral, vertical and horizontal approaches to the NTB negotiations. For example, many Members are raising issues bilaterally with their trading partners. Vertical initiatives are ongoing on automobiles, electronic products and wood products. There have been some proposals of a horizontal nature concerning export taxes, export restrictions and remanufactured products. On export taxes, some Members have expressed the view that such measures fall outside the mandate of the NAMA negotiations. Some Members have also raised in other Negotiating Groups some of the NTBs they had notified initially in the context of the NAMA negotiations. For example, a number of trade facilitation measures are now being examined in the Negotiating Group on Trade Facilitation. Some other Members have also indicated their intention to bring issues to the regular WTO Committees. NTBs currently proposed for negotiation in the NAMA Group are contained in document JOB(05)/85/Rev.3.

27. Some proposals have been made of a procedural nature in order to expedite the NTB work, including a suggestion to hold dedicated NTB sessions. Further consideration will need to be given to this and other proposals. Members will also need to begin considering some time-lines for the submission of specific negotiating proposals and NTB outcomes.

Appropriate Studies and Capacity Building Measures (paragraph 15 of the NAMA framework)

28. There has been no discussion as such on this element as it is an ongoing and integral part of the negotiating process. Several papers have been prepared by the Secretariat during the course of the negotiations and capacity building activities by the Secretariat have increased considerably since the launch of the

Doha Development Agenda. Such activities will need to continue taking into account the evolution of the negotiations.

Non-reciprocal Preferences (paragraph 16 of the NAMA framework)

29. In response to calls by some Members for a better idea of the scope of the problem, the ACP Group circulated an indicative list of products (170 HS 6-digit tariff lines) vulnerable to preference erosion in the EC and US markets as identified through a vulnerability index. Simulations were also submitted by the African Group. Some developing Members expressed concern that the tariff lines listed covered the majority of their exports, or covered critical exports to those markets and were also precisely the lines on which they sought MFN cuts. As a result, for these Members, it was impossible to entertain any solution which related to less than full formula cuts or longer staging. In this regard, concern was expressed by them that non-trade solutions were not being examined. For the proponents of the issue, a trade solution was necessary as this was a trade problem. According to them, their proposal would not undermine trade liberalization because they were seeking to manage such liberalization on a limited number of products.

30. This subject is highly divisive precisely because the interests of the two groups of developing Members are in direct conflict. Additionally, it is a cross-cutting issue which makes it even more sensitive. While, the aforementioned list of products has been helpful in providing a sense of the scope of the problem and may help Members to engage in a more focused discussion, it is clear that pragmatism will need to be shown by all concerned.

Environmental Goods (paragraph 17 of the NAMA framework)

31. Since the adoption of the July framework in 2004, limited discussions have been held on this subject in the Group. However, it is noted that much work under paragraph 31(iii) of the Doha Ministerial Declaration has been undertaken by the Committee on Trade and Environment in Special Session. There would need to be close coordination between the two negotiating

groups and a stock taking of the work undertaken in that Committee would be required at the appropriate time by the NAMA Negotiating Group.

Other Elements of the NAMA Framework

32. On the other elements of the NAMA framework, such as supplementary modalities (paragraph 12), elimination of low duties (paragraph 13) and tariff revenue dependency (paragraph 16) the Group has not had a substantive debate. This has in part to do with the nature of the issue or because more information is required from the proponents. Regarding supplementary modalities, such modalities will become more relevant once the formula has been finalized. On elimination of low duties, this issue may be more suitable to consider once there is a better sense of the likely outcome of the NAMA negotiations. On tariff revenue dependency, more clarity is required from the proponents on the nature and scope of the problem.

C. FINAL REMARKS

33. As may be observed from the above report, Members are far away from achieving full modalities. This is highly troubling. It will take a major effort by all if the objective of concluding the NAMA negotiations by the end of 2006 is to be realized.

34. To this end, I would highlight as a critical objective for Hong Kong a common understanding on the formula, paragraph 8 flexibilities and unbound tariffs. It is crucial that Ministers move decisively on these elements so that the overall outcome is acceptable to all. This will give the necessary impetus to try and fulfil at a date soon thereafter the objective of full modalities for the NAMA negotiations.

35. Specifically, Ministers should :

- Obtain agreement on the final structure of the formula and narrow the range of numbers.
- Resolve their basic differences over paragraph 8 flexibilities.
- Clarify whether the constant mark-up approach is the way forward, and if so, narrow the range of numbers.

ANNEX C

Services

Objectives

1. In order to achieve a progressively higher level of liberalization of trade in services, with appropriate flexibility for individual developing country Members, we agree that Members should be guided, to the maximum extent possible, by the following objectives in making their new and improved commitments :

(a) Mode 1

(i) commitments at existing levels of market access on a non-discriminatory basis across sectors of interest to Members

(ii) removal of existing requirements of commercial presence

(b) Mode 2

(i) commitments at existing levels of market access on a non-discriminatory basis across sectors of interest to Members

(ii) commitments on mode 2 where commitments on mode 1 exist

(c) Mode 3

(i) commitments on enhanced levels of foreign equity participation

(ii) removal or substantial reduction of economic needs tests

(iii) commitments allowing greater flexibility on the types of legal entity permitted

(d) Mode 4

(i) new or improved commitments on the categories of Contractual Services Suppliers, Independent Professionals and Others, de-linked from commercial presence, to reflect *inter alia* :

— removal or substantial reduction of economic needs tests

— indication of prescribed duration of stay and possibility of renewal, if any

(ii) new or improved commitments on the categories of Intra-corporate Transferees and Business Visitors, to reflect *inter alia* :

— removal or substantial reduction of economic needs tests

— indication of prescribed duration of stay and possibility of renewal, if any

(e) MFN Exemptions

(i) removal or substantial reduction of exemptions from most-favoured-nation (MFN) treatment

(ii) clarification of remaining MFN exemptions in terms of scope of application and duration

(f) Scheduling of Commitments

(i) ensuring clarity, certainty, comparability and coherence in the scheduling and classification of commitments through adherence to, *inter alia*, the Scheduling Guidelines pursuant to the Decision of the Council for Trade in Services adopted on 23 March 2001

(ii) ensuring that scheduling of any remaining economic needs tests adheres to the Scheduling Guidelines pursuant to the Decision of the Council for Trade in Services adopted on 23 March 2001.

2. As a reference for the request-offer negotiations, the sectoral and modal objectives as identified by Members may be considered.[22]

3. Members shall pursue full and effective implementation of the Modalities for the Special Treatment for Least-Developed Country Members in the Negotiations on Trade in Services (LDC Modalities) adopted by the Special Session of the Council for Trade in Services on 3 September 2003, with a view to the beneficial and meaningful integration of LDCs into the multilateral trading system.

4. Members must intensify their efforts to conclude the negotiations on rule-making under GATS Articles X, XIII, and XV in accordance with their respective mandates and timelines :

(a) Members should engage in more focused discussions in connection with the technical and procedural questions relating to the operation and application of any possible emergency safeguard measures in services.

(b) On government procurement, Members should engage in more focused discussions and in this context put greater emphasis on proposals by Members, in accordance with Article XIII of the GATS.

(c) On subsidies, Members should intensify their efforts to expedite and fulfil the information exchange required for the purpose of such negotiations, and should engage in more focused discussions on proposals by Members, including the development of a possible working definition of subsidies in services.

5. Members shall develop disciplines on domestic regulation pursuant to the mandate under Article VI : 4 of the GATS before the end of the current round of negotiations. We call upon Members to develop text for adoption. In so doing, Members shall consider proposals and the illustrative list of possible elements for Article VI : 4 disciplines.[23]

Approaches

6. Pursuant to the principles and objectives above, we agree to intensify and expedite the request-offer negotiations, which shall remain the main method of negotiation, with a view to securing substantial commitments.

7. In addition to bilateral negotiations, we agree that the request-offer negotiations should also be pursued on a plurilateral basis in accordance with the principles of the GATS and the Guidelines and Procedures for the Negotiations on Trade in Services. The results of such negotiations shall be extended on an MFN basis. These negotiations would be organized in the following manner :

(a) Any Member or group of Members may present requests or collective requests to other Members in any specific sector or mode of supply, identifying their objectives for the negotiations in that sector or mode of supply.

(b) Members to whom such requests have been made shall consider such requests in accordance with paragraphs 2 and 4 of Article XIX of the GATS and paragraph 11 of the Guidelines and Procedures for the Negotiations on Trade in Services.

(c) Plurilateral negotiations should be organised with a view to facilitating the participation of all Members, taking into account the limited capacity of developing countries and smaller delegations to participate in such negotiations.

8. Due consideration shall be given to proposals on trade-related concerns of small economies.

9. Members, in the course of negotiations, shall develop methods for the full and effective implementation of the LDC Modalities, including expeditiously :

(a) Developing appropriate mechanisms for according special priority including to sectors and modes of supply of interest to LDCs in accordance with Article IV : 3 of the GATS and paragraph 7 of the LDC Modalities.

(b) Undertaking commitments, to the extent possible, in such sectors and modes of supply identified, or to be identified, by LDCs that represent priority in their development policies in accordance with paragraphs 6 and 9 of the LDC Modalities.

(c) Assisting LDCs to enable them to identify sectors and modes of supply that represent development priorities.

(d) Providing targeted and effective technical assistance and capacity building for LDCs in accordance with the LDC Modalities, particularly paragraphs 8 and 12.

(e) Developing a reporting mechanism to facilitate the review requirement in paragraph 13 of the LDC Modalities.

10. Targeted technical assistance should be provided through, *inter alia*, the WTO Secretariat, with a view to enabling developing and least-developed countries to participate effectively in the negotiations. In particular and in accordance with paragraph 51 on Technical Cooperation of this Declaration, targeted

technical assistance should be given to all developing countries allowing them to fully engage in the negotiation. In addition, such assistance should be provided on, *inter alia*, compiling and analyzing statistical data on trade in services, assessing interests in and gains from services trade, building regulatory capacity, particularly on those services sectors where liberalization is being undertaken by developing countries.

Timelines

11. Recognizing that an effective timeline is necessary in order to achieve a successful conclusion of the negotiations, we agree that the negotiations shall adhere to the following dates :

(a) Any outstanding initial offers shall be submitted as soon as possible.

(b) Groups of Members presenting plurilateral requests to other Members should submit such requests by 28 February 2006 or as soon as possible thereafter.

(c) A second round of revised offers shall be submitted by 31 July 2006.

(d) Final draft schedules of commitments shall be submitted by 31 October 2006.

(e) Members shall strive to complete the requirements in 9(a) before the date in 11(c).

Review of Progress

12. The Special Session of the Council for Trade in Services shall review progress in the negotiations and monitor the implementation of the Objectives, Approaches and Timelines set out in this Annex.

ANNEX D

Rules

I. Anti-Dumping and Subsidies and Countervailing Measures including Fisheries Subsidies

We :

1. *acknowledge* that the achievement of substantial results on all aspects of the Rules mandate, in the form of

amendments to the Anti-Dumping (AD) and Subsidies and Countervailing Measures (SCM) Agreements, is important to the development of the rules-based multilateral trading system and to the overall balance of results in the DDA;

2. *aim* to achieve in the negotiations on Rules further improvements, in particular, to the transparency, predictability and clarity of the relevant disciplines, to the benefit of all Members, including in particular developing and least-developed Members. In this respect, the development dimension of the negotiations must be addressed as an integral part of any outcome;
3. *call on* Participants, in considering possible clarifications and improvements in the area of anti-dumping, to take into account, *inter alia*, (a) the need to avoid the unwarranted use of anti-dumping measures, while preserving the basic concepts, principles and effectiveness of the instrument and its objectives where such measures are warranted; and (b) the desirability of limiting the costs and complexity of proceedings for interested parties and the investigating authorities alike, while strengthening the due process, transparency and predictability of such proceedings and measures;
4. *consider* that negotiations on anti-dumping should, as appropriate, clarify and improve the rules regarding, *inter alia*, (a) determinations of dumping, injury and causation, and the application of measures; (b) procedures governing the initiation, conduct and completion of antidumping investigations, including with a view to strengthening due process and enhancing transparency; and (c) the level, scope and duration of measures, including duty assessment, interim and new shipper reviews, sunset, and anti-circumvention proceedings;
5. *recognize* that negotiations on anti-dumping have intensified and deepened, that Participants are showing a high level of constructive engagement, and that the process of rigorous discussion of the issues based on

specific textual proposals for amendment to the AD Agreement has been productive and is a necessary step in achieving the substantial results to which Ministers are committed;

6. *note* that, in the negotiations on anti-dumping, the Negotiating Group on Rules has been discussing in detail proposals on such issues as determinations of injury/causation, the lesser duty rule, public interest, transparency and due process, interim reviews, sunset, duty assessment, circumvention, the use of facts available, limited examination and all others rates, dispute settlement, the definition of dumped imports, affiliated parties, product under consideration, and the initiation and completion of investigations, and that this process of discussing proposals before the Group or yet to be submitted will continue after Hong Kong;
7. *note*, in respect of subsidies and countervailing measures, that while proposals for amendments to the SCM Agreement have been submitted on a number of issues, including the definition of a subsidy, specificity, prohibited subsidies, serious prejudice, export credits and guarantees, and the allocation of benefit, there is a need to deepen the analysis on the basis of specific textual proposals in order to ensure a balanced outcome in all areas of the Group's mandate;
8. *note* the desirability of applying to both anti-dumping and countervailing measures any clarifications and improvements which are relevant and appropriate to both instruments;
9. *recall* our commitment at Doha to enhancing the mutual supportiveness of trade and environment, *note* that there is broad agreement that the Group should strengthen disciplines on subsidies in the fisheries sector, including through the prohibition of certain forms of fisheries subsidies that contribute to overcapacity and over-fishing, and *call on* Participants promptly to undertake further detailed work to, *inter alia*, establish the nature

and extent of those disciplines, including transparency and enforceability. Appropriate and effective special and differential treatment for developing and least-developed Members should be an integral part of the fisheries subsidies negotiations, taking into account the importance of this sector to development priorities, poverty reduction, and livelihood and food security concerns;

10. *direct* the Group to intensify and accelerate the negotiating process in all areas of its mandate, on the basis of detailed textual proposals before the Group or yet to be submitted, and complete the process of analysing proposals by Participants on the AD and SCM Agreements as soon as possible;

11. *mandate* the Chairman to prepare, early enough to assure a timely outcome within the context of the 2006 end date for the Doha Development Agenda and taking account of progress in other areas of the negotiations, consolidated texts of the AD and SCM Agreements that shall be the basis for the final stage of the negotiations.

II. Regional Trade Agreements

1. We welcome the progress in negotiations to clarify and improve the WTO's disciplines and procedures on regional trade agreements (RTAs). Such agreements, which can foster trade liberalization and promote development, have become an important element in the trade policies of virtually all Members. Transparency of RTAs is thus of systemic interest as are disciplines that ensure the complementarity of RTAs with the WTO.

2. We commend the progress in defining the elements of a transparency mechanism for RTAs, aimed, in particular, at improving existing WTO procedures for gathering factual information on RTAs, without prejudice to the rights and obligations of Members. We instruct the Negotiating Group on Rules to intensify its efforts to resolve outstanding issues, with a view to a provisional decision on RTA transparency by 30 April 2006.

3. We also note with appreciation the work of the Negotiating Group on Rules on WTO's disciplines governing RTAs, including *inter alia* on the "substantially all the trade" requirement, the length of RTA transition periods and RTA developmental aspects. We instruct the Group to intensify negotiations, based on text proposals as soon as possible after the Sixth Ministerial Conference, so as to arrive at appropriate outcomes by end 2006.

ANNEX E

Trade Facilitation

Report by the Negotiating Group on Trade Facilitation to the TNC

1. Since its establishment on 12 October 2004, the Negotiating Group on Trade Facilitation met eleven times to carry out work under the mandate contained in Annex D of the Decision adopted by the General Council on 1 August 2004. The negotiations are benefiting from the fact that the mandate allows for the central development dimension of the Doha negotiations to be addressed directly through the widely acknowledged benefits of trade facilitation reforms for all WTO Members, the enhancement of trade facilitation capacity in developing countries and LDCs, and provisions on special and differential treatment (S&DT) that provide flexibility. Based on the Group's Work Plan (TN/TF/1), Members contributed to the agreed agenda of the Group, tabling 60 written submissions sponsored by more than 100 delegations. Members appreciate the transparent and inclusive manner in which the negotiations are being conducted.

2. Good progress has been made in all areas covered by the mandate, through both verbal and written contributions by Members. A considerable part of the Negotiating Group's meetings has been spent on addressing the negotiating objective of improving and clarifying relevant aspects of GATT Articles V, VIII and X, on which about 40 written submissions[24] have been tabled by Members representing the full spectrum of the WTO's Membership. Through discussions on these submissions and related questions and answers (JOB(05)/222), Members have

advanced their understanding of the measures in question and are working towards common ground on many aspects of this part of the negotiating mandate. Many of these submissions also covered the negotiating objective of enhancing technical assistance and support for capacity building on trade facilitation, as well as the practical application of the principle of S&DT. The Group also discussed other valuable submissions dedicated to these issues.[25] Advances have also been made on the objective of arriving at provisions for effective cooperation between customs or any other appropriate authorities on trade facilitation and customs compliance issues, where two written proposals have been discussed.[26] Members have also made valuable contributions on the identification of trade facilitation needs and priorities, development aspects, cost implications and inter-agency cooperation.[27]

3. Valuable input has been provided by a number of Members in the form of national experience papers[28] describing national trade facilitation reform processes. In appreciation of the value to developing countries and LDCs of this aspect of the negotiations, the Negotiating Group recommends that Members be encouraged to continue this information sharing exercise.

4. Building on the progress made in the negotiations so far, and with a view to developing a set of multilateral commitments on all elements of the mandate, the Negotiating Group recommends that it continue to intensify its negotiations on the basis of Members' proposals, as reflected currently in document TN/TF/W/43/Rev.4, and any new proposals to be presented. Without prejudice to individual Member's positions on individual proposals, a list of (I) proposed measures to improve and clarify GATT Articles V, VIII and X; (II) proposed provisions for effective cooperation between customs and other authorities on trade facilitation and customs compliance; and, (III) cross-cutting submissions; is provided below to facilitate further negotiations. In carrying out this work and in tabling further proposals, Members should be mindful of the overall deadline for finishing the negotiations and the resulting need to move into focussed drafting mode early enough after the Sixth Ministerial Conference

so as to allow for a timely conclusion of text-based negotiations on all aspects of the mandate.

5. Work needs to continue and broaden on the process of identifying individual Member's trade facilitation needs and priorities, and the cost implications of possible measures. The Negotiating Group recommends that relevant international organizations be invited to continue to assist Members in this process, recognizing the important contributions being made by them already, and be encouraged to continue and intensify their work more generally in support of the negotiations.

6. In light of the vital importance of technical assistance and capacity building to allow developing countries and LDCs to fully participate in and benefit from the negotiations, the Negotiating Group recommends that the commitments in Annex D's mandate in this area be reaffirmed, reinforced and made operational in a timely manner. To bring the negotiations to a successful conclusion, special attention needs to be paid to support for technical assistance and capacity building that will allow developing countries and LDCs to participate effectively in the negotiations, and to technical assistance and capacity building to implement the results of the negotiations that is precise, effective and operational, and reflects the trade facilitation needs and priorities of developing countries and LDCs. Recognizing the valuable assistance already being provided in this area, the Negotiating Group recommends that Members, in particular developed ones, continue to intensify their support in a comprehensive manner and on a long-term and sustainable basis, backed by secure funding.

7. The Negotiating Group also recommends that it deepen and intensify its negotiations on the issue of S&DT, with a view to arriving at S&DT provisions that are precise, effective and operational and that allow for necessary flexibility in implementing the results of the negotiations. Reaffirming the linkages among the elements of Annex D, the Negotiating Group recommends that further negotiations on S&DT build on input presented by Members in the context of measures related to GATT Articles V, VIII and X and in their proposals of a cross-cutting nature on S&DT.

I. PROPOSED MEASURES TO IMPROVE AND CLARIFY GATT ARTICLES V, VIII AND X

A. Publication and Availability of Information :

- Publication of Trade Regulations
- Publication of Penalty Provisions
- Internet Publication
  - (a) of elements set out in Article X of GATT 1994
  - (b) of specified information setting forth procedural sequence and other requirements for importing goods
- Notification of Trade Regulations
- Establishment of Enquiry Points/SNFP/Information Centres
- Other Measures to Enhance the Availability of Information

B. Time Periods Between Publication and Implementation :

- Interval between Publication and Entry into Force

C. Consultation and Comments on New and Amended Rules :

- Prior Consultation and Commenting on New and Amended Rules
- Information on Policy Objectives Sought

D. Advance Rulings

- Provision of Advance Rulings

E. Appeal Procedures

- Right of Appeal
- Release of Goods in Event of Appeal

F. Other Measures to Enhance Impartiality and Non-Discrimination :

- Uniform Administration of Trade Regulations
- Maintenance and Reinforcement of Integrity and Ethical Conduct Among Officials
  - (a) Establishment of a Code of Conduct
  - (b) Computerized System to Reduce/Eliminate Discretion

(c) System of Penalties

(d) Technical Assistance to Create/Build up Capacities to Prevent and Control Customs Offences

(e) Appointment of Staff for Education and Training

(f) Coordination and Control Mechanisms

G. Fees and Charges Connected with Importation and Exportation :

- General Disciplines on Fees and Charges Imposed on or in Connection with Importation and Exportation

  (a) Specific Parameters for Fees/Charges

  (b) Publication/Notification of Fees/Charges

  (c) Prohibition of Collection of Unpublished Fees and Charges

  (d) Periodic Review of Fees/Charges

  (e) Automated Payment

- Reduction/Minimization of the Number and Diversity of Fees/Charges

H. Formalities Connected with Importation and Exportation :

- Disciplines on Formalities/Procedures and Data/ Documentation Requirements Connected with Importation and Exportation

  (a) Non-discrimination

  (b) Periodic Review of Formalities and Requirements

  (c) Reduction/Limitation of Formalities and Documentation Requirements

  (d) Use of International Standards

  (e) Uniform Customs Code

  (f) Acceptance of Commercially Available Information and of Copies

  (g) Automation

  (h) Single Window/One-time Submission

  (i) Elimination of Pre-Shipment Inspection

(j) Phasing out Mandatory Use of Customs Brokers

I. Consularization :

- Prohibition of Consular Transaction Requirement

J. Border Agency Cooperation :

- Coordination of Activities and Requirement of all Border Agencies

K. Release and Clearance of Goods :

- Expedited/Simplified Release and Clearance of Goods
  - (a) Pre-arrival Clearance
  - (b) Expedited Procedures for Express Shipments
  - (c) Risk Management /Analysis, Authorized Traders
  - (d) Post-Clearance Audit
  - (e) Separating Release from Clearance Procedures
  - (f) Other Measures to Simplify Customs Release and Clearance
- Establishment and Publication of Average Release and Clearance Times

L. Tariff Classification :

- Objective Criteria for Tariff Classification

M. Matters Related to Goods Transit :

- Strengthened Non-discrimination
- Disciplines on Fees and Charges
  - (a) Publication of Fees and Charges and Prohibition of Unpublished ones
  - (b) Periodic Review of Fees and Charges
  - (c) More effective Disciplines on Charges for Transit
  - (d) Periodic Exchange Between Neighbouring Authorities
- Disciplines on Transit Formalities and Documentation Requirements
  - (a) Periodic Review
  - (b) Reduction/Simplification
  - (c) Harmonization/Standardization

(d) Promotion of Regional Transit Arrangements
(e) Simplified and Preferential Clearance for Certain Goods
(f) Limitation of Inspections and Controls
(g) Sealing
(h) Cooperation and Coordination on Document Requirements
(i) Monitoring
(j) Bonded Transport Regime/Guarantees

- Improved Coordination and Cooperation
  (a) Amongst Authorities
  (b) Between Authorities and the Private Sector
- Operationalization and Clarification of Terms

II. PROPOSED PROVISIONS FOR EFFECTIVE COOPERATION BETWEEN CUSTOMS AND OTHER AUTHORITIES ON TRADE FACILITATION AND CUSTOMS COMPLIANCE

- Multilateral Mechanism for the Exchange and Handling of Information

III. CROSS-CUTTING SUBMISSIONS

1. Needs and Priorities Identification

- General tool to assess needs and priorities and current levels of trade facilitation
- Take result of assessment as one basis for establishing trade facilitation rules, arranging S&D treatment and providing technical assistance and capacity building support

2. Technical Assistance and Capacity Building

— Technical Assistance and Capacity Building in the Course of the Negotiations

  - Identification of Needs and Priorities
  - Compilation of Needs and Priorities of Individual Members

- Support for Clarification and Educative Process Including Training

— Technical Assistance and Capacity Building Beyond the Negotiations Phase

- Implementation of the Outcome
- Coordination Mechanisms for Implementing Needs and Priorities as well as Commitments

3. Multiple-Areas

- Identification of Trade Facilitation Needs and Priorities of Members
- Cost Assessment
- Inter-Agency Cooperation
- Links and Inter-relationship between the Elements of Annex D
- Inventory of Trade Facilitation Measures
- Assessment of the Current Situation
- Timing and Sequencing of Measures

ANNEX F

Special and Differential Treatment

LDC Agreement-Specific Proposals

23) Understanding in Respect of Waivers of Obligations under the GATT 1994

(i) We agree that requests for waivers by least-developed country Members under Article IX of the WTO Agreement and the Understanding in respect of Waivers of Obligations under the GATT 1994 shall be given positive consideration and a decision taken within 60 days.

(ii) When considering requests for waivers by other Members exclusively in favour of least-developed country Members, we agree that a decision shall be taken within 60 days, or in exceptional circumstances as expeditiously as possible thereafter, without prejudice to the rights of other Members.

36) Decision on Measures in Favour of Least-Developed Countries

We agree that developed-country Members shall, and developing-country Members declaring themselves in a position to do so should :

(a)(i) Provide duty-free and quota-free market access on a lasting basis, for all products originating from all LDCs by 2008 or no later than the start of the implementation period in a manner that ensures stability, security and predictability.

(ii) Members facing difficulties at this time to provide market access as set out above shall provide duty-free and quota-free market access for at least 97 per cent of products originating from LDCs, defined at the tariff line level, by 2008 or no later than the start of the implementation period. In addition, these Members shall take steps to progressively achieve compliance with the obligations set out above, taking into account the impact on other developing countries at similar levels of development, and, as appropriate, by incrementally building on the initial list of covered products.

(iii) Developing-country Members shall be permitted to phase in their commitments and shall enjoy appropriate flexibility in coverage.

(b) Ensure that preferential rules of origin applicable to imports from LDCs are transparent and simple, and contribute to facilitating market access.

Members shall notify the implementation of the schemes adopted under this decision every year to the Committee on Trade and Development. The Committee on Trade and Development shall annually review the steps taken to provide duty-free and quota-free market access to the LDCs and report to the General Council for appropriate action.

We urge all donors and relevant international institutions to increase financial and technical support aimed at the diversification of LDC economies, while providing additional financial and technical assistance through appropriate delivery mechanisms to meet their implementation obligations, including fulfilling SPS and TBT requirements, and to assist them in managing their adjustment processes, including those necessary to face the results of MFN multilateral trade liberalisation.

38) Decision on Measures in Favour of Least-Developed Countries

It is reaffirmed that least-developed country Members will only be required to undertake commitments and concessions to the extent consistent with their individual development, financial or trade needs, or their administrative and institutional capacities.

Within the context of coherence arrangements with other international institutions, we urge donors, multilateral agencies and international financial institutions to coordinate their work to ensure that LDCs are not subjected to conditionalities on loans, grants and official development assistance that are inconsistent with their rights and obligations under the WTO Agreements.

84) Agreement on Trade-Related Investment Measures

LDCs shall be allowed to maintain on a temporary basis existing measures that deviate from their obligations under the TRIMs Agreement. For this purpose, LDCs shall notify the Council for Trade in Goods (CTG) of such measures within two years, starting 30 days after the date of this declaration. LDCs will be allowed to maintain these existing measures until the end of a new transition period, lasting seven years. This transition period may be extended by the CTG under the existing procedures set out in the TRIMs Agreement, taking into account the individual financial, trade, and development needs of the Member in question.

LDCs shall also be allowed to introduce new measures that deviate from their obligations under the TRIMs Agreement. These new TRIMs shall be notified to the CTG not later than six months after their adoption. The CTG shall give positive consideration to such notifications, taking into account the individual financial, trade, and development needs of the Member in question. The duration of these measures will not exceed five years, renewable subject to review and decision by the CTG.

Any measures incompatible with the TRIMs Agreement and adopted under this decision shall be phased out by year 2020.

88) Decision on Measures in Favour of Least-Developed Countries–Paragraph 1

Least-developed country Members, whilst reaffirming their commitment to the fundamental principles of the WTO and relevant provisions of GATT 1994, and while complying with the general rules set out in the aforesaid instruments, will only be required to undertake commitments and concessions to the extent consistent with their individual development, financial and trade needs, and their administrative and institutional capabilities. Should a least-developed country Member find that it is not in a position to comply with a specific obligation or commitment on these grounds, it shall bring the matter to the attention of the General Council for examination and appropriate action.

We agree that the implementation by LDCs of their obligations or commitments will require further technical and financial support directly related to the nature and scope of such obligations or commitments, and direct the WTO to coordinate its efforts with donors and relevant agencies to significantly increase aid for trade-related technical assistance and capacity building.

NOTES

1. On the proposed basis that cut remains to be determined for those developing countries with an AMS. In any case, there is a view (not shared by all) that cuts for developing countries should be less than 2/3 of the cut for developed countries.
2. The exact extent of the flexibility to be provided pursuant to paragraph 15 of the July 2004 Framework remains to be agreed.
3. Of course, this needs to be viewed as illustrative rather than overly literally, if for no other reason than that these are conditional figures. For instance, while the European Communities has indicated it could be prepared to go as far as 70% in the top tier, they make it clear that this is acceptable only if the United States will go to 60% in the second tier. The United States for its part, however, has only indicated preparedness to go to that 60% if the European Communities is prepared to go as high as 83% — which it has not indicated it is prepared to do.
4. One Member has proposed the year 2010 for "export subsidies", with accelerated elimination for "specific" products. Another group of Members

have proposed a period "no longer than five years" for all forms of export subsidies, with "direct" export subsidies subject to front-loading within that period.

5. This includes, but is not limited to : exemptions, if any, to the 180 day rule; whether the disciplines should allow for pure cover only or also permit direct financing; the appropriate period for programmes to fully recover their costs and losses through the premia levied from the exporters (principle of self-financing — there needs to be convergence between position which range from one year to fifteen years); the disciplines regarding special circumstances; and the question of special and differential treatment, including whether, as some Members argue, developing countries should be allowed longer repayment terms for export credits extended by them to other developing countries and the specifics of differential treatment in favour of least-developed and net food-importing developing countries.
6. This fundamental divergence has effectively precluded convergence on such matters as what disciplines, if any, should be established with respect to monetization of food aid or the question of the provision of food aid in fully grant form only. The importance of operationally effective transparency requirements is generally acknowledged, but details have still to be developed, particularly those relating to the role of the WTO in this context. Further work is required to clarify the role of recipient countries and relevant international organizations or other entities in triggering or providing food aid.
7. The method for calculating the AVEs for the sugar lines is still to be established.
8. At one end of the spectrum, as it were, a "harmonisation" formula within the bands; at the other end "flexibility" within the formula.
9. The matrix below is an illustrative table that portrays the extent of divergences that remain, even on the basis of post-August 2005 proposals. This does not entirely cover all the subtleties of those proposals to utilize a "pivot" (although most are in fact within the ranges tabulated), but is intended to convey a snapshot of the status of average cuts proposed post-August.

	Thresholds	Range of cuts (%)
Band 1	0% - 20/30%	20-65
Band 2	20/30% - 40/60%	30-75
Band 3	40/60% - 60/90%	35-85
Band 4	>60/90%	42-90

10. As an element in certain conditional proposals on overall market access, tabled post-July 2005.

11. Some see this as being tariff quota based and expressed as a percentage of domestic consumption, with proposals of up to 10%. Others propose *pro rata* expansion on an existing trade basis, including taking account of current imports. Some also propose no new TRQs, with sensitivity in such cases to be provided through other means, *e.g.* differential phasing. There is also a proposal for a "sliding scale" approach.

12. In this pillar, as well as in the other two, there is general convergence on the point that developing countries will have entitlement to longer implementation periods, albeit that concrete precision remains to be determined.

13. The matrix below is an illustrative table that portrays the extent of divergences that remain, just on the basis of post-August 2005 proposals.

	Thresholds	Range of cuts (%)
Band 1	0% - 20/50%	15-25*
Band 2	20/50% - 40/100%	20-30*
Band 3	40/100% - 60/150%	25-35*
Band 4	>60-150%	30-40*

*There is also a proposal that cuts for developing countries should be "slightly lesser" than the upper tariff cuts for developed countries shown in the preceding table (*i.e.* "slightly lesser" than 65, 75, 85 and 90%).

14. As an element in certain conditional proposals on overall market access, tabled post-July 2005.

15. While the eventual zone of convergence for developed countries undoubtedly has a bearing in this area, it has been proposed by a group of Members that the principles of sensitive products generally and for TRQs specifically should be different for developing countries. Another group of Members has proposed, in the post-August period, an entitlement for developing countries of at least 50% more than the maximum number of lines used by any developed Member. This would (based on developed country proposals) amount to a potential variation between 1.5% and 22.5% of tariff lines. This latter group has also proposed that products relating to long-standing preferences shall be designated as sensitive and that any TRQ expansion should not be "at the detriment of existing ACP quotas". This particular view has been, however, strongly opposed by other Members which take the firm position that tropical and diversification products should not at all be designated as sensitive products.

16. It is argued by some Members that this is to be interpreted as meaning full duty- and tariff quota-free access, but by others as less than that.

17. Note 15 above refers.
18. It is also proposed that this should be accompanied by simple and transparent rules of origin and other measures to address non-tariff barriers.
19. Concrete proposals have been made, with a three-step approach : 80% on day one, an additional 10% after 12 months and the last 10% a year later.
20. A Member has indicated that it is prepared to implement all its commitments from day one and, in any case, to autonomously ensure that its commitments on eliminating the most trade-distorting domestic support, eliminating all forms of export subsidies and providing mfn duty- and quota-free access for cotton will take place from 2006.
21. This would appear to include in particular such a matter as tariff escalation, where it discourages the development of processing industries in the commodity producing countries. The idea of a review and clarification of what the current status is of GATT 1994 provisions relating to the stabilisation of prices through the adoption of supply management systems by producing countries, and the use of export taxes and restrictions under such systems is also on the table. Proponents would seek something more than this such as more concrete undertakings in the area of non-tariff measures and actual revision of existing provisions. There is, at this point, no consensus in these latter areas, but an appreciation at least of the underlying issues at stake.
22. As attached to the Report by the Chairman to the Trade Negotiations Committee on 28 November 2005, contained in document TN/S/23. This attachment has no legal standing.
23. As attached to the Report of the Chairman of the Working Party on Domestic Regulation to the Special Session of the Council for Trade in Services on 15 November 2005, contained in document JOB(05)/280.
24. TN/TF/W/6-W/15, W/17-W/26, W/28, W/30-W/32, W/34-36, W/38-W/40, W/42, W/44-W/49, W/53, W/55, W/58, W/60-W/62, W/64-W/67, W/69, W/70.
25. TN/TF/W/33, W/41, W/56, W/63, W/73 and W/74.
26. TN/TF/W/57 and W/68.
27. TN/TF/W/29, W/33, W/41, W/62 and W/63.
28. TN/TF/W/48, W/50 , W/53, W/55, W/58, W/60, W/61, W/65, W/69 and W/75.

Appendix-IV

CANCÚN WTO MINISTERIAL STATEMENT, 2003

(Adopted on 14 September 2003)

1. As we conclude our Fifth Ministerial Conference in Cancún, we would like to express our deep appreciation to the Government and people of Mexico for the excellent organization and warm hospitality we have received in Cancún.

2. At this meeting we have welcomed Cambodia and Nepal as the first least-developed countries to accede to the WTO since its establishment.

3. All participants have worked hard and constructively to make progress as required under the Doha mandates. We have, indeed, made considerable progress. However, more work needs to be done in some key areas to enable us to proceed towards the conclusion of the negotiations in fulfilment of the commitments we took at Doha.

4. We therefore instruct our officials to continue working on outstanding issues with a renewed sense of urgency and purpose and taking fully into account all the views we have expressed in this Conference. We ask the Chairman of the General Council, working in close cooperation with the Director-General, to coordinate this work and to convene a meeting of the General Council at Senior Officials level no later than 15 December 2003 to take the action necessary at that stage to enable us to move towards a successful and timely conclusion of the negotiations. We shall continue to exercise close personal supervision of this process.

5. We will bring with us into this new phase all the valuable work that has been done at this Conference. In those areas where we have reached a high level of convergence on texts, we undertake to maintain this convergence while working for an acceptable overall outcome.

6. Notwithstanding this setback, we reaffirm all our Doha Declarations and Decisions and recommit ourselves to working to implement them fully and faithfully.

Appendix-V

DOHA WTO MINISTERIAL 2001: MINISTERIAL DECLARATION, 2001

(Adopted on 14 November 2001)

1. The multilateral trading system embodied in the World Trade Organization has contributed significantly to economic growth, development and employment throughout the past fifty years. We are determined, particularly in the light of the global economic slowdown, to maintain the process of reform and liberalization of trade policies, thus ensuring that the system plays its full part in promoting recovery, growth and development. We, therefore, strongly reaffirm the principles and objectives set out in the Marrakesh Agreement Establishing the World Trade Organization, and pledge to reject the use of protectionism.

2. International trade can play a major role in the promotion of economic development and the alleviation of poverty. We recognize the need for all our peoples to benefit from the increased opportunities and welfare gains that the multilateral trading system generates. The majority of WTO members are developing countries. We seek to place their needs and interests at the heart of the Work Programme adopted in this Declaration. Recalling the Preamble to the Marrakesh Agreement, we shall continue to make positive efforts designed to ensure that developing countries, and especially the least-developed among them, secure a share in the growth of world trade commensurate with the needs of their economic development. In this context, enhanced market access, balanced rules, and well targeted, sustainably financed technical assistance and capacity-building programmes have important roles to play.

3. We recognize the particular vulnerability of the least-developed countries and the special structural difficulties they face in the global economy. We are committed to addressing the marginalization of least-developed countries in international trade and to improving their effective participation in the multilateral trading system. We recall the commitments made by ministers at our meetings in Marrakesh, Singapore and Geneva, and by the international community at the Third UN Conference on Least-Developed Countries in Brussels, to help least-developed countries secure beneficial and meaningful integration into the multilateral trading system and the global economy. We are determined that the WTO will play its part in building effectively on these commitments under the Work Programme we are establishing.

4. We stress our commitment to the WTO as the unique forum for global trade rule-making and liberalization, while also recognizing that regional trade agreements can play an important role in promoting the liberalization and expansion of trade and in fostering development.

5. We are aware that the challenges members face in a rapidly changing international environment cannot be addressed through measures taken in the trade field alone. We shall continue to work with the Bretton Woods institutions for greater coherence in global economic policy-making.

6. We strongly reaffirm our commitment to the objective of sustainable development, as stated in the Preamble to the Marrakesh Agreement. We are convinced that the aims of upholding and safeguarding an open and non-discriminatory multilateral trading system, and acting for the protection of the environment and the promotion of sustainable development can and must be mutually supportive. We take note of the efforts by members to conduct national environmental assessments of trade policies on a voluntary basis. We recognize that under WTO rules no country should be prevented from taking measures for the protection of human, animal or plant life or health, or of the environment at the levels it considers appropriate, subject to the requirement that they are not applied in a manner which would constitute a means of arbitrary or unjustifiable discrimination

between countries where the same conditions prevail, or a disguised restriction on international trade, and are otherwise in accordance with the provisions of the WTO Agreements. We welcome the WTO's continued cooperation with UNEP and other intergovernmental environmental organizations. We encourage efforts to promote cooperation between the WTO and relevant international environmental and developmental organizations, especially in the lead-up to the World Summit on Sustainable Development to be held in Johannesburg, South Africa, in September 2002.

7. We reaffirm the right of members under the General Agreement on Trade in Services to regulate, and to introduce new regulations on, the supply of services.

8. We reaffirm our declaration made at the Singapore Ministerial Conference regarding internationally recognized core labour standards. We take note of work under way in the International Labour Organization (ILO) on the social dimension of globalization.

9. We note with particular satisfaction that this conference has completed the WTO accession procedures for China and Chinese Taipei. We also welcome the accession as new members, since our last session, of Albania, Croatia, Georgia, Jordan, Lithuania, Moldova and Oman, and note the extensive market-access commitments already made by these countries on accession. These accessions will greatly strengthen the multilateral trading system, as will those of the 28 countries now negotiating their accession. We, therefore, attach great importance to concluding accession proceedings as quickly as possible. In particular, we are committed to accelerating the accession of least-developed countries.

10. Recognizing the challenges posed by an expanding WTO membership, we confirm our collective responsibility to ensure internal transparency and the effective participation of all members. While emphasizing the intergovernmental character of the organization, we are committed to making the WTO's operations more transparent, including through more effective and prompt dissemination of information, and to improve dialogue

with the public. We shall, therefore, at the national and multilateral levels continue to promote a better public understanding of the WTO and to communicate the benefits of a liberal, rules-based multilateral trading system.

11. In view of these considerations, we hereby agree to undertake the broad and balanced Work Programme set out below. This incorporates both an expanded negotiating agenda and other important decisions and activities necessary to address the challenges facing the multilateral trading system.

WORK PROGRAMME

Implementation-Related Issues and Concerns

12. We attach the utmost importance to the implementation-related issues and concerns raised by members and are determined to find appropriate solutions to them. In this connection, and having regard to the General Council Decisions of 3 May and 15 December 2000, we further adopt the Decision on Implementation-Related Issues and Concerns in document WT/MIN(01)/17 to address a number of implementation problems faced by members. We agree that negotiations on outstanding implementation issues shall be an integral part of the Work Programme we are establishing, and that agreements reached at an early stage in these negotiations shall be treated in accordance with the provisions of paragraph 47 below. In this regard, we shall proceed as follows : (a) where we provide a specific negotiating mandate in this declaration, the relevant implementation issues shall be addressed under that mandate; (b) the other outstanding implementation issues shall be addressed as a matter of priority by the relevant WTO bodies, which shall report to the Trade Negotiations Committee, established under paragraph 46 below, by the end of 2002 for appropriate action.

Agriculture

13. We recognize the work already undertaken in the negotiations initiated in early 2000 under Article 20 of the Agreement on Agriculture, including the large number of negotiating proposals submitted on behalf of a total of 121 members. We recall the long-term objective referred to in the Agreement to

establish a fair and market-oriented trading system through a programme of fundamental reform encompassing strengthened rules and specific commitments on support and protection in order to correct and prevent restrictions and distortions in world agricultural markets. We reconfirm our commitment to this programme. Building on the work carried out to date and without prejudging the outcome of the negotiations we commit ourselves to comprehensive negotiations aimed at : substantial improvements in market access; reductions of, with a view to phasing out, all forms of export subsidies; and substantial reductions in trade-distorting domestic support. We agree that special and differential treatment for developing countries shall be an integral part of all elements of the negotiations and shall be embodied in the schedules of concessions and commitments and as appropriate in the rules and disciplines to be negotiated, so as to be operationally effective and to enable developing countries to effectively take account of their development needs, including food security and rural development. We take note of the non-trade concerns reflected in the negotiating proposals submitted by Members and confirm that non-trade concerns will be taken into account in the negotiations as provided for in the Agreement on Agriculture.

14. Modalities for the further commitments, including provisions for special and differential treatment, shall be established no later than 31 March 2003. Participants shall submit their comprehensive draft Schedules based on these modalities no later than the date of the Fifth Session of the Ministerial Conference. The negotiations, including with respect to rules and disciplines and related legal texts, shall be concluded as part and at the date of conclusion of the negotiating agenda as a whole.

Services

15. The negotiations on trade in services shall be conducted with a view to promoting the economic growth of all trading partners and the development of developing and least-developed countries. We recognize the work already undertaken in the negotiations, initiated in January 2000 under Article XIX of the General Agreement on Trade in Services, and the large number of proposals submitted by members on a wide range of sectors and

several horizontal issues, as well as on movement of natural persons. We reaffirm the Guidelines and Procedures for the Negotiations adopted by the Council for Trade in Services on 28 March 2001 as the basis for continuing the negotiations, with a view to achieving the objectives of the General Agreement on Trade in Services, as stipulated in the Preamble, Article IV and Article XIX of that Agreement. Participants shall submit initial requests for specific commitments by 30 June 2002 and initial offers by 31 March 2003.

Market Access for Non-agricultural Products

16. We agree to negotiations which shall aim, by modalities to be agreed, to reduce or as appropriate eliminate tariffs, including the reduction or elimination of tariff peaks, high tariffs, and tariff escalation, as well as non-tariff barriers, in particular on products of export interest to developing countries. Product coverage shall be comprehensive and without prior exclusions. The negotiations shall take fully into account the special needs and interests of developing and least-developed country participants, including through less than full reciprocity in reduction commitments, in accordance with the relevant provisions of Article XXVIII bis of GATT 1994 and the provisions cited in paragraph 50 below. To this end, the modalities to be agreed will include appropriate studies and capacity-building measures to assist least-developed countries to participate effectively in the negotiations.

Trade-Related Aspects of Intellectual Property Rights

17. We stress the importance we attach to implementation and interpretation of the Agreement on Trade-Related Aspects of Intellectual Property Rights (TRIPS Agreement) in a manner supportive of public health, by promoting both access to existing medicines and research and development into new medicines and, in this connection, are adopting a separate declaration.

18. With a view to completing the work started in the Council for Trade-Related Aspects of Intellectual Property Rights (Council for TRIPS) on the implementation of Article 23.4, we agree to negotiate the establishment of a multilateral system of notification and registration of geographical indications for wines and spirits by the Fifth Session of the Ministerial Conference. We note that

issues related to the extension of the protection of geographical indications provided for in Article 23 to products other than wines and spirits will be addressed in the Council for TRIPS pursuant to paragraph 12 of this declaration.

19. We instruct the Council for TRIPS, in pursuing its work programme including under the review of Article 27.3(b), the review of the implementation of the TRIPS Agreement under Article 71.1 and the work foreseen pursuant to paragraph 12 of this declaration, to examine, *inter alia*, the relationship between the TRIPS Agreement and the Convention on Biological Diversity, the protection of traditional knowledge and folklore, and other relevant new developments raised by members pursuant to Article 71.1. In undertaking this work, the TRIPS Council shall be guided by the objectives and principles set out in Articles 7 and 8 of the TRIPS Agreement and shall take fully into account the development dimension.

Relationship between Trade and Investment

20. Recognizing the case for a multilateral framework to secure transparent, stable and predictable conditions for long-term cross-border investment, particularly foreign direct investment, that will contribute to the expansion of trade, and the need for enhanced technical assistance and capacity-building in this area as referred to in paragraph 21, we agree that negotiations will take place after the Fifth Session of the Ministerial Conference on the basis of a decision to be taken, by explicit consensus, at that session on modalities of negotiations.

21. We recognize the needs of developing and least-developed countries for enhanced support for technical assistance and capacity building in this area, including policy analysis and development so that they may better evaluate the implications of closer multilateral cooperation for their development policies and objectives, and human and institutional development. To this end, we shall work in cooperation with other relevant intergovernmental organisations, including UNCTAD, and through appropriate regional and bilateral channels, to provide strengthened and adequately resourced assistance to respond to these needs.

22. In the period until the Fifth Session, further work in the Working Group on the Relationship between Trade and Investment will focus on the clarification of : scope and definition; transparency; non-discrimination; modalities for pre-establishment commitments based on a GATS-type, positive list approach; development provisions; exceptions and balance-of-payments safeguards; consultation and the settlement of disputes between members. Any framework should reflect in a balanced manner the interests of home and host countries, and take due account of the development policies and objectives of host governments as well as their right to regulate in the public interest. The special development, trade and financial needs of developing and least-developed countries should be taken into account as an integral part of any framework, which should enable members to undertake obligations and commitments commensurate with their individual needs and circumstances. Due regard should be paid to other relevant WTO provisions. Account should be taken, as appropriate, of existing bilateral and regional arrangements on investment.

Interaction between Trade and Competition Policy

23. Recognizing the case for a multilateral framework to enhance the contribution of competition policy to international trade and development, and the need for enhanced technical assistance and capacity-building in this area as referred to in paragraph 24, we agree that negotiations will take place after the Fifth Session of the Ministerial Conference on the basis of a decision to be taken, by explicit consensus, at that session on modalities of negotiations.

24. We recognize the needs of developing and least-developed countries for enhanced support for technical assistance and capacity building in this area, including policy analysis and development so that they may better evaluate the implications of closer multilateral cooperation for their development policies and objectives, and human and institutional development. To this end, we shall work in cooperation with other relevant intergovernmental organisations, including UNCTAD, and through appropriate regional and bilateral channels, to provide strengthened and adequately resourced assistance to respond to these needs.

25. In the period until the Fifth Session, further work in the Working Group on the Interaction between Trade and Competition Policy will focus on the clarification of : core principles, including transparency, non-discrimination and procedural fairness, and provisions on hardcore cartels; modalities for voluntary cooperation; and support for progressive reinforcement of competition institutions in developing countries through capacity building. Full account shall be taken of the needs of developing and least-developed country participants and appropriate flexibility provided to address them.

Transparency in Government Procurement

26. Recognizing the case for a multilateral agreement on transparency in government procurement and the need for enhanced technical assistance and capacity building in this area, we agree that negotiations will take place after the Fifth Session of the Ministerial Conference on the basis of a decision to be taken, by explicit consensus, at that session on modalities of negotiations. These negotiations will build on the progress made in the Working Group on Transparency in Government Procurement by that time and take into account participants' development priorities, especially those of least-developed country participants. Negotiations shall be limited to the transparency aspects and therefore will not restrict the scope for countries to give preferences to domestic supplies and suppliers. We commit ourselves to ensuring adequate technical assistance and support for capacity building both during the negotiations and after their conclusion.

Trade Facilitation

27. Recognizing the case for further expediting the movement, release and clearance of goods, including goods in transit, and the need for enhanced technical assistance and capacity building in this area, we agree that negotiations will take place after the Fifth Session of the Ministerial Conference on the basis of a decision to be taken, by explicit consensus, at that session on modalities of negotiations. In the period until the Fifth Session, the Council for Trade in Goods shall review and as appropriate, clarify and improve relevant aspects of Articles V, VIII and X of the GATT

1994 and identify the trade facilitation needs and priorities of members, in particular developing and least-developed countries. We commit ourselves to ensuring adequate technical assistance and support for capacity building in this area.

WTO Rules

28. In the light of experience and of the increasing application of these instruments by members, we agree to negotiations aimed at clarifying and improving disciplines under the Agreements on Implementation of Article VI of the GATT 1994 and on Subsidies and Countervailing Measures, while preserving the basic concepts, principles and effectiveness of these Agreements and their instruments and objectives, and taking into account the needs of developing and least-developed participants. In the initial phase of the negotiations, participants will indicate the provisions, including disciplines on trade distorting practices, that they seek to clarify and improve in the subsequent phase. In the context of these negotiations, participants shall also aim to clarify and improve WTO disciplines on fisheries subsidies, taking into account the importance of this sector to developing countries. We note that fisheries subsidies are also referred to in paragraph 31.

29. We also agree to negotiations aimed at clarifying and improving disciplines and procedures under the existing WTO provisions applying to regional trade agreements. The negotiations shall take into account the developmental aspects of regional trade agreements.

Dispute Settlement Understanding

30. We agree to negotiations on improvements and clarifications of the Dispute Settlement Understanding. The negotiations should be based on the work done thus far as well as any additional proposals by members, and aim to agree on improvements and clarifications not later than May 2003, at which time we will take steps to ensure that the results enter into force as soon as possible thereafter.

Trade and Environment

31. With a view to enhancing the mutual supportiveness of trade and environment, we agree to negotiations, without prejudging their outcome, on :

(i) the relationship between existing WTO rules and specific trade obligations set out in multilateral environmental agreements (MEAs). The negotiations shall be limited in scope to the applicability of such existing WTO rules as among parties to the MEA in question. The negotiations shall not prejudice the WTO rights of any Member that is not a party to the MEA in question;

(ii) procedures for regular information exchange between MEA Secretariats and the relevant WTO committees, and the criteria for the granting of observer status; and

(iii) the reduction or, as appropriate, elimination of tariff and non-tariff barriers to environmental goods and services.

We note that fisheries subsidies form part of the negotiations provided for in paragraph 28.

32. We instruct the Committee on Trade and Environment, in pursuing work on all items on its agenda within its current terms of reference, to give particular attention to :

(i) the effect of environmental measures on market access, especially in relation to developing countries, in particular the least-developed among them, and those situations in which the elimination or reduction of trade restrictions and distortions would benefit trade, the environment and development;

(ii) the relevant provisions of the Agreement on Trade-Related Aspects of Intellectual Property Rights; and

(iii) labelling requirements for environmental purposes.

Work on these issues should include the identification of any need to clarify relevant WTO rules. The Committee shall report to the Fifth Session of the Ministerial Conference, and make recommendations, where appropriate, with respect to future action, including the desirability of negotiations. The outcome of this work as well as the negotiations carried out under paragraph 31(i) and (ii) shall be compatible with the open and non-discriminatory nature of the multilateral trading system, shall not add to or diminish the rights and obligations of members under existing WTO agreements, in particular the Agreement on the

Application of Sanitary and Phytosanitary Measures, nor alter the balance of these rights and obligations, and will take into account the needs of developing and least-developed countries.

33. We recognize the importance of technical assistance and capacity building in the field of trade and environment to developing countries, in particular the least-developed among them. We also encourage that expertise and experience be shared with members wishing to perform environmental reviews at the national level. A report shall be prepared on these activities for the Fifth Session.

Electronic Commerce

34. We take note of the work which has been done in the General Council and other relevant bodies since the Ministerial Declaration of 20 May 1998 and agree to continue the Work Programme on Electronic Commerce. The work to date demonstrates that electronic commerce creates new challenges and opportunities for trade for members at all stages of development, and we recognize the importance of creating and maintaining an environment which is favourable to the future development of electronic commerce. We instruct the General Council to consider the most appropriate institutional arrangements for handling the Work Programme, and to report on further progress to the Fifth Session of the Ministerial Conference. We declare that members will maintain their current practice of not imposing customs duties on electronic transmissions until the Fifth Session.

Small Economies

35. We agree to a work programme, under the auspices of the General Council, to examine issues relating to the trade of small economies. The objective of this work is to frame responses to the trade-related issues identified for the fuller integration of small, vulnerable economies into the multilateral trading system, and not to create a sub-category of WTO Members. The General Council shall review the work programme and make recommendations for action to the Fifth Session of the Ministerial Conference.

Trade, Debt and Finance

36. We agree to an examination, in a Working Group under the auspices of the General Council, of the relationship between trade, debt and finance, and of any possible recommendations on steps that might be taken within the mandate and competence of the WTO to enhance the capacity of the multilateral trading system to contribute to a durable solution to the problem of external indebtedness of developing and least-developed countries, and to strengthen the coherence of international trade and financial policies, with a view to safeguarding the multilateral trading system from the effects of financial and monetary instability. The General Council shall report to the Fifth Session of the Ministerial Conference on progress in the examination.

Trade and Transfer of Technology

37. We agree to an examination, in a Working Group under the auspices of the General Council, of the relationship between trade and transfer of technology, and of any possible recommendations on steps that might be taken within the mandate of the WTO to increase flows of technology to developing countries. The General Council shall report to the Fifth Session of the Ministerial Conference on progress in the examination.

Technical Cooperation and Capacity Building

38. We confirm that technical cooperation and capacity building are core elements of the development dimension of the multilateral trading system, and we welcome and endorse the New Strategy for WTO Technical Cooperation for Capacity Building, Growth and Integration. We instruct the Secretariat, in coordination with other relevant agencies, to support domestic efforts for mainstreaming trade into national plans for economic development and strategies for poverty reduction. The delivery of WTO technical assistance shall be designed to assist developing and least-developed countries and low-income countries in transition to adjust to WTO rules and disciplines, implement obligations and exercise the rights of membership, including drawing on the benefits of an open, rules-based multilateral trading system. Priority shall also be accorded to small, vulnerable, and transition economies, as well as to members and observers

without representation in Geneva. We reaffirm our support for the valuable work of the International Trade Centre, which should be enhanced.

39. We underscore the urgent necessity for the effective coordinated delivery of technical assistance with bilateral donors, in the OECD Development Assistance Committee and relevant international and regional intergovernmental institutions, within a coherent policy framework and timetable. In the coordinated delivery of technical assistance, we instruct the Director-General to consult with the relevant agencies, bilateral donors and beneficiaries, to identify ways of enhancing and rationalizing the Integrated Framework for Trade-Related Technical Assistance to Least-Developed Countries and the Joint Integrated Technical Assistance Programme (JITAP).

40. We agree that there is a need for technical assistance to benefit from secure and predictable funding. We therefore instruct the Committee on Budget, Finance and Administration to develop a plan for adoption by the General Council in December 2001 that will ensure long-term funding for WTO technical assistance at an overall level no lower than that of the current year and commensurate with the activities outlined above.

41. We have established firm commitments on technical cooperation and capacity building in various paragraphs in this Ministerial Declaration. We reaffirm these specific commitments contained in paragraphs 16, 21, 24, 26, 27, 33, 38-40, 42 and 43, and also reaffirm the understanding in paragraph 2 on the important role of sustainably financed technical assistance and capacity-building programmes. We instruct the Director-General to report to the Fifth Session of the Ministerial Conference, with an interim report to the General Council in December 2002 on the implementation and adequacy of these commitments in the identified paragraphs.

Least-Developed Countries

42. We acknowledge the seriousness of the concerns expressed by the least-developed countries (LDCs) in the Zanzibar Declaration adopted by their ministers in July 2001. We recognize that the integration of the LDCs into the multilateral trading system

requires meaningful market access, support for the diversification of their production and export base, and trade-related technical assistance and capacity building. We agree that the meaningful integration of LDCs into the trading system and the global economy will involve efforts by all WTO members. We commit ourselves to the objective of duty-free, quota-free market access for products originating from LDCs. In this regard, we welcome the significant market access improvements by WTO members in advance of the Third UN Conference on LDCs (LDC-III), in Brussels, May 2001. We further commit ourselves to consider additional measures for progressive improvements in market access for LDCs. Accession of LDCs remains a priority for the Membership. We agree to work to facilitate and accelerate negotiations with acceding LDCs. We instruct the Secretariat to reflect the priority we attach to LDCs' accessions in the annual plans for technical assistance. We reaffirm the commitments we undertook at LDC-III, and agree that the WTO should take into account, in designing its work programme for LDCs, the trade-related elements of the Brussels Declaration and Programme of Action, consistent with the WTO's mandate, adopted at LDC-III. We instruct the Sub-Committee for Least-Developed Countries to design such a work programme and to report on the agreed work programme to the General Council at its first meeting in 2002.

43. We endorse the Integrated Framework for Trade-Related Technical Assistance to Least-Developed Countries (IF) as a viable model for LDCs' trade development. We urge development partners to significantly increase contributions to the IF Trust Fund and WTO extra-budgetary trust funds in favour of LDCs. We urge the core agencies, in coordination with development partners, to explore the enhancement of the IF with a view to addressing the supply-side constraints of LDCs and the extension of the model to all LDCs, following the review of the IF and the appraisal of the ongoing Pilot Scheme in selected LDCs. We request the Director-General, following coordination with heads of the other agencies, to provide an interim report to the General Council in December 2002 and a full report to the Fifth Session of the Ministerial Conference on all issues affecting LDCs.

Special and Differential Treatment

44. We reaffirm that provisions for special and differential treatment are an integral part of the WTO Agreements. We note the concerns expressed regarding their operation in addressing specific constraints faced by developing countries, particularly least-developed countries. In that connection, we also note that some members have proposed a Framework Agreement on Special and Differential Treatment (WT/GC/W/442). We therefore agree that all special and differential treatment provisions shall be reviewed with a view to strengthening them and making them more precise, effective and operational. In this connection, we endorse the work programme on special and differential treatment set out in the Decision on Implementation-Related Issues and Concerns.

Organization and Management of the Work Programme

45. The negotiations to be pursued under the terms of this declaration shall be concluded not later than 1 January 2005. The Fifth Session of the Ministerial Conference will take stock of progress in the negotiations, provide any necessary political guidance, and take decisions as necessary. When the results of the negotiations in all areas have been established, a Special Session of the Ministerial Conference will be held to take decisions regarding the adoption and implementation of those results.

46. The overall conduct of the negotiations shall be supervised by a Trade Negotiations Committee under the authority of the General Council. The Trade Negotiations Committee shall hold its first meeting not later than 31 January 2002. It shall establish appropriate negotiating mechanisms as required and supervise the progress of the negotiations.

47. With the exception of the improvements and clarifications of the Dispute Settlement Understanding, the conduct, conclusion and entry into force of the outcome of the negotiations shall be treated as parts of a single undertaking. However, agreements reached at an early stage may be implemented on a provisional or a definitive basis. Early agreements shall be taken into account in assessing the overall balance of the negotiations.

48. Negotiations shall be open to :

(i) All members of the WTO; and

(ii) States and separate customs territories currently in the process of accession and those that inform members, at a regular meeting of the General Council, of their intention to negotiate the terms of their membership and for whom an accession working party is established.

Decisions on the outcomes of the negotiations shall be taken only by WTO members.

49. The negotiations shall be conducted in a transparent manner among participants, in order to facilitate the effective participation of all. They shall be conducted with a view to ensuring benefits to all participants and to achieving an overall balance in the outcome of the negotiations.

50. The negotiations and the other aspects of the Work Programme shall take fully into account the principle of special and differential treatment for developing and least-developed countries embodied in : Part IV of the GATT 1994; the Decision of 28 November 1979 on Differential and More Favourable Treatment, Reciprocity and Fuller Participation of Developing Countries; the Uruguay Round Decision on Measures in Favour of Least-Developed Countries; and all other relevant WTO provisions.

51. The Committee on Trade and Development and the Committee on Trade and Environment shall, within their respective mandates, each act as a forum to identify and debate developmental and environmental aspects of the negotiations, in order to help achieve the objective of having sustainable development appropriately reflected.

52. Those elements of the Work Programme which do not involve negotiations are also accorded a high priority. They shall be pursued under the overall supervision of the General Council, which shall report on progress to the Fifth Session of the Ministerial Conference.

Appendix-VI

GENEVA WTO MINISTERIAL DECLARATION, 1998

(Adopted on 20 May 1998)

1. This Second Session of the Ministerial Conference of the WTO is taking place at a particularly significant time for the multilateral trading system, when the fiftieth anniversary of its establishment is being commemorated. On this occasion we pay tribute to the system's important contribution over the past half-century to growth, employment and stability by promoting the liberalization and expansion of trade and providing a framework for the conduct of international trade relations, in accordance with the objectives embodied in the Preambles to the General Agreement on Tariffs and Trade and the World Trade Organization Agreement.

2. We underline the crucial importance of the multilateral rule-based trading system. We reaffirm the commitments and assessments we made at Singapore, and we note that the work under existing agreements and decisions has resulted in significant new steps forward since we last met. In particular, we welcome the successful conclusion of the negotiations on basic telecommunications and financial services and we take note of the implementation of the Information Technology Agreement. We renew our commitment to achieve progressive liberalization of trade in goods and services.

3. The fiftieth anniversary comes at a time when the economies of a number of WTO Members are experiencing difficulties as a result of disturbances in financial markets. We take this opportunity to underline that keeping all markets open

must be a key element in a durable solution to these difficulties. With this in mind, we reject the use of any protectionist measures and agree to work together in the WTO as in the IMF and the World Bank to improve the coherence of international economic policy-making with a view to maximizing the contribution that an open, rule-based trading system can make to fostering stable growth for economies at all levels of development.

4. We recognize the importance of enhancing public understanding of the benefits of the multilateral trading system in order to build support for it and agree to work towards this end. In this context we will consider how to improve the transparency of WTO operations. We shall also continue to improve our efforts towards the objectives of sustained economic growth and sustainable development.

5. We renew our commitment to ensuring that the benefits of the multilateral trading system are extended as widely as possible. We recognize the need for the system to make its own contribution in response to the particular trade interests and development needs of developing-country Members. We welcome the work already underway in the Committee on Trade and Development for reviewing the application of special provisions in the Multilateral Trade Agreements and related Ministerial Decisions in favour of developing country Members, and in particular the least-developed among them. We agree on the need for effective implementation of these special provisions.

6. We remain deeply concerned over the marginalization of least-developed countries and certain small economies, and recognize the urgent need to address this issue which has been compounded by the chronic foreign debt problem facing many of them. In this context we welcome the initiatives taken by the WTO in cooperation with other agencies to implement in an integrated manner the Plan of Action for the least-developed countries which we agreed at Singapore, especially through the High-Level Meeting on Least-Developed Countries held in Geneva in October 1997. We also welcome the report of the Director-General on the follow-up of this initiative, to which we attach great importance. We commit ourselves to continue to improve market access conditions for products exported by the

least-developed countries on as broad and liberal a basis as possible. We urge Members to implement the market-access commitments that they have undertaken at the High-Level Meeting.

7. We welcome the WTO Members who have joined since we met in Singapore: Congo, Democratic Republic of Congo, Mongolia, Niger and Panama. We welcome the progress made with 31 applicants currently negotiating their accession and renew our resolution to ensure that the accession processes proceed as rapidly as possible. We recall that accession to the WTO requires full respect of WTO rules and disciplines as well as meaningful market access commitments on the part of acceding candidates.

8. Full and faithful implementation of the WTO Agreement and Ministerial Decisions is imperative for the credibility of the multilateral trading system and indispensable for maintaining the momentum for expanding global trade, fostering job creation and raising standards of living in all parts of the world. When we meet at the Third Session we shall further pursue our evaluation of the implementation of individual agreements and the realization of their objectives. Such evaluation would cover, *inter alia*, the problems encountered in implementation and the consequent impact on the trade and development prospects of Members. We reaffirm our commitment to respect the existing schedules for reviews, negotiations and other work to which we have already agreed.

9. We recall that the Marrakesh Agreement Establishing the World Trade Organization states that the WTO shall provide the forum for negotiations among its Members concerning their multilateral trade relations in matters dealt with under the agreements in the Annexes to the Agreement, and that it may also provide a forum for further negotiations among its Members concerning their multilateral trade relations, and a framework for the implementation of the results of such negotiations, as may be decided by the Ministerial Conference. In the light of paragraphs 1-8 above, we decide that a process will be established under the direction of the General Council to ensure full and faithful implementation of existing agreements, and to prepare for the

Third Session of the Ministerial Conference. This process shall enable the General Council to submit recommendations regarding the WTO's work programme, including further liberalization sufficiently broad-based to respond to the range of interests and concerns of all Members, within the WTO framework, that will enable us to take decisions at the Third Session of the Ministerial Conference. In this regard, the General Council will meet in special session in September 1998 and periodically thereafter to ensure full and timely completion of its work, fully respecting the principle of decision-making by consensus. The General Council's work programme shall encompass the following:

(a) recommendations concerning:

   (i) the issues, including those brought forward by Members, relating to implementation of existing agreements and decisions;

   (ii) the negotiations already mandated at Marrakesh, to ensure that such negotiations begin on schedule;

   (iii) future work already provided for under other existing agreements and decisions taken at Marrakesh;

(b) recommendations concerning other possible future work on the basis of the work programme initiated at Singapore;

(c) recommendations on the follow-up to the High-Level Meeting on Least-Developed Countries;

(d) recommendations arising from consideration of other matters proposed and agreed to by Members concerning their multilateral trade relations.

10. The General Council will also submit to the Third Session of the Ministerial Conference, on the basis of consensus, recommendations for decision concerning the further organization and management of the work programme arising from the above, including the scope, structure and time-frames, that will ensure that the work programme is begun and concluded expeditiously.

11. The above work programme shall be aimed at achieving overall balance of interests of all Members.

Appendix-VII

TEXT : SINGAPORE WTO MINISTERIAL DECLARATION

(Adopted on 13 December 1996)

Singapore — Trade ministers from more than 120 countries have concluded a week-long ministerial that reached agreement in a number of key areas, topped by an Information Technology Agreement (ITA) among a number of the major participants to eliminate tariffs on a range of high-technology goods by the year 2000.

In a final communique issued on the final day of the World Trade Organization's (WTO) December 9-13 first ministerial meeting, the ministers also committed to conclude by next February an agreement on basic telecommunication services.

There was little progress on discussions to allow more countries to join the 128-member WTO, the most prominent of the accession applications coming from China. The communique states that it is important that the applicants offer "meaningful market access commitments," and that the WTO would work "expeditiously" to bring these countries into the WTO system.

On a U.S. initiative to include labor standards in the WTO work program, the communique includes a brief statement that the International Labor Organization "is the competent body to set and deal with these standards," but that the WTO members also "reject the use of labor standards for protectionist purposes."

The ministers agreed to set up a working group to examine the relationship between trade and investment and another to study issues relating to trade and competition policy, including anti-competitive practices.

And they agreed to another group that would study transparency in government procurement practices, with the idea of moving toward an international agreement on this issue.

The ministers further agreed to uphold commitments made in the Uruguay Round global trade accord that calls for moving forward with new agricultural trade liberalization negotiations beginning in 1999.

The WTO members approved a plan of action to help the poorest countries that includes technical assistance but makes no mention of a proposal by WTO Director General Renato Ruggiero to eliminate tariffs for the world's poorest countries.

The WTO said it would organize a meeting in 1997 with the United Nations Conference on Trade and Development (UNCTAD) that would examine how to improve trade opportunities for these poorest members.

The ministers expressed disappointment that a number of member countries have failed to notify the WTO, as required under the Uruguay Round accords, when trade measures or legislation are enacted.

Following is the text of the final communique :

Purpose

1. We, the Ministers, have met in Singapore from 9 to 13 December 1996 for the first regular biennial meeting of the WTO at Ministerial level, as called for in Article IV of the Agreement Establishing the World Trade Organization, to further strengthen the WTO as a forum for negotiation, the continuing liberalization of trade within a rule-based system, and the multilateral review and assessment of trade policies, and in particular to :

— assess the implementation of our commitments under the WTO Agreements and decisions;

— review the ongoing negotiations and Work Programme;

— examine developments in world trade; and

— address the challenges of an evolving world economy.

Trade and Economic Growth

2. For nearly 50 years Members have sought to fulfill, first in the GATT and now in the WTO, the objectives reflected in the preamble to the WTO Agreement of conducting our trade relations with a view to raising standards of living worldwide.

The rise in global trade facilitated by trade liberalization within the rules-based system has created more and better-paid jobs in many countries. The achievements of the WTO during its first two years bear witness to our desire to work together to make the most of the possibilities that the multilateral system provides to promote sustainable growth and development while contributing to a more stable and secure climate in international relations.

Integration of Economics; Opportunities and Challenges

3. We believe that the scope and pace of change in the international economy, including the growth in trade in services and direct investment, and the increasing integration of economies offer unprecedented opportunities for improved growth, job creation, and development. These developments require adjustment by economies and societies. They also pose challenges to the trading system. We commit ourselves to address these challenges.

Core Labor Standards

4. We renew our commitment to the observance of internationally recognized core labour standards. The International Labour Organization (ILO) is the competent body to set and deal with these standards, and we affirm our support for its work in promoting them.

We believe that economic growth and development fostered by increased trade and further trade liberalization contribute to the promotion of these standards. We reject the use of labour standards for protectionist purposes, and agree that the comparative advantage of countries, particularly low-wage developing countries, must in no way be put into question. In this regard, we note that the WTO and ILO Secretariats will continue their existing collaboration.

Marginalization

5. We commit ourselves to address the problem of marginalization for least-developed countries, and the risk of it for certain developing countries. We will also continue to work for greater coherence in international economic policy-making and for improved coordination between the WTO and other agencies in providing technical assistance.

Role of WTO

6. In pursuit of the goal of sustainable growth and development for the common good, we envisage a world where trade flows freely. To this end we renew our commitment to :

- — a fair, equitable and more open rule-based system;
- — progressive liberalization and elimination of tariff and non-tariff barriers to trade in goods;
- — progressive liberalization of trade in services;
- — rejection of all forms of protectionism;
- — elimination of discriminatory treatment in international trade relations;
- — integration of developing and least-developed countries and economies in transition into the multilateral system; and
- — the maximum possible level of transparency.

Regional Agreements

7. We note that trade relations of WTO Members are being increasingly influenced by regional trade agreements, which have expanded vastly in number, scope and coverage. Such initiatives can promote further liberalization and may assist least-developed, developing and transition economies in integrating into the international trading system.

In this context, we note the importance of existing regional arrangements involving developing and least-developed countries. The expansion and extent of regional trade agreements make it important to analyze whether the system of WTO rights and obligations as it relates to regional trade agreements needs to be further clarified. We reaffirm the primacy of the multilateral trading system, which includes a framework for the development of regional trade agreements, and we renew our commitment to ensure that regional trade agreements are complementary to it and consistent with its rules. In this regard, we welcome the establishment and endorse the work of the new Committee on Regional Trade Agreements. We shall continue to work through progressive liberalization in the WTO as we are committed in the WTO Agreement and Decisions adopted at Marrakesh, and in so doing facilitate mutually supportive processes of global and regional trade liberalization.

Accession

8. It is important that the 28 applicants now negotiating accession contribute to completing the accession process by accepting the WTO rules and by offering meaningful market access commitments. We will work to bring these applicants expeditiously into the WTO system.

Dispute Settlement

9. The Dispute Settlement Understanding (DSU) offers a means for the settlement of disputes among Members that is unique in international agreements. We consider its impartial and transparent operation to be of fundamental importance in assuring the resolution of trade disputes, and in fostering the implementation and application of the WTO agreements. The Understanding, with its predictable procedures, including the possibility of appeal of panel decisions to an Appellate Body and provisions on implementation of recommendations, has improved Members' means of resolving their differences. We believe that the DSU has worked effectively during its first two years. We also note the role that several WTO bodies have played in helping to avoid disputes. We renew our determination to abide by the rules and procedures of the DSU and other WTO agreements in the conduct of our trade relations and the settlement of disputes. We are confident that longer experience with the DSU, including the implementation of panel and appellate recommendations, will further enhance the effectiveness and credibility of the dispute settlement system.

Implementation

10. We attach high priority to full and effective implementation of the WTO Agreement in a manner consistent with the goal of trade liberalization. Implementation thus far has been generally satisfactory, although some Members have expressed dissatisfaction with certain aspects. It is clear that further effort in this area is required, as indicated by the relevant WTO bodies in their reports. Implementation of the specific commitments scheduled by Members with respect to market access in industrial goods and trade in services appears to be proceeding smoothly. With respect to industrial market access, monitoring of implementation would be enhanced by the timely availability of trade and tariff data. Progress has been made also in advancing the WTO reform programme in agriculture, including in implementation of agreed market access concessions and domestic subsidy and export subsidy commitments.

Notifications and Legislation

11. Compliance with notification requirements has not been fully satisfactory. Because the WTO system relies on mutual monitoring as a means to assess implementation, those Members which have not submitted notifications in a timely manner, or whose notifications are not complete, should renew their efforts. At the same time, the relevant bodies should take appropriate steps to promote full compliance while considering practical proposals for simplifying the notification process.

Developing Countries

12. Where legislation is needed to implement WTO rules, Members are mindful of their obligations to complete their domestic legislative process without further delay. Those Members entitled to transition periods are urged to take steps as they deem necessary to ensure timely implementation of obligations as they come into effect. Each Member should carefully review all its existing or proposed legislation, programmes and measures to ensure their full compatibility with the WTO obligations, and should carefully consider points made during review in the relevant WTO bodies regarding the WTO consistency of legislation,

programmes and measures, and make appropriate changes where necessary.

13. The integration of developing countries in the multilateral trading system is important for their economic development and for global trade expansion. In this connection, we recall that the WTO Agreement embodies provisions conferring differential and more favourable treatment for developing countries, including special attention to the particular situation of least-developed countries. We acknowledge the fact that developing country Members have undertaken significant new commitments, both substantive and procedural, and we recognize the range and complexity of the efforts that they are making to comply with them. In order to assist them in these efforts, including those with respect to notification and legislative requirements, we will improve the availability of technical assistance under the agreed guidelines. We have also agreed to recommendations relative to the decision we took at Marrakesh concerning the possible negative effects of the agricultural reform programme on least-developed and net food-importing developing countries.

Least-Developed Countries

14. We remain concerned by the problems of the least-developed countries and have agreed to :

— a Plan of Action, including provision for taking positive measures, for example duty-free access, on an autonomous basis, aimed at improving their overall capacity to respond to the opportunities offered by the trading system;

— seek to give operational content to the Plan of Action, for example, by enhancing conditions for investment and providing predictable and favourable market access conditions for LLDCs' products, to foster the expansion and diversification of their exports to the markets of all developed countries; and in the case of relevant developing countries in the context of the Global System of Trade Preferences; and

— organize a meeting with UNCTAD and the International Trade Centre as soon as possible in 1997, with the participation of aid agencies, multilateral financial institutions and least-developed countries to foster an integrated approach to assisting these countries in enhancing their trading opportunities.

Textiles and Clothing

15. We confirm our commitment to full and faithful implementation of the provisions of the Agreement on Textiles and Clothing (ATC). We stress the importance of the integration of textile products, as provided for in the ATC, into GATT 1994 under its strengthened rules and disciplines because of its systemic significance for the rule-based, non-discriminatory trading system and its contribution to the increase in export earnings of developing countries. We attach importance to the implementation of this Agreement so as to ensure an effective transition to GATT 1994 by way of integration which is progressive in character. The use of safeguard measures in accordance with ATC provisions should be as sparing as possible. We note concerns regarding the use of other trade distortive measures and circumvention. We reiterate the importance of fully implementing the provisions of the ATC relating to small suppliers, new entrants and least-developed country Members, as well as those relating to cotton-producing exporting Members. We recognize the importance of wool products for some developing country Members. We reaffirm that as part of the integration process and with reference to the specific commitments undertaken by the Members as a result of the Uruguay Round, all Members shall take such action as may be necessary to abide by GATT 1994 rules and disciplines so as to achieve improved market access for textiles and clothing products. We agree that, keeping in view its quasi-judicial nature, the Textiles Monitoring Body (TMB) should achieve transparency in providing rationale for its findings and recommendations. We expect that the TMB shall make findings and recommendations whenever called upon to do so under the Agreement. We emphasize the responsibility of the Goods Council in overseeing, in accordance with Article IV : 5 of the WTO Agreement and Article 8 of the ATC, the functioning of the ATC, whose implementation is being supervised by the TMB.

Trade and Environment

16. The Committee on Trade and Environment has made an important contribution towards fulfilling its Work Programme. The Committee has been examining and will continue to examine, inter alia, the scope of the complementarities between trade liberalization, economic development and environmental protection. Full implementation of the WTO Agreements will make an important contribution to achieving the objectives of sustainable development. The work of the Committee has underlined the importance of policy coordination at the national level in the area of trade and environment. In this connection, the work of the Committee has been enriched by the participation of environmental as well as trade experts from Member governments and the further participation of such experts in the Committee's deliberations would be welcomed. The breadth and complexity of the issues covered by the Committee's Work Programme shows that further work needs to be undertaken on all items of its agenda, as contained in its report. We intend to build on the work accomplished thus far, and therefore direct the Committee to carry out its work, reporting to the General Council, under its existing terms of reference.

Services Negotiations

17. The fulfillment of the objectives agreed at Marrakesh for negotiations on the improvement of market access in services — in financial services, movement of natural persons, maritime transport services and basic telecommunications — has proved to be difficult. The results have been below expectations. In three areas, it has been necessary to prolong negotiations beyond the original deadlines. We are determined to obtain a progressively higher level of liberalization in services on a mutually advantageous basis with appropriate flexibility for individual developing country Members, as envisaged in the Agreement, in the continuing negotiations and those scheduled to begin no later than 1 January 2000. In this context, we look forward to full MFN agreements based on improved market access commitments and national treatment. Accordingly, we will :

— achieve a successful conclusion to the negotiations on basic telecommunications in February 1997; and

— resume financial services negotiations in April 1997 with the aim of achieving significantly improved market access commitments with a broader level of participation in the agreed time frame.

With the same broad objectives in mind, we also look forward to a successful conclusion of the negotiations on Maritime Transport Services in the next round of negotiations on services liberalization.

In professional services, we shall aim at completing the work on the accountancy sector by the end of 1997, and will continue to develop multilateral disciplines and guidelines. In this connection, we encourage the successful completion of international standards in the accountancy sector by IF AC, IASC, and IOSCO. With respect to GATS rules, we shall undertake the necessary work with a view to completing the negotiations on safeguards by the end of 1997. We also note that more analytical work will be needed on emergency safeguards measures, government procurement in services and subsidies.

ITA and Pharmaceuticals

18. Taking note that a number of Members have agreed on a Declaration on Trade in Information Technology Products, we welcome the initiative taken by a number of WTO Members and other States or separate customs territories which have applied to accede to the WTO, who have agreed to tariff elimination for trade in information technology products on an MFN basis as well as the addition by a number of Members of over 400 products to their lists of tariff-free products in pharmaceuticals.

Work Programme and Built-in Agenda

19. Bearing in mind that an important aspect of WTO activities is a continuous overseeing of the implementation of various agreements, a periodic examination and updating of the WTO Work Programme is a key to enable the WTO to fulfill its objectives. In this context, we endorse the reports of the various WTO bodies. A major share of the Work Programme stems from

the WTO Agreement and decisions adopted at Marrakesh. As part of these Agreements and decisions we agreed to a number of provisions calling for future negotiations on Agriculture, Services and aspects of TRIPS, or reviews and other work on Anti-Dumping, Customs Valuation, Dispute Settlement Understanding, Import Licensing, Preshipment Inspection, Rules of Origin, Sanitary and Phyto-Sanitary Measures, Safeguards, Subsidies and Countervailing Measures, Technical Barriers to Trade, Textiles and Clothing, Trade Policy Review Mechanism, Trade-Related Aspects of Intellectual Property Rights and Trade-Related Investment Measures. We agree to a process of analysis and exchange of information, where provided for in the conclusions and recommendations of the relevant WTO bodies, on the Built-in Agenda issues, to allow Members to better understand the issues involved and identify their interests before undertaking the agreed negotiations and reviews. We agree that :

— the time frames established in the Agreements will be respected in each case;

— the work undertaken shall not prejudge the scope of future negotiations where such negotiations are called for; and

— the work undertaken shall not prejudice the nature of the activity agreed upon *(i.e.* negotiation or review).

Investment and Competition

20. Having regard to the existing WTO provisions on matters related to investment and competition policy and the built-in agenda in these areas, including under the TRIMs Agreement, and on the understanding that the work undertaken shall not prejudge whether negotiations will be initiated in the future, we also agree to :

— establish a working group to examine the relationship between trade and investment; and

— establish a working group to study issues raised by Members relating to the interaction between trade and competition policy, including anti-competitive practices, in order to identify any areas that may merit further consideration in the WTO framework.

These groups shall draw upon each other's work if necessary and also draw upon and be without prejudice to the work in UNCTAD and other appropriate intergovernmental fora. As regards UNCTAD, we welcome the work under way as provided for in the Midrand Declaration and the contribution it can make to the understanding of issues. In the conduct of the work of the working groups, we encourage cooperation with the above organizations to make the best use of available resources and to ensure that the development dimension is taken fully into account. The General Council will keep the work of each body under review, and will determine after two years how the work of each body should proceed. It is clearly understood that future negotiations, if any, regarding multilateral disciplines in these areas, will take place only after an explicit consensus decision is taken among WTO Members regarding such negotiations.

Transparency in Government Procurement

21. We further agree to :

— establish a working group to conduct a study on transparency in government procurement practices, taking into account national policies, and, based on this study, to develop elements for inclusion in an appropriate agreement; and

Trade Facilitation

— direct the Council for Trade in Goods to undertake exploratory and analytical work, drawing on the work of other relevant international organizations, on the simplification of trade procedures in order to assess the scope for WTO rules in this area.

22. In the organization of the work referred to in paragraphs 20 and 21, careful attention will be given to minimizing the burdens on delegations, especially those with more limited resources, and to coordinating meetings with those of relevant UNCTAD bodies. The technical cooperation programme of the Secretariat will be available to developing and, in particular,

least-developed country Members to facilitate their participation in this work.

23. Noting that the 50th anniversary of the multilateral trading system will occur early in 1998, we instruct the General Council to consider how this historic event can best be commemorated.

Finally, we express our warmest thanks to the Chairman of the Ministerial Conference, Mr. Yeo Cheow Tong, for his personal contribution to the success of this Ministerial Conference. We also want to express our sincere gratitude to Prime Minister Goh Chok Tong, his colleagues in the Government of Singapore and the people of Singapore for their warm hospitality and the excellent organization they have provided. The fact that this first Ministerial Conference of the WTO has been held at Singapore is an additional manifestation of Singapore's commitment to an open world trading system.

GLOSSARY OF TERMS

GENERAL

GATT General Agreement on Tariffs and Trade, which has been superseded as an international organization by the WTO. An updated General Agreement is now one of the WTO's agreements.

GATT 1947 The old (pre-1994) version of the GATT.

GATT 1994 The new version of the General Agreement, incorporated into the WTO, which governs trade in goods.

Members WTO governments (first letter capitalized, in WTO style).

MFN Most-favoured-nation treatment (GATT Article I, GATS Article II and TRIPS Article 4), the principle of not discriminating between one's trading partners.

National Treatment The principle of giving others the same treatment as one's own nationals. GATT Article III requires that imports be treated no less favourably than the same or similar domestically-produced goods once they have passed customs. GATS Article XVII and TRIPS Article 3 also deal with national treatment for services and intellectual property protection.

TPRB, TPRM The Trade Policy Review Body is General Council operating under special procedures for meetings to review trade policies and practices of individual WTO members under the Trade Policy Review Mechanism.

Transparency Degree to which trade policies and practices, and the process by which they are established, are open and predictable.

Uruguay Round Multilateral trade negotiations launched at Punta del Este, Uruguay in September 1986 and concluded in Geneva in December 1993. Signed by Ministers in Marrakesh, Morocco, in April 1994.

TARIFFS

Binding, Bound see "tariff binding".

Electronic Commerce The production, advertising, sale and distribution of products via telecommunications networks.

Free-rider A casual term used to infer that a country which does not make any trade concessions, profits, nonetheless, from tariff cuts and concessions made by other countries in negotiations under the most-favoured-nation principle.

Harmonized System An international nomenclature developed by the World Customs Organization, which is arranged in six digit codes allowing all participating countries to classify traded goods on a common basis. Beyond the six digit level, countries are free to introduce national distinctions for tariffs and many other purposes.

ITA Information Technology Agreement, or formally the Ministerial-Declaration on Trade in Information Technology Products, under which participants will remove tariffs on IT products by the year 2000.

ITA II Negotiations aimed at expanding ITA's product coverage.

Nuisance Tariff Tariff so low that it costs the government more to collect it than the revenue it generates.

Schedule of Concessions List of bound tariff rates.

Tariff Binding Commitment not to increase a rate of duty beyond an agreed level. Once a rate of duty is bound, it may not be raised without compensating the affected parties.

Tariff Escalation Higher import duties on semi-processed products than on raw materials, and higher still on finished products. This practice protects domestic processing industries and discourages the development of processing activity in the countries where raw materials originate.

Tariff Peaks Relatively high tariffs, usually on "sensitive" products, amidst generally low tariff levels. For industrialized countries, tariffs of 15 per cent and above are generally recognized as "tariff peaks".

Tariffs Customs duties on merchandise imports. Levied either on an ad valorem basis (percentage of value) or on a specific basis (*e.g.* $7 per 100 kgs.). Tariffs give price advantage to similar locally-produced goods and raise revenues for the government.

WCO World Customs Organization, a multilateral body located in Brussels through which participating countries seek to simplify and rationalize customs procedures.

NON-TARIFF MEASURES

Anti-dumping Duties Article VI of the GATT 1994 permits the imposition of anti-dumping duties against dumped goods, equal to the difference between their export price and their normal value, if dumping causes injury to producers of competing products in the importing country.

Circumvention Measures taken by exporters to evade anti-dumping or countervailing duties.

Countervailing Measures Action taken by the importing country, usually in the form of increased duties to offset subsidies given to producers or exporters in the exporting country.

Dumping Occurs when goods are exported at a price less than their normal value, generally meaning they are exported for less than they are sold in the domestic market or third-country markets, or at less than production cost.

NTMs Non-tariff measures such as quotas, import licensing systems, sanitary regulations, prohibitions, etc.

Price Undertaking Undertaking by an exporter to raise the export price of the product to avoid the possibility of an anti-dumping duty.

PSI Preshipment inspection — the practice of employing specialized private companies to check shipment details of goods ordered overseas — *i.e.* price, quantity, quality, etc.

QRs Quantitative restrictions — specific limits on the quantity or value of goods that can be imported (or exported) during a specific time period.

Rules of Origin Laws, regulations and administrative procedures which determine a product's country of origin. A decision by a customs authority on origin can determine whether a shipment falls within a quota limitation, qualifies for a tariff preference or is affected by an anti-dumping duty. These rules can vary from country to country.

Safeguard Measures Action taken to protect a specific industry from an unexpected build-up of imports — governed by Article XIX of the GATT 1994.

Subsidy There are two general types of subsidies: export and domestic. An export subsidy is a benefit conferred on a firm by the government that is contingent on exports. A domestic subsidy is a benefit not directly linked to exports.

Tariffication Procedures relating to the agricultural market-access provision in which all non-tariff measures are converted into tariffs.

Trade Facilitation Removing obstacles to the movement of goods across borders (*e.g.* simplification of customs procedures).

VRA, VER, OMA Voluntary restraint arrangement, voluntary export restraint, orderly marketing arrangement. Bilateral arrangements whereby an exporting country (government or industry) agrees to reduce or restrict exports without the importing country having to make use of quotas, tariffs or other import controls.

TEXTILES AND CLOTHING

ATC The WTO Agreement on Textiles and Clothing which integrates trade in this sector back to GATT rules within a ten-year period.

Carry Forward When an exporting country uses part of the following year's quota during, the current year.

Carry Over When an exporting country utilizes the previous year's unutilized quota.

Circumvention Avoiding quotas and other restrictions by altering the country of origin of a product.

CTG Council for Trade in Goods — oversees WTO agreements on goods, including the ATC.

Integration Programme The phasing out of MFA restrictions in four stages starting on 1 January 1995 and ending on 1 January 2005.

ITCB International Textiles and Clothing Bureau — Geneva-based group of some 20 developing country exporters of textiles and clothing.

MFA Multifibre Arrangement (1974-94) under which countries whose markets are disrupted by increased imports of textiles and clothing from another country were able to negotiate quota restrictions.

Swing When an exporting country transfers part of a quota from one product to another restrained product.

TMB The Textiles Monitoring Body, consisting of a chairman plus ten members acting in a personal capacity, oversees the implementation of ATC commitments.

Transitional Safeguard Mechanism Allows members to impose restrictions against individual exporting countries if the importing country can show that both overall imports of a product and imports from the individual countries are entering the country in such increased quantities as to cause — or threaten — serious damage to the relevant domestic industry.

AGRICULTURE/SPS

Agenda 2000 EC's financial reform plans for 2000-06 aimed at strengthening the union with a view to receiving new members. Includes reform of the CAP (see below).

Border Protection Any measure which acts to restrain imports at point of entry.

BSE Bovine spongiform encephalopathy, or "mad cow disease".

Box Category of domestic support. **Green Box:** supports considered not to distort trade and therefore permitted with no limits. **Blue Box:** permitted supports linked to production, but subject to production limits and therefore minimally trade-distorting. **Amber Box:** supports considered to distort trade and therefore subject to reduction commitments.

Cairns Group Group of agricultural exporting nations lobbying for agricultural trade liberalization. It was formed in 1986 in Cairns, Australia just before the beginning of the Uruguay Round. Current membership: Australia, Argentina, Brazil, Canada, Chile, Colombia, Fiji, Indonesia, Malaysia, New Zealand, Paraguay, the Philippines, South Africa, Thailand and Uruguay.

CAP Common Agricultural Policy — The EU's comprehensive system of production targets and marketing mechanisms designed to manage agricultural trade within the EU and with the rest of the world.

Codex Alimentarius FAO/WHO commission that deals with international standards on food safety.

Distortion When prices and production are higher or lower than levels that would usually exist in a competitive market.

Deficiency Payment Paid by governments to producers of certain commodities and based on the difference between a target price and the domestic market price or loan rate, whichever is the less.

EEP Export enhancement programme — programme of US export subsidies given generally to compete with subsidized agricultural exports from the EU on certain export markets.

Food Security Concept which discourages opening the domestic market to foreign agricultural products on the principle that a country must be as self-sufficient as possible for its basic dietary needs.

Internal Support Encompasses any measure which acts to maintain producer prices at levels above those prevailing in international trade; direct payments to producers, including deficiency payments, and input and marketing cost reduction measures available only for agricultural production.

International Office of Epizootics Deals with international standards concerning animal health.

Multifunctionality idea that agriculture has many functions in addition to producing food and fibre, *e.g.* environmental protection, landscape preservation, rural employment, etc.

Peace Clause Provision in Article 13 of the Agriculture Agreement says agricultural subsidies committed under the agreement cannot be challenged under other WTO agreements, in particular the Subsidies Agreement and GATT. Expires at the end of 2003.

Reform Programme Programme for reducing subsidies and protection and other reforms under the Agriculture Agreement.

SPS Regulations Sanitary and Phytosanitary regulations — government standards to protect human, animal and plant life and health, to help ensure that food is safe for consumption.

Variable Levy Customs duty rate which varies in response to domestic price criterion.

INTELLECTUAL PROPERTY

Berne Convention Treaty, administered by WIPO, for the protection of the rights of authors in their literary and artistic works.

CBD Convention on Biological Diversity.

Counterfeit Unauthorized representation of a registered trademark carried on goods identical or similar to goods for which the trademark is registered, with a view to deceiving the purchaser into believing that he/she is buying the original goods.

Geographical Indications Place names (or words associated with a place) used to identify products (for example, "Champagne", "Tequila" or "Roquefort") which have a particular quality, reputation or other characteristic because they come from that place.

Intellectual Property Rights Ownership of ideas, including literary and artistic works (protected by copyright), inventions (protected by patents), signs for distinguishing goods of an enterprise (protected by trademarks) and other elements of industrial property.

IPRs Intellectual property rights.

Lisbon Agreement Treaty, administered by WIPO, for the protection of geographical indications and their international registration.

Madrid Agreement Treaty, administered by WIPO, for the repression of false or deceptive indications of source on goods.

Mailbox Refers to the requirement of the TRIPS Agreement applying to WTO Members which do not yet provide product patent protection for pharmaceuticals and for agricultural chemicals. Since 1 January 1995, when the WTO agreements entered into force, these countries have to establish a means by which applications of patents for these products can be filed. (An additional requirement says they must also put in place a system for granting "exclusive marketing rights" for the products whose patent applications have been filed.)

Paris Convention Treaty, administered by WIPO, for the protection of industrial intellectual property, *i.e.* patents, utility models, industrial designs, etc.

Piracy Unauthorized copying of copyright materials for commercial purposes and unauthorized commercial dealing in copied materials.

Rome Convention Treaty, administered by WIPO, UNESCO and ILO, for the protection of the works of performers, broadcasting organizations and producers of phonograms.

TRIPS Trade-Related Aspects of Intellectual Property Rights.

UPOV International Union for the Protection of New Varieties of Plants (Union internationale pour la protection des obtentions vegetales)

Washington Treaty Treaty for the protection of intellectual property in respect of lay-out designs of integrated circuits.

WIPO World Intellectual Property Organization.

INVESTMENT

Export-performance Measure Requirement that a certain quantity of production must be exported.

FDI Foreign direct investment.

Local-Content Measure Requirement that the investor purchase a certain amount of local materials for incorporation in the investor's product.

Product-Mandating Requirement that the investor export to certain countries or region.

Trade-Balancing Measure Requirement that the investor use earnings from exports to pay for imports.

TRIMS Trade-related investment measures.

DISPUTE SETTLEMENT

Appellate Body An independent seven-person body that, upon request by one or more parties to the dispute, reviews findings in panel reports.

Automaticity The "automatic" chronological progression for settling trade disputes in regard to panel establishment, terms of reference, composition and adoption procedures.

DSB Dispute Settlement Body — when the WTO General Council meets to settle trade disputes.

DSU The Uruguay Round Understanding on Rules and Procedures Governing the Settlement of Disputes.

Nullification and Impairment Damage to a country's benefits and expectations from its WTO membership through another country's change in its trade regime or failure to carry out its WTO obligations.

Panel Consisting of three experts, this independent body is established by the DSB to examine and issue recommendations on a particular dispute in the light of WTO provisions.

SERVICES

Accounting Rate In telecoms, the charge made by one country's telephone network operator for calls originating in another country.

Commercial Presence Having an office, branch, or subsidiary in a foreign country.

GATS The WTO's General Agreement on Trade in Services.

General Obligations Obligations which should be applied to all services sector at the entry into force of the agreement.

Initial Commitments Trade liberalizing commitments in services which members are prepared to make early on.

Modes of Delivery How international trade in services is supplied and consumed. Mode 1: cross border supply; mode 2: consumption abroad; mode 3: foreign commercial presence; and mode 4: movement of natural persons.

Multi-Modal Transportation using more than one mode. In the GATS negotiations, essentially door-to-door services that include international shipping.

National Schedules The equivalent of tariff schedules in GATT, laying down the commitments accepted — voluntarily or through negotiation — by WTO members.

Natural Persons People, as distinct from juridical persons such as companies and organizations.

Offer A country's proposal for further liberalization.

Protocols Additional agreements attached to the GATS. The Second Protocol deals with the 1995 commitments on financial services. The Third Protocol deals with movement of natural persons.

Prudence, Prudential In financial services, terms used to describe an objective of market regulation by authorities to protect investors and depositors, to avoid instability or crises.

Schedule "Schedule of Specific Commitments" — A WTO member's list of commitments regarding market access and bindings regarding national treatment.

Specific Commitments See "schedule".

REGIONALISM/TRADE AND DEVELOPMENT

ACP African, Caribbean and Pacific countries. Group of 71 countries with preferential trading relation with the EU under the Lome Treaty.

Andean Community Bolivia, Colombia, Ecuador, Peru and Venezuela.

APEC Asia Pacific Economic Cooperation forum.

ASEAN Association of Southeast Asian Nations. The seven ASEAN members of the WTO — Brunei, Indonesia, Malaysia, Myanmar, the Philippines, Singapore and Thailand — often speak in the WTO as one group on general issues. The other ASEAN members are Laos and Vietnam.

Caricom The Caribbean Community and Common Market comprises 15 countries.

CTD The WTO Committee on Trade and Development.

Customs Union Members apply a common external tariff (*e.g.* the EC).

EC European Communities (official name of the European Union in the WTO).

EFTA European Free Trade Association.

Free Trade Area Trade within the group is duty free but members set own tariffs on imports from non-members (*e.g.* NAFTA).

G15 Group of 15 developing countries acting as the main political organ for the Non-Aligned Movement.

G77 Group of developing countries set up in 1964 at the end of the first UNCTAD (originally 77, but now more than 130 countries).

G7 Group of seven leading industrial countries: Canada, France, Germany, Italy, Japan, United Kingdom, United States.

GRULAC Informal group of Latin-American members of the WTO.

GSP Generalized System of Preferences — programmes by developed countries granting preferential tariffs to imports from developing countries.

HLM WTO High-Level Meeting for LDCs, held in October 1997 in Geneva.

ITC The International Trade Centre, originally established by the old GATT and is now operated jointly by the WTO and the

UN, the latter acting through UNCTAD. Focal point for technical cooperation on trade promotion of developing countries.

LDCs Least-developed countries.

Mercosur Argentina, Brazil, Paraguay and Uruguay.

NAFTA North American Free Trade Agreement of Canada, Mexico and the US.

Quad Canada, EC, Japan and the United States.

SACU Southern African Customs Union comprising Botswana, Lesotho, Namibia, South Africa and Swaziland.

S&D "Special and differential treatment" provisions for developing countries. Contained in several WTO agreements.

UNCITRAL United Nations Centre for International Trade Law, drafts model laws such as the one on government procurement.

UNCTAD The UN Conference on Trade and Development.

TRADE AND ENVIRONMENT

Agenda 21 The Agenda for the 21st Century — a declaration from the 1992 Earth Summit (UN Conference on the Environment and Development) held in Rio de Janeiro.

Article XX GATT Article listing allowed "exceptions" to the trade rules.

Basel Convention An MEA dealing with hazardous waste.

BTA Border tax adjustment.

CITES Convention on International Trade in Endangered Species. An MEA.

CTE The WTO Committee on Trade and Environment.

EST Environmentally-sound technology.

EST&P EST and products.

Ex Ante, Ex Post Before and after a measure is applied.

LCA Life cycle analysis — a method of assessing whether a good or service is environmentally friendly.

MEA Multilateral environmental agreement.

Montreal Protocol An MEA dealing with the depletion of the earth's ozone layer.

PPM Process and production method.

TBT The WTO Agreement on Technical Barriers to Trade.

Waiver Permission granted by WTO members allowing a WTO member not to comply with normal commitments. Waivers have time limits and extensions have to be justified.

SELECTED BIBLIOGRAPHY

Aaronson, S.A., *Trade and the American Dream : A Social History of Postwar Trade Policy* (Lexington, KY : University of Kentucky Press, 1996).

Alam, Riley, "Delivering E-Commerce", *EIU European Policy Analyst,* 1st Qr., 1999.

Annan, K., *Wall Street Journal,* 29 November 1999.

Bhagwati, J. and Hudec, R.E. (eds.), *Fair Trade and Harmonization : Prerequisites for Free Trade?* (Cambridge, MA : MIT Press, 1996).

Bhattacharyya, B. and Pal, Parthapratim, "Opening up of Indian Agriculture : Implications for Food Security", mimeo, Indian Institute of Foreign Trade, New Delhi, 1999.

Bhattacharyya, B. *Chinese Response to Asian Economic Crisis : Implications for India's Trade,* IIFT Occasional Paper, 1998.

Bourgeois, J.H.J., Berrod, F., and Fournier, E.G. (eds.), *The Uruguay Round Results : A European Lawyers' Perspective* (Brussels : European Interuniversity Press, 1995).

Business Guide to the Uruguay Round, ITC, UNCTAD/WTO, Commonwealth Secretariat, 1996.

China 2020 : Integration with the Global Economy : China Engaged, The World Bank, 1997, Washington.

Coppock, Joseph D. *International Economic Instability* 1962, McGraw Hill, New York.

Correa M., Carlos and Yusuf, Abdulqawi A. (ed.), *Intellectual Property and International Trade.*

Croley, S. and Jackson, J.H., "WTO Dispute Procedures, Standard of Review and Deference to National Governments", *American Journal of International Law* 90 (1997) : 2.

Croome, J., *Reshaping the World Trading System : A History of the Uruguay Round* (Geneva : WTO, 1995).

Das, Bhagirath Lai, *The WTO Agreements : Deficiencies, Imbalances and Required Changes.*

Davey, W.J., *Pine and Swine : Canada-United States Trade Dispute Settlement — the FTA Experience and NAFTA Prospects* (Ottawa : Centre for Trade Policy and Law, 1996).

David Palmeter and Petros C. Mavroidis, *Dispute Settlement in the World Trade Organisation* (Kluwer Law International, The Hague, 1999).

Deepak Nayyar and Abhijit Sen (1994), "International Trade and the Agricultural Sector in India", *Economic Liberalization and Indian Agriculture,* ed. by G.S. Bhalla.

Ernst Ulrich Petersmann, *The GATT/WTO Dispute-Settlement System* (Kluwer Law International, The Hague, 1997).

Fretillet, J.P., and Veglio, C., *Le GATT demystifie* (Paris : Syros, 1994).

GATT (1992), *Trade and the Environment,* GATT/1529, February.

Gervais, Daniel, *The TRIPs Agreement : Drafting History and Analysis.*

Gopalsamy, N., *GATT/WTO : TRIPs, TRIMs and Trade in Services.*

Gulati, Ashok (1998), "Indian Agriculture in an Open Economy" in *India's Economic Reforms and Development. Essays for Manmohan Singh,* ed. by Isher Judge Ahluwalia and I.M.D. Little.

Gulati, Ashok and Kelley, Tim, 1999, *Trade Liberalisation and Indian Agriculture,* Oxford University Press, India.

Gulati, Ashok and Narayanan, Sudha 1999, *Negotiating for Indian Agriculture in the Millennium Round* (Mimeo).

Gulati, Ashok, 1998, "Indian Agriculture in an Open Economy : Will it Prosper?" Isher Judge Ahluwalia and I.M.D. Little (eds.), *India's Economic Reforms and Development : Essays for Manmohan Singh,* Oxford University Press, India.

Hart, M., *Canadian Economic Development and the International Trading System : Constraints and Opportunities* (Toronto : University of Toronto Press, 1985).

Hart, M., *Decision at Midnight : Inside the Canada-U.S. Free Trade Negotiations* (Vancouver : UBC Press, 1994).

Hathaway, Dale, E. and Ingco, Merlinda, D., 1995, *Agricultural Liberalisation and the Uruguay Round* (Mimeo).

Hoekman, B.M., and Kostecki, M.M., *The Political Economy of the World Trading System : From GATT to the WTO* (Oxford and New York : Oxford University Press, 1995).

Hudec, M.E., *Enforcing International Trade Law, The Evolution of the Modern GATTLegal System* (Salem, MA : Butterworth Legal Publishers, 1993).

Hudec, R.E., *The GATT Legal System and World Trade Diplomacy,* 2nd edn (Salem, MA : Butterworth Legal Publishers, 1990).

Hudec, Robert (1997), "Comment on 'Environmental Standards : An International Trade", *Annual World Bank Conference on Develop Economics 1996,* Washington : World Bank.

IMF, 1992, *Issues and Developments in International Trade Policy.*

"India Cotton and Textile Industries Reforming to Compete", Rural Development Sector Unit, South Asia Region, World Bank, January 1999.

"India's Commodity Exports : A Post-Uruguay Round Appraisal", prepared for ESCAP, IIFT, New Delhi, July 1999.

India Grains, June 1999, p. 22.

International Telecommunication Union, "Policy Considerations for Electronic Commerce", May 1999 (downloaded from ITU website).

International Trade Centre, *Forum,* January 1999.

Iwasawa, Y., *WTO No Funso Shori* (The Dispute Settlement of the World Trade Organization) (in Japanese) (Tokyo : Sanseido, 1995).

Jackson, J.H., "The Legal Meaning of a GATT Dispute Settlement Report : Some Reflections", in N. Blokker and S. Muller (eds.), *Towards More Effective Supervision by International Organizations, Essays in Honor of Henry G. Schermers,* Vol. I (Boston, MA : Kluwer Academic, 1994).

Jackson, J.H., "The World Trade Organization : Watershed Innovation or Cautious Small Step Forward", *World Economics,* II (1995) : pp. 11-31.

Jackson, J.H., "The WTO Dispute Settlement Understanding — Misunderstandings on the Nature of Legal Obligation", *American Journal of International Law,* 90 (1997) : 60.

Jackson, J.H., and Sykes, A.O., *Implementing the Uruguay Round* (Oxford : Clarendon Press, 1997).

Jackson, J.H., Davey, W.J., and Sykes, A.O., *Legal Problems of International Economic Relations : Cases, Materials and Text on the National and International Regulation of Transnational Economic Relations* (St Paul, MN : West Publishing, 1995).

Jackson, J.H., *Restructuring the GATT System* (London : Royal Institute of International Affairs/Pinter, 1990).

Jackson, J.H., *The World Trading System : Law and Policy of International Economic Relations* (Cambridge, MA : MIT Press, 1989; 2nd edn 1997).

Jackson, J.H., *World Trade and the Law of GATT : Treaties on a Legal Analysis of the General Agreement on Tariffs and Trade* (Indianapolis, IN : Bobbs-Merrill, 1969).

Jaffe, A., S. Peterson, P. Portney, and R. Stavins, 1995, "Environmental Regulation and the Competitiveness of US Manufacturing : What Does the Evidence Tell Us?", *Journal of Economic Literature,* Vol. XXXIII (March), pp. 132-63.

Jha, Ashok (1997), "Protection of the Environment, Trade and India's Leather Exports" in Veena Jha, Grant Hewison and Maree Underhill (ed.) *Trade, Environment and Sustainable Development : A South Asian Perspective,* UNCTAD.

John H. Jackson, *The World Trading System* (Second Edition, MIT, 1997).

Kathuria, S. and Bhardwaj, A., "Export Quotas and Policy Constraints in the Indian Textile and Garment Industries", *SASPR,* World Bank, New Delhi, 27 May 1998.

Katti, V., "Opportunities in the Areas of Agriculture, Manufacturing and Services", Paper presented in National Seminar organised by IIFT in collaboration with SCOPE, New Delhi, 29 May 1999.

Katti, V., *Competition Policy and IPRs,* Paper presented in National Seminar on World Trade Organisation : Implications for Business, organised by SCOPE in collaboration with IIFT, New Delhi.

Kenen, P.B. (ed.), *Managing the World Economy : Fifty Years after Bretton Woods* (Washington, DC : Institute for International Economics, 1994).

Kotwal and Ramaswami (1999), *op. cit.*

Kotwal, Ashok and Ramaswami, Bharat, "Economic Reforms in Agriculture and Rural Growth", *India in the Era of Economic Reforms,* ed. by Jeffery Sachs, Asutosh Varshney and Nirupam Bajpai Oxford University Press, New Delhi: 1999.

Legal Text, *Uruguay Round of Multilateral Trade Negotiations.*

Low, Olarreaga and Saurez (1998), "Does Globalisation Cause a Higher Concentration of International Trade and Investment Flows?" WTO Staff Working Paper.

Majumdar, M. "The MFA Phase-out and EU Clothing Sourcing : Forecasts to 2005", *Textile Outlook International,* March 1996.

Martin and Winter, "The Abolition of the Multi-Fibre Arrangement and Its Implications for Fibre Markets", International Trade Division, World Bank, 26 April 1996.

Mattoo, Subramanian, Multilateral Rules for International Competition Law, *World Economy,* Vol. 21, No. 8, pp. 1129-1150.

Multilateralisation of Sovereignty, Discussion Paper, Center for International Trade, Economics & Environment (CUTS), July 1998, pp. 61-73.

OECD, 1998, *Producer and Consumer Subsidy Equivalent.*

Organization for Economic Cooperation and Development, *Assessing the Effects of the Uruguay Round* (Paris : OECD, 1993).

Paemen, H., and Bensch, A., *From GATT to the WTO : The European Community in the Uruguay Round* (Leuven : Leuven University Press, 1995).

Parikh, Kirit S. (1998), "Food Security : Individual and National", *op. cit.*

Per Pinstrup-Anderson, Rajul Pandya-Lorch and Mark W. Rosegrant, *The World Food Situation : Recent Developments, Emerging Issues and Long-Term Prospects* IFPRI, December 1997.

Perroni and Whalley, Competition Policy and the Developing Countries, by Carlo Perroni and John Whalley in *Uruguay Round Results and the Emerging Trade Agenda* by UNCTAD, Geneva, 1998, pp. 493-512.

Pescatore, P., Davey, W.J., and Lowenfeld, A., *Handbook of GATT Dispute Settlement* (Irvington-on-Hudson, NY : Kluwer Law International, 1995).

Petersmarnn, E.-U., "How to Promote the International Rule of Law? Contributions by the World Trade Organization Appellate Review System", *Journal of International Economic Law,* I (1998) : 25.

Pigato, Miria *et al., South Asia's Integration into the World Economy,* World Bank, 1997.

Prasad, HAC and Katti, V., *Non-conventional Technology Based Services,* Commonwealth, New Delhi, 1998.

Preeg, E., *Traders in a Brave New World : The Uruguay Round and the Future of the International Trading System* (Chicago, IL : University of Chicago Press, 1995).

Publication, Vol. XXXIII, No. 9, Mumbai, 28 Feb.-6 March 1998.

Qureshi, A.H., *The World Trade Organization : Implementing International Trade Norms* (Manchester and New York : Manchester University Press, 1996).

Radhakrishna, R. and Ravi, C. "Food Demand and the Poor in India : Emerging Trends and Perspectives with Liberalization", *Economic Liberalization in South Asia,* ed. by Ric Shand, Macmillan India, New Delhi: 1999.

Raed Safadi, "The Uruguay Round Agreements : Impact on Developing Countries", *World Development,* Vol. 24, No. 7.

Report of Expert Group on Interaction between Trade and Competition Policy, Ministry of Commerce, Government of India, New Delhi, January 1999.

Reported in *Asian Wall Street Journal,* 30 November 1999.

Ricupero, R., Statement at the opening of the Seattle Ministerial Conference, 30 Nov. 1999 (Website of UNCTAD).

S.L. Rao, (1998), Towards a National Competition Policy for India. *Economic and Political Weekly,* Sameeksha Trust.

Schott, J.J. (ed.), *The World Trading System : Challenges Ahead* (Washington, DC : Institute for International Economics, 1996).

Schott, J.J., *The Uruguay Round : An Assessment* (Washington, DC : Institute for International Economics, 1994).

Srinivasan, T.N. (1998), *Developing Countries and the Multilateral Trading System : From the GATT to the Uruguay Round and the Future,* Oxford University Press.

Stewart, T. (ed.), *The World Trade Organization : The Multilateral Trade Framework for the 21st Century and US Implementing Legislation* (Washington DC : American Bar Association, 1996).

Sumantra Ghosal, "Borders Essential for a Pluralistic Society", *The Economic Times,* 14 December 1999.

Sumitra Chishti, "India-China Economic and Political Relation", mimeograph, 1999.

Swacker, F.W., Redden, K., and Wenger, L., *World Trade without Barriers : The World Trade Organization (WTO) and Dispute Resolution* (Charlottesville, VA : Michie Co./Butterworth, 1995).

"The Future of China", a speech by Joseph Stiglitz, Senior Vice President and Chief Economist, The World Bank Annual Meetings Programme of Seminars, "China : Challenges and Prospects."

"The Results of the Uruguay Round of Multilateral Trade Negotiations : The Legal Texts", 1995, WTO, Geneva.

"The Role of Rice in India's Food Security : Projections and Future Directions", *India Grains,* June 1999.

The State of Food Insecurity in the World 1999 — FAO Report. *The Times of India,* 7 December 1999.

The TRIPs Agreement and Developing Countries, prepared by UNCTAD Secretariat.

UN Conference on the RBPs as quoted in *Multilateralisation of Sovereignty,* Discussion Paper, Center for International Trade, Economics & Environment (CUTS), July 1998, pp. 61-73.

US Department of Commerce (1998), *The Emerging Digital Economy.*

Venkatesan, R. and Katti, V., *India's Textile Policy for the 21st Century,* BR Publishers, New Delhi : 1999.

Watal, Jayashree, "TRIPS, Implementing the Agreement : Policy Options for India", *Economic and Political Weekly,* September 27, 1997.

Website of US Department of Commerce.

Wheat (US), No. 2, soft red winter, export price delivered at the Gulf port for prompt or 30 days shipment, World Bank Pink Sheet data.

Working Group on the Interaction between Trade & Competition Policy.

Working Group on the Interaction between Trade and Competition Policy, Competition-Related Provisions in Existing WTO Agreements, World Trade Organisation, No. 3347, 17 June 1997.

World Bank site http ://www.worldbank.org

World Trade Organisation, WT/WGTCP/104, 16 October 1998, Working Group on the Interaction between Trade & Competition Policy.

World Trade Organisation, WT/WGTCP/M/2, 12 Nov. 1997, Working Group on the Interaction between Trade & Competition Policy.

World Trade Organisation, WT/WGTCP/M/4, 24 June 1998.

World Trade Organisation, WT/WGTCP/W, 8 Dec. 1998, Working Group on the Interaction between Trade & Competition Policy.

World Trade Organisation, WT/WGTCP/W/22, July 1997, Working Group on the Interaction between Trade and Competition Policy, Communication from the World Bank.

World Trade Organisation, WT/WGTCP/W1, 11 June 1997, Working Group on the Interaction between Trade and Competition Policy, Communication from the European Community and its Member States.

World Trade Organisation, WT/WGTCP/W6, 19 June 1997, Working Group on the Interaction between Trade and Competition Policy, Communication from the United States.

WTO (1998), *"GATT/WTO Dispute Settlement Practice Relating to Article XX, Paragraphs (b), (d) and (g) of GATT"*, WT/ CTE/W/ 53/Rev.l, 26 October (98-4148).

WTO (1999), *Trade and Environment,* Special Studies 4, October, WTO.

WTO Documents on Accession. WTO Website.

WTO, "Seminar on Electronic Commerce and Development", February 1999 (WT/COMTTJ/18).

WTO, 1995, *Legal Texts of the Uruguay Round.* WTO, 1997, *Trade Policy Review — Various Countries.*

WTO, *Development Implications of Electronic Commerce,* November 1998.

WTO, *Dispute Settlement Decision,* Vol. I (Bernan Press, Lahman, Maryland, USA, 1998).

Zarrelli, Simonetta (1997), "Trade in Eco-Labelled Products : Developing Country Participation and the Need for Increased Transparency", Zarrilli, Simonetta, Jha, Veena and Vossenaar, Rene (ed.s) *Eco-Labelling and International Trade* (UNCTAD), 1ac Millan Press.